Stream of Consciousness

What is the basic architecture of consciousness? How are time and space manifest in conscious experience? Is consciousness really like a stream, as William James famously argued?

Although there has recently been a massive upsurge of interest in consciousness, most of this has been focused on the relationship between consciousness and the brain. This has meant that important and intriguing questions concerning the fundamental characteristics of consciousness itself have not received the attention they deserve. *Stream of Consciousness* is devoted to these questions, presenting a systematic, phenomenological inquiry into the most general features of conscious life: the nature of awareness, introspection, phenomenal space and time-consciousness.

Barry Dainton shows us that a stream of consciousness is not a mosaic of discrete fragments of experience, but rather an interconnected flowing whole. This is due to a single primitive experiential relationship which he calls 'co-consciousness', a relationship which holds between those experiences that are had together, both at a time and over time.

Stream of Consciousness will interest anyone concerned with the current debates on consciousness in philosophy, psychology and neuroscience.

Barry Dainton is Senior Lecturer in Philosophy at the University of Liverpool.

International Library of Philosophy

Edited by José Bermúdez, Tim Crane and Peter Sullivan

Recent titles in the ILP include:

Personal Identity and Self-consciousness
Brian Garrett

The Sceptical Challenge
Ruth Weintraub

Dispositions: A Debate
D. M. Armstrong, C. B. Martin and U. T. Place
Edited by Tim Crane

Psychology from an Empirical Standpoint
Franz Brentano

G. E. Moore: Selected Writings
G. E. Moore
Edited by Thomas Baldwin

The Facts of Causation
D. H. Mellor

Real Time II
D. H. Mellor

The Conceptual Roots of Mathematics
J. R. Lucas

Knowledge and Reference in Empirical Science
Jody Azzouni

Reason without Freedom
David Owen

Stream of Consciousness

Unity and continuity in
conscious experience

Barry Dainton

Routledge
Taylor & Francis Group

LONDON AND NEW YORK

First published 2000
by Routledge
2 Park Square, Milton Park, Abingdon, Oxon, OX14 4RN

Simultaneously published in the USA and Canada
by Routledge
270 Madison Ave, New York, NY 10016

Revised paperback edition published 2006

Routledge is an imprint of the Taylor & Francis Group

© 2000, 2006 Barry Dainton

Typeset in Times by Taylor & Francis Books Ltd

Printed and bound in Great Britain by St Edmundsbury Press,
Bury St Edmunds, Suffolk

British Library Cataloguing in Publication Data
A catalogue record for this book is available from the British Library

Library of Congress Cataloging in Publication Data
Dainton, Barry, 1958–
Stream of consciousness: unity and continuity in conscious
experience/Barry Dainton.
p. cm – (International library of philosophy)
Includes bibliographical references and index.
1. Consciousness. 2. Philosophy of mind. I. Title. II. Series.
B808.9.D35 2000
126–dc21   99–059597

Hardback ISBN 0–415–22382–2
Paperback ISBN 0–415–37929–6

For my parents

Contents

List of figures   xi
Preface   xii

1 Introduction   **1**
   1.1 The phenomenal 1
   1.2 The phenomenal and the physical 5
   1.3 Understanding 10
   1.4 Perception and projection 14
   1.5 Phenomenology 18
   1.6 Reality, appearance and phenomenal truths 21
   1.7 Questions of demarcation and individuation 23
   1.8 A look ahead 25

2 Unity, introspection and awareness   **28**
   2.1 Awareness 28
   2.2 The phenomenal background 29
   2.3 Unity and introspection 34
   2.4 Pure awareness 41
   2.5 The A-thesis and common sense 44
   2.6 Variations on a theme 48
   2.7 Simplicity 57

3 Phenomenal space   **60**
   3.1 Consciousness, co-consciousness and space 60
   3.2 Non-spatial consciousness? 63
   3.3 Dis-integration 65
   3.4 Phenomenal spaces 72
   3.5 The S-thesis reconsidered 78
   3.6 V-spaces: further issues 80
   3.7 Co-consciousness 84

4   Transitivity   **88**

4.1 *Co-consciousness as a relation 88*

4.2 *Streams and their parts 90*

4.3 *Unity and transitivity 95*

4.4 *Transitivity: the case against 97*

4.5 *Transitivity: the case for 103*

4.6 *A question of interpretation 109*

5   Phenomenal time: problems and principles   **113**

5.1 *Time in experience 113*

5.2 *Continuity in question 117*

5.3 *Experience, the present, and presence 120*

5.4 *Memory and the experience of time 123*

5.5 *Pulses and binding 128*

5.6 *A conflict of principles 131*

6   Broad and Husserl   **136**

6.1 *A curious tale 136*

6.2 *Broad: the early account 137*

6.3 *Broad: the later account 142*

6.4 *Connectedness and presentedness 145*

6.5 *Husserl on the 'consciousness of internal time' 150*

6.6 *New words, old problems 154*

6.7 *Husserl's change of view 159*

7   The overlap model   **162**

7.1 *Foster on the time within experience 162*

7.2 *Innocent curiosities 167*

7.3 *Durations and thresholds 169*

7.4 *Symmetry, flow and mode 173*

7.5 *Passage within a four-dimensional world 177*

7.6 *Time, awareness and simultaneity 179*

8   Phenomenal interdependence   **183**

8.1 *Bundles and bonds 183*

8.2 *Wholes and parts 185*

8.3 *Mereological essentialism 187*

8.4 *Phenomenal interdependence 190*

8.5 *Interdependence and its limits: sensory wholes 195*

8.6 *Strong Impingement 201*

8.7 *Interdependence and its limits: meaning 207*

9 The ramifications of co-consciousness **214**

   9.1 Co-conscious wholes 214
   9.2 Global character: type holism and token holism 218
   9.3 Space and character 224
   9.4 C-holism and succession 227
   9.5 C-holism and temporal modes of presentation 229
   9.6 Transitivity revisited 232
   9.7 Conclusion 235

Postscript 240

Notes 260
Bibliography 267
Index 270

Figures

4.1 Exotic experiential structure   97
4.2 Suggested effect of gradual commissurotomy on consciousness   100
4.3 Weak dissociations within consciousness   103
4.4 A natural way of thinking of the unity within experience   106
4.5 A better way   106
6.1 Temporal awareness: Broad's early view   138
6.2 Core contents: O_1-O_4 = Q-R, O_2-O_3 = P-S   140
6.3 Temporal awareness: Broad's later view   144
6.4 Husserl's diagram of time   152
6.5 A continuum of continua   158
8.1 A case of partial phenomenal interdependence   194
8.2 Two perceptual gestalts   198
8.3 Müller-Lyer   199
8.4 Perceptual bias: Weak Impingement   200
8.5 Gestalt-switching   203
8.6 Kanisza's Triangle   206
9.1 Holism: the overall picture   235

Preface

> But all my hopes vanish, when I come to explain the principles, that unite our successive perceptions in our thought or consciousness.
>
> Hume

The principal aim of this book is to provide an account of the unity and continuity to be found within our streams of consciousness. Since I confine my attention to what occurs within experience, my approach is phenomenological: I try to describe and make sense of the experienced relationships between the contents of consciousness – items such perceptual experiences, thoughts, feelings, mental images and bodily sensations. Inevitably, in addressing these issues I will also be concerned with the general nature and structure of conscious awareness.

In talking of the 'experienced relationship' between the contents of consciousness I am not referring to anything mysterious or unfamiliar. To illustrate: look at your hand and snap your fingers. What happens? You see and feel a movement, and hear a sound. These three experiences – one auditory, one visual and one tactile – do not occur in isolation from one another, they occur together within your consciousness, you are aware of them all at once (along with a good deal else). Moreover, these experiences are not momentary, they each have some duration; you are aware not only of their duration but of the way each is preceded and followed by other experiences. Experiences that occur simultaneously can be experienced together, but so can experiences that occur successively.

The fact that experiences occur together in these ways is so obvious and familiar that it may not seem to give rise to any interesting or significant problems or puzzles. This changes as soon as one looks at the matter more closely. When you see and hear your finger move, just what is the relationship between the visual experience and the auditory experience? Are the auditory and visual contents separate from your awareness of them? If so, what is your awareness like in itself? Could these same contents exist independently of your awareness? Alternatively, perhaps these different contents are simply parts of a single complex experience, one which does not involve a separation of awareness and content. If so, what is the relationship between these parts, what is it that binds them together? Does being connected in this way affect the character of the parts – would the visual component of your experience have been just the same if the auditory component had been absent? The sound and the movement seem to be located at roughly the same place. Does this mean consciousness is in some manner spatial? Given that we directly experience change, our awareness cannot be confined to a durationless present, but how can we be directly aware of what is in the past? What must consciousness be like if immediate experience encompasses a temporal interval?

Questions such as these are far from trivial. Space and time were long seen as jointly constituting a fixed arena which both contained and constrained all that exists and occurs; they were viewed as the frame of the world. But there is another framework, one we are more directly acquainted with, phenomenal rather than physical, but no less central to our lives: it consists of the sorts of space, time, unity and continuity to be found within our own experience, rather than between atoms, stars, tables and chairs. In investigating this framework we are probing some of the most general and basic features of conscious life.

While the topics I will be dealing with have not been ignored in recent years, they have not received a great deal of attention either. This is largely because many philosophers until recently assumed that consciousness could be ignored, explained away, or analysed in terms of something else. The climate has now changed and there is a widespread (though far from universal) acceptance that consciousness is not only real, but too important to ignore or explain away, and that attempts to reduce it to something quite different will not succeed (a view I share and assume to be true throughout, but will not try to defend). As a consequence of this climatic change, interest in consciousness has soared, and not only among philosophers: people working in fields such as psychology, biology, neuroscience and physics have taken an interest too, which has led to a burgeoning literature. However, comparatively little of this new work has been concerned with phenomenological issues; most of it has been devoted to the relationship between consciousness and the brain, or consciousness and the physical world. This is understandable, for as soon as experience is taken seriously – taken to be an irreducible ingredient of reality in its own right – the difficulty of understanding how anything material could generate experience becomes all too apparent, and long-neglected metaphysical options have to be taken seriously again: perhaps we are not wholly physical beings; perhaps our conception of the physical requires radical revision; perhaps the problem only seems so hard because of our cognitive limitations. But while the interest in these questions is legitimate and understandable, it is to some extent premature. To understand the relationship between consciousness and matter we need an understanding of the nature of both. That physicists are still some way from completing their business is well known, but there are fundamental questions about experience that are somewhat less well known, and which have yet to be answered. As long as the matter–consciousness relationship remains problematic, the only way these questions can be answered is by inspecting consciousness itself, from the inside. Some of these questions, those concerning the ways experiences are interrelated within streams of consciousness, are the sole subject matter of this book.

A word of warning: although my approach is largely phenomenological, any reader looking for an introduction to the relevant views of the major figures of the classical phenomenological tradition will be disappointed. My interest in the stream of consciousness stemmed originally from an inquiry into the self and the problem of personal identity. Having come round to the view that a promising approach to the latter problem would focus on the ways capacities for conscious experience have to be related to belong to a single subject, I came to consider how experiences have to be related in order to constitute a stream of consciousness, and at this point, not previously having given the question much thought, I embarked on exploratory forays into the phenomenological literature. I found stimulation and obscurity in roughly equal measure; one thing I did not find were satisfactory answers to the questions I brought with me. Consequently, although borrowing from other writers (of whatever tradition) whenever possible, I have at times found myself obliged to carve out a path of my own. This said, my engagement with the phenomenological literature did not leave me entirely unscathed. There is a discussion of Husserl's views on time-consciousness in Chapter 6, and my treatment of introspective awareness in Chapter 2 was influenced by Brentano and Sartre; the alert reader will detect occasional echoes of Heidegger. My interest in the relationship between experiential wholes and their parts was to some degree provoked by one of Husserl's *Logical Investigations*, certain doctrines of the gestalt psychologists, and passages to be found in that great source of phenomenological insights and descriptions, James' *Principles of Psychology*.

Sadly, the list of neglected topics does not end here. Apart from one brief detour, I have made no mention of the voluminous Eastern writings on the ways consciousness can be transformed by meditative practices, and I have made no mention at all of the various writings devoted to the consequences of ingesting hallucinogens. Nor have I taken much account of the neurological data about the fascinating effects brain disorders can have on experience. But while a fuller and better treatment would no doubt incorporate material from all of these sources, there is something to be said for trying to achieve a clear picture of typical streams of consciousness, of the sort most of us have for most of the time. This is what I have tried to provide, although even within this constraint I have further narrowed the focus. In restricting my attention to the most general features of experience, I have made no attempt to do justice to its variety and richness, and so to this extent plead guilty to the charge of ignoring everything that makes human life interesting and distinctive. Most of what I have to say would probably apply to far more primitive creatures, incapable of conceptual thought and moral or aesthetic responses, creatures who can only enjoy the simplest forms of sensory experience. But only if the experiences of these creatures unfold within the same framework of unity and continuity as our own experience, in all its richness and complexity. And as I have already suggested, though familiar, this framework poses problems aplenty.

Whatever errors and infelicities remain in what follows, there would have been more were it not for the assistance I have received from others. My thanks to: John Foster, for invaluable guidance and encouragement when I first started thinking about these questions; Nicholas Nathan, for both his enthusiastic support and his determined attempts to make me aware of the inadequacies of my position; Howard Robinson, for helpful advice on a recent draft and many enjoyable discussions on related topics; Michael McGhee, for his assistance on Eastern matters; Stephen Clark, Brendan Larvor and John Williamson for reading and commenting on Chapters 8 and 9; Tim Crane, for not reading more than he did; Gwynneth Knowles, whose suggestions for stylistic improvements I have not always followed, but which nonetheless made a difference.

1   Introduction

1.1 The phenomenal

Since my main topic is the way experiences are interrelated within streams of consciousness, some preliminary clarifications concerning what I mean by 'experience' and 'consciousness' are in order. There is of course a limit on what can be said on this topic: if you do not know what it is like to have experience, words will not help, and there is probably no 'you' there to find out. But although 'consciousness' and 'experience' are to some extent primitive notions, they are also as hotly contested as any in philosophy. The literature is full of distinctions between different types of consciousness, theories about what can and cannot be said about consciousness, and the relationship between consciousness and the physical world. In this opening chapter I will indicate where I stand on a few of these issues, those that are relevant to what follows. In particular, I will have something to say about two distinctive types of experience, the experience of understanding and perceptual experience. I focus on the latter to avoid possible misunderstandings, and on the former because it is often ignored altogether. Also, as I will be spending a good deal of time trying to describe various features of our experience, I make some general comments on phenomenology and related matters.

I shall not try to defend the positions I endorse here in any detail, partly because some of issues I mention will be taken up in subsequent chapters, but more importantly, because defending the general policy I adopt of taking experience seriously is a considerable undertaking in its own right. By 'taking experience seriously' I mean adopting a stance of robust, full-blooded realism about consciousness. This means taking consciousness as seriously as we take science. From this perspective, sensory experiences, bodily sensations and conscious thoughts are regarded as just as real as paradigmatic physical things such as mountains, houses and trees, and perhaps more real than the some of the currently postulated occupants of the microphysical realm. It also means rejecting all attempts to reduce the experiential to the non-experiential. (So, for example, contrary to what some functionalists would say, there is more to being an experiential state than being a state with certain causal powers; an experience has certain intrinsic features over and above any causal powers it may have.) A good many philosophers think there are good reasons for *not* taking experience seriously. Although I think these philosophers are wrong, I will not engage with their arguments here. This has been done effectively by others, for example Foster (1991), McGinn (1991), Searle (1992), Flanagan (1992), Robinson (1994), Strawson (1994) and Chalmers (1996).

By 'consciousness' I mean *phenomenal* consciousness; by 'experiences' I mean states or items with a phenomenal character. The 'phenomenal character' of an experience refers to the distinctive *feel* the experience has. A state has a phenomenal character when there is something that it is like to have or undergo that state. A sudden severe stomach cramp that causes one to bend over double feels very different from a gentle tickle; the cramp and the tickle are sensations with a different phenomenal character. There is 'something it is like' to feel a raging anger, to see a magnolia coloured wall, to hear a cello tone, to struggle with a piece of mental arithmetic, to remember one's first day at school, to smell a roasting chicken, to imagine the flavour of ginger. These are all experiences, they all have different phenomenal characters.

Some experiences are more noticeable than others. In thinking of 'experiences' we tend to think first of what we can see and hear, our thoughts or memories, our more memorable pains and pleasures. We easily overlook the presence of those *bodily* sensations that form the backdrop of our consciousness: gentle sensations of texture and pressure (e.g. from our clothing), feelings of warmth or coolness, along with feelings in our muscles, organs and joints, and our sense of balance (standing upright feels different from standing on one's head). But these various bodily feelings all have their own distinctive phenomenal character, they all belong to the realm of experience.

As examples of items possessing phenomenal character I have referred to particular experiences, but experiences do not typically occur in isolation from one another. A stream of consciousness is an ensemble of experiences that is unified both at and over time, both synchronically and diachronically. The expression 'the unity of consciousness' is occasionally used to refer to the unity of the mind as a whole. Taken in this way, the topic is the way in which mental states of all kinds, experiential and non-experiential, are inter-related when they belong to the same mind. Since by 'consciousness' I mean phenomenal consciousness, by the 'unity of consciousness' I mean the unity of experience. Let us pause to consider this unity in a little more detail.

Imagine a party game: participants are blindfolded and handed an object, and they have to work out what the object is relying on touch alone. It is your turn, and panic is starting to set in; your three minutes are nearly up and you still have no idea what your object is; the taunts and laughter from your audience are starting to annoy. The thing you are handling is quite small, made of plastic, and obviously a contraption of some kind, it has several moveable parts, some hinged. You suspect there is a way to get the whole thing to fold up, but the various extremities can move in a bewildering number of directions, and you have been unable to manoeuvre them into any recognizable shape. Your best guess is that it is some sort of puzzle, an executive toy or some such thing. But too late: jeers erupt, your time has run out. Tearing off the blindfold you look at the mysterious object, only to find that you are still no wiser. Anger now surges – how could you hope to identify by touch an object you don't recognize when you see it?

Consider a few snapshots of your stream of consciousness during these few minutes; each snapshot consists of your experience over a brief interval.

1   As you start to manipulate the object you have tactile sensations in your hands and fingers. These do not occur by themselves, but are continuous with the rest of your bodily experience (e.g. your body-image: sitting hunched in a chair). You are also having some thoughts – 'What is this damned thing?' – emotional feelings (mounting frustration), and mental images (you are trying to find an image to fit the feel). These thoughts and images do not occur in isolation from one another, they are experienced together – they are *co-conscious* – both with one another (thought + emotional feeling + mental image) and your various bodily experiences.

2   The audience was silent at first, but has now started to make its presence felt; you try not to pay attention to the racket they are making, but can hear them nonetheless. So now there are auditory experiences which are co-conscious with your thoughts, mental images, emotional feelings and bodily sensations.

3   You have just removed the blindfold, so visual experiences now enter the mix; these are co-conscious with all your other experience: what you hear and feel in your body, what you are thinking and feeling emotionally (a mixture of anger, frustration and puzzlement).

Each of these brief cross-sections is an instance of simultaneous experiences being experienced together, or bearing the relationship of co-consciousness to one another. As the example makes plain, experiences of different sorts can be, and typically are, co-conscious; indeed, at least as a first approximation, it seems likely that all our experiences at any given moment are mutually co-conscious.

But experience is also unified over time, at least over fairly brief intervals, of the duration of the so-called specious present. Handling the contraption while blindfolded produced a sequence of tactile sensations. As you trace a contour with a finger you feel a continuous sensation of smoothness, not a succession of discrete bursts of sensation. As you try to visualize what you are holding you imagine one object after another; each image lasts a short while, and when one object replaces another the transition itself is experienced. When the audience becomes restless you hear a rumbling of muttering and murmuring, a flow of sound which as it runs on is continually renewed. And all the while, there is the constant presence of bodily feeling and emotion: these too constitute a continuous presence. This constant flow or turnover of experience is one reason the 'stream' metaphor seems apt. A stream of consciousness is a continuous succession of experiences, and what gives the stream its unity from one moment to the next is the fact that this succession is itself experienced.

My main concern in this book is co-consciousness, in both its synchronic and diachronic forms. I shall try to elucidate its characteristics, and see what can be said about it. As I noted in the Preface, a phenomenological approach is unavoidable, for the unity I am concerned with is a unity in consciousness itself. There is no denying that our streams of consciousness do display a distinctive sort of unity, and this unity does not just consist in a relationship between certain experiences, it consists in a relationship between experiences that is itself experienced. To investigate this unity I do not need to suppose that anything external to my consciousness exists at all. Irrespective of whether I am a human being, a brain-in-a-vat or an immaterial soul, I have certain experiences which, as they occur, are experienced together. The question is: when experiences are co-conscious, what is the nature of this relationship, what can be said about this purely experiential phenomenon? Scientific studies of the brain are largely irrelevant to this question. Consider the so-called binding problem with which neuroscientists are currently wrestling (cf. Horgan 1994: 72–8). At the most general level, the problem is how the scattered neuronal activity within a single brain manages to generate unified states of consciousness. Given that the neural processes known to be associated with auditory, bodily and visual experience are located in different parts of the brain, how (or where) do these processes manage to create a single unified experience? Then there are more specific problems. When I hear you speak I hear your words as meaningful; there are a number of different neural processes involved in speech perception – how do they manage to integrate their outputs? When I see a blue cube, how do parts of the brain responsible for shape perception and colour perception get their act together so as to produce what I see? These are all interesting problems. But it is clear that while solutions to these problems might tell us something about the physical conditions that are sufficient (and perhaps necessary) for human beings to enjoy unified streams of consciousness, they would not tell us much about what the unity and continuity of consciousness involves at a purely experiential level. For this we need to turn to phenomenology.

Experience gives rise to a more familiar and more widely discussed puzzle: what is the relationship between phenomenal consciousness and the physical world? So far as I can see, at the present time this relationship remains as mysterious as ever, but we do not need to resolve this mystery in order to describe and try to make sense of our experience. This said, the general stance taken on the matter–consciousness question is relevant to certain issues with which I will be concerned – one such is the issue of how experiences are to be individuated. Since this question cannot be ignored altogether, I will briefly sketch the general position which seems to me most reasonable, and which I will be assuming henceforth.

1.2 The phenomenal and the physical

The matter–consciousness problem is easy to state: how can physical particles and fields, when organized as they are in living brains, manage to produce experiences possessing phenomenal characteristics? Where do the phenomenal characteristics come from? Think back to the time before matter had collapsed into the first stars. Since the universe at this time consisted of simple particles randomly scattered through vast reaches of space, it seems unlikely that there was experience anywhere to be found. If the universe in this condition was wholly experience-free, how can simply re-arranging the same elementary particles have given birth to something fundamentally new and different: consciousness? How can the bringing together of non-experiential things ever produce an experience? Even the simplest experience seems to be something wholly *other* than a collection of physical atoms. Yet, if the evolutionary story is to be believed, this is precisely what did happen: consciousness (of a rudimentary kind) abruptly emerged on the scene as soon as matter achieved a certain type of organization. This aspect of the mind–brain problem seems uniquely baffling. The relationship between matter and experience can seem utterly mysterious in a way that the relationship between matter and computation, or matter and cognition, is not. Hence the claim that the matter–cognition problem is trivial in comparison with the matter–consciousness problem. The latter is so hard the former can seem relatively easy.[1]

As for solutions to the matter–consciousness problem, the history of philosophy is littered with them; but if we adopt a robust realism about both the physical world and experience, which I do here, some can be ignored. Experiential realism rules out eliminativism and reductionism: it is not an option to say experiences do not exist, or are identical with physical processes which lack phenomenal characteristics. Accepting physical realism means it is not an option to say the physical world does not exist at all (e.g. some idealisms) or that all physical facts can in some manner be reduced to purely experiential facts (e.g. classical phenomenalism). But this leaves a good many other options open.

Dualism is one such. Substance dualism is the doctrine that experiences are states of objects which are non-physical or immaterial; property dualism, in one common form, is the doctrine that experiences are immaterial particulars which are generated by (or at least correlated) with physical occurrences. Both versions of dualism hold that experiences are non-physical; the divergence occurs over whether or not experiences are attributes or modes of a non-physical substance. Given that the relationship between matter and consciousness is at present an unresolved mystery, I do not think that we are in a position to rule out any half-way intelligible theory about this relationship with any confidence. This said, I will generally assume that Cartesian-style substance dualism is false. Not because I think the doctrine is less than half-way intelligible – it has its problems, but so do the alternatives – but because the doctrine has distinctive implications concerning the unity of consciousness, and so far as possible, I want to see what can be said about the unity of consciousness without committing myself to any particular view of the matter–consciousness relationship.

It is easy to see why substance dualists tend not to regard the unity of consciousness as especially problematic. If we are immaterial substances whose essence is to be conscious, experiences that belong to the same subject are modes of a single immaterial substance; since the essence of this substance is consciousness, it is not surprising that our experiences are unified – they are unified because they are coinstantiated in the same conscious substance. But this is too quick and easy. The availability of coin-stantiation as an explanation of the unity in consciousness means substance dualists tend not to inquire any further into the nature of this unity, which – as we shall see – has some strange and remarkable properties, properties which only come to light when the easy answer to the question is not taken as the last word on the matter. Dualists also tend to ignore certain other relevant questions. If experiences are properties of immaterial substances, is it impossible for a single immaterial substance to sustain two distinct streams of consciousness at a given time? If this is not impossible, then coin-stantiation cannot explain the unity of the experiences in each of the two streams and some further explanation is needed. If it is impossible, why is it impossible? I have one further reason for regarding substance dualism with suspicion: like Hume, I think the doctrine is suspect on purely phenomeno-logical grounds – a point I will be returning to in Chapter 2.

If we leave substance dualism out of the picture, what other options remain? Property dualism is one possibility, but there are non-dualistic approaches which are live options too. One of these non-dualistic approaches is rooted in the fact that the scientific picture of the world is in one respect a very limited one. Physics has a lot to say about the size, shape and causal powers of different sorts of physical item, but what does it have to say about the intrinsic nature of space-time, or of fundamental particles such as electrons or neutrinos? Strange as it may initially seem, it has nothing whatsoever to say about these matters. General relativity tells us that space-time is a medium whose intrinsic geometry is partly dependent upon the distribution of mass-energy within it; it tells us nothing of the intrinsic nature of space-time itself. Physics tells us of the size and mass of particles, it tells us of the various ways they causally interact with other particles (and each other), but this is all: it has nothing to say about the nature of the stuff from which these particles are constituted. The same will surely apply to as-yet undiscovered particles (and fields), including those which turn out to be basic. Assuming that at least some physical items must have *some* sort of intrinsic character, an intriguing possibility opens up:

what is there to rule out the possibility that the intrinsic character of at least some physical items is phenomenal? The obvious candidates are the parts of the nervous system that we know to be correlated with the occurrence of experiences.

This view, which for obvious reasons I will call *phenomenalized* materialism (or *P-materialism* for short) solves several problems at once. It situates the experiential firmly within the physical realm; it explains how the phenomenal can causally interact with the physical and vice-versa; it also allows us to say something about the intrinsic nature of at least some parts of the physical world.[2]

But the theory also faces a number of difficulties. Is P-materialism committed to panpsychism? Do rocks and puddles possess even a faint glimmer of consciousness? Most people find this idea very strange. But if the matter in the brain is conscious, can we be certain that puddles do not possess some slight degree of consciousness? After all, brains and puddles are constructed from the same basic material constituents, elementary particles and their associated fields. If matter is intrinsically conscious, then must not these elementary ingredients possess phenomenal features in some form, no matter how dim? In which case, will not every material thing possess some form of consciousness? Then there is the so-called 'grain problem'.[3] What portion of the brain could be identical with the visual experience one has when one looks at a white sheet of paper? Whereas the relevant visual experience is a smooth region of phenomenal whiteness, the neural structures associated with this experience are far from homogeneous (just think what a tangle of neurones looks like). The same applies to the elementary particles neurones are composed of. Where in the brain do we find something with the same structure as a smooth expanse of pure phenomenal white? The physical constituents of the brain seem too uneven, too granular (hence the label 'grain problem'). There is also the difficulty of accommodating the sheer variety of phenomenal features. There is all the difference in the world between a visual experience of white, the smell of herring, and the sound of birdsong. Yet, so far as we know, the neural structures associated with these different sorts of experience are quite similar; they are merely slightly different configurations of the same kinds of elementary ingredients. How could physical structures which are so similar possess intrinsic natures that differ so completely? It may be that future discoveries about matter (specifically about the matter that constitutes brains) will provide solutions to these problems. Or perhaps the granularity problem at least will simply be side-stepped: suppose experiences are identical with regions of space. Perhaps experiences correspond to the intrinsic character of those regions of space that are energized or distorted by the neuronal activity within brains. Since space itself is smooth, except perhaps at the very, very small scale, the granularity of matter no longer poses a problem. Whether the various patterns of disruption produced in space by neural activity are such as to dispose of the problem of phenomenal variety is another question.

The P-materialist starts from the premise that our current conception of matter is along roughly the right lines, and tries to find a route which allows the phenomenal to slot into this conception; if P-materialism is true, the phenomenal lies right at the heart of the material. Another option, one which is necessarily rather less specific, is to hold that our current conception of matter is radically mistaken, or at least hopelessly incomplete. I call this *liberalized*, or *L-materialism*. For the L-materialist, all bets are off as to what the real nature of the physical world really is. The positive suggestion is that the matter–consciousness problem seems so hard only because our understanding of the nature of matter is so partial. If we had a more adequate understanding of matter, the problem would either go away altogether or at least not seem so hopeless. Strawson adopts essentially this position, and calls it *agnostic materialism*. He writes

> the idea that the mind–body problem is particularly perplexing flows from our unjustified and relatively modern faith that we have an adequate grasp of the fundamental nature of matter at some crucial general level of understanding, even if we are still uncertain about many details. Agnosticism seems called for because it seems so clear that this cannot be right if materialism is true.
>
> (1994: 105)

In a similar vein, McGinn argues that the brain must have properties other than those currently recognized,

> since these are insufficient to explain what it can achieve, namely the generation of consciousness. The brain must have aspects that are not represented in our current physical world-view, aspects we do not understand, in addition to all those neurones and electro-chemical processes. There is, on this view, a radical incompleteness in our view of reality, including physical reality.
>
> (1995: 157)

Failing to recognize that physical things might have phenomenal intrinsic natures is one way our current view of physical reality might be incomplete (we do not usually suppose that elementary physical phenomena have phenomenal characteristics). So P-materialism is one form L-materialism might take, but it is not the only form. The L-materialist is open to the possibility that matter might prove to be even stranger than the P-materialist maintains, and given the objections that can be levelled against P-materialism, this extra degree of freedom is a useful thing to have. This said, what version of physicalism could be stranger than P-materialism?

There are several possibilities. One option runs along the following lines. The physical world contains both experiential and non-experiential items, but there is a connection between them of a kind that makes it reasonable to hold that the experiential is nonetheless a part of the material (in the sense of 'non-mental') world: there are properties or entities that are neither wholly phenomenal nor wholly physical, but which are such that they can interact or combine so as to yield the kinds of physical and phenomenal properties we are familiar with, and do so in a regular law-like manner. These *ur*-qualities might reasonably be thought to be more fundamental than either the phenomenal or the physical (as we currently recognize it to be). The physical and the phenomenal, in a world like this, are merely two different guises the fundamental qualities can adopt. The same *ur*-qualities that constitute a particular experience, could – were they differently configured – constitute something non-experiential. In an attempt to flesh out a proposal of this sort, McGinn has suggested that the emergence of consciousness from matter strikes us as mysterious because our common-sense conception of the physical is informed by a defective conception of (physical) space. Consciousness seems to be non-spatial, in that experiences do not occupy or compete for space in the way ordinary physical objects do. How can something non-spatial arise from something spatial? If we are to hold onto the view that consciousness is not radically autonomous with respect to the physical, it seems reasonable to speculate that some pre- or sub-spatial aspect of physical reality is associated with the generation of consciousness. The idea that physical space is itself the product of interactions among pre-spatial particulars is one that physicists have been toying with. Although the spatial dimensions we are familiar with are commonly supposed to have originated with the big bang, if the physical has pre-spatial ingredients, these could easily have pre-dated the big bang, and perhaps explain why it occurred at all. Suppose these same pre-spatial ingredients are responsible for the generation of consciousness, a proposal which cannot be dismissed out of hand, given the non-spatial characteristics of at least some sorts of experience. These suppositions lead to the striking conclusion that 'consciousness turns out to be older than matter in space, at least as to its raw materials' (McGinn 1995: 155).

Needless to say, such proposals are highly speculative, but there is nothing wrong with this. When physicists talk of the Final Theory or the 'theory of everything', they are talking about a theory which will explain the behaviour of matter alone – matter conceived in wholly experience-free terms. Since this theory has yet to be formulated we have as yet no firm idea as to what its general form will be like. If present trends are anything to go by, the Final Theory will end up attributing to the physical world features that are exotic to say the least by everyday standards. The weird ideas that are already in play in contemporary physics need no introduction: non-locality, the multiple concealed spatial dimensions of string theory, the branching (or non-branching) multi-verse. But these are all theories which treat the physical as experience-free. If we make the assumption that experience is an integral part of the physical realm, that phenomenal characteristics are as fundamental as mass or charge, or even more fundamental than mass or charge, there is plenty of scope for physics to get stranger still. We can at present do little more than speculate as to what a *real* theory of everything might look like.

I offer no opinion about which of these various approaches is closest to the truth of the matter; I think it is too early to tell. Although dualism has its drawbacks, it also has its advantages. Materialism – whether phenomenalized or liberalized – may seem more appealing. The idea that our universe is a deeply unified whole is aesthetically attractive; materialism offers the prospect of a unified cosmos, dualism does not. Also, both P-materialism and L-materialism offer the prospect of a more satisfying explanation of the matter–experience relationship than any form of dualism. The basic psychophysical laws between matter and mind that the dualist posits may not be absurd from a metaphysical standpoint, since some laws must be unexplainable in terms of other laws, but if some form of materialism is true we have the prospect of a more detailed explanation of the matter–consciousness relationship. Basic laws would figure in this explanatory scheme too, but at a deeper level.

However, we have at present no way of knowing whether any form of materialism will prove viable, so although I will be saying a lot about experience, with one exception I will endeavour to maintain remain neutral as to the details of the matter–consciousness relationship, the one exception being substance dualism of the traditional Cartesian type. I will call this position *moderate naturalism*. 'Naturalism' because it seems clear that experience is profoundly interwoven with the physical world, 'moderate' because I have no idea as to the precise nature of the relationship between the two. If either L- or P-materialism is true, the natural (or physical) world is in part an experiential world. If some form of property dualism is true, experience cannot be naturalized very deeply at all, but it nonetheless remains deeply integrated with the physical world: at the very least, the character of our consciousness depends on the activity within our nervous systems, and unless epiphenomenalism obtains, some of the activity within our nervous systems depends on what goes on within our consciousness.

1.3 Understanding

In thinking about the various forms consciousness takes, it is natural to draw a rough distinction between 'inner' and 'outer' experiences. The distinction is not very clear-cut, and is in some ways misleading, but it does correspond with a common way of thinking. By 'outer' experience I mean *sensory* experience, the experiences of the surrounding world our sense organs give us, the deliverances of sight, hearing, touch, taste and smell. I will say more about these shortly. The realm of 'inner' experience includes all forms of consciousness that *seem* to be located wholly within our bodies. These seemingly interior experiences can be divided into two categories. On the one hand, there is the range of easily overlooked experiences of a bodily kind, such as warmth, pain, hunger, nausea, kinaesthetic sensations and our sense of balance. (There is a case for including smell and taste in this list.) On the other hand, there is the range of experiences that seem to occur within our heads, those which we take to be most intimately associated with our minds, with what is distinctively mental as opposed to bodily: memories, mental images, emotional feelings, such as fear or regret, and conscious thinking. Closely associated with the latter, and also often overlooked, is the experience of *understanding*. This is the distinctive sort of experience that occurs when we read or hear (or think) a symbol or sentence and understand what it means. I will follow Strawson and call this 'understanding-experience' (1994: §§1.4, 7.2). Because this sort of experience is often overlooked, or ignored, I will say a little more about it.

I think it is clear that there is something it is like to understand the spoken and written word. Compare what it is like to listen to a conversation in your mother tongue (English, let us suppose), with what it is like to listen to a conversation in a language you cannot understand at all (e.g. Finnish). There are two differences. The English conversation will consist of sequences of familiar words, words you recognize as soon as you hear them. The Finnish conversation will seem to consist of a flow of speech-sounds; there will be no recognizable words; for the most part you will not be able to tell with any confidence where one word or sentence begins and another ends. A Finn, listening to the same conversation, would hear familiar words, packaged into sentences, clearly and distinctly. The conversation will *sound* different to you than it does to the Finn. But there is a second difference. As the English conversation proceeds, you understand it, automatically and involuntarily. You hear the words 'Cats make you sneeze, don't you just hate them?' and you immediately know what is being said; the meaning of the utterance is as present within your experience as the sound of the words. If you were to hear the same sentiment expressed in Finnish, you would understand nothing. This difference, the presence and absence of the experience of understanding, amounts to a clear difference in the character of your consciousness as a whole in the two situations just envisaged. In the one case, you hear a sentence and *understand its meaning*, in the other case, you hear a sentence (or a pattern of sound) and *understand nothing*. In the latter case, the meaning of what is said is wholly absent from your consciousness, in the former case it is present.

The difference is perhaps even more marked in the case of reading. Due to the peculiarities of speech-perception, a given utterance will be perceived to possess very different auditory qualities by different people, depending on their familiarity with the language being spoken. But scanning a printed page, trying to read what is written, will probably result in visual experience of a broadly similar character, irrespective of whether what is read is understood or not. There will be *some* difference here, but of a lesser degree than in the auditory case. When scanning a passage written in Finnish you will not see familiar words, in the way a literate Finn would, but at least you will see familiar letters, organized into words and sentences. The following is a simple recipe for vanilla ice-cream:

> Take 1 pint of milk, 1 pint of double cream, a pod of vanilla (split lengthwise), 7 egg yolks and half a pound of caster sugar. Heat the milk and the vanilla, whisking as it comes to the boil. Remove from the heat and leave for half an hour. Beat the sugar and egg yolks together, and pour the milk (now vanilla flavoured) onto this mixture. Put the mixture into a saucepan. Cook gently, stirring all the while, until the mixture thickens. Pour the mixture through a strainer into a bowl, and stir in the cream. Leave the mixture to cool, then freeze it.

As you read through this passage, you understand the instructions; you know what it is that you are being told to do. It is not merely that you are able to *do* something after reading the passage that you were unable to do before, i.e. the difference is not merely an alteration in your behavioural dispositions and abilities. You are aware of the content or meaning of the passage as you read through it; as a result, the character of your experience is quite different from what it would have been if you had merely stared at the writing rather than reading it. To see this, it suffices to imagine what the experience of someone able to read and understand Finnish but not English would be like as they read through the same recipe. The visual experience of this reader might be fairly similar to yours, but there would be no understanding-experience at all.

It would be wrong to suppose that understanding-experience occurs separately from our perception of speech and writing. Focusing on the case of speech, when I hear you talk to me, I do not hear the sound of your voice, and while this is going on have a separate experience of the content of what you are saying. I do not hear your words as mere *sounds* at all. In hearing you talk, I hear meaningful words and sentences. Meaning is as much a phenomenal feature of what I hear as the timbre and pitch of your voice. Hence the uncanny experience most people have had of finding that a word sometimes loses its meaning when repeated over and over. As the meaning drains away we are left with the pure sound, a sound that is quite devoid of its usual meaning; when this happens, a word we are perfectly familiar is transformed into something, a *noise*, that strikes us as quite alien. If we did not usually perceive words as intrinsically meaningful we could not experience the meaning evaporating in this fashion. McCulloch observes: 'In ordinary communication in our own language with our familiars, then, it seems that the transmission is direct: your words load their significance directly into my consciousness, and are in that sense themselves "transparent"' (1995: 152). This has to be interpreted in the right way. Your words are not transparent in the sense that they are lacking perceived auditory qualities (or else I would not hear what you are saying at all). Your words are sounds, but they are sounds which, as I hear them, are intrinsically imbued with meaning. Your words are not something I have to get through or around to get at your meaning – as is the case with coded messages.

There is another mistake to avoid. Understanding-experience is not a sensory phenomenon in this sense: it does not consist of mental images of a sensory sort (visual, acoustic, tactile) that accompany what is read or heard. While reading through the recipe above, you may have visualized certain culinary operations. These imagined images do not constitute understanding-experience. You could have understood the passage just as well if while reading it you had imagined nothing at all. As Strawson remarks, in the reading case 'there is perhaps a rapid and diaphanous process of forming acoustic mental images. But this is not all, for – *barath abalori trafalon* – one can have all this without the experience of understanding' (1994: 8).

The experience of meaning is not restricted to spoken words and symbols. There is also thought to consider. It is here that the experience of meaning is at once manifestly obvious and alarmingly elusive. Sometimes conscious thought takes a verbal form: sentences spoken 'silently', in the acoustic imagination. (Recall what it was like, as a child learning to read, to be forced to read silently to oneself rather than aloud.) Understanding-experience in this case is similar to ordinary speech-perception: meaning is experienced as present in words and sentences, the only difference is that the words and sentences are now imagined rather than heard or read. But not all thought is like this. Thoughts often occur without any distinctive sensory garb. I am walking out of the house and suddenly remember that I have left the cooker on and have to go back to turn it off – the thought flashes through my consciousness, it is not 'spoken' inwardly, it is not verbalized at all. Yet its content could not be clearer. In cases like this, we experience meaning in a pure form (or so it seems). According to Vygotsky, 'Inner speech, is speech almost without words. ... While in external speech thought is embodied in words, in inner speech words die as they bring forth thought. Inner speech is to a large extent thinking in pure meanings' (1997: 249). The idea that occurrent thoughts can be wholly determinate in their content yet quite diaphanous, lacking any experiential character other than the meaning they carry, can seem quite puzzling. How could there be such a thing as 'pure meaning'? How would we detect thoughts of this sort – would they not be invisible? We do not need to be able to answer these questions in order to recognize that the kind of experience in question exists: there are non-verbal and non-imagistic conscious thoughts, thoughts that are diaphanous and fleeting, yet whose content is clear.[4] If meaning were not present in our consciousness in this fashion, the character of our experience, taken as a whole, would be very different from how it is.

Contentful thought that seems wholly transparent is an extreme case; often our thinking consists of images of various sorts, fragments of sub-vocal inner speech. Understanding-experience comes in many forms. It should also be noted that 'thought' here should be interpreted quite generally, to include the way in which our beliefs, hopes, fears and intentions manifest themselves in our stream of consciousness. Propositional attitudes are dispositional states which exist when we are not conscious of them, but they can and do manifest themselves in consciousness, and when they do, we experience their content. 'Meaning' is a complex concept. In saying that meaning is present in understanding-experience, I do not mean to suggest that every aspect of meaning is to be found there. The referential component clearly is not. My twin on Twin-Earth has, let us suppose, a stream of experience which is indistinguishable from mine, in all qualitative or phenomenal respects. When I think 'I must give Bob a ring' (whether verbalized or not), an exactly similar thought occurs in my twin's stream of consciousness. But my thought is about the Bob I know, the Bob I have met, who lives round the corner on this planet, whereas my twin's thought is about the Bob he knows, who lives round the corner on his planet. So 'Bob' in my thought does not have the same meaning (or reference) as 'Bob' does in my twin's thought. This is a familiar point. But just as there is more to meaning than what is present in understanding-experience, there is more to meaning than reference. The important point is that one important aspect of meaning *is* present in understanding-experience. I will not attempt to characterize this aspect. My aim here has been the very limited one of making it clear that there is more to consciousness than the sensory. A creature lacking language and concepts can have a rich variety of sensory experience, but they would not have understanding-experience. In talking about 'experience' I mean to refer to both sensory and non-sensory consciousness.

1.4 Perception and projection

A central category of experience is perceptual experience: the experiences we have when we look at things, hear things and taste things. Although everyone agrees that our perceptual organs provide us with experiences, there is a good deal of controversy as to what exactly perceptual experience amounts to. There are many analyses of perceptual experience and perceptual content, but I am not going to enter into these debates in any detail; all we need here is a very general idea as to what perceptual experience involves. My starting assumptions do most of the work. The combination of full-blooded experiential realism together with moderate naturalism cuts out many options, and (so far as I can see) makes some sort of Lockean account of perception inevitable. This general view of perception goes by a variety of names: 'indirect realism', 'the error theory', the 'representative theory', 'projectivism'. For reasons which will become plain, I shall use the latter label.

According to the general lines of this account, a common-sense way of thinking about a good deal of our perceptual experience is dramatically mistaken. In everyday life we negotiate our way about a world of familiar objects, things we can see or hear, and sometimes smell, touch and taste. Concentrating on what is – for present purposes – the most important case, vision, we naturally suppose these familiar objects possess as intrinsic characteristics the contours and colours we see them as possessing. When in this 'natural attitude' of 'naive realism', we take our eyes to be quite literally windows onto the world. If I see a red vase on a table in front of me I take it for granted that the vase's surface possesses just the same redness that I am aware of in my experience. The vase's colour seems as independent of me and my consciousness as its shape and mass. I have no sense of my consciousness *extending outwards*, as it were, and furnishing the vase with its perceived properties. On this view, opening and closing our eyes is rather like opening and closing the curtains in a room. When the curtains are open we can see the house opposite; close the curtains and we can't see out at all. The house opposite remains just the same whether our curtains our closed or open. The glass in a window gives us a transparent access to the world outside, provided we are awake and able to take advantage of it. It is natural to think our eyes work in somewhat the same way. Closing our eyes is like closing the curtains, it prevents our seeing out. Just as a window allows us to see what lies beyond a room, our eyes allow us to see what lies outside our bodies.

This natural picture of the relationship between ourselves and the objects of our perceptual awareness does not survive a combination of philosophical reflection and scientifically informed common sense. There are a number of related reasons for this – but since this is familiar philosophical territory I will not go into them all or in any detail. To begin with, if we believe what contemporary physics tells us about the composition of material objects, it is not easy to see how they (or their surfaces) could possess so-called secondary properties such as colour as intrinsic, non-relational, properties. The matter constituting an object like a vase is nearly all empty space, dotted through which are unimaginably tiny particles embedded within force-fields of various types. There is no reason to think these field-filled regions of space are wholly permeated by colour (as we know it from our experience) or anything like it. Much the same applies to the light entering our eyes when we see.[5] But more damaging to naive realism is the general picture of the perceptual process itself that science provides us with. By opening my eyes and looking about I allow streams of photons reflected and refracted by the objects in my vicinity to stimulate my retina, and so my nervous system, which in turn causes my brain to produce visual experiences. The phenomenal character of our experience depends only upon the final stages of this causal process. As a consequence, when I see a red vase, there is a very real sense in which the existence of the vase itself is irrelevant to the character of my experience. If the series of neural changes brought on by looking at the vase were to occur in the absence of the vase – which seems perfectly possible – I would have a visual experience indistinguishable (in all phenomenal respects) from a genuine perception of the vase. This is a familiar point, and one hardly anyone would deny. Wholly life-like perceptual illusions happen, and there is no more reliable way of bringing them about than inducing changes in the perceptual organs of the sort that would be induced by veridical perception. But this simple point has far-reaching ramifications.

Suppose I have a hallucination of a red vase induced (we can suppose) by direct electro-chemical retinal stimulation rather than by light emanating from a vase. Since this hallucination is wholly realistic, it seems to me that I am seeing a red vase a few feet away from me sitting on a table. Although there is no physical vase present in front of me, the vase I am staring at appears to be wholly 'out there'; it seems to be as mind-independent as anything could be. I have no sense of my consciousness extending outward into space and creating a vase-like appearance. But something like this must be happening: the vase I am experiencing as sitting a few feet away from me is nothing but a mental projection into external space. I am not saying that this projected image really occupies external space (space external to our bodies), but it seems to (and the image does not seem to be a mental projection at all). There is nothing terribly surprising here – after all we are dealing with a case of hallucination, and it is well known that hallucinations are creatures of the mind. But once this is accepted, it becomes hard to believe that the immediate objects of ordinary, non-hallucinatory, perceptual experience are significantly different: these too are mental projections, even though they don't seem to be. For what is going on when I really see a vase? Light from the vase falls on my retina, causing just the same sorts of experience-producing neural activity that was responsible for my hallucination. If this type of neural activity produces a vase-like mental projection in the hallucination case, won't it do so in the ordinary perceptual case too? What is to prevent it doing so? This line of reasoning generalizes: what is true of the vase is true of everything I visually perceive, and everything I perceive with any other sense too. According to this projectivist account of perception, all perceptual experience is like this: without exception it is all projection.

So far as touch, taste and smell are concerned, the projectivist view is easy to accept, and probably accords with common sense. It is easy to believe that the distinctive smell and flavour of a lemon are properties of experiences which lemons cause us to have. It is easy to believe that the warmth we feel in a radiator is a sensation in our hand – and so akin to a pain or an itch. Smells, flavours and suchlike do not strike us as being 'out there' and independent of us in the same way as the immediate or direct objects of visual perception – auditory experience comes somewhere in between. But the projectivist account of vision is undeniably counterintuitive. When I look at the moon on a clear night, it is hard to believe that the moon is not itself present in my experience. It is hard to believe that what is present is nothing but an internally generated and outwardly projected phenomenal image, something ontologically akin to an itch or a pain. If projectivism is true, the boundary between inner and outer has to be revised: the realm of the inner (construed as that which belongs to my consciousness) expands to incorporate the entirety of the (seemingly) outer world as I experience it.

In saying all this I do not want to deny that veridical perception differs from hallucination. Projectivism is quite compatible with the idea that vase-like perceptual experience caused (in the normal sort of way) by light from a vase should be placed into a different category of experience from vase-like hallucinations. If we put veridical perceptual experience in a different category from hallucinations, we might go on to say that veridical perceptions and hallucinations are ontologically distinct kinds of experience. This too is compatible with projectivism, provided it is recognized that hallucinations and veridical perceptions have something important in common: they both involve the production of internally generated phenomenal images, strange though this seems from the standpoint of common sense.

Projectivism is counterintuitive in other ways. If the phenomenal properties we encounter in perceptual experience are not part of the external physical world, how is it that the brain manages to produce them? After all, the brain too is a physical thing. While this remains a deep mystery, it is not a reason for adopting a different view of perception. We already know the brain can generate phenomenal properties; to suppose that phenomenal properties such as colour are also possessed by ordinary physical things such as tables and vases simply multiplies the mystery. (Eliminating the mystery by denying the existence of phenomenal properties, or reducing them to something else, is not an option, given the experiential realism I am presupposing here.) If there is no reason to think ordinary physical objects possess anything resembling phenomenal colour, projectivism has the consequence that the familiar objects in the world about us are probably quite unlike how they appear to be. There is a very real sense in which the world is a place of silence and darkness. This can be a perturbing thought. But there is this consoling thought: things may not be as they appear, but there is no possibility of our seeing them as they really are, bereft of the secondary qualities we project onto them. If we did not see things clothed in projected secondary qualities, we would not see them at all.

This is not the place for a deeper treatment of these issues. As in the case of understanding-experience, my only reason for raising the issue of the general nature of perception is to help make clear how I am using terms like 'experience' and 'phenomenal contents'. When I talk about 'visual experience' I am talking about the visual field and its contents. This field, and its contents, I take to be wholly experiential items, parts of a person's total state of consciousness at a given time. When naive realists talk about the visual field and its contents, they are talking about physical objects out in the world that lie within someone's field of vision; 'experience' enters this picture only as a direct unmediated awareness of these outer objects. But when I talk about the relationship between auditory and visual experiences, I will usually be talking about contents occurring within the auditory and visual sense-fields. Some of these contents will be items we do not ordinarily think of as *experiential* at all.

1.5 Phenomenology

It might be thought that the projectivist view of perception is incompatible with adopting a phenomenological approach to our experience as a whole. Projectivism requires us to regard certain objects as being experiential in character, objects which we would ordinarily – whilst in the grip of the natural attitude – take to be non-experiential, so it might seem that by assuming projectivism I am starting off by misdescribing the phenomena. In one sense this is true, in another it is not.

Although I am rejecting the idea that veridical perception is a direct unmediated awareness of outer things, as should be clear by now I am not denying that this is how perception seems to us to be. Perceptual experience is *world-presenting*. By which I mean: the things we see (or seem to see in realistic hallucinations) seem to be out there in the world; the world seems to be directly revealing itself to us as soon as we open our eyes. Because of this, it is sometimes said that perceptual experience is transparent. We do not ordinarily think of the objects we see around us (i.e. the immediate objects of our experience) as experiential phenomena; we unthinkingly interpret our experience in a worldly manner. As a result, there is a sense in which experience itself is usually invisible. We take ourselves to be directly perceiving the world; we do not (while in the natural attitude) detect the presence of an experiential medium which lies between ourselves and the things in the world we see, hear and touch. Yet if projectivism is true, there is a sense in which we are all enclosed in spheres of virtual reality, phenomenal spheres somehow produced by activities within our brains: all we are directly aware of are the contents within these spheres. But this is not how it seems. Even when I am dwelling on the absurdities of naive realism I do not seem to be enclosed in a virtual world, I seem to be surrounded by ordinary material things, tables, chairs, walls, not experience.

That perceptual experience is world-presenting is a phenomenological truth, no doubt one of the most important of such truths. How, then, can we conduct a phenomenological investigation into the stream of consciousness while simultaneously embracing projectivism? The problem here is more apparent than real. We need to distinguish between two general sorts of phenomenology. On the one hand there is *naive* or *pre-critical* phenomenology, on the other there is *informed* or *critical* phenomenology. Someone engaged in pre-critical phenomenology tries to describe the character of their experience without making any explicit assumptions of a broadly philosophical sort about what 'experience' is. Someone engaged in critical phenomenology also tries to describe the character of their experience, but does so while allowing philosophical (or scientific) doctrines to influence what 'experience' is taken to be. Once this distinction is drawn, it becomes easier to understand how it is that some self-professed phenomenologists find themselves immediately presented with a world filled mainly with resonantly familiar things (such as houses and hammers) with scarcely an experience to be found, and others find themselves immediately presented with nothing but experience, in the form of phenomenal objects, sense-data, qualia-patterns and suchlike. Both sorts of phenomenology are probably worth pursuing (although there is room to question the degree to which a truly presupposition-less or theory-free phenomenology is really possible). The sort of phenomen-ology I will be pursuing in what follows will usually be of the critical variety.

Chalmers draws a useful distinction between three types of *phenomenal judgments* (1996: 175–6). A phenomenal judgment is a judgment made about experience; 'judgment' here can refer to spoken or written reports, or to thoughts one has about one's experience. A *first-order* judgment about expe-rience is about the objects or states of affairs the experience is of, i.e. the external objects that are presented. In talking about what we perceive, in ordinary world-presenting experience, we do not normally intend to talk about our *experience* as such at all. If I ask you to tell me what you can see I will usually want you to tell me about the objects you can perceive. Can you see the missing slate on the roof of the house opposite? Can you see the number on the front of the approaching bus which is still some distance away? If you tell me 'I can't see the number very clearly, but it might be the 125', you are making a first-order phenomenal judgment. Although you are talking about what you can see, and so are reporting on your experience, you are talking about the bus, you are reporting on the representational content of your experience rather than its phenomenal character. When we engage in phenomenology of the naive sort, we will for the most part be making first-order judgments. In making *second-order* judgments, we focus on our experience as such. In ordinary life, we most commonly make judgments of this type about bodily sensations. Focusing on my headache, I might wonder whether it is severe enough to warrant taking an aspirin. After a meal, I might detect a lingering flavour in my mouth and not be sure what it is a flavour of, so I focus my attention on its phenomenal character, trying to identify the kind of flavour it is. In doing so, I deliberately focus my atten-tion onto the character of (a part of) my current experience, and I realize that it is my experience that I am making a judgment about. To make second-order judgments about visual perceptual experience is not so common in everyday life, since we are usually concerned with what we can see, rather than with the character of our visual experience itself. But we can easily make the switch. One way to do it is to imagine that one's current visual experience is a hallucination, and describe how things *seem* without making any assumptions as to how things really are. Another way is to adopt the standpoint of a critical phenomenology informed by projectivism. From this standpoint, ordinary perceptual experience loses its transparency; everything that is immediately present in experience is regarded as an experi-ence. When I see the bus approaching, I regard the bus (the direct object of my visual experience) as a part of my consciousness. What Chalmers calls *third-order* phenomenal judgments are generalizations about types of experi-ence. If I say 'pains are more noticeable than sensations of pressure' or 'experiences within a stream of consciousness are usually unified diachronically and synchronically', I am making third-order judgments. Since I will be operating in the critical phenomenological mode, most of the claims I will be making about consciousness will be second- and third-order judgments.

Engaging in any sort of phenomenology is a risky business. When I refer to the character of what 'we' experience, what I am usually talking about is my experience, and the best way of describing it. Any claims I make about 'our' experience involve generalizations from these first-personal results, and this prompts the question: how do I know everyone (or *anyone*) else's inner conscious life is like mine? Since here is not the place to refute the sceptic concerning other minds (the sort of sceptic who denies we are justified in believing other people have consciousness at all, or consciousness in any way resembling our own), I shall be brief on this topic. We unthinkingly assume that our conscious lives are broadly similar, and this unthinking assumption receives confirmation over and over again in daily life, in our interactions with others, simply because we rarely (if ever) have occasion to question it. Whenever writers of any kind attempt to describe the general character of human consciousness, whatever the differences in fine details, we can usually recognize them as attempts to describe a mental landscape of a sort we are ourselves acquainted with. This is surely not coincidental. This is not to say there are no intersubjective differences at all. What does seem plausible (setting radical scepticism aside) is that what differences there are will tend to be minor rather than major, at least for those of us who are not mentally or physically impaired or otherwise significantly unusual. This suggests that we are most likely to find agreement on phenomenological issues when we focus on the general characteristics of consciousness, than we are when we probe its more specific modalities (as is done in oenology, for example). But this agreement may not be served up on a plate, it may be something we have to struggle to achieve. Although it is true to say that we know what it is like to be conscious simply in virtue of being conscious (and there is no other way to know this), it does not follow that we automatically know the most appropriate way to describe what it is like to be conscious, to put experience into words. But the fact that phenomenology can be difficult does not mean that it is impossible. For the most part I will be concerned only with the most general structural characteristics of streams of consciousness. On the assumption, which I think (and here assume) is justified, that everyone's consciousness shares the same general structural traits, when presented with competing descriptions of these it is reasonable to suppose that we should be able to recognize, compare and finally agree on the description which does most justice to the most basic facts concerning our experience. It may well be that in so doing we will become cognizant of aspects of our consciousness we were not explicitly aware of previously, but if so, we should be able to agree on their character too. As Dennett (1991: 80) says in this context: 'in crashing obviousness lies objectivity'.

1.6 Reality, appearance and phenomenal truths

The experiential realm is often equated with the realm of appearance. Taken in one way, this is unobjectionable. The surrounding world presents itself to us in perceptual experience, but it does so only partially – I cannot see the underside, or the inside, of the table in front of me – and not always accurately; things are not always how they appear to be. But taken in another way, the idea that experience is nothing more than appearance is wrong. Why? Because from the standpoint of moderate naturalism, experience itself is an unreduced and irreducible component of reality. This means our introspective knowledge of the character of our experience provides us with knowledge about how some small portion of reality really is – experience itself is a part or aspect of the real, not merely an appearance of the real. This knowledge may not be complete – experiences may have properties which are not discernible in their phenomenal character – but it cannot and should not be ignored, for there is unlikely to be any other way of acquiring it.

This point is sometimes overlooked, even by writers who take experience seriously. Unger argues that certain propositions about the nature of both consciousness and subjects of consciousness can come to seem very appealing when one reflects on one's own conscious experience. The relevant propositions may seem not only to be true, but necessarily true, perhaps even to be deep metaphysical truths. He maintains, however, that when these same propositions are considered from a viewpoint informed by a 'robust sense of reality', the situation changes: it becomes evident that the relevant propositions do not express deep metaphysical truths, indeed, it becomes hard to see how they could be true at all. What is this robust sense of reality? Unger suggests that in part

> it is a healthy epistemological scepticism: It cannot be nearly so easy as this to uncover deep truths about main aspects of reality. As with other psychological phenomena, an adequate understanding of conscious experience requires experiment, observation and theorizing that is both protracted and painstaking.
>
> (1990: 43)

He further suggests that this healthy epistemological scepticism may in turn be partly rooted in the belief that concrete reality is wholly physical in nature: we should not take seriously doctrines about experience (or subjects of experience) which are clearly in conflict with the 'objective' view of ourselves, namely that we are complex physical beings composed of very many simpler physical things.

I do not at this point want to consider the merits or otherwise of the various doctrines Unger is concerned to undermine, namely that consciousness is all or nothing, completely private to a single subject, and absolutely indivisible. What I do want to question is his assumption that truths about 'main aspects of concrete reality' cannot be discovered using the tools available to phenomenology, but only by the sorts of observation and experiment that are used in the natural sciences. Let us suppose there are some facts about experience which can be established solely by introspecting and formulating third-order phenomenal judgments. For want of a better term, we might call these *phenomenal truths*. Since, from the standpoint of moderate naturalism, experience is itself an ingredient of concrete reality, it is clearly a mistake to think phenomenal truths are anything other than truths about concrete reality. So should we be suspicious of the very idea of phenomenal truths? Unger holds that phenomenal truths are suspect because they are easily discovered, and 'deep' truths about reality cannot be easily discovered. But this claim is itself suspect, on several grounds. So far as the physical world is concerned, any number of truths are very easy to discover: objects fall when dropped, water boils and evaporates when heated, solid objects cannot occupy the same place at the same time. Truths such as these may only hold within restricted domains and with appropriate qualifications, and they may not be deep, since a theoretical story can be told (or desired) about why these empirical generalizations obtain, but they are certainly worth knowing. Perhaps there are phenomenal truths of comparable interest that are equally easy to discover. If so, the fact that they are easily discovered is irrelevant to their interest, or their truth. As for depth, it is true that phenomenology is primarily descriptive; it is certainly not in the business of formulating explanatory hypotheses, often concerning unobservable forces and entities, that are commonplace in the natural sciences. Depth in this form is not a phenomenological goal, or an attribute of phenomenal truths. But depth comes in other forms. Unger tacitly assumes that whatever phenomenal truths there are can easily be discovered. This is yet another suspect assumption: why assume that phenomenology is easy? I suggested above that the task of putting experience into words may sometimes prove difficult. Perhaps some phenomenal truths can only be discovered when unobvious questions are asked, or when appropriate concepts are brought to bear. As it happens, some aspects of our experience are easily described, but we shall see that others are not.

One last point. Suppose we believe the world to be wholly physical. Does this belief have any implications for what we can or cannot say about the character of our experience? Unger suggests that it does: if any putative phenomenal truth cannot be reconciled with the idea that we are wholly composed of small physical things, which are in turn composed of smaller physical things, the phenomenal claim must be rejected. But if we take experience seriously, and combine experiential realism with materialism, we can turn this argument on its head. If a claim about experience is both firmly grounded in the phenomenological data and in conflict with the picture of ourselves that is provided by one or other of the natural sciences, questioning the relevant science is at least as reasonable as questioning the relevant phenomenology. For if P-materialism is true, phenomenology is our only mode of access to the intrinsic nature of the material world; if truths about the phenomenal are truths about the physical, such truths can properly be regarded as data to which scientific theories are answerable.[6] The situation is similar if L-materialism is true. The L-materialist accepts that experience is an ingredient of the physical world, and also accepts that current physical science is radically incomplete. From this perspective, situations in which the phenomenological data conflict with accepted science may well provide valuable clues as to how the relevant science might be revised and improved. In making these remarks I am not suggesting that phenomenological claims are privileged and above suspicion. If putting experience into words is not always easy, mistakes are inevitable; so if a hypothesis about experience deriving from phenomenology turns out to be in conflict with some piece of scientific data, whether the latter derives from physics, psychology or neurophysiology, then it is certainly worth subjecting the phenomenological claim to renewed scrutiny. My point is simply that it is also reasonable to work in the other direction as well. And if, after due scrutiny, it turns out that the phenomenological claim is not one that can easily be given up, then we have reason to question the relevant scientific hypotheses.

1.7 Questions of demarcation and individuation

How are experiences to be classified into types? Upon what factors does the identity of a particular token experience depend? Before looking into these questions we must first decide what counts as 'an experience'.

I will adopt a flexible approach to this question: I will regard any experiential component of a stream of consciousness as 'an experience'. A complete momentary cross-section of a stream is an experience, the complete content of a stream over a given interval is an experience, any combination of co-occurring contents within a stream is an experience, e.g. the sensations of pressure on my back, and the right-hand side of my visual field together count as an experience. A typical stream of consciousness can be divided into particular experiences in many different ways. Although some divisions are more well founded than others, I will not assume that there is any one best way of dividing a given stream into its constituent parts. This flexible policy will prove useful later on, when we look at streams of consciousness and their parts in more detail. (Rather than provide a defence of this policy now I will wait until §4.2, by which time a clearer picture of streams and their contents will have emerged.) Since most experiences have some duration, the time at which an experience takes place will usually be a temporal interval rather than a durationless moment.

The phenomenal character of an experience consists of all its various phenomenal features. In referring to the character of an experience I will usually be referring to what the experience is like, exactly like, phenomenologically. So my current visual field, taken as a whole, has at this moment a certain phenomenal character, as do its various component regions – e.g. the region that consists of my perception of the illuminated part of the computer screen I am looking at. If my visual field were in any way different, it would have a different phenomenal character. If my visual field had a different character, my overall consciousness would also have a different character. For the sake of variety as much as convenience, as well as referring to experiences and their phenomenal characters I will sometimes refer to 'phenomenal objects' and 'phenomenal properties'. By 'object' here I mean any part of an experience; a phenomenal 'property' is any feature of a phenomenal object. So a pain I feel in my leg is a phenomenal object, and the felt quality of this pain is a phenomenal property. I shall use 'phenomenal content' to refer to both phenomenal objects and properties.

In talking about types of experience, I will usually assume that experiences with the same phenomenal character are of the same type. We could, if we wanted, classify experiences in narrower, more discriminating ways. We could, for example, take various non-phenomenal factors as relevant to the type of an experience. Experiences with the same phenomenal character can have different causes, and this difference can matter. You and your counterpart on Twin-Earth have phenomenally indistinguishable streams of consciousness, but the representational content of many of your world-related thoughts and perceptions are different. We could take the content (in this sense) of qualitatively indistinguishable experiences to be relevant to their identity. Similarly for causal role. Suppose someone were to 're-wire' your brain in such a way that everything you previously saw as blue you now see as orange, and vice-versa. Under these circumstances, phenomenal blue and phenomenal orange would come to possess different causal roles in your mind. Phenomenal orange would be caused by seeing objects that would previously have produced phenomenal blue, and vice-versa. After becoming accustomed to the alteration, on seeing a sky that (to you) looks bright orange, you might declare 'Another blue sky – global warming is not all bad', while thinking to yourself, silently, that the sky looked better when it *was* blue. If we opted to individuate experiences in terms of their causal role, then experiences with exactly the same intrinsic phenomenal character but different causal roles would be counted as different types of experience. However, since my concerns in what follows will for the most part be purely phenomenological, I will ignore these alternative or finer-grained ways of classifying experiences.

The identity of a token experience is commonly held to depend upon on its subject, its phenomenal character, and its time of occurrence. The rationale for this tri-partite identity criterion is readily understandable. Take two experiences, e_1 and e_2. If they differ in their intrinsic phenomenal character (if one is a pain, the other a smell sensation), then it is obvious that e_1 and e_2 are distinct experiences. Likewise if e_1 has already occurred and so is wholly in the past by the time e_2 happens. But what if e_1 and e_2 have exactly the same phenomenal character and occur at precisely the same time? Could they still be distinct? Of course they could: provided they were had by different people, or to speak more generally, provided they have different subjects. It may not happen very often that two subjects have experiences with exactly the same character at precisely the same time, but it is conceivable that they might. However, although the subject/time/character criterion is in many ways a natural one, it is not one which I will adopt.

The idea that co-conscious experiences belong to the same subject – are consubjective – is certainly an important idea, although whether it is always or necessarily true is another matter. The same applies to the notion that a single subject has only a single stream of consciousness at any one time. Interesting though these themes are, they will not play any significant role in what follows. The thesis that co-conscious experiences are consubjective may be true, but it is not very informative. Accepting the thesis does not tell us what kinds of purely experiential relationships hold among co-conscious experiences, and we do not need to know what kind of thing selves or subjects are – or even assume there are such things – to embark on a phenomenological inquiry into these relationships. For this reason I will adopt a policy of strict neutrality on the relationship between subjects and experiences. Having adopted this policy, I am no longer in a position to subscribe to any particular principle concerning the sorts of experience a subject could have at any one time, and this in turn means that a policy of individuating experiences in terms of their subjects is as close to vacuous as makes no difference, for present purposes if not for others.

So, in order to accommodate the possibility of numerically distinct experiences which are both qualitatively indistinguishable and simultaneous, we need to introduce an alternative third ingredient. If we assume some form of materialism is true, we can treat experiences like any other physical occurrence and individuate them in terms of their spatial location – or, possibly, their sub-spatial material ingredients. If some form of property dualism is true, we can individuate in terms of physical causes and effects, or – more radically – take token experiences to be primitive particulars. Hence my policy. I will assume that token experiences owe their individuality to three factors: their exact phenomenal character, their time of occurrence, and their physical basis. In keeping with my stance of moderate naturalism, I will not speculate exactly what form this physical basis takes. If token experiences should prove to be primitive particulars, nothing I have to say will be affected.

1.8 A look ahead

For the benefit of those who like to know where they are going before they set off, I will conclude these preliminaries by providing a brief outline of the way the discussion will proceed.

I begin by considering the synchronic unity of consciousness. When simultaneous experiences are co-conscious, what is the nature of this relationship, what can be said about it from a purely experiential perspective? My answer to the latter question will be: nothing. I will argue that synchronic co-consciousness is a primitive feature of experience, one which cannot be analysed or reduced to anything else. This result emerges from a process of elimination. Chapter 2 is devoted to examining two superficially similar (but in reality quite different) accounts of co-consciousness: one of these appeals to introspection, the other to a special form of awareness. According to the latter view, co-consciousness is a product of the essentially bi-polar nature of consciousness itself: any experiencing consists of a phenomenal object falling within an act of awareness; when a multiplicity of experiences falls under the scope of a single awareness, these experiences are automatically unified. Uncovering the inadequacies of these accounts prepares the ground for the examination of a third: the idea that phenomenal contents are co-conscious in virtue of occurring within a unified phenomenal space. I tackle this idea in Chapter 3. Here, in addition to arguing that co-consciousness does not necessarily take a spatial form, I take a more general look at the notion of a sensory field (or space). Just as different accounts can be given of physical space – think of the relationist/substantivalist dispute – so different accounts can be given of phenomenal space. Or rather, there are different kinds of phenomenal space, and these can be construed in ways which correspond to some of the different ways in which physical space has been conceived.

Whatever account can be given of co-consciousness at-a-time, it will be only half the story. There is also the unity of experience across time to consider: diachronic co-consciousness. What we are thinking, feeling and perceiving is usually changing, in one way or another, from one moment to the next. Present experiences slip into the past and are replaced by new experiences. The contents of the present moment of consciousness are continually changing or being renewed, and this continual change is itself an experienced feature of consciousness. I start to look at this diachronic unity in Chapter 5.

The step-by-step approach makes for simplicity, but may also appear artificial, in that to focus initially on synchronic unity independently of diachronic unity might seem phenomenologically unrealistic. Consciousness, it could be objected, is temporal through and through: our thoughts and experiences are never static, but constantly and continually flowing. While this seems true, there is no denying that we are aware of experiences happening simultaneously as well as successively. Experience may always be flowing, but we can nonetheless distinguish between the unity which cuts across a stream, and holds between simultaneously occurring experiences, and the unity which runs through a stream and binds non-simultaneous successive experiences. Since the unity of consciousness has these two dimensions, there is no reason why we should not deal with them separately, although we will only have a full understanding of the phenomenon when we have investigated both.

Chapter 5 consists of a general overview of the problems phenomenal temporality poses, and of some of the key assumptions made by those who have tried to provide an account of it. In Chapter 6 the focus is on C. D. Broad and E. Husserl, both of whom wrestled with the topic at different stages of their respective careers. Their work is of special interest because of the way their views evolved. Broad rejected his initial account in favour of a theory similar to one Husserl advocated in some of his earlier writings on time-consciousness, whereas Husserl in turn found fault with this earlier work and moved in a direction reminiscent of the theory Broad had initially advocated, but later came to reject. The reason for this curious pattern of reversals lies, I suggest, in the fact that both writers were influenced by certain erroneous but influential assumptions, and so failed to notice a comparatively simple solution to the problem. In Chapter 7 I expound this simple solution (which has been advocated on several occasions by John Foster, and is briefly mentioned by Russell), argue for a further simplification (the rejection of the bi-polar model of consciousness) and attempt to overcome the various objections which can be levelled against it. I conclude that the same basic relationship of co-consciousness is responsible for the unity of consciousness both at and over time. Our streams of consciousness have but one unifying agent.

Although my main concern is with the binding agent within consciousness, the phenomenal glue, as it were, which is responsible for experiential unity, I will also be looking at various different but related issues. In Chapter 4, by way of an interlude before embarking on the examination of phenomenal temporality, I consider whether synchronic co-consciousness is a transitive relationship. Is it possible for there to be three simultaneous experiences, such that the first is co-conscious with the second, and the second is co-conscious with the third, but the first is not co-conscious with the third? It is certainly difficult to imagine such a state of affairs, but is imaginability here a reliable guide to possibility? Familiar results from neuroscience concerning split-brains suggest it may not be; I tentatively argue the opposite.

The final two chapters are devoted to another difficult issue, that of phenomenal interdependence. When experiences are co-conscious, does the fact that they are so unified affect the experiences in question? If so, in what ways and to what extent? How would your overall experience have been different if, when reading *these italicized words* you had heard a loud noise? Some authors have argued that consciousness is profoundly holistic, such that any particular experience is in some manner affected or altered by the other experiences with which it is co-conscious. These claims are scrutinized in Chapter 8, where I distinguish different forms of phenomenal interdependence, and argue that it is a real but limited occurrence, one that is exhibited most clearly in certain sorts of perceptual wholes or gestalts. In Chapter 9 I explore the same issue from another direction, and suggest that co-consciousness is indeed responsible for a form of holism within experience, but a holism of a rather more subtle variety than any of those previously discussed.

2 Unity, introspection and awareness

2.1 Awareness

The unity within consciousness is something we experience, something we have an awareness of, something we can notice. This may suggest that co-consciousness is in some manner bound up with, dependent upon, or even created by, awareness. This is the idea I will be evaluating in this chapter, albeit in a restricted form: I will be concerned only with synchronic unity, with the way simultaneous experiences are related to one another within a stream of consciousness.

The term *awareness* is used in different ways, and not all of these uses specifically concern consciousness, let alone the unity of consciousness. Sometimes the term is effectively synonymous with knowledge or belief. We say such things as 'I wasn't aware that Britain has so few high mountains', or 'Were you aware that Susan and David have divorced?'. In this sense, 'awareness' is not directly concerned with experience at all. I may have been aware of Susan and David's divorce without consciously thinking about it. My interlocutor was not querying whether I happened to be currently thinking about this state of affairs; the question was about whether I knew about it, whether I had this piece of information stored away somewhere. As far as specifically conscious awareness is concerned, several further uses of the term need to be distinguished. Sometimes, the presence of conscious awareness is taken simply to indicate the presence of experience, in any form. 'Consciousness first appeared on the scene with simple organic life-forms, previously the universe was wholly devoid of awareness'. When 'awareness' is used in this way it is virtually synonymous with 'conscious-ness' and 'experience', as I use the terms. But this is not the most common use of 'awareness' in relation to experience. 'I watched a dog stroll across the street, but I wasn't aware it was Seamus'. Here the lack of awareness indicates the failure to recognize an individual (an individual that one would recognize ordinarily or in other circumstances). We sometimes say we are aware of something if and when we notice or pay attention to it. 'It had been getting dark for some time, but I only became aware of it when I started to read the newspaper'. Recognition usually involves concepts: I can only recognize (be aware) that the tea I have been given is Earl Grey if I have the concept of *Earl Grey* tea. But recognition does not always require concepts: when a mother picks up her young child, the child may recognize who it is that has picked them up (be aware that it is a familiar visual presence) without having the concept 'mother' or 'person'. Similarly, animals may recognize all manner of things for which they have no concepts (of a linguistic sort at least). We also use awareness in relation to introspection. When we want to find out about our current experience, we introspect: we deliberately focus our attention and see what we find. Think of what you do when you wonder whether your toothache is getting better or worse. As you scrutinize your toothache, you become *introspectively aware* of it. There are also some purely philosophical uses of 'awareness'. According to one influential doctrine, consciousness has a two-level structure: all experiencing consists of an awareness of some content.

So far as the unity of consciousness is concerned, only the last two uses of 'awareness' are of direct relevance. If all experiencing consists of an awareness of some content, then presumably the unity of consciousness is a product of different experiential contents falling within the scope of a single centre of awareness. A large part of this chapter will be taken up with evaluating this view. However, before embarking on this investigation it will be useful to explore some related themes, namely the relationship between the unity of consciousness and the sorts of awareness involved in attention, introspection and recognition. Of particular interest here is the relationship between unity and introspection, which I will be looking at in §2.3. But first I want to take a closer look at some of the different ways in which we can notice or pay attention to the different parts of our experience. Doing so not only sheds light on the relationship between introspective awareness and unity, it suggests that introspection itself comes in different forms.

2.2 The phenomenal background

Imagine taking a brief look at a row of books on a shelf. Suppose the shelf contains about twenty books, and you allow your eyes to sweep across them all, without pausing on any particular one. You may notice and read only a couple of titles; a few moments later, if you try, you may be able to remember these titles along with a couple more (you can probably recognize some books by their jacket colours, which you may be able to remember seeing on the shelf). But it is obvious that your overall visual experience as you looked at the bookshelf was a good deal richer than what you can now remember: the entire row of books registered in your experience. You are unlikely to have read the title of each book, and your perception of some may well have been blurred, as in an indistinct photograph, but most (probably all) of the books featured in your visual experience, and so contributed to its overall phenomenal character. If the shelf had contained one book more, or one book fewer, your experience would probably have had a different phenomenal character, even if this difference is one you would not have noticed, and one you would not remember (so you would never be in a position to describe or talk about it). The shelf may have contained a book with a brightly coloured dust-jacket in a quite unfamiliar colour; this colour formed part of your visual experience, even though you would not have recognized it (you would have had no specific name or concept for it) if you had noticed it.

This case illustrates the way the phenomenal content of experience is not restricted to or exhausted by what we notice or are able to remember or describe in any detail. We can all see colours (or hear sounds, detect smells, etc.) for which we have no specific name or concept. The example also suggests that purely phenomenal consciousness has a robust independence from awareness of the attentive and recognitional kind. This is not to say that the character of our experience is wholly independent of attention. Suppose that on looking at the row of books you had allowed your gaze to rest on the book on the extreme right; suppose you had focused your attention on this book. You almost certainly have read its title, and by virtue of paying attention to this book the others would have registered in your experience to a lesser degree, and you would remember less about them. But the important point remains: the content of our experience at a given moment is not restricted to whatever it is we are paying attention to at the time in question.

This point has a bearing on the status of marginal or peripheral experience. Imagine what it is like to read a book, a sometimes boring book, while listening to some music in the background. From time to time your attention wanders, you start to daydream; although your attention is taken up with whatever it is that you are imagining, your eyes remain open and fixed on the page. What are you seeing and hearing while in this distracted state of mind? This much at least seems evident: you clearly continue to have *some* visual and auditory experiences. As you become immersed in your daydream you no longer pay attention to the book; you doubtless cease to focus your eyes upon the page, so you no longer see the words on the page clearly, but you continue to have visual experience: it is not as though all the lights go out, plunging you into total darkness. Suppose this were to occur, suppose the room *were* plunged into total darkness. You would surely notice the change. Moreover, you would not merely think to yourself, 'What's happened? The room wasn't like this a few moments ago', you would see the change, the sudden transition from light to dark. If you see this transition you must have been seeing something throughout. The same applies to the music in the background, though perhaps not so obviously. You are probably having some auditory experience all the time, even though you were not paying any attention to it – if the sound had suddenly doubled in volume you would probably have heard it do so.

Perhaps it is possible to be conscious without being attentively aware of any part of one's experience. William James suggests that

Most people fall several times a day into a fit of something like this: The eyes are fixed on vacancy, the sounds of the world melt into confused unity, the attention is dispersed so that the whole body is felt, as it were, at once, and the foreground of consciousness is filled, if by anything, by a sort of solemn sense of surrender to the empty passing of time.

(1952: 261)

I expect most of us have experienced something approaching this.

In all these cases there is experience that goes unnoticed; there is experience without conscious awareness, in the sense of 'awareness' as attention or recognition. But experience that is not attended to is still experience. Indeed, it is plausible to suppose that the bulk of our consciousness consists of this sort of unnoticed experience. I will call this sphere of experience the *phenomenal background*. The phenomenal background goes largely unnoticed because it is constantly present for as long as we are awake (and often while we dream). Most experiences that go on long enough for us to become habituated to them (but which do not cease altogether) will sink into this background, for example the sound of a refrigerator, or the noise of a car engine.

The phenomenal background has three main components. One such is the diverse range of bodily experience (I have already remarked on our tendency to overlook these). Another is world-presenting perceptual experience, what we see, hear, touch, smell and taste. The content of this experience is nothing less than the surrounding world: the ground underfoot, rooms, walls and furniture, streets, fields and trees, animals and people, the sky above – these are all parts of the phenomenal background, they all feature in our experience, for the most part unnoticed, as we go about our ordinary business. Needless to say, this is not apparent while we are in the ordinary mode of the natural attitude of naive realism. It is only when we shift to the informed phenomenological mode, and make second- or third-order phenomenal judgments, that we view the background as part of our experience at all. For the most part, we regard the background as a part of the world.

The third component of the phenomenal background is in some ways the most elusive of all: our overall mood, our sense of self, what it feels like to be the conscious being we are. One aspect of the sense of self is bodily, but there is another distinctively mental or psychological aspect. When I wake up on an average morning, the room I find myself in, what I can smell and see, the noises I can hear, the feel of my body as a whole – this is all familiar. But something else, something inner is familiar too, the overall character of my stream of consciousness. If I were to think about it, I would recognize that the sort of consciousness I currently have (as I awake) is similar to that which I usually have. This is not just a matter of what I think and remember, it concerns what I feel like *as* I think, remember, and try to decide what to do next: the ambient background against which my stream of thought unfolds. When people speak of their 'sense of self', at least part of what they are referring to is this ambient inner background, the intangible *atmosphere* of the conscious mind. This inner background is not constant, it changes with our mood, but perhaps not very dramatically. Perhaps there are significant differences between individuals: the atmosphere of the Buddha's consciousness might have been very different from that of Vlad the Impaler. Or perhaps not; perhaps the ambient background of most human consciousness is much the same for most of the time. The important thing is simply to acknowledge the phenomenon in question: there is something that it feels like to be oneself, and this is part of the overall phenomenal background, and is constantly present along with the other components – the feel of one's body and the presence of the surrounding world.

With this fuller characterization of the phenomenal background in mind, consider a variant of the scenario sketched above. You are sitting in an armchair, you have stopped daydreaming and have become engrossed in your book, which has taken an interesting turn, when suddenly the *entire* phenomenal background disappears, not just peripheral sound and vision, but mood and bodily experience too. The effect would be dramatic: it would seem as though the surrounding world had vanished, and your body with it. You would not feel the surrounding and supporting armchair, and since the surrounding room would no longer be present in your experience – save for the page of the book you were reading – you would be both surrounded and filled by void, physically and emotionally. As this example makes plain, the sense we have of being embodied beings-in-a-world is due almost entirely to the presence of the phenomenal background.

Since the phenomenal background is not usually the object of our attention, we are rarely attentively aware of it. But it would be odd to say we have no awareness of it whatsoever, of any kind; it is, after all, a constant presence in our experience. This reveals a further flexibility in the notion of 'awareness': we can be *inattentively aware* of things, ourselves and our surroundings. Switching to the informed phenomenological mode, this means we can be inattentively aware of our experience. I will refer to this mode of consciousness as *passive* awareness.

Exploring the phenomenal background

Having recognized the importance of the phenomenal background, a methodological question arises. How can we conduct a phenomenological investigation into this part of our experience? By definition, the background is not something to which we pay attention. If I deliberately attend to the character of the sensations in my lower back, these sensations are no longer part of the phenomenal background. In making phenomenal judgments, especially second- and third-order judgments, we rely on introspection. Given that introspection involves attentive awareness, how can we possibly make phenomenal judgments about the phenomenal background? If we cannot make such judgments, how can we know there is such a thing at all?

The answer to this should already be plain: we *can* make phenomenal judgments about the peripheral regions of our experience. We can register and report on the contents of our passive awareness (either verbally or in thought), and we can do so without focusing our attention onto the phenomena in question. One way of doing this is to rely on short-term memory. We can 'replay', perhaps repeatedly, the past few moments of our experience, trying to remember it as best we can. In so doing, we can notice or direct our attention onto aspects of this stretch of experience that went unnoticed and unattended at the time.

But we do not need to rely only on memory – there is a more direct route. We can make judgments about the phenomenal background more or less as it happens. Try the following experiment. Focus your attention as hard as you can onto the page in front of you, onto its colour or texture; keep your attention focused here, and while doing so describe out loud something else you can perceive, e.g. the colour of the walls that you can see in your peripheral vision, or any sounds you can hear. Suppose the walls are green: you can notice and report on this without significantly lessening the degree of attention you are paying to the page in front of you. There will probably be some reduction in the degree of attention you are paying to the page, but not a great deal. The important point is that you can register something of the character of the contents of your peripheral experience without focusing your attention onto your peripheral experience itself. We can call this procedure *passive introspection*. (Not to be confused with the sort of passive awareness I mentioned above, which is non-selective and non-introspective.) Of course, ordinarily, if we wanted to make a second-order judgment about some aspect of our current experience, we would deliberately turn our attention onto it: we would actively introspect. Passive introspection is certainly less informative than active introspection, but memory aside, there is no other route of access to the phenomenal background.[1]

In passive introspection we focus our attention away from the content we wish to describe or take note of; in this manner, we can (in a manner of speaking) attend to what we are *not* paying attention to. There may seem to be more than a whiff of paradox here. How can we pay attention to something we are deliberately not paying attention to? But the problem is only verbal. We can distinguish between *primary* and *secondary* attention. Primary attention is what we ordinarily mean by attention. The objects of secondary attention are the parts of the phenomenal background we choose to register or make a judgment about while deliberately keeping our (primary) attention fixed elsewhere.

It might be objected that this distinction, along with the corresponding distinction between active and passive introspection, is confused. The objection runs thus: 'We can only pay attention to one thing at a time; when we try to attend to two different things we find ourselves quickly switching our attention back and forth. There is only one form of introspection, and one form of attention.' But while it is true that we can, if we choose, quickly move our attention back and forth between two objects, we can also choose to keep our attention locked onto just one thing, and while doing so take note of some aspect of our experience that we are deliberately not attending to. Moreover, we can do so in a selective way: I could, for example, decide on a policy of keeping my attention fixed on my annoying toothache while taking note, in a repeated sequence, of what I can feel in my feet, see at the upper right corner of my visual field, and hear to my left. Given that when I am registering what I can feel in my feet I am not registering, in the same way, what I can see or hear, it is reasonable to say that I am paying attention (of a sort) to my feet, but not to what I can see or hear, even though my full attention (in the ordinary sense) remains locked firmly onto my toothache. It should also be noted that a policy of selectively attending, in a secondary way, to different aspects of our experience, can be accompanied by a deliberate switching of our primary attention back and forth between two distinct targets.

One last point. Although we often make judgments or form beliefs about what we introspect, it is important to note that not all introspection, whether passive or active, is judgmental. Sometimes we introspect in a purely exploratory way: we focus on some part of our experience with the intention of merely making ourselves open to whatever is there. Indeed, this exploratory kind of introspection will often precede any attempt at coming to a belief or forming a judgment.

2.3 Unity and introspection

The relationship between the unity of consciousness and introspection is a somewhat tangled one. In part this is because, as we have just seen, there are different kinds of introspection. For present purposes I will take it that we are introspectively aware of an experience when we attend to it, actively or passively, usually (though not always) with a view to forming a judgment or belief about it on the basis of the direct or non-inferential access that we have to our own experiences. But there is another reason why the relationship between unity and introspection is somewhat complicated: there are different questions to be addressed and answered. As should by now be clear, the idea that introspection (of whatever kind) is responsible for the unity of consciousness is a non-starter. Introspection is something we engage in only sporadically, whereas our typical streams of consciousness are unified (to some degree) all the time; so it is clearly not the case that experiences are co-conscious only when they are actually introspected. A more interesting issue is whether experiences are co-conscious when or because they *could* be introspected. On the face of it, although the vast majority of our experiences go by without being the objects of introspective scrutiny, all these non-introspected experiences were available to introspection as they occurred, they were all *introspectible*. What is the connection between unity and introspectibility? I will call the claim that synchronic co-consciousness and introspectibility are essentially bound up with one another the *I-thesis*. The I-thesis comes in two forms:

Strong I-thesis   Co-consciousness is constituted by introspectibility: experiences are co-conscious *because* they are introspected or introspectible. A group of token experiences are co-conscious if and only if they are either the actual or potential objects of a single introspective awareness.

Weak I-thesis   Co-consciousness is not constituted by introspectibility, but the two are correlated: if a group of experiences are co-conscious they are all actual or potential objects of a single introspective awareness.

Since for both theses the sort of introspectibility at issue can be active or passive, there are really four distinct theses to consider. The Strong I-thesis, in either form, is not a plausible one, but is nonetheless worth considering. For in coming to understand exactly why the Strong I-thesis is false, a significant aspect of the unity of consciousness comes into clearer focus.

The Strong I-thesis

Consider first the Strong I-thesis and the role of active introspection. Is there any reason to believe experiences are only co-conscious because they can be actively introspected? I cannot see that there is. The unity of the phenomenal background is something we are passively aware of; although we can turn our attention onto it if we wish, it remains resolutely present and unified when our active attention is focused elsewhere. The unity of the background seems wholly independent of active introspection; it is something active introspection can *reveal*, when it is appropriately directed, but it is there anyway. The same considerations apply to passive introspection. Although we can probe the phenomenal background by using this technique, it is not something we do very often, and yet we have a constant passive awareness of the background and its unity. Again, the unity of the background is something that we can discover by using passive introspection, but this 'discovery' only amounts to a recognition of what was there anyway. The *unity* of the background, and hence co-consciousness, is a feature of our experience that seems to be more basic than any sort of introspection. Another example will help make this clear, if it is not already.

Imagine walking through a park. As you stroll along, various things and happenings attract your attention. You see a shrub that you do not recognize in the border; you stare at it for a minute or two, trying to identify it. As you do so a child a few yards ahead starts to cry. A little while later you hear a birdcall which may have been a cuckoo; you pause to listen to it more carefully. Now imagine what your experience would be like, as a whole, on these two occasions. When you pause to concentrate on the mysterious shrub, what happens to the various plants surrounding the shrub, the ground underfoot, the sky above? Well, nothing happens to them; they do not vanish as your attention becomes focused on the shrub; you see the shrub and you also see whatever surrounds it, even if only in a blurred fashion. While this is going on the child starts to cry; after an initial moment of annoyance, you manage to return your attention to the shrub. But the child's crying does not disappear; you continue to hear it, even though you have succeeded in not paying attention to it. Similarly, when you strain your ears trying to identify the birdcall, you continue to see the park all about you: the trees, the path, the fields, the sky – they do not all suddenly vanish into thin air. What of bodily experience, does this vanish when you pay attention to what you are seeing or hearing? Of course not. You are standing upright, weighted to the ground as you always are, perhaps leaning forward slightly to get a better look – it *feels* like something to be in this condition, and you continue to have these feelings. Then there is what you are thinking – 'What sort of shrub is it? I think I've seen that shape of leaf before' – and your overall mood. But I shall not go on. We all know what it is like to walk through a park and pause to look at something. The point I want to get across is that the overall experience here is *unified*. As your attention flits from one thing to another, you perceive more than you attend to, you continue to have thoughts, emotions and bodily sensations, and you have these while feeling situated in your environment. The phenomenal background is not just a constant presence in ordinary experience, it is a unified presence.

I have been describing matters from the naive standpoint, but the same applies if we move to the critical standpoint. Focusing one's attention is not like closing down the stops on a camera; one's experience does not shrink or contract. But one thing of significance does change. From the naive standpoint, the unity of your experience is a consequence of the fact that you are part of a unified world. The things you see, hear and touch are things in your environment; they are all things in the space surrounding you, the space within which you are situated. From the informed standpoint, this unity is in the first instance a feature of your experience: you are having a variety of co-conscious experiences. Your bodily experiences are co-conscious with your perceptual experience, and these are both co-conscious with your conscious thoughts, decisions, imaginings, memories and emotions. The co-consciousness of these various experiences registers only in passive awareness.

As this example makes clear, the overall unity of consciousness is independent of both passive and active introspection. However, while this is a significant result, there is a further limitation on the scope of introspective awareness that is worth noting.

Suppose you do introspect some part of your current experience, actively or passively. This introspected experience remains co-conscious with the remainder of your experience, or at least a large part of it (the world does not vanish when you introspect). Given this, what is responsible for the unity of the introspected experience with the non-introspected experiences with which it is co-conscious? One thing seems certain: it cannot be any form of introspection. When you focus your active attention onto the shrub your thoughts, bodily feelings and auditory experiences all remain co-conscious with your visual experience. These experiential relationships cannot be explained in terms of introspectibility, for they are not even *potential* objects of introspection. If you were to try to actively introspect these relationships you would have to stop introspecting your experience of the shrub. As this example makes plain, the co-consciousness of experiences which are not being actively introspected with experiences which are, is not something which can be actively introspected. The same applies in the case of passive introspection. An experience that is the object of secondary attention is co-conscious with both the rest of the phenomenal background and the object of primary attention. This overall unity is something of which we have a passive awareness, but it is not something of which we could have a passive introspective awareness.

This is not to say that we cannot passively introspect the experiential relationship between an experience we are actively introspecting and some region of the phenomenal background. I can be actively introspecting my auditory experience of the child's crying whilst at the same time passively introspecting the fact that this auditory experience is co-conscious with my visual experience. But even in this sort of case there will usually be experiences and experiential relationships which are not introspected, for example the co-consciousness of my bodily experiences with my auditory and visual experiences. So the point remains: with the exception of the sort of case just noted, the co-consciousness of introspected and non-introspected experience necessarily eludes introspection. This provides another reason for rejecting the Strong I-thesis: there is at least one form of co-consciousness that is in principle non-introspectible.

The Weak I-thesis

According to the Weak I-thesis, introspectibility and co-consciousness are correlated: any experiences that are co-conscious could be introspected. We have just seen that in one case at least, this is not true. But with this exception noted, might it not be that all the other parts of our experience are introspectible? At first sight this seems plausible enough, but there are complications. I will start by looking at the Weak I-thesis in connection with active introspection.

The idea that we could have introspected experiences we did not in fact introspect only makes sense if the sort of introspection in question does not alter the character of the relevant experiences. Since the identity of an experience depends in part on its phenomenal character, if introspection affected the character of an experience we clearly could not introspect experiences that we did not in fact introspect. It is also clear that *active* introspection does influence the character of experience. Think of the effects of dwelling on one's physical discomforts. A headache which while unnoticed was no more than a nagging irritation can become a genuine torment when we start paying attention to it, and in so doing the pain undergoes a change in phenomenal character. Suppose that five minutes ago I was not actively introspecting my slight headache. According to the version of Weak I-thesis, I could have been attentively aware of this sensation if I had chosen to be. But if I had so chosen my headache would very probably have intensified, and so the pain I would have been reflectively aware of would not have been numerically the same pain as I actually had. Pain is a type of experience whose phenomenal character is *attention-dependent*. It is not alone. Auditory experience in the form of background noise is also attention-dependent, but here the alterations can be more dramatic. Directing attention onto the sounds impinging on the edges of one's awareness turns a vague humming and buzzing into a combination of distinct and familiar noises. The 'cocktail party effect' is a well known example of this: on first entering a room full of a crowd of conversing people we hear nothing but the noise created by many raised competing voices. By turning our attention onto a particular face and listening hard, we can often begin to hear what this person is saying quite distinctly. As we do so, the hubbub of other voices recedes deeper into the phenomenal background.

For illustrative purposes I have deliberately chosen two cases where attention-dependency is particularly evident; although less evident in other sorts of case, it is there nonetheless. There is nothing deeply mysterious about attention-dependency. When we focus our attention onto some part of our experience, or on some part of the environment that we are perceiving with one of our senses, it seems that our brains react by allowing more of the stimuli pouring through the relevant sensory channel to be processed; this results in a more noticeable and more detailed experience. This change is due solely to (active) attention – it occurs whether or not we shift the focus of our eyes, or change the orientation of our heads so as to listen more effectively. There may be some conscious subjects whose minds are not like ours this respect, so attention-dependency is certainly a contingent phenomenon. But since our experience does exhibit this dependency, it will often be the case that experiences we did not introspect could not have been introspected.

What of passive introspection? Passive introspection is an unusual activity to engage in, to say the least. Most of the introspection we under-take is of the active variety, which is not surprising: if you want to find out about some part of your experience, why divert your attention away from it? Passive introspection may be unusual, but it can reach places active intro-spection cannot: into the recesses of the phenomenal background. The question we need to consider is not whether we actually passively introspect all our experience (we do not), but whether all our experience could be passively introspected.

We have already noted a general limitation on passive introspection: the co-consciousness of experiences that are passively introspected with those that are not cannot itself be an object of passive introspection. This point aside, the question we need to ask is whether passive introspection induces the same attention-dependent alterations in the character of experience as active introspection. This seems unlikely. If I want to investigate the auditory component of my current phenomenal background, I will keep my primary attention focused elsewhere – for example onto the fine detail of the wallpaper in front of me – and direct my secondary attention onto what I am hearing. I can then make a variety of phenomenal judgments about this part of the background. The fact that my primary attention is not directed onto the items I am making judgments about means the risk of attention-induced changes in phenomenal character is reduced, if not wholly eliminated. If this is true more generally, the idea that the bulk of our experience could be passively introspected, as it occurs, seems quite plausible. Since passive introspection is a delicate affair – it is all too easy to allow one's primary attention to drift over to the intended target – many actual attempts at passive introspection will fail. That is, the intended target will undergo some slight attention-induced alteration in phenomenal character. Perhaps most attempts will fail. But there is also the possibility of success, and to this extent, in the case of passive introspection, the Weak I-thesis may well be largely true – for beings whose minds are like ours.

The unspeakable

I have suggested that we are aware of the unity of the phenomenal background, even when we are not paying attention to it. What kind of awareness of this unity do we have? Obviously, an awareness of the passive sort, but a form of passive awareness which is distinct from what I have been calling passive introspection, which involves the deployment of secondary attention. To clearly mark this fact, I will use the term *wholly passive* awareness, or *WP-awareness*, to refer to the sort of non-attentive and non-selective awareness that we have of the unity of the phenomenal background.

WP-awareness is more closely bound up with co-consciousness than any other form of awareness: not only is the awareness we have of the phenomenal background when we are not interrogating it of the wholly passive kind, as we have already noted, but when we do interrogate our experience, either by actively or passively introspecting some part of it, the introspected experience typically remains co-conscious with non-introspected experiences. This experiential relationship cannot possibly be introspected, passively or actively, since attention (whether primary or secondary) is directed elsewhere, hence the awareness we have of the unity of introspected and non-introspected contents is of the wholly passive kind. If anything could be said to constitute co-consciousness, it is WP-awareness. This sort of awareness seems both sufficient and necessary for co-consciousness.

Although WP-awareness plays a unique role in our consciousness, it is also uniquely elusive. Any part or feature of our experience that we formulate first- or second-order judgments about will be introspected, either actively or passively. Any part or feature of our experience that is the object of primary or secondary attention is likewise introspected, either actively or passively. As a result there is a limited amount we are able to say or consciously believe about the contents or objects of WP-awareness. To a large extent, what we are aware of in non-attentive awareness belongs to the realm of the unmentionable or indescribable. The same applies to the unity of consciousness itself, since this is only fully manifest at the level of WP-awareness.

This is not as mysterious as it may seem. If we cannot frame first- or second-order judgments about experiences to which we are not attending, it is because these kinds of judgment are selective. At a minimum, making such judgments involves taking note of certain features of an experience at the expense of others. This 'taking note' may amount to no more than selective attention: imagine listening to a police siren in order to ascertain whether it is getting louder or softer. Or it may involve simple recognition, as in 'I know that face', or it may involve the formation of beliefs and the application of concepts – 'That colour is vermilion'. When we make judgments like this there are inevitably aspects of our experience that are not being attended to or judged in the same way (assuming that our experience has some degree of complexity, which it usually has). But again, the experiences that are not attended to are perfectly real; they make up the phenomenal background, which in turn makes up the bulk of our experience. In saying that the experiences we make first- and second-order judgments about are just as real as the constituents of the phenomenal background, I am making a third-order judgment, a judgment about experience in general. The contents of WP-awareness may elude introspection, but we nonetheless know what they are like; the contents of WP-awareness are experiences that we have or undergo, and the phenomenal character of these experiences is as real as that of any other kind of experience. True, we cannot make the kinds of judgment about the phenomenal background which require attention or introspection, but to describe or form beliefs about its general features we do not need to introspect. When we do introspect some particular part of our consciousness, we have a wholly passive awareness that the non-introspected parts are just as real as the introspected part. We can know this much, even though we are not in a position to make detailed judgments about the non-introspected parts.

By way of conclusion, it seems that all versions of the I-thesis are false. Neither active nor passive introspection or introspectibility are constitutive of co-consciousness, so the Strong I-thesis is false. Since there is a general limitation on introspectibility – due to the impossibility of introspecting the unity of introspected and non-introspected experiences – the Weak I-thesis is also false. This general limitation aside, the phenomenon of attention-dependence means that a good part of our experience is not actively introspectible, even if most of it is passively introspectible. As for co-consciousness itself, it is independent of introspection in all its forms. If co-consciousness is correlated with or constituted by anything, it is WP-awareness. But since the latter is wholly independent of introspection and attention, nothing said so far takes us closer to a positive understanding of what this sort of awareness involves.

2.4 Pure awareness

There is another, more influential, awareness-based account of experiential unity that I want to consider. I mentioned earlier the idea that consciousness harbours a division between awareness and content (or act and object). The doctrine in question can come in different forms, but the basic idea is that consciousness is inherently bi-polar: any experiencing has two components, on the one hand there is an awareness, an act of pure sensing, and on the other the phenomenal contents or objects that are presented to this awareness. The awareness itself is usually taken to be a simple locus of bare apprehension, it is has no parts or complexity, no phenomenal content of its own. Any conscious episode, whether a single token sensation or a cross-section of an entire stream of consciousness, consists of the sensing of some experiential content, where the sensing and the content are distinct (or at least clearly distinguishable) aspects of the episode as a whole. The passage below (Deikman 1996: 351) is a clear exposition of the doctrine:

> Awareness cannot itself be observed, it is not an object, not a thing. Indeed, it is featureless, lacking form, texture, colour, spatial dimensions. These characteristics indicate that awareness is of a different nature than the contents of the mind; it goes beyond sensations, emotions, ideation, memory. Awareness is at a different level, it is prior to contents, more fundamental. Awareness has no intrinsic content, no form, no surface characteristics – it is unlike everything else we experience, unlike objects, sensations, emotions, thoughts, or memories.
>
> Thus experience is dualistic, not the dualism of mind and matter, but the dualism of awareness and the contents of awareness. To put it another way, experience consists of the observer and the observed. Our sensations, our images, our thoughts – the mental activity by which we engage and define the world – all are part of the observed. In contrast, the observer – the 'I' – is prior to everything else; without it there is no experience of existence. If awareness did not exist in its own right there would be no 'I' … no transparent centre of my being.

For the remainder of this section, when I use the term 'awareness' I will usually be referring to the distinctive kind of awareness mentioned in this passage – on occasion I shall signal this with an asterisk – awareness[*].

If consciousness does possess an awareness–content structure, we clearly have a non-trivial account of the unity of consciousness, and hence of co-consciousness. If two or more phenomenal objects are presented to a single awareness these objects will automatically be co-conscious – they will be experienced together. Moreover, if we take it that there is no other way for phenomenal contents to be experienced together, falling under a single awareness turns out to be both sufficient and necessary for co-consciousness. I will call the doctrine that consciousness has an awareness–content (or act–object) structure, and that the unity of consciousness consists of diverse contents falling under a single awareness, the *awareness-* or *A-thesis*.[2]

Some preliminary clarifications are in order. The awareness in question is experiential rather than cognitive. It is not a matter of being able to think about, or form conscious beliefs about, one's current experiences. For the A-theorist, a thought – even a 'higher order' thought about a thought – is just one more phenomenal object or content, and a thought is conscious in virtue of being sensed, i.e. being an object of awareness*. The A-thesis should be distinguished from a familiar ownership principle: the claim that experience is necessarily owned, that every experience belongs to a subject. The A-theorist is not obliged to take the view that the posited awareness is an entity which has the experience, or which the experience is for, or alternatively, that the awareness in question is owned by a something whose awareness it is. The A-thesis, considered as a doctrine concerning the nature and unity of consciousness, is ontologically neutral on the topic of the subject/experience relationship. This said, there is an obvious kinship between the A-thesis and the ownership doctrine. Given the plausibility of the ownership doctrine, it would be quite natural for the A-theorist to ascribe the posited awareness to a subject, conceived as something over and above any phenomenal content. Looking at things from the other direction, a subscriber to the ownership principle might well be tempted to say that a token experience is something which happens to a particular subject in virtue of that subject being aware of a phenomenal object. On this view, an entity is a subject of experience in virtue of its possessing the capacity to be aware of presented contents.

The relationship between the A-thesis and the I-thesis is somewhat nuanced. At first sight awareness* looks to be very different from the kinds of introspective awareness we looked at earlier. Introspection involves a focusing of the attention; it is something we can control, something we do from time to time. But according to the A-theorist we are always and continually aware*, since every experience consists of an awareness* of a content – even the unnoticed experiences in the phenomenal background. Moreover, awareness* is not under the control of the will, it is not something we can turn on or off by choice. We can influence the course of our experience by choosing what we look at or listen to, what we smell or taste, but we cannot *stop experiencing* at will. The Strong I-thesis is implausible because the unity of consciousness is continuous and independent of attention and volition; since awareness* is held to have just these features, the A-thesis is far more plausible as an account of co-consciousness. However, the gap may not be so large. A-theorists differ as to what precisely they take awareness* to be.

One option is to say that awareness* is a form of attention, and that introspection – at least the active sort – is simply a focusing of the overall attentive field.[3] A-theorists who take this line will regard the Strong I-thesis as an imperfectly formulated version of their own position.

The A-thesis faces an obvious objection: why believe there is such a thing as awareness* at all? Since it has no phenomenal features of its own, how could we possibly detect such a thing in our experience? G. E. Moore, perhaps unwittingly, illustrates the problem in this well known passage:

> though philosophers have recognised that something distinct is meant by consciousness, they have never yet had a clear idea of what that something is. They have not been able to hold it and blue before their minds and compare them in the same way as they compare blue and green. And for [this reason]: the moment we try to fix our attention upon consciousness, and to see what, distinctly, it is, it seems to vanish. It seems as if we had before us a mere emptiness. When we try to introspect the sensation of blue, all we can see is the blue; the other element is ... diaphanous. Yet it can be distinguished, if we look attentively enough, and know that there is something to look for.
>
> (1922: 25)

Moore's 'consciousness', our awareness*, only becomes fully diaphanous when its scope is generalized so as to include everything that we would ordinarily regard as inner and experiential in nature. Moore claims to be able to discern this diaphanous awareness* as a distinct and distinguishable component of his overall consciousness. But how could he? If awareness* is wholly diaphanous, wholly without phenomenological content, what is it that he is finding, what is there for him to find? To be sure, Moore finds that he is conscious, he is experiencing. But why should we believe that he can detect a wholly contentless awareness* in addition to the phenomenal objects that comprise the contents of his experience?

Although this objection has considerable force when directed at Moore's somewhat confusing (or confused) remarks, it has none whatsoever when directed against the A-theorist who maintains that awareness* is a featureless locus of pure apprehension. By its very nature, awareness* is not something which can be detected or discerned within experience; it is not a content present in consciousness, rather it is that *to which* contents are presented. Consequently, the A-theorist will maintain that to doubt the existence of awareness* on the grounds that it does not appear among the contents of one's consciousness, is as misguided as doubting that one has eyes just because one cannot see them.

This reply brings the status of the A-thesis into clearer focus. While its opponents can rightly claim that nothing to be found within experience supports the doctrine, its supporters can rightly maintain that nothing in experience can refute it either. Given this stand-off, it is clear phenomenology will be of little or no use in determining the outcome of the debate. If the A-thesis is to be refuted, considerations of a different sort will have to be deployed.

I will say at the outset that the A-thesis strikes me as very implausible; I am with James when he wrote:

> I believe that 'consciousness', when once it has evaporated to this estate of pure diaphaneity, is on the point of disappearing altogether. It is the name of a non-entity. ... Those who still cling to it are clinging to a mere echo, the faint rumour left behind by the disappearing 'soul' upon the air of philosophy.
>
> (1995: 100)

But since the doctrine has seemed plainly true to some people, people who have devoted a great deal of thought to experience, more needs saying if a case against the A-thesis is to be made. I will begin by making some suggestions about how one might be misled into supposing consciousness is inherently bi-polar. I will then move on to consider the main variants of the A-thesis – so far I have only characterized the doctrine in a general way. We shall see that the different variants are all problematic, albeit in different ways.

2.5 The A-thesis and common sense

The A-thesis has a certain degree of intuitive plausibility. The idea that we are always 'aware' of our experiences could even be regarded as plain common sense. But only until we look at the issue more closely.

If I have a raging toothache and someone asks me 'Are you aware of your pain?', I will reply 'Of course I am, what do you think?'. But by this I will (probably) simply mean that I can feel the pain – the pain hasn't gone away. There is no implication here that consciousness involves a dualism of aware-ness and content. As I noted in §2.1, we sometimes use 'awareness' simply to indicate the existence of experience, but more often we use it to refer to what we notice, or pay attention to. If I am asked 'Are you aware of both your auditory and visual experience?', I will probably pause for a moment and say 'Yes'. The question will have drawn my attention to these aspects of my consciousness, and I will have noted that they are indeed co-conscious. The question has brought me to notice and so form a conscious belief about something I was previously not paying attention to at all. However, there is no support for the A-thesis here: since according to the A-theorist we are always aware of all our experience, the notion of 'awareness' in play here is far removed from what we usually mean by the term.

Some of the intuitive appeal the A-thesis has may derive from a natural but mistaken way of thinking about how we are aware of our experiences when we notice them or pay them attention. It is easy to lapse into talking as though experiences are things we perceive or observe, in essentially the same way as we perceive or observe ordinary physical things. On entering a room

I will look about, my gaze will sweep from side to side, from the front of the room to the back, pausing here and there. If I decide to take note of my various bodily sensations I can start at the soles of my feet, focusing my attention tightly onto what I feel there, and gradually work upwards; next I focus on my ankles, then my calves, then my knees, and so on. At any point I can direct my attention away from my bodily sensations and pay attention to what I can see or hear. So one moment I might be scrutinizing the faint sensations on my neck caused by the pressure of my collar, the next moment I might be scrutinizing the different shades of colour on the carpet. When I change the focus of my attention in this way it is almost as if I am *looking* at different things. It might seem as though I have a single sensory faculty, akin to an eye, a sensory organ of a special kind which I can point or focus wherever I like. This inner 'eye' is quite unlike the other sensory faculties, since it can apprehend experiences of different kinds – it is not restricted to sound, vision or touch. Just like the ordinary eye, the field of 'vision' of the inner eye has a centre or focus and a periphery. Unlike the ordinary eye, the inner eye's focus can be any kind of experience, and the periphery consists of the remainder of our experience – the entire phenomenal background. So when I focus my attention on the bodily feelings in my ankle, my auditory and visual experiences retreat to the periphery of my awareness, the periphery of my inner eye's field of vision.

This line of thinking may be quite a natural one, but it also seems plainly wrong, at least if taken literally. Our eyes and ears provide us with auditory and visual experiences, our skin and muscles provides us tactile sensations, but we do not have an additional sensory organ which perceives the various experiences provided by our eyes, ears and other sensory organs. If we really did have this additional organ, and if it worked like our other sensory organs, our sensory experiences would be items that causally interacted with this additional organ to generate a *second* set of experiences – everything would be experienced twice over. Or rather, it would be more correct to say that the only experiences we would have – if we regard ourselves as the inner eye – would be the experiences generated by the additional organ. After all, the experiences produced by our eyes and ears would be as absent from our consciousness as the physical things in the environment which causally stimulate these organs. These absurdities are the result of taking introspection to be a form of sensory perception, on a par with ordinary sense perception. But it seems clear that we do not observe our experiences in this sort of way. We have experiences, we can direct our attention onto them, and we can form beliefs about them; it is wrong, however, to think that in directing our attention at experiences we are turning a multi-modal sensory organ onto them. There is no such thing.

Of course, most A-theorists would agree with this verdict. The inner eye of awareness[*] is a point of pure apprehension; contents of all sorts are 'observed' in a direct and unmediated fashion – the A-thesis can be construed as the doctrine of naive realism applied *within* the realm of experience.

Consequently, no additional level of content is involved; there is just one level of content which is directly apprehended. Once we start thinking in this way we might identify ourselves with this faculty; we might regard the inner eye as nothing less than the 'I' itself, and so reach the doctrine articulated in the quotation given above: the self is a locus of pure awareness*, and all experiencing necessarily involves an awareness–content duality. I will be investigating the intelligibility of this model in the next section. My present concern is merely to clarify the doctrine and assess the degree to which it is supported by more or less obvious features of ordinary experience. I have suggested that the intuitive appeal of the A-thesis may (in part) derive from mistakenly construing attention to be a form of observation; this appeal is diminished (to some extent) as soon as it is pointed out that the sort of 'observation' in question is of a very distinctive kind. But a further question remains: if attention is *not* a roving searchlight-like awareness involving a separate and additional level of consciousness, what account can we give of it?

A more realistic picture starts with the observation that for the most part attention involves performing some action with more care than usual. As Lyons says, to perceive a beaker on a table and then to pay attention to one's perceiving of it

> is not to engage in two processes or activities but to modify one's approach to the one and only one activity. Attention is an adverbial modification of some first-level experience or activity. ... One can perceive the beaker, and then one can do it attentively – that is, with care, banishing distractions, with alertness, concentration and so on.
>
> (1986: 107)

Just as one can perceive carefully and with concentration, so can one think carefully and deliberately. On this view, paying attention is usually a matter of the manner in which we do something rather than the willed movement of an inner ray of awareness. When we pay attention to experience, as we do when engaged in active introspection, we are usually trying to arrive at some judgment about some aspect of the experience's character. In doing so, we stop doing what we were previously doing with care and concentration, diverting our cognitive resources to the task in hand. When we engage in passive introspection, we try to formulate a snap judgment about some part of the phenomenal background while also trying to do something else with care and attention. We can decide to make a succession of judgments about different parts of our experience. For example, I can pay attention for a few seconds to the faint pains in my lower back, then deliberately switch my attention to the tactile sensations caused by the pressure of my feet on the floor; after a few seconds, I can return my attention to my back pain. But in so doing I am simply registering the character of the relevant experiences with a view to forming a judgment or belief about them – I am not wielding a beam of separate awareness.

I suggested above that the A-thesis can be construed as naive realism applied within the realm of experience, and it may well be that much of the appeal the A-thesis has derives from this source, for there is no denying that naive realism has a certain appeal. When I look at a vase on the table before me I seem have a direct unmediated awareness of something that is both external to me and independent of me; I do not have any sense of my consciousness reaching out through space and touching (or surrounding or permeating) the vase. But of course this is only how things seem (or can seem) from the standpoint of naive phenomenology; the situation is quite different from the perspective of phenomenology informed by projectivism. Now, the vase I am immediately visually aware of, the vase that looks to be several feet away from me, is recognized as being itself a component part of my overall consciousness, and the same applies to all the immediate objects of world-presenting visual and auditory perception. When we adopt this projectivist position, any motivation for adopting the awareness-object model provided by how things naively seem vanishes.

In fact, when considered more closely, the notion that the A-thesis is simply naive realism applied to phenomenal rather than wordly objects may be an oversimplification. Whereas the A-theorist's distinction between aware-ness and its objects is strict – awareness* is pure apprehension and nothing more – it is not clear that the same applies to the distinction between content and awareness which is sustained by a pre-theoretical conception of ordi-nary perception. Although when I look at the vase in front of me I do not have any sense of my awareness extending outward and constituting what I see, if I stretch my arm out to take hold of the vase then I *do* have the sense of my awareness stretching out into space: my arm is the source of various spatially extended bodily sensations, and these sensations seem to be part of my total field of consciousness in a way the vase I see is not. Suppose now that I take hold of the vase, in a slow deliberate way; I feel my fingers gradu-ally closing in, until the vase's narrow neck is completely encircled. It now seems as though this part of the vase is contained within my field of bodily awareness. But as soon as I actually touch the surface of the vase this changes: I now feel something which seems completely external to me, for my bodily awareness does not extend *into* the vase, it stops at the surface. When we look at things in this way it can seem quite natural to think that consciousness as a whole has an awareness–content structure: the awareness component consists of everything that seems inner, i.e. thoughts, feelings, bodily sensations, whereas the corresponding contents are those outer things we perceive through sight, hearing and touch. Since this division between awareness and content is very different from that posited by the A-thesis, the latter once again proves to be more distant from our ordinary ways of thinking than it might initially have seemed.

Perhaps some of the people who are attracted to a dualism of awareness and content have been influenced by one or more of these considerations I have just outlined; if so they may wish to think again. In any event, it is time to assess the intelligibility of the thesis in question. To this end it will be useful to distinguish in a more systematic fashion the different forms the A-thesis can take.

2.6 Variations on a theme

The idea that consciousness is inherently bi-polar can be elaborated in different ways. One question is where to draw the line between awareness and content: which sorts of mental item fall on the *awareness* side of the line, and which fall on the *content* side? The most common option, and the one I want to consider first, is to regard seemingly inner items such as thoughts, decisions, memories and emotions, to be just as separate from awareness as the immediate objects of perceptual experience. The resulting awareness is divested of all ordinary phenomenal characteristics; it is the pure contentless awareness* that we have already encountered. Proponents of this doctrine fall into different camps, depending upon whether or not they believe that awareness* can or cannot exist independently of content, and whether content can or cannot exist independently of awareness*. This gives us four positions to consider:

S1   awareness* cannot exist independently of content, and content cannot exist independently of awareness*
S2   awareness* cannot exist independently of content, but content can exist independently of awareness*
S3   awareness* can exist independently of content, and content can exist independently of awareness*
S4   awareness* can exist independently of content, but content cannot exist independently of awareness*

Each of these positions affirms an awareness–content dualism. Both S1 and S2 deny the possibility of awareness* occurring in the absence of content, whereas S3 and S4 affirm this possibility. S1 and S2 differ over whether phenomenal content can exist independently of awareness, as do S3 and S4. Since the idea of a wholly bare awareness* – an awareness that has no object or content whatsoever – looks highly suspect, the most plausible variants would seem to be S1 and S2, so I will begin by looking at these. There is a second reason for starting here. Suppose we find reason to reject the idea that content is awareness-dependent, and hence S1, and suppose also that we find reason to reject the idea that content is awareness-independent, and hence S2, then without further ado we also have reasons for rejecting S3 and S4, irrespective of the intelligibility or otherwise of the notion of a bare awareness*.

According to S1, phenomenal contents cannot exist except as objects of awareness*. This has some plausibility, in that it seems odd to think of items such as pains, perceptions and thoughts existing when no one is experiencing them. But in recognizing this we must remember the distinction between the A-thesis and the ownership principle, the claim that every experience belongs to some subject. Suppose we accept the ownership doctrine, and so accept that any experience is always an experience some subject is having. It does not follow from this that experience has an awareness–content structure. The subject might be an animal, a brain, a soul, or a system of interrelated mental states. Think now of Moore's patch of blue. This token of blueness, a region within a visual field, is a phenomenal content. According to S1, an experience results when the blue patch is combined with an awareness*, and in the absence of awareness*, the blue patch cannot exist. But why not? Since awareness* itself is devoid of phenomenal features, what ingredient does it bring to the experience of blueness? Certainly not the phenomenal quality of blueness itself. If awareness* does not itself contain this instance of phenomenal blue, why should the latter not be able to exist in the absence of awareness? The problem runs deeper. For what applies to phenomenal blue applies to all other phenomenal contents. If we hold that phenomenal contents in general cannot exist independently of awareness*, and that this is so because of their very nature, it seems that awareness* must in some manner be directly responsible for bringing all the *diversity* of different phenomenal characteristics into being. But given the diaphanous character of awareness* itself, this seems impossible. If awareness* is in itself diaphanous, perfectly transparent, bringing the same intangible illumination to all its objects, how can it bring such diverse phenomenal properties as colour and sound into the world? Supposing a transparent awareness* could be responsible for phenomenal diversity is as absurd as thinking one could convert a television from black-and-white to colour by holding a sheet of plain glass in front of the screen.

Perhaps S2 is a better option. According to S2, awareness* does not create phenomenal characteristics or contents, it merely reveals or discloses them. On this view, phenomenal contents can, and do, exist when they are not the object of awareness*. Here is how Lockwood (1989: 162–3) describes the position:

> phenomenal qualities are, on the disclosure view, simply intrinsic attributes as disclosed by awareness. They are not self-revealing; it is awareness that reveals them. … On this view, phenomenal qualities are neither realized by being sensed nor sensed by being realized. They are just realized, and sensed or not as the case may be. The realization of a phenomenal quality is one thing, I contend; its being an object of awareness is something else, albeit something for which its realization is a necessary condition. … As a first approximation, one could think of awareness as a kind of searchlight, sweeping around an inner landscape. … The searchlight may be thought of, in part, as revealing qualities that were already part of this landscape, rather than as bringing these qualities into being.

But while this view avoids the difficulty with S1, it is problematic for a different reason. The idea that awareness can sweep across independently existing phenomenal contents and 'disclose' their character to a subject, is similar to the absurd view that there is an 'inner eye' which observes experiences in just the same manner that we observe physical objects. But at least the 'inner eye' theory – for all its absurdity – provides us with an informative picture of what awareness* does. Once we reject the notion that awareness is akin to an ordinary form of perception we are left with a puzzle. If phenomenal contents can exist independently of awareness*, if these awareness*-free contents can possess phenomenal characteristics, what reason is there to suppose anyone's experience would be different if awareness* itself were absent? The A-theorist will presumably insist that in the absence of awareness* there simply is no experience. Take awareness* away and all the lights go out, so to speak. But it is not at all clear how this could be the case. Suppose you are staring at a white ceiling; your visual field is filled with a white expanse. This white expanse is a phenomenal object. The supposed awareness* is contributing nothing to the intrinsic experiential character of this object: this object could exist independently of awareness* with all its phenomenal qualities intact. But if this is true, then would not this object constitute an *experience* even in the absence of awareness*?

The point is perhaps clearer if we consider a typical complex experience, rather than a single simple experience. So consider your own current experience, as a whole – a combination of thought, feeling, perceptions, bodily sensations, and so forth. Now subtract from them the supposed wholly diaphanous awareness*. Can you imagine all the phenomenal characteristics of this experience being realized, just as they are in your actual experience, yet no experience occurring? But this is just what the proponent of S2 maintains would occur. The point can be made in a more picturesque way. Suppose a pure awareness is gazing down upon your current stream of consciousness; suppose too that all the phenomenal characteristics of your current experience are completely independent of this awareness*. How would things be different for you if this awareness* were absent or extinguished? How *could* things be different, experientially? Given that exactly the same phenomenal characteristics are realized irrespective of whether the awareness* is present or not, there would surely be no difference at all. Consequently, even if a pure awareness* is now gazing down upon your consciousness and is in some manner apprehending the character of your experience as it unfolds, what has this entity got to do with you? The answer seems to be: nothing whatsoever. The idea that you would cease to experience anything if this awareness* were to vanish seems quite absurd. Once again the difficulty lies with the featureless character of awareness*: if awareness* is wholly without phenomenal features it is hard to see that anything would be lost if it were to disappear, and it is very hard to see why experience itself should be impossible in its absence.

So both S1 and S2 seem problematic. As far as the objects of awareness* are concerned, the A-theorist faces a dilemma. If we say the objects of awareness* cannot exist in the absence of awareness*, we face the problem of explaining why not, given that awareness* brings nothing tangible to the contents. If we say the objects of awareness* can exist independently of awareness*, we face the problem of explaining why these contents are not themselves experienced, since it is hard to see what the absence of awareness* could take away from the contents.

A tangible awareness?

In response to these difficulties, the A-theorist could insist that the awareness component of experience does have some specific discernible phenomenological character. This amounts to giving up the dubious notion of a wholly transparent awareness*. The trouble is that it is not easy to see what this character could be.

The most obvious option would be to say that awareness is a form of attention. The claim of the A-theorist now becomes: all experiences contain a *volitional* element, for consciousness in all its forms is an attending to a content or contents. The A-theory in this guise allows the objects of awareness to possess, as intrinsic characteristics, phenomenal properties such as colour and taste. These objects are not, however, experiences in their own right; rather, they form parts of experiences when combined with an attentive awareness.

We know what it is like to focus our attention on something, so this proposal at least has the merit of providing awareness with some distinct phenomenological content. But it is not very plausible in other respects. Adherents of S1 and S2 (and S3 and S4) differ over whether phenomenal contents can exist independently of attention, but they will agree that experience occurs only when attention and contents are combined. But for a now-familiar reason this is hard to believe: most of our experience occurs without being the object of attention. Even if we accept the idea that we are always attending to something – and this is itself questionable – it does not seem plausible to suppose we are always attending to all our current experience. The notion of attention is essentially contrastive. If we are paying attention to one aspect of our overall experience, we are neglecting to pay attention to some other part. Our interest in the A-thesis is primarily as an account of co-consciousness and the unity of experience. But as we have already seen in connection with the various versions of the I-thesis, the experienced unity in experience seems wholly independent of attention. The unity of the phenomenal background is quite independent of active or primary attention, since it is precisely that part of our experience to which we are not attending. It is true that we can passively introspect the phenomenal background, and in doing so we employ a secondary form of attention. But there is no reason to think the unity of consciousness is constituted by this ability – it is there when the ability is not being exercised. And then there is the point that the co-consciousness of introspected and non-introspected experience cannot itself be the object of either active or passive attention.

The A-theorist could try a different line. It might be argued that in any experiencing there is a clear distinction between the phenomenal content itself and our *engagement* with this content. This engagement can take different forms. Paying attention to an experience is one form of engagement, as is forming a belief or judgment in direct response to it. Feeling our limbs move in response to a decision to act is another. A pain is something we would usually prefer to be rid of, but it continues to hurt anyway – it impresses itself on us against our will. It might be argued that sensory experience as a whole is something that impresses itself upon us: we cannot stop it by will-power alone, nor can we control the course it takes (save in the minimal sense of putting ourselves in a position to perceive one thing rather than another). In virtue of pressing in upon us, perceptual experience is something we are constantly engaged with, as conscious agents. All these forms of engagement are aspects of experiencing which have a phenomenal character (there is something it is like to have sensory experience pour in on one). Consequently, we can reconstrue the awareness–content distinction thus: in any experiencing, there is a distinction between phenomenal content and *an awareness of being engaged with this content*, in one or other of the ways just mentioned.[4]

This version of the A-thesis is the volitional theory in another form, but it is considerably more plausible than the version which restricts the volitional aspect of experience to attention. There is no denying that we often are engaged with our experience – we do not passively witnesses the world, we take an active interest, we intervene, and even when we are not actively intervening, what happens – the course our experience takes – is of some concern, it matters to us. However, there are problems. Even if under normal circumstances we are always in some manner engaged with our experience, might there not be certain special states of consciousness, achievable through meditation or similar procedures, in which this engagement ceases? There are people who claim to have achieved such a condition. If this is the case, experience does not necessarily possess an awareness–content structure (where awareness = engagement). This point aside (it will come up again shortly in a rather different context), there are other reasons for rejecting the engagement theory. Consider sensory experience. I have stressed the importance of not overlooking the phenomenal background, and this is another case in point. Do we have any sense of engagement with the unnoticed parts of the phenomenal background? There are occasions when we might, but for the most part surely we do not. The various elements that make up the background (which for the most part we do not think of as experiences at all) are simply there, they are not bothering us, they are of no concern to us whatsoever. For the past few minutes the books on the shelf to my right have featured in my passive awareness; they are just within the periphery of my visual field; if they were not there the general character of my experience – of sitting here in this room in this position – would be different. But although present, these books (or my passive experiences of them) have not been pressing in on me, I have not been engaged with them in any way. The same is generally true of the contents of the phenomenal background.

Although this fact alone suffices to refute the engagement theory, it is worth pausing a moment to consider the extent to which we could reasonably be said to be 'engaged' with other parts of our experience. Take the stream of conscious thought and understanding-experience. Some sorts of thinking certainly can be described as activities we engage in. If I decide to recall a memorized quotation or poem, or decide to carry out a long division in my head, I will be deliberately engaging in a particular kind of mental activity, and this kind of activity has a particular phenomenal character. But not all our 'inner' experience is like this. Memories (more particularly, memory-images) sometimes just occur, unwanted and unbidden; remembering in this form is something which happens to us, rather than something we actively undertake. For the most part, the direction our thought takes from one moment to the next seems quite out of our control, at least in the sense that we have not usually chosen the line our thinking is taking. We do not decide to think about this or that, we just find ourselves thinking about this or that. (And if we do suddenly decide to think about this rather than that, where did *this* thought come from?) At times we are wholly passive, non-engaged, participants in the course of our inner life. The same applies to how we act. If we had to consciously choose which limb to move next, few of us would be capable of walking and chewing gum at the same time. When we absent-mindedly go about our daily business, how often do we have the *feeling* that we are actively engaged in what we are doing? If the engagement theory is correct, we always have this feeling, to some degree or another. I am not at all sure this is true.

A bare awareness?

Having found reasons for rejecting S1 and S2, we are left with S3 and S4. But given what has already been said, these positions look to be even more problematic than S1 and S2. Both S3 and S4 affirm the possibility of awareness* existing independently of any contents – a bare awareness. This is obviously a very dubious proposition indeed. What would a wholly contentless awareness* be like? A bare awareness would be wholly devoid of thoughts, feelings, sensory experience of any kind. What would differentiate a bare awareness from nothing at all? I cannot see that anything would. In response, the A-theorist could opt for one of the manoeuvres we have just discussed: perhaps pure awareness has a volitional character. But I cannot see that this is any improvement. The idea of a *naked will* is as strange as that of a bare awareness. What would a consciousness that consisted of nothing but an objectless, contentless *willing* be like? It is one thing to exert one's will while one has a stream of consciousness, but if we remove everything from one's consciousness save the willing (or attending or sense of engagement), what would be left?

It might be objected that the notion of a pure consciousness of a non-volitional kind cannot be dismissed so easily, on the grounds that many people claim to have experienced just such a state themselves. The concept of a 'pure consciousness state' plays a role in certain Eastern mystical traditions. One of the goals of certain meditative practices is the attainment of abnormal states of consciousness which are often described as 'pure' or 'contentless' or 'empty' or 'non-volitional'. Although not everyone is able to achieve these unusual states, presumably some people have. If this is so, it is something we need to take into account, for it is reasonable to suppose that abnormal states of consciousness can further our understanding of consciousness in general. After all, our understanding of matter has progressed because we took the trouble to study it in the abnormal conditions that are routinely created in laboratories. Since the Eastern meditative traditions have been engaged in systematically exploring consciousness under unusual conditions for many centuries, it would be foolhardy to dismiss their results.

However, from what I can gather – I am no expert in these matters – it is far from clear that what the Eastern traditions refer to as a 'pure consciousness' is what I have called a bare awareness. In fact, the reverse seems to be the case. This is obviously true when the state so-called is said to have the character of a luminous radiant field, which it sometimes is. Luminescence is a phenomenal characteristic. But more generally, meditation is often conducted with the aim of achieving a non-conceptual awareness: experience continues, but one tries not to interpret it in terms of everyday concepts. This means, amongst other things, trying to stop conceptualizing experience in subject-object terms. At a more advanced stage the aim is to bring about a non-dualistic state of consciousness in which there is no awareness of any kind of a distinction between experiencing self and experienced world. It is one thing to accept the proposition that the awareness–content division is unreal, or not representative of consciousness in general; it is another thing altogether to experience a state of consciousness in which there does not *seem* to be any difference whatsoever between inner and outer, or subject and object. A non-dualistic consciousness of this type is often what is meant by a 'pure consciousness'. Such a consciousness is not wholly devoid of phenomenal contents; content is present, but distributed through a conscious field that lacks the usual division between inner and outer.[5] This sort of experience is clearly quite different from a bare awareness or a naked will. So far as I can see, the thesis that the awareness–content distinction is in some way or other illusory is a common theme of most if not all of these schools of thought. To this extent the Eastern traditions support (rather than undermine) the line I have been arguing for in connection with the A-thesis.

If any of the so-called 'pure' conscious states resembles bare awareness, it may be the condition of 'cessation' that is described in certain Buddhist texts. In the Theravada tradition (Griffiths 1986: 17), the state of cessation is the culmination of an ascending series of altered states of consciousness:

1 By the transcendence of all the conceptualizations of form, by the disappearance of conceptualizations based upon sense-data, by paying no attention to conceptualizations of manifoldness, having attained the sphere of infinite space [the practitioner] remains therein, thinking 'space is unending'.
2 By entirely transcending the sphere of infinite space, having attained to the sphere of infinite consciousness, [the practitioner] remains therein, thinking 'consciousness is infinite'.
3 By entirely transcending the sphere of infinite consciousness, having attained to the sphere of nothing at all, [the practitioner] remains therein, thinking 'there is nothing'.
4 By entirely transcending the sphere of nothing at all, having entered the sphere of neither conceptualization nor non-conceptualization, [the practitioner] remains therein.
5 By entirely transcending the sphere of neither conceptualization nor non-conceptualization, having attained the cessation of sensation and conceptualization, [the practitioner] remains therein.

By dwelling intently on nothingness, in these various ways, the aim is to reach a state where one's consciousness comes to resemble what one is imagining: nothingness. If the state of cessation were experienced, it would clearly be far more extreme than what we might call 'everyday' experiences of nothingness: if one's lower body is anaesthetized, it seems that a disturbing nothingness has invaded one's lower portions, but it only seems like this because one's consciousness is otherwise perfectly normal. Cessation is supposed to result in the *complete* annihilation of consciousness, it is 'a condition in which no mental events of any kind occur, a condition distinguishable from death only by a certain residual warmth and vitality in the unconscious practitioner's body'.[6] If this is right, it seems clear that this condition is indistinguishable from ordinary dreamless sleep, and is not a form of consciousness at all.

Substantival awareness?

Before moving on, it is worth considering a position which is similar to the A-thesis in one respect – it posits a sharp distinction between awareness and content – but which is quite different in other respects. The A-theorist's pure awareness* is wholly distinct from the entire range of conscious mental contents. An alternative option is to take all conscious mental contents to be constituents or features of awareness itself. So in addition to my thoughts, volitions and bodily sensations being components of my awareness, so are the immediate objects of my auditory and visual experience. Taking this line might seem to collapse the distinction between awareness and content: if everything in experience is a component of awareness, how can there be room for a content–awareness distinction? The answer is a familiar one: we take awareness to be a substance, and phenomenal objects and properties to be modifications of this substance.

The A-thesis in this form is a version of the Cartesian conception of consciousness. The dualism of awareness and content is transformed into the dualism of substance and mode. It might seem peculiar to regard this position as a variation on the theme that consciousness harbours an awareness–content dualism, but looked at in one way this construal is quite natural. If, like Descartes, we want to say that a substance has a single essential attribute, of which all its particular states are modes, what do we take the essential attribute of a conscious substance to be? One obvious answer is: *awareness*. Since the Cartesian regards conscious substances as simple and without parts, a Substantival awareness too is simple and without parts. This is not the only way the Cartesian position can be developed, but it is one way.

However, this Substantivalist position looks as implausible as any we have considered so far. What would experience have to be like if the positing of a Substantival awareness were to be justified? We would have to be able to make sense of the idea that all the phenomenal objects (or properties) with which we are acquainted are qualitative modifications of a single sort of experiential medium. We could then reasonably identify this medium with awareness. So far as I can see, there is no possibility of this: the differences between the intrinsic characteristics of phenomenal items are simply too big. What does a conscious thought have in common with an experience of phenomenal purple? What does a phenomenal sound have in common with a smell? How does a feeling of sullen melancholy resemble the experience of drinking champagne? The idea that experiences as different as these are qualitative modifications of a single form of experience is very hard to believe.[7]

One further possibility should be mentioned. According to a familiar piece of traditional metaphysics, the *inherence doctrine*, any property must inhere in some substance. This doctrine might seem to provide a motivation for the Substantival conception. If phenomenal objects are realizations of phenomenal properties, then the latter must inhere in some substance. So if the inherence doctrine is true, there must be some substance within which our experience unfolds, and what could this substance be other than consciousness itself? We are back with the notion of a Substantival awareness.

But this argument moves far too quickly. For one thing, there are alternatives to the inherence doctrine: it could be that experiences are particulars in their own right, inhering in no substance whatsoever. Streams of consciousness, on this view, consist of bundles of interrelated particulars. Even if we accept the inherence doctrine, and accept that phenomenal states are realizations of phenomenal properties in some substance or other, there are alternatives to a Substantival awareness. If some form of materialism is true, whether L-materialism or P-materialism, phenomenal properties inhere in physical substances, possibly in physical space itself. In keeping with moderate naturalism, I remain open to any of these options.

There is, however, one option to which I do take exception: the idea that experiences inhere in a featureless substratum, or bare particular. The notion of a bare particular is invoked for several reasons, one of which is to serve as that in which properties inhere, another of which is to explain how properties come to be instantiated together. Since bare particulars are featureless, they are ideally suited to performing the task of being the thing phenomenal properties belong to, given that it seems difficult to see how the latter could be adjectival modifications of anything else. Since any phenomenal properties that inhere in a single bare particular would automatically be co-instantiated, it would be natural to think they would thereby be co-conscious. However, the idea of a wholly featureless particular is as obscure and problematic as anything in metaphysics. Why believe there are such things? A bare particular, in virtue of its complete lack of features, is not something we could be aware of, it is not something which could be phenomenologically real. It is no less dubious than the notions of a bare awareness and a naked will. Moreoever, if a Substantival awareness were to take the form of a bare particular, then it is hard to avoid the conclusion that *every* object in existence harbours an awareness. If our experiences inhere in a Substantival awareness, and if the latter is a bare particular, then since every bare particular is (intrinsically) exactly alike, how can we avoid the conclusion that an awareness lurks at the heart of literally every thing?

2.7 Simplicity

Returning to our main theme, since no version of the A-thesis looks to be viable, we should reject the idea that consciousness harbours a dualism of awareness and content. What model of consciousness can we put in its place?

The A-theorist tried to keep awareness distinct from content, but since this has turned out to be a mistake we must accept that awareness and content are not distinct ingredients within experience. It follows that consciousness is inseparable from phenomenal contents: when a given phenomenal item comes into being, it comes into being as a conscious experience; to be an experience it does not need to fall under any separate awareness*, or inhere in any Substantival awareness. In other words, contents are themselves intrinsically conscious, and hence – in a manner of speaking – they are self-revealing or self-intimating. That is, phenomenal contents become conscious simply by coming into existence. Whenever phenomenal properties are realized, or phenomenal objects come into existence, conscious experience occurs. I shall call this non-dualistic model of consciousness the *Simple Conception* of experience.

In saying that experience is self-revealing, I do not mean to suggest that we are always cognitively or introspectively aware of our experience as it occurs. The bulk of our experience goes largely if not completely unnoticed; we only rarely make judgments about the phenomenal background, the contents of which are not usually the object of conscious belief. Nonetheless, the phenomenal background is real, and we have a wholly passive awareness of its phenomenal character. This wholly passive awareness should not be confused with the awareness of the A-theorist – it is not something that is in any way separate from the contents which comprise the phenomenal background.

The Simple Conception may at first sight seem implausible. Reflecting on the problems facing the different versions of the A-thesis may make it seem less so. But still, the idea that our experience is all of a piece, all on one plane or level, so to speak, may well seem odd: are there not striking differences within experience? There are indeed, but the Simple Conception is quite compatible with this fact. To start with, there is the division I have stressed between seemingly outer, world-presenting perceptual experiences, and seemingly inner experiences, such as bodily sensations, thoughts, volitions, mental images, and so forth. If the Simple Conception seems counterintuitive, I suspect this is in large part due to the expansion of the domain of experience that projectivism brings: the idea that the immediate objects of auditory and visual perception are in fact experiences is itself counterintuitive. There is also the fact that attention is selective, and we can (within limits) direct our attention where we choose; some parts of our consciousness are the objects of attention, some are not. This distinction within experience is also compatible with the Simple Conception. It is only if attention is taken to consist in a second and separate level of consciousness that the Simple Conception is undermined, and as I pointed out in §2.5, there is no justification for viewing attention in this way.

Another source of resistance to the Simple Conception may stem from a widely held principle concerning the ownership of experience. Is the claim that phenomenal content is intrinsically conscious compatible with the idea that experiences cannot just *be*, that any experience is necessarily an experience *for* someone or something? The answer is that there is no incompatibility here at all. Saying that consciousness is built into phenomenal contents is quite compatible with the view that consciousness is something subjects have, or that there cannot be consciousness without some subject whose consciousness it is. If any awareness is always, necessarily, the awareness of some subject, then since awareness is an intrinsic feature of phenomenal contents, the latter too always, necessarily, belong to some subject. But a further difficulty is lurking hereabouts. In accepting that phenomenal contents are intrinsically conscious items, we seem to be opening the door to the possibility that something as insignificant as Moore's patch of blue, or a single itch or twinge, could wholly constitute a subject's experience at a given moment. Consider a single twinge of pain. If a subject's consciousness consisted of nothing more than this fleeting pain, does it make sense to say that this pain is something a subject feels? Must there not be something more, a richer centre of experience, in order for the pain to produce suffering in the subject who feels it? It is not clear that this is so. But in any event, the problem posed by simple, solitary experiences is not a problem for the Simple Conception as such. Suppose that isolated phenomenal contents, such as a single pain or a patch of blue, cannot exist.

All this means is that there are limits on how simple a subject's experience can be. Whenever pains or patches of blue occur, they do so as components of a more complex experience.

However, while the Simple Conception may look viable in the light of the discussion thus far, there are considerations, notably concerning temporal awareness, which may alter the picture, and we have not yet exhausted the topic of synchronic unity.

3 Phenomenal space

3.1 Consciousness, co-consciousness and space

If co-consciousness cannot be explained in terms of introspection or awareness (of the pure sort), should we conclude that it is a basic relationship, a
relationship about which nothing informative can be said? This conclusion
would only be justified if there were no prospect of an alternative explanation, and there is at least one further approach that is worth looking into, an
approach which appeals to the spatial character of consciousness.

The very idea that consciousness has a spatial character might seem
bizarre: according to a long-standing tradition consciousness is essentially
temporal but wholly non-spatial. This view is not absurd, but it must be
interpreted correctly. The space which has traditionally been denied to
consciousness is *physical* space; since we have no idea of the precise relationship between matter and experience, it is not surprising that we have no idea
of the precise relationship between experience and the physical space which
matter occupies; from here it is but a short step to holding that experience
does not occupy physical space at all. This is a questionable but respectable
position. But from a phenomenological perspective, it would be absurd to
deny that a good deal of our experience has a spatial character. Indeed, if
we set aside projectivism and adopt the naive stance, there is a case for
saying that all our experience, without exception, seems to be located somewhere in physical space, the same space as is occupied by tables and cups,
mountains and stars.

This applies most obviously to perceptual experience. We can see the
stars, touch tables, taste the coffee in cups, and hear the noise made when a
cup is dropped. Normal perceptual experience is world-presenting, the world
presented to us is spatial, and the space in question seems to be physical
space. But other kinds of experience seem to be located within this space
too. If I focus on my own conscious thinking, it apparently occurs somewhere within my head – between my ears, behind my eyes. Although I cannot
usually see my head, the latter is part of my body, most of which I can both
see and touch, and sometimes hear. When viewed in this way, my body is
just one object among many others in a common spatial world, a world we

can see, hear, smell, taste, touch and move about in. But my body is not just an object I can see and touch, it is a source of bodily experience, which has several components: tactile sensations, feelings of warmth and cold, sensations of pain, pleasure and bodily activities, feelings deriving from muscles and joints, and the vestibular sense of balance. Together these provide us with a bodily sense-field, within which more localized experiences take place. Whereas sight, hearing and touch tell us that we are three-dimensional physical objects among others, these senses do not tell us what it is like to *be* such an object; bodily experience is different: it seems to tell us what one particular region of physical space, that occupied by our bodies, is like 'on the inside'. Despite this difference, bodily experience is fully integrated with the rest of our sensory experience. The arm I feel as my own, which moves in accord with my will, is an object I can see (and touch, with my other arm). If I click my fingers, the noise seems to be produced at the same region of space where I can both see and feel my fingers. To recall our earlier example of the party game, as you frantically tried to identify the puzzling object, you were aware (passively) of sitting hunched in an armchair, surrounded by a jeering crowd of people.

While this is roughly how things seem from within the natural attitude, things change as soon as we adopt projectivism, and shift to the standpoint of critical rather than naive phenomenology. The physical world now drops out of the picture, at least as something that is immediately presented to us in experience, but this much remains the same: what we are immediately presented with is a closely integrated three-dimensional world, albeit a wholly phenomenal world. If I hear a fly buzzing behind me, there is an auditory phenomenal object (the buzzing) apparently located within the same space as my bodily sense-field and the objects present in my visual field. If I turn around I can see the fly; when I move to catch it I can both see and feel my arm extending out before me; when I catch the fly I see my hand close around it, and feel and hear the fly buzzing within my loosely clenched fist. When I reflect on these events, my thinking seems to be going on in the head-region of my bodily sense-field. Having now shifted into the critical phenomenological mode, my conscious thoughts, the visual appearance, feel and sound of the fly, these are all conceived as parts of my overall experience. They are all experiences and all co-conscious.

This fact suggests the following idea: simultaneous experiences are co-conscious solely by virtue of occurring at the same time within a single unified three-dimensional phenomenal space; being thus spatially connected is both sufficient and necessary for co-consciousness. Call this the *S-thesis*.

An alternative label for the S-thesis would be the K- or *Kantian*-thesis, as Kant is perhaps the best known advocate of the idea that our experience necessarily has a unified three-dimensional spatial form.[1] But since Kant restricted this claim first to human experience (rather than experience in general), and second to 'outer' or perceptual experiences, this would be somewhat misleading, since I take the S-thesis to apply to both outer and inner sense. Michael Ayers has recently stressed the unified spatial character of experience:

> in order to do justice to the scope of perceptual knowledge it is neces-
> sary to develop the conception of an integrated sense-field. It is wrong
> to think of the senses as in general the source of disparate streams of
> information or content, each discrete from the deliverances of the other
> senses which it is left to some superior intellectual faculty to relate to
> one another in constructing knowledge of objects in space.
>
> (1991: vol. I, 153–4)

But while Ayers would, I think, agree that thoughts, mental images and suchlike are part of the same spatially integrated sense-field as 'outer' or perceptual experience, it is not clear whether or not he believes – as Kant did – that our experience is necessarily spatially unified.

There is no denying that the S-thesis has a certain intuitive rationale. Being located in a common space is one way for things to be together – it is a way in which diverse things can co-exist. Since our (normal) experience is spatially distributed and integrated, it seems natural to suppose that this spatial integration is responsible for the mode of co-existence that is co-consciousness. Moreover, since the occupants of a single *phenomenal* space would necessarily be co-conscious, it seems that the notion of a phenomenal space is doing useful explanatory work: it is telling us how and why diverse phenomenal contents can be co-conscious. There are further advantages. First, a phenomenal space provides a metaphysical underpinning for the intuitively compelling idea that experiences are logically non-transferable between subjects. Experiences belonging to different subjects occur within different phenomenal spaces, and we might plausibly take the identity of a particular experience to be determined, in part, by the phenomenal space within which it occurs. One way for (simultaneous) experiences to be distinct is by possessing different phenomenal characters; another is by occurring at different places within the same phenomenal space; another is by occurring within different phenomenal spaces. Second, the S-thesis does not suffer from the same difficulties as the Strong I-thesis. This thesis was undermined by the fact that experiences remain resolutely co-conscious irrespective of whether or not they are the objects of active introspective scrutiny. This is not a problem for the S-thesis: the spatial organization of our consciousness is clearly independent of which regions (if any) of our overall experience we are attending to. The noises of the passing cars to my left do not change or lose their location when I am not paying attention to them – if I hear these noises at all, I hear them on my left. Third, surprising though it might seem, the idea that the unity of consciousness is underpinned by a spatial field of awareness, bears some similarities with the Cartesian doctrine that partic-ular experiences are modifications of a conscious substance. The substance in question is a substantival phenomenal space; particular experiences are localized qualities inhering in this space.[2] Those who find the Cartesian position appealing may well have reason to look favourably upon the S-thesis.

However, despite its intuitive appeal, the S-thesis is no more successful than the Strong I-thesis, albeit for different reasons. There are three main difficulties. First, is it really the case that experience in all its forms is necessarily spatial? Second, given that much of our experience is spatial and spatially integrated, is it necessarily so? Or can we imagine circumstances in which we continue to have co-conscious experiences, but where spatial integration collapses? Third, can we really make sense of the notion of a phenomenal space of the kind the S-theorist needs? And if we can, is there such a thing within our experience? Although different considerations can be brought to bear on each of these questions, the second and third are interdependent, in that answering either in the negative strengthens the case for answering the other in the negative.

3.2 Non-spatial consciousness?

Since the S-thesis stresses the spatial character of consciousness, let us begin by considering the extent to which it is true that all forms of consciousness have a spatial character. This question has two aspects. Do *all* forms of consciousness possess an intrinsic spatial character (the way a patch of blue does)? Do all forms of consciousness exist within a broader and more encompassing phenomenal space? I noted earlier that consciousness has often been held to be essentially non-spatial in nature, and while this does not seem at all plausible when we think of sensory experience, while distinguishing phenomenal from physical spatiality, the doctrine becomes rather more plausible if we discount sensory awareness in all its forms (imagination and memory included), and think only of 'inner', or 'intellectual' consciousness: e.g. our thoughts and deliberations, our conscious desires and intentions. Although this type of consciousness usually seems to have a spatial location (within the head-region of the bodily sense-field), it does not seem to possess much – if anything – by way of intrinsic phenomeno-spatial extension. To make these matters a little more concrete, consider a thought experiment.

Suppose all sensory input to your brain is swiftly cut off. You immediately lose all five senses, along with all bodily awareness – your sense of balance included – leaving you with only your thoughts, memories, emotions, powers of imagination and volition. You no longer have any sense of having a body or of being embodied: this sense depends on having bodily sensations along with kinaesthetic and vestibular awareness, and these are all gone. Our brains do not provide us with any distinctive sensations of a 'bodily' or 'brainy' sort; you have no more sensory awareness of your brain than you have of your liver or spleen. Once all your sensory inputs are severed, your brain could be removed from your body and envatted, then taken to the moon, but provided it is kept healthy and functions normally, you would be none the wiser. Although you might well believe that your thinking was still taking place in your brain – as opposed to a disembodied soul killing time in limbo – you have no definite feeling or sensation of *having* or *being* a brain. In addition to having no way of keeping track of your (or your brain's) whereabouts, your sense of having a spatial position – or of occupying a volume of space – is drastically attenuated, if not eliminated entirely. As Oliver Sacks points out, this might well be a deeply disturbing experience:

> If one is given a spinal anesthetic that brings to a halt neural traffic in the lower half of the body, one cannot feel merely that this is paralyzed and senseless; one feels that it is wholly, impossibly, 'non-existent', that one has been cut in half, and that the lower half is absolutely missing – not in the familiar sense of being somewhere, elsewhere, but in the uncanny sense of not-being, or being nowhere. The terms that patients use communicate something of this incommunicable nothing. They may say that part of them is 'missing', 'evacuated', 'gone'. ... One such patient, trying to formulate the unformulable, finally said that his lost limbs were 'nowhere to be found', and that they were 'like nothing on earth'. Hearing such phrases, as one will hear from every patient who finds himself in such a situation – or more properly, 'situationless' – ... one is reminded of the words of Hobbes: 'That which is not Body ... is no part of the Universe: and since the Universe is all, that which is not Body ... is Nothing, and Nowhere.' Spinal anesthesia is common – perhaps a million women have had it for painless childbirth – but descriptions are most rare, partly because the experience is so abhorrent that it is instantly banished from the memory and mind, and partly because the experience (or non-experience) is an experience of nothing. How can one describe nothingness, non-being, non-entity, when there is, literally, nothing to describe?
>
> (1987: 564)

Our imaginary case is more extreme that that reported by Sacks' patients: they have lost only parts of their bodily sense-field; you have lost yours in its entirety. It is not just the odd limb you feel to have disappeared into nothingness, it is your entire body – along with vision, hearing, taste and smell.

But we have not yet taken our thought experiment as far into the realm of the non-spatial as it is possible to go. Thus far your links with your sensory organs (body included) have been lost, but you have retained your powers of sensory imagination and recall. Now imagine that you lose these abilities, in their entirety. Some people who become blind can still remember what it is like to see, and are able to conjure up visual images at will; others gradually lose this ability, and are left in an utterly non-visual, colourless, experiential world. Let us suppose that this is what it is like for you – except you lose not only the ability to remember and imagine visual experience, you lose the ability to remember and imagine all forms of sensory experience. Yet your mental life, rarefied though it now is, carries on – as a flow of thought, cogitation and largely impotent desire and intent. A mental life of this purely intellectualized form is hard for us to imagine clearly, but I think we can imagine it dimly. (According to one theological tradition, this is all we can expect by way of a mental life should we find ourselves in heaven – but not, perhaps, hell.) The pertinent question is: in what manner would this form of consciousness be spatial? Would it possess anything by way of intrinsic spatial extension? Would it seem to be occurring in a more extensive phenomenal space? The answer to both questions is: very probably not.

If non-imagistic conscious thinking is wholly non-spatial, the S-thesis is clearly in trouble. If a purely intellectual consciousness could be non-spatial, the idea that co-consciousness requires spatial connectedness is undermined: could not such a consciousness have more than one thing going on within it, for example a feeling of dread accompanied by a succession of non-imagistic thoughts, and would not these goings-on be co-conscious?

However, a response is available to the S-theorist. Since under normal conditions we are aware of our intellectual consciousness occurring inside our heads, perhaps we should regard this form of consciousness as a part of the bodily sense-field. This proposal has the merit of explaining why it is that we usually feel our thinking to be located within our bodies. As for the thought experiment we have just been considering, it could be argued that the total loss of normal sensory input merely results in a dramatic *shrinking* of the bodily sense-field, rather than its complete annihilation. Since we cannot imagine clearly what it would feel like to be in the envisaged condition, the idea that we would still feel some residual spatial extension, albeit nebulous, cannot be dismissed with complete confidence. In response, it could be argued that the difficulty we have in imagining a wholly non-spatial experience is due to the fact that our actual experience is so profoundly spatial, and the claim that all possible experience must have some spatial character is an illegitimate extrapolation from ordinary everyday experience. Since it is hard to see how to resolve this issue, I will move on. But I think this much at least has been established: we cannot be confident that a non-spatial consciousness is an impossibility. This alone does something to undermine the S-thesis.

3.3 Dis-integration

The S-theorist claims that co-conscious experiences necessarily belong to a single phenomenal space. Perhaps this claim is open to a more straightforward refutation than the one we have just been considering: can we conceive of ordinary experiences, experiences which have spatial characteristics, being co-conscious but not spatially connected? I have already granted that our normal experience is spatially integrated. Can we imagine a subject's experiences being or becoming spatially *dis*-integrated while remaining co-conscious?

Some writers are of the opinion that we all began life in just such a condition. Piaget held that infants initially live in a number of separate sensory universes: a tactile world, a visual world, an auditory world. It is only with time and experience that events within these sensory spaces become coordinated, and as a result, the infant's phenomenal worlds gradually coalesce into the unitary space we adults are familiar with from our own experience. But the empirical evidence for this claim is controversial.[3] And since no one (so far as I am aware) has claimed to be able to remember being in such a condition, it seems we need to turn to thought experiments. By way of background preparation, it is useful to recall the scenario described in Dennett's entertaining and intriguing 'Where Am I?' (1981).

For reasons I will not go into here, Dennett finds himself in an unusual predicament: he has to embark on a dangerous underground mission, but has to leave his brain behind. Happily, thanks to advances in surgery and micro-electronics, it is now possible to remove and envat someone's brain without seriously disrupting the connections linking body and brain. Before the brain is removed from the body, the nerves connecting body to brain are severed one by one. As each nerve is severed, a tiny two-way radio transceiver is fitted to the nerve endings; these transceivers allow electrical signals to pass from brain to body and from body to brain just as they would if the relevant nerve were in one piece. When the process is complete, and the brain is removed from the body, the two-way communication between them is scarcely impaired. Thanks to the millions of efficient transceivers, it is as though the nerves connecting body and brain have been stretched rather than cut. Dennett undergoes the operation. On waking he finds himself feeling surprisingly normal; he looks in the mirror and sees a familiar face – altered only by the presence of two small radio antennae sticking out of his head. He asks to see his brain, and is led to a vat filled with a fluid the colour of ginger ale and containing what looks to be a human brain connected up to a vast array of electronic paraphernalia. At which point a disturbing thought occurs to him:

> I thought to myself: 'Well, here I am sitting on a folded chair, staring through a piece of plate glass at my own brain. ... But wait', I said to myself, 'shouldn't I have thought "Here am I suspended in a bubbling fluid, being stared at by my own eyes."?' I tried thinking this latter thought. I tried to project it into the tank, offering it hopefully to my brain, but I failed to carry off the exercise with any conviction. I tried again. 'Here am I, Daniel Dennett, suspended in a bubbling fluid, being stared at by my own eyes.' No, it just didn't work. Most puzzling and confusing. Being a philosopher of firm physicalist conviction, I believed unswervingly that the tokening of my thoughts was occurring somewhere in my brain: yet when I thought 'Here I am', where the thought

occurred to me was here, outside the vat, where I, Dennett, was standing staring at my brain.

(Dennett 1981: 219)

This is an arresting image, and a noteworthy instance of a full-scale locational delusion. Since the case is an imaginary one, Dennett is not describing an experience anyone has actually had; he is making a phenomenological prediction: he is suggesting that this is how things would seem to anyone in his imagined predicament. I think he is almost certainly right. I for one cannot imagine my sensory experience being just like it is now yet it seeming to me that my thinking is taking place somewhere other than inside my head. Since all Dennett's sensory experience is just as it would be if his brain were in his head, it is not surprising that it seems to him that his thinking is going on in his head – and that he himself, *qua* experiencing subject, is where his body is, rather than where he knows his brain to be.

This case illustrates the role sensory experience plays in our having a sense of 'being somewhere'; it reinforces the idea that our sense of where our thinking is taking place is anchored in our bodily sense-field. It also illustrates something else. When it seems to him that he is not where his brain is, Dennett is certainly deluded: his brain is where his experience is being produced, and so where he is, even though this is not how things seem. Dennett's story demonstrates that we could (conceivably) suffer a fully convincing *locational* hallucination without suffering from any *perceptual* hallucination – as Dennett looks down on his envatted brain he is wide awake and his senses are working perfectly. But I want to use some variations of the basic scenario to illustrate another possibility: a spatially dis-integrated consciousness. To render these rather unusual scenarios vivid I will supply rather more by way of detail.

Story of a head

Suppose then, that your brain has been removed from your body, à la Dennett. Before allowing data to flow back and forth between your body and brain, the team of pioneering neural engineers decides to conduct some tests. To start with, they equip an artificial head – call it simply 'the Head' – with auditory and visual receptors that exactly mimic the receptive powers of your biological eyes and ears; they connect these artificial sense organs to radio transceivers, tuned so their emissions will be received by the transceivers fitted to the visual and auditory nerves dangling from your brain. The nerves leading to the motor centres of your brain that control your eye movements are also fitted with transceivers, which are put in communication with tiny servo-motors able to move the 'eyes' in the Head. As soon as this artificial head is switched on you can see and hear; your visual and auditory experience is just as it usually is, save that you cannot move your head to follow what is going on – you are restricted to moving your eyes. The neural engineers engineer a surprise for you. Knowing of your passion for loud rock music, rather than using the Head to show you your envatted brain, they decide to give you a free front-row seat at a heavy metal concert – one of your favourite bands is playing locally. Only when the Head is firmly fixed onto its tripod right in front of the band, which has just started its first number, are the switches thrown. For the past few days you have had nothing by way of sensory experience at all – save for your dreams and the odd hallucination. Suddenly, you are catapulted from this dark and lonely silence into the deafening noise and glare of the concert hall. You understand at once what must have happened – you were forewarned of the tests that would be carried out before your full re-embodiment. You silently express appreciation for the engineers' taste in music, but wish they had set the gain on the transceivers rather lower: all this raucous noise and brilliant light is a bit overpowering after all that darkness and silence.

As these thoughts pass through your mind, where does it seem to you that you are? Where does your thinking seem to be going on? The answer seems plain. It would seem to you that you were in the concert hall; it would seem to you that your thinking was going on just where it usually does: some-where just behind your eyes and between your ears. The idea that thinking requires a sensory anchor in order to be felt as 'situated' in the external world was one of the lessons we drew from our earlier consideration of Dennett's imagined predicament. What we now see is that this anchor need not involve bodily experience. Your thinking does have a sensory anchor – of a violent and overpowering sort, but of a wholly audio-visual character. True, you would not feel yourself to be normally embodied, since you have nothing by way of bodily sensations. But then, most of us have had the misfortune of leaving our dentist's surgery with half our head feeling completely numb – the after-effect of a local anaesthetic. Would an even stronger anaesthetic, one which rendered one's entire head (and body) utterly numb, significantly reduce the sense that one's thinking was taking place just behind one's eyes and in between one's ears? I do not think it would.

Our playful neural engineers are not yet through. When your brain and body were separated, your breathing and other basic body functions came under the control of a basic-body-functions programme (your body would have died otherwise). This programme has been running on a computer in continuous radio contact with your body, via the transceivers fitted to your body's severed nerve endings. For their second test, the engineers decide to disconnect the Head and basic-body-programme, and switch on the trans-ceivers connecting your brain to your body. They will not activate transceivers connecting your brain with your eyes, ears, nose and tongue. You will now have a full range of bodily experience, but be effectively blind and deaf. You will be able move at will, and examine what you bump into by touch, but you will not smell or taste anything. Knowing of your passion for sub-aqua diving, the engineers engineer another surprise for you. They kit out your body with breathing apparatus and dump it into the sea, not far offshore, but in an area particularly favoured by sub-aquatic explorers for the rich variety of flora and fauna. Only when your body has touched the seabed do they throw the switches which restore communication between your brain and body. As soon as they do, you immediately feel the bitterly cold water pressing in all around (the engineers did not go so far as to provide a wetsuit); you feel the weight of the breathing equipment on your back, and the mouthpiece between your lips. It's clear that you are underwater. As this realization dawns you erupt into a violent fit of coughing: the basic-body-function programme was not designed to handle underwater breathing. Cursing the engineers' carelessness, once the coughing fit has passed you start to explore your new environment. Being an accomplished undersea explorer you have no difficulty in navigating your way about over the seabed, blind though you are. As you swim along, tentatively so as not to bang your head too hard on rocky outcrops, you can feel the fronds of seaweed caressing your skin, and the gentle nibblings of curious fish. You can only hope that no sharks are about. Now, in this case too it is clear where you would seem to be, and where your thinking would seem to be taking place. You would feel yourself to be re-embodied; it would seem as though *you* were moving along on the seabed; your thinking would seem to be going on within your head. Although you still *believe* that your experience is being produced by activity within your brain, your brain does not constitute a sensory anchor for your consciousness. Consequently, the idea that your consciousness is located within your brain – in a vat of warm nutrient fluid, rather than the cold salty sea – would carry no phenomenological conviction whatsoever.

At this point the neural engineers conduct their final test. As you continue with your tentative examination of your undersea environment, the Head is taken from the laboratory to the top of a nearby mountain. It is a warm sunny day. The switches are thrown, and all of a sudden – while swimming through the dark silent ocean – you find sound and vision have been restored. The ensuing barrage of contradictory experience is confusing in the extreme. To make matters worse, your concentration having been rudely disrupted, you now bang your head, with some force, as you swim into a sharp piece of rock jutting up from the seabed. As you feel the warmth of the blood trickle down your cheek, a new experience is introduced into the already baffling mix: pain. You realize you had better stop moving. So, focusing all your attention on your bodily feelings, trying to ignore your visual experience altogether (you only partly succeed), you try to find a safe place to deposit your body. Fortunately, you soon come across a large smooth rock, and you wedge yourself between it and the seabed. You now set about exploring your newly enriched sensory world. Or rather, your sensory *worlds*. Focusing your attention firmly on your visual and auditory experience, you find that you recognize the view. You have often taken a hike to the top of this mountain. As you listen to the sounds of the occasional bird call, and the strong wind whistling through the pines, you can almost (but not quite) taste the warm, fresh, alpine-flowery character of the mountain air. It is as though you were standing there yourself, on that familiar summit. But your contemplation of this splendour is interrupted: something has taken a grip on your ankle, and is starting to pull. Trying with all your might to ignore the mountain scenery, you focus hard on your bodily experience. You soon find yourself returning to the dark, cold, silent seabed. The tugging on your ankle continues. You feel a slimy suckered tentacle coiling itself around your lower leg. It does not feel quite so large and threatening as it first did – you opt to engage your aggressor. Reaching down, you try to remove the tentacle; as you do, you feel another two tentacles trying to wrap themselves around your arm. As you bring your other arm into action, you encounter another two tentacles – or perhaps it's three. Grabbing hold of one, you give a sharp pull. The beast tries to pull free, but you hold on tightly. Pulling again, you feel the squirming mass attached to the tentacle move closer. Reaching out to touch with your other hand you find your suspicions confirmed: a smallish octopus, nothing worse.

But now something is changing on the auditory and visual front. You hear a loud engine start up. Before you know it, your visual point of view is moving. The engineering team has played its final card. The Head was not sitting on its usual tripod on the mountain top, but attached atop a small radio-controlled plane. This plane has just been launched over the vertiginous cliff-face on the north side of the summit. Casting the octopus away into the passing underwater currents, your attention is now grabbed by the audio-visual treat provided by the flying Head. As the plane swoops and dives in response to the whims of the engineer with the control box, you are captivated by the visual spectacle. You feel yourself swooping and diving through the clouds, firmly rooted in your visual viewpoint. After an enjoyable few minutes of aerial acrobatics – during which the dark coldness of the ocean floor seems far away, despite being constantly present in the background of your awareness – you hear the plane's engine begin to splutter, and then cut out altogether. Perhaps the plane has run out of fuel – perhaps the neural engineers are having a last laugh at your expense. In any event, you are plunging fast and Headfirst towards the ground. You stare at the rapidly approaching valley floor. And then, abruptly and silently, the lights go out. Much to your relief you feel nothing whatsoever – save for the cold waters pressing on your body, in darkness, wedged under a rock on the ocean bed.

Diagnosis

I would not pretend that the predicaments I have been describing are easy to imagine oneself into with any great clarity. They are too far removed from the sort of experience we are accustomed to. But they are clearly possible forms someone's experience *could* take, and I think we can anticipate with some confidence roughly what it would be like if our own experience were to take these forms. Perhaps the most dubious aspect of the cases, as I have described them, is the assumption that one would have the feeling of oneself *shifting* back and forth between body and Head, merely by concentrating hard and shifting one's attention. But I do not think this is too unrealistic. After all, if we concentrate on a piece of music our bodily and visual experiences lose all prominence, although they do not vanish altogether. Similarly, if we focus all our (active) attention on our bodily experience, we barely notice what we are seeing and hearing. So, returning to the third scenario, it does not seem too implausible to suppose that if one were to concentrate on one's bodily experience, one would have the impression that one's thinking was going on underwater, and if one were to concentrate on one's audio-visual experience, one would have the impression that one's thinking was taking place up on a mountain top. But perhaps it would take time and practice to be able to focus one's attention in this way. In any event, this is a side issue. The main purpose of the scenarios will doubtless be evident.

In each of the first two scenarios you are provided with a single unified phenomenal space: in the first case audio-visual, in the second case bodily. In the third scenario, these phenomenal 'worlds' are both present at the same time. Your overall experience comprises a full range of bodily experience and a full range of auditory and visual experience; these experiences are all mutually co-conscious, all the time. But they are not integrated so as to constitute a common phenomenal space. Rather, they are split into two disjoint spaces: one wholly bodily, one formed by a fusion of sound and vision. The octopus that you feel attaching itself to your leg is not something you can see or hear; the bird you can see and hear circling over a nearby tree is manifestly not something you could approach and touch – your body is underwater on the ocean floor. It is true that all your perceptions, bodily and audio-visual, are of events occurring within physical space, and so these events are spatially related. But these physical spatial relations have no phenomenal reality for you. Not only are you unable to see any ocean from your mountain-top vantage point, you have no idea of how far away or in which direction your body lies; likewise, from your bodily point of view, you have no idea how far you would have to swim, or in which direction, to move closer to the site of your auditory and visual viewpoint. There are no *experienced* spatial relations between your bodily experiences and your audio-visual experiences. Yet both sets of experiences are nonetheless co-conscious.

A variant of the third scenario may make it easier to appreciate the extent to which the phenomenal spaces in question really are unconnected. Instead of going to the trouble of lugging the Head up a mountain, the neural engineers simply play back to you a recording they made of your experiences at the heavy metal concert, i.e. a perfect recording of the patterns of radio signals sent from the Head to your brain. So while you are swimming tentatively and blindly through the sea, you suddenly find yourself returned to the cacophonous concert hall, the light-show blazing away. But returned only in part – you are still aware of the sea pressing around your body. Naturally, you recognize what you are seeing and hearing, and realize that it must be a recording. Nonetheless, the experience is just as vivid and realistic as it was first time around. Visually speaking, the band are up there on stage, performing away. But this audio-visual experience does not correspond with anything currently going on – the scene you are witnessing exists only within your consciousness. Your body, however, really is on the seabed – or so you believe. Given this, you have no sense at all that your bodily and audio-visual experiences are taking place within a common space, whether phenomenal or physical. Yet both sets of experiences are co-conscious.

3.4 Phenomenal spaces

The thought experiments we have been considering amount to counter-examples to the S-thesis. Since it seems possible to imagine co-conscious experiences which are not confined to a single unified phenomenal space, there is reason to reject the claim that phenomeno-spatial connectedness is necessary for co-consciousness. However, resting as it does on imaginary cases which are not only highly speculative but hard to imagine, this result is not as secure as it might be. It can be reinforced by considerations of a different, more metaphysical kind. But the S-thesis is not my only reason for introducing these considerations. The terms 'sensory field' and 'phenomenal space' have been bandied about frequently in the last couple of sections. I have not said exactly what I take these things to be. Before concluding this discussion of phenomenal spatiality I will try to clarify just what sort of thing, just what sort of space, a phenomenal space is. After all, although I have argued that co-consciousness is not essentially spatial, I have also acknowledged that to a very large extent our consciousness *is* spatial. If we want an understanding of the unity of consciousness we need an understanding of phenomenal space.

A distinction drawn in connection with physical space provides a useful starting point. The physical world is a spatio-temporal world: it consists of physical things spread through space and time. For present purposes, to simplify matters, we can suppose time is a dimension distinct from space and leave it out of the picture. We can now ask: What are the most basic constituents of the physical world? Assuming a realistic attitude to the physical world *per se*, there are three options. Physical space could be onto-logically basic, with physical objects possessing an ontologically derivative status. Or physical objects could be basic, with physical space possessing an ontologically derivative status. Or physical space and physical things could both be ontologically basic physical items. Anyone who adopts either the first or the third of these options is committed to the view that physical space is an ontologically basic particular in its own right. This view goes by a variety of names: spatial realism, absolutism, or substantivalism. Anyone who adopts the second option is committed to the view that physical space is not an ontologically basic particular. This view is commonly known as spatial anti-realism, relationism, or relationalism. To minimize terminological confusion I will talk of substantivalism and relationism.

The substantivalist position is easy to characterize. Space exists, as a concrete (i.e. non-abstract) thing. Space is just as real as any material object. Since the space we are concerned with at the moment is physical space, this space is a physical object in its own right. Substantivalism comes in two strengths. Standard-strength substantivalism is the view that space is just as real as its material occupants (i.e. physical particles or bodies), while accepting that the latter are just as real as the space they exist within. This position corresponds with the third option outlined above. The strong or *super*-substantivalist holds that space is ontologically more fundamental than the objects it contains. On this view, physical bodies are adjectival on space; physical bodies exist when space takes on certain qualities; a physical body is nothing more than a region of space endowed with certain properties. For the super-substantivalist, there is, strictly speaking, only one physical particular, space itself.

Relationism is rather harder to characterize. The typical relationist does not deny that material objects are separated by space. Obviously, there are spatial relations among objects (hence 'relationism'). Moreover, talk of places (in space) where there are no material objects seems to make sense. Most relationists are reluctant to deny these hard-to-deny facts. What relationists do want to deny is the thesis that space exists as something separate from and independent of material objects. To achieve this, the relationist will try to show that the truth of propositions about distances, movements and locations depends exclusively on facts concerning actual and (nomologically) possible spatial relations between material objects. There are various ways this might be done, and consequently different versions of relationism, but there is no need to go any further into these issues here. Our concern is with phenomenal space, and in this context, a clear difference can be discerned between two fundamentally different types of space, one substantival and one not.

Fields of presence

The idea that space could be substantival, even in the weakest sense of 'something other than nothing', initially strikes many people as implausible. Is not space by itself, i.e. empty space, just nothingness? How can any amount of nothingness add up to anything substantial (or substantival)? Since we are concerned with phenomenal space, the sorts of consideration which are relevant to establishing substantivalism with regard to physical space are not relevant (e.g. explanatory simplicity in physical science). I will make this assumption: for a phenomenal space to merit the label 'substantival', the space in question should possess some phenomenal reality – the space in question must possess some intrinsic phenomenal characteristics of its own. It is easy to see that such spaces can exist: a certain kind of sense-field fits the bill. I will call the relevant types of sense-field *P-fields*; the 'P' is for *presence* or *plenum*. By way of an example, imagine a subject whose sensory experience is wholly visual, and whose visual experience resembles what we experience when looking at a slightly misted stained glass window: flat, lacking any depth, a mosaic of translucent coloured shapes appearing within a medium possessing inherent luminosity. Our imaginary subject's visual field, when empty, is a luminous, pale white expanse. Phenomenal objects, i.e. coloured shapes, are literally parts of the sense-field – parts of the field which happen to be endowed with certain distinctive visual qualities. The sense-field itself possesses an intrinsic phenomenal character: it is a field of two-dimensional luminosity, two-dimensional visual presence. This sort of sense-field is the sort of thing I mean by a P-field. A P-field is spatially extended (hence a 'field'), possessing a certain dimensionality and size (not necessarily constant), and possesses its own intrinsic phenomenal character. If we take a P-field to be a phenomenal space – call it a *P-space* – the size and structure of the space is fixed by the intrinsic phenomenal characteristics of the corresponding sense-field. It is clear that a P-space possesses the sort of properties one would expect a substantival phenomenal space to have. It is intrinsically spatial, and possesses an intrinsic phenomenal character throughout. The existence and structure of this spatial medium is independent of any objects located within it.

Now, our imaginary subject's P-field qualifies as a *super*-substantival space. Phenomenal objects are adjectival on the space, since they consist of a spatial medium taking on certain qualitative features, of a visual sort, at certain locations within it. But a weaker type of P-space is possible, corresponding to the standard-strength substantivalism mentioned earlier. To see this, suppose our imaginary subject's sensory experience is audio-visual, rather than simply visual. Our subject is sometimes aware of discrete sounds as well as colour and light. When our subject hears these sounds, they always seem to be located (phenomenologically speaking) somewhere within a 2-D visual P-field. Although these sounds have a location within the background visuo-phenomenal field, they are not adjectival on this field in the same way as are coloured shapes. A coloured shape consists of a qualitative modification in the intrinsic character of the background P-field. Or, to put it less strongly, it is at least an option to regard these items in this way. This is not an option for auditory objects, which are of a different sensory-modal type from the background P-field. Auditory qualities can spatially coincide with visual properties, but they cannot be intrinsic features of a visual plenum. When a sound exists in a visual plenum, it does not exist as a component part of the plenum; a coloured shape does.

Phenomenal voids

While P-fields are certainly possible, a quite different type of sense-field is also possible. Consider the contents of our own experience, phenomenal particulars such as itches, sounds, and the immediate objects of visual experience. While these contents are typically spatial and spatially located, they are not located within a three-dimensional spatial medium possessing an intrinsic phenomenal character. We do not find ourselves immersed within a phenomenological plenum of any kind – for the most part, the space we find ourselves in, the space our experiences appear to be located within, is a phenomenal vacuum, empty of intrinsic phenomenal characteristics. If this is not obvious, consider ordinary auditory experience. We can hear sounds all about us (and occasionally within us); we hear sounds at varying distances from both one another and ourselves. Assuming projectivism, these sounds – the immediate objects of auditory perception – are not located in physical space, they are phenomenal and exist only within our consciousness; so the space we hear sounds as occurring in is a phenomenal space. Unlike the flat visual sense-field we considered above, the typical auditory sense-field is far from being a plenum: the bulk of it is a phenomenal void. Imagine you are in bed, in a house in the country, in the dead of night. No matter how hard you strain your ears you can hear nothing at all; you are surrounded by silence. You then hear a dog emit a single howl, some distance away – a couple of hundred yards at least. This noise might seem to echo around for a short while, but does it fill your auditory field? Does it seem to be coming from all directions and from all distances? Of course not – most of your auditory field is still filled with silence, auditory nothingness. The same holds under more normal circumstances, when we can hear several sounds coming from different directions and distances – even when the auditory field is quite busy, it is rarely full (in the way it is when one is wearing a pair of headphones emitting loud white noise). Unlike the imagined two-dimensional visual field, the auditory field seems to have no intrinsic phenomenal qualities; it is a phenomenological void or vacuum. Call sense-fields with this nature *V-fields*, and the phenomenal spaces they constitute *V-spaces*.

On some occasions a V-space can be completely filled by phenomenal content (e.g. the auditory experience one has when wearing headphones emitting loud white noise). But the typical V-space is not empty: it contains phenomenal objects, and these objects can take up room within the V-space. Imagine listening to an orchestra on a good stereo: the sound from the string section seems to fill up a certain volume of space in between the speakers. To keep things simple I have been concentrating on a single modality – auditory experience – but the typical V-space is multi-modal: it comprises phenomenal contents of diverse kinds, spread through a phenomenal void. Earlier I used visual experience to illustrate what P-space could be like. But the contents of our ordinary visual experience are located in a V-space. In the case of the imagined two-dimensional plenum, the subject's visual space is wholly filled; our ordinary three-dimensional visual space is not. If I hold my hands up in front of me, with my right hand a foot or so behind my left, I can see that one hand is farther away than the other.

I do not see the space between them as possessing any intrinsic visuo-phenomenal characteristics. The space between them is filled in one sense – I can see the wall against which both appear – but the wall appears to be behind both hands, not between them. We can of course see objects that extend through the depth-dimension, as when I hold my arm up before me and look along it. Here a portion of visual space is filled in the third dimension of depth. But the normal visual field is not wholly filled – there are visual vacua. Bodily experience provides a better approximation to a three-dimensional P-field, but only an approximation. Muscular kinaesthetic sensations possess some phenomenal depth – they exist some way beneath the skin. But it would be a mistake to think bodily experience as a whole has the character of a P-field. There are regions within our bodies (e.g. our bones and brain) which are not usually sensation-filled: a phenomenal void lurks within each of us. And there is a bodily space around us which is not filled with any bodily sensations, the space we can move our limbs about in. If I close my eyes and hold up my two hands, palms facing, leaving a few inches between them, I am aware of the distance between them, but this distance is not filled with any intrinsic phenomenal features.

In distinguishing between P-spaces and V-spaces, the phenomenal character of *empty* space is paramount: V-spaces can possess phenomenal voids, P-spaces cannot. This difference can be brought out in a slightly different way. In the case of a P-space, we do not merely sense objects as occurring in space, we sense the space between objects, and this empty space possesses intrinsic phenomenal characteristics. Imagine looking at two black circles on an otherwise white wall – you can see the whiteness surrounding and filling the circles. The entire visual expanse can be regarded as a P-field, and within this field there are no regions that are empty of visual content. In a V-space, on the other hand, we experience objects as occurring at various spatial locations, but we do not experience the space between them as having any intrinsic phenomenal character. Imagine hearing a dog bark to your left, and a door shut to your right – and nothing else; in this case there is no auditory experience of the space in between – the space is an auditory void. This is quite unlike the two-dimensional visual case, in which there is a luminous expanse between any two co-existing visual objects.

I have suggested that it would be natural to regard P-spaces as instances of substantival spaces. V-spaces are most naturally regarded as relational. What could justify regarding them as substantival? Empty space within a V-space lacks any inherent phenomenal characteristics, so there are no grounds for regarding this space as possessing anything by way of phenomenal substance – so to speak. Moreover, when contents occur within a V-field, it seems we can express everything we want by referring only to the contents and their spatial relations. For example, if you hear two sounds, you could identify them thus: a rifle shot to my right, about a hundred yards away, a car passing on my left, about ten yards away. These phenomenal objects occur at certain (only vaguely specifiable) distances, and in certain directions, from the subject. But they do not occur within a phenomenal medium of the sort there would have to be to justify talking of a substantival phenomenal space. Since there exists no such medium, there are no facts about it to be described.

In characterizing V-spaces, it would be wrong to focus solely on the actual spatial relations between phenomenal contents. A V-space is constituted of places where phenomenal objects *might* be, as well as places where phenomenal objects actually are. As I noted earlier, relationists often view space as a domain of nomological possibilities. When you hear the rifle shot on your right and a car passing by on the left, there is plenty of empty space where you could be hearing (or seeing or touching) other things – e.g. a second rifle shot right in front of you. Similarly, when I hold my right hand a foot further away from me than my left, although I see nothing in the empty space in between, there is space there where I could see (or hear or touch) something, for example one of your hands. A more interesting point is that there are constraints on the places where we can sense phenomenal objects. Perhaps the most blatant constraint is dimensionality. We are aware of one-, two- and three-dimensional phenomenal contents and phenomeno-spatial relations, but we have no four-dimensional spatial awareness. We cannot perceive or imagine hyperspheres or hypercubes; we can hear things happening behind and in front of us, to our left and right, or above or below us, but we cannot hear things taking place in any other directions. Other constraints are modality-specific. The field of vision is limited in a way the field of hearing is not – we can hear all around us, but see only in front of us (roughly speaking). Tactile sensations are restricted to the bodily sense-field, which itself has a distinctive shape.

These constraints might suggest this thought: If our experience is restricted to a three-dimensional array of places, places which can be empty of phenomenal contents, can we not regard this array as a substantival V-space? I think not. The fact that there are constraints on the sorts of spatial relations phenomenal contents can enter into does not in itself justify regarding V-spaces as anything other than relational. For although these constraints are real enough, and are nomological rather than logical, *they are not the product of the phenomenal space itself*. Recall the visual P-space we considered earlier. In this case, the location and movements of visual contents are restricted to two dimensions. But this restriction is a direct consequence of the background spatial medium: this medium is two-dimensional, and particular visual contents (such as a filled blue triangle) come into being when a region of this medium becomes endowed with the relevant visuo-phenomenal properties. In this case, the constraints on spatial relatedness are an expression of the structure of a phenomenal space – a phenomenal space possessing its own intrinsic phenomenal character. Things are quite different in the case of V-spaces. The contents that exist within a V-space may possess their own intrinsic phenomeno-spatial extension, but this extension is not the result of some region of a background spatial medium being

endowed with localized phenomenal characteristics. Whatever may be responsible for the constraints operative within a V-space, it is not the V-space
itself. If we elect to regard a V-space as a structured domain of possibilia, a
domain consisting of a set of places where contents can be sensed, this
domain is the product of the constraints governing the experiences a subject
is capable of having. If these constraints were other than they are, which
they could be, logically speaking, the structure of the subject's global V-
space would be different. Now, in the case of a P-space too, the shape, size
and dimensionality of this space are the products of the constraints on the
kinds of experience a subject can have. If these constraints were relevantly
different, the P-space would be different too. We gave our imaginary subject
a 2-D visual field; we could as easily envisage a subject with a 3-D visual P-
field. But in envisaging such variations, the experiential constraints operate
on (or create) a substantival phenomenal space. This space then acts as a
constraint on the phenomenal objects which can exist within it. This is the
reverse of the way experiential constraints work in the case of a V-space. A
V-space only exists because of the experiential constraints on phenomenal
objects, and these objects are not adjectival on, or constrained by, a more
basic phenomenal space. The existence of experiential constraints of this
kind may justify the claim that a V-space is not just nothing, pure and
simple, but it does not follow that a V-space is a something in the way a P-
space is. By virtue of possessing an intrinsic phenomenal character, P-spaces
are phenomenally real in a way V-spaces are not.

3.5 The S-thesis reconsidered

Since the basic differences between substantival and non-substantival
phenomenal spaces should now be reasonably clear, we can move on to
reconsider the S-thesis, i.e. the claim that phenomeno-spatial connectedness
is both sufficient and necessary for co-consciousness. Since the sufficiency
claim is uncontroversial – any phenomenal contents that are sensed as being
in a phenomeno-spatial relation are automatically co-conscious – what is at
issue is the necessity claim. We are now in a better position to appreciate just
how implausible this necessity claim is, partly because we can now see more
clearly what would have to be the case for it to be true.

   Imagine a subject whose experience is confined to a single P-field. Any
simultaneous phenomenal objects falling within this subject's awareness
would necessarily be spatially related. This subject can only be aware of
different phenomenal objects if these objects occur within the P-field. For
this subject, co-consciousness is an essentially spatial relationship. The S-
thesis would be true for such a subject. We might go so far as to say that the
very consciousness of such a subject is spatial in form, for whenever this
subject is experiencing anything it is experiencing a spatially extended
phenomenal plenum, and whatever else it experiences occurs within this
plenum. But although there might be subjects of this kind, it is clear that we

are not like this. Not only is our consciousness not confined to a single P-field, none of our sense-fields is a P-field (assuming I am right in claiming that there are phenomenal voids within the bodily sense-field). So what we need to consider is the S-thesis in relation to phenomenal spaces of the V-variety. But before doing so, note this: although the S-thesis would be true for subjects whose experience is restricted to a single P-field, can we not conceive of subjects whose simultaneous experience fills two (or more) spatially unconnected yet co-conscious P-fields? So far as I can see, there is nothing to rule out such a possibility. If there could be such subjects, the S-thesis is false even for subjects whose experience is confined to P-fields.

But rather than dwell on this rather remote possibility, let us turn to subjects rather more akin to ourselves, subjects whose experience occurs within V-spaces. Our own experience is, typically, multi-modal and spatially unified. The deliverances of our senses are combined with bodily sensations, thoughts, emotions and imaginings in a single V-space. But is there any reason whatsoever to suppose that V-spaces must be unified in this way? I cannot see that there is. The structure of a V-space depends ultimately upon the constraints governing the sorts of experience a subject can have. There is no *a priori* reason to suppose these constraints can take only one form. As I noted earlier, although our experience is confined to three spatial dimensions, we can conceive of subjects whose experience is confined to two spatial dimensions, as well as subjects capable of experiences possessing more than three spatial dimensions, e.g. subjects who can perceive or imagine 4-D hyperspheres. Dimensionality is one way space-relevant experiential constraints can differ; there are indefinitely many others. Some of these variations will generate V-spaces with unfamiliar geometries. There are possible beings whose auditory experience is confined to a circular region in front of them (like our field of vision) and whose visual field extends for a full 360 degrees (they have several spherical eyes, and their bodies are translucent). There are possible beings whose audio-visual field is shaped like a torus, and like a familiar mint is holed in the middle. There are possible beings whose bodily experience is spatially disjointed. One such species is a type of sentient plant. Each plant comprises several bulbs, connected to one another by underground nerves; the plants can feel the warmth of the sun on their leaves and petals, but have no awareness of the space separating their scattered stalks and shoots. And then there are possible beings with multiple sense-fields, each of a different modality, each of which generates a separate V-space; yet despite this spatial disunity, these separate V-spaces are mutually co-conscious. There is no need to describe such beings: this is precisely the possibility already explored in our earlier thought experiment.

In thinking about V-fields and co-conscious unity, the important point is this. For a subject whose experience occurs within a V-space, the characteristics of this space are determined by the phenomeno-spatial relations among the phenomenal objects that can be present in the subject's experience.

These spatial relations are not constrained by any background spatial medium – there is no P-field. Since these relations possess no intrinsic phenomenal character, since they are so tenuous (phenomenologically speaking), it seems quite conceivable that types of content which are experienced as spatially related could also be experienced in the absence of these relations, and hence as co-conscious but spatially unconnected. Hence it is plausible to think that in the absence of a P-field, co-consciousness itself places no spatial constraints on phenomenal contents. Given that experience is not confined to P-fields, and there is no reason to think the phenomeno-spatial relations among co-conscious experiences will necessarily warrant the postulation of a single unified V-field within which all the subject's experience can be located, there is no reason to accept the S-thesis.

In §2.6 I argued against the idea that our experiences are qualitative modifications of a Substantival awareness: our experiences have such different phenomenal characteristics it is hard to see how they could all be qualitative modifications of a single underlying experiential medium, or modes of a phenomenal substance. Our discussion of phenomenal space reinforces this conclusion. If an individual consciousness took the form of a single P-space, it would be natural to take this underlying phenomenal space to be a substance, a substantival phenomenal space. If the phenomenal items featuring in this space were all of the same modal type as the P-field, we might well be justified in taking them to be adjectival modifications of the P-field. (Remember the example of a super-substantival phenomenal space, the flat visual field of luminosity, whose sole occupants are regions of colour.) But our consciousness is not like this. The space our experience occurs within is a V-space; since V-spaces lack any inherent phenomenal character, there is no justification for taking them to have a substantival nature. So I do not think there are any phenomenological grounds for accepting the substantival conception as a general truth about consciousness. At most, it might be true for subjects whose experience has the form of a single P-field.

3.6 V-spaces: further issues

Questions can be posed about V-spaces (and no doubt P-spaces too) which I have not yet mentioned, let alone considered. Two are of sufficient importance to merit a brief examination.

Are spatial relations between objects in a V-space absolute or relative? I suspect there are many possibilities. Imagine waking up to find yourself in total darkness tied down to a chair. After a while, a vertical white line appears, apparently floating in mid-air, somewhere on your left; you can see nothing whatsoever but this line. Although the line is clearly vertical, and clearly in front of you and on your left, would it appear to be at any definite distance from you? I expect not. If you entertain the hypothesis that the line is a few inches long, you can infer that it is quite close to you – a matter of inches. If you suppose the line is several feet long, it is clearly some yards from you. But both these hypotheses, and many others, are compatible with what you can actually see. Under these circumstances, the line might not appear to be at a determinate distance from you at all. We vary the scenario, and suppose that you wake up to find your body completely numb and paralysed, so that you have no sense of being embodied, no sense of right and left, no sense of up and down (the systems responsible for your sense of balance have been disabled). In this condition, you would be unable to tell whether the line is horizontal, vertical or somewhere in between. Nor would you be able to tell whether the line is right in front of you, or somewhere to one side, since you are unable to move either your head or eyeballs, and have no idea at all as to whether your eyes are pointing straight ahead or not. As soon as the lights come on, and you see that you are in a room, and that the line is in fact a thin white rod hanging from the ceiling, everything changes: the size, orientation and location of the rod will be immediately apparent.

This sort of case may suggest the spatial properties of V-field occupants are relative, to a large extent if not completely. But other examples suggest otherwise: size, distance, direction and orientation may be relative in some V-fields but not in others. Imagine what it would be like to be floating naked in a dark weightless environment. If you were sufficiently relaxed, and attempted no movements, given that there is nothing touching or pressing on your skin you might be quite unable to detect any bodily sensations. Let us suppose this is the case. Despite the absence of bodily sensations, you would still have a sense of the disposition of your limbs, for example you would have an intuitive sense of whether your arms are bent or straight. If someone were to prick your skin with a needle, you would immediately know the chosen location; you would feel the pain as situated on the back of your thigh, or on the palm of your hand. The location of the pain is thus absolute rather than relative, in that the pain has a definite location within an otherwise empty bodily V-field. Although our bodily V-fields are non-substantival, the locations, orientations and sizes of bodily sensations are absolute rather than relative. There may well be subjects whose visual fields have similar properties: such subjects would have an intuitive sense of the size, direction and distance of visuo-phenomenal objects, irrespective of what other experiences – whether visual or otherwise – they have at the same time.

Another issue worthy of further attention concerns a distinction between what I will call *real* and *imaginary* V-spaces. I have suggested that the struc-ture of a V-space is determined by the constraints on the sorts of experience available to a subject. While there is undeniably a sense in which this is true, it is also something of an oversimplification. Suppose I wake up one morning in a darkened room. Although I can see nothing, I know the shape and width of my usual field of vision – roughly semi-spherical – and I have corresponding expectations as to where visual sensations will occur when I turn on the light. I do not expect to see anything that is going on behind my head, I do not expect my visual field to extend further behind me than it usually does. Unbeknownst to me, my optical nerves have been damaged by a viral infection during the night, and my visual capacities have altered. I now have tunnel vision; my field of vision has shrunk from 180 degrees to 30 degrees. Although I will find out about my altered condition as soon as I turn on the light, before doing so I am completely unaware of it. Since the range of possible visual experiences available to me is not what it was, my visual V-field has changed, but since I am oblivious to this fact, my expectations as to what I will be able to see do not conform to the reality of the situation. In other words, my real visual V-field has a span of 30 degrees, whereas my imaginary visual V-field still has a span of 180 degrees. When I do turn on the light, I will feel myself to be partially blinded, in that I will have a sense that my actual visual field is surrounded by a region of darkness into which I cannot see, but I will not feel that this new darkness extends behind me, into the regions where I have never been able to see. Since this feeling may continue for months or years, long after I have become fully accustomed to my tunnel vision, it is clear that the structure of imaginary V-fields is not determined by 'expectations' in quite the usual sense. Memory, instinct and what remains imaginable – each of these factors no doubt plays a role.

I shall not try to specify exactly what does determine the structure of imaginary V-fields. The point to which I want to draw attention is the fact that we have an instinctive sense of the size, shape and structure of our sensory fields, even when these fields lack any intrinsic phenomenal characteristics, as V-fields do. Indeed, it is precisely because V-fields themselves lack intrinsic phenomenal characteristics that the distinction between their imaginary structure and their real structure has the significance it does. V-fields (unlike P-fields) have no intrinsic features, there is a sense in which they are pure nothingness, but they are not unstructured nothingness; we do not feel ourselves surrounded by a void of four or *n* dimensions. The boundaries of a V-field are fixed as much by instinctive expectations and what is imaginable as by the actual constraints on our sensory experience.[4]

This fact strengthens the conclusion I reached earlier concerning the possibility of spatially unconnected but co-conscious contents. The fact that we find it so difficult to imagine such contents can be plausibly be put down to contingent features of our perceptual systems and histories. Since beings with differently organized perceptual systems (e.g. spatially scattered sense-organs) would have different instincts and expectations about the spatial structure of their experience, the possibility of spatially disjoint V-spaces, both imaginary and real, is very real indeed.

Having recognized the existence and significance of imaginary V-spaces, we are in a position to counter an objection to the lesson drawn from the thought experiment introduced in §3.3. I suggested that in the situation envisaged, as you survey some mountain scenery from the vantage point of the Head, you would have no sense that your audio-visual experiences were spatially related (in a phenomenal way) to your bodily experience, as you crawl along the seabed, despite the fact that all the experiences involved are co-conscious. It could be objected: 'No: even though the *contents* of your audio-visual and bodily experiences would be spatially unconnected, it would still seem to you that your visual experience (or its content) was located in front of your body, as per usual. Is this not precisely the feeling we sometimes have when we listen to a radio broadcast of a piece of music on headphones? If the microphones have been well placed we have a fairly clear sense of the size of the venue (which may be much larger than the room we are actually in) and the locations within it of the various instruments. Although we know full well that the sounds we are hearing are not occurring in our immediate environment, they nonetheless appear to be spatially related to the rest of our experience. If you hear a clash of cymbals to your right you could point in the direction the sound seems to be coming from'. While this objection may seem to have some force, it nonetheless fails, and we are now in a position to see why.

In my earlier diagnosis of the final stage of the thought experiment, I assumed that the normal phenomeno-spatial connections between your bodily and audio-visual experience would be absent. Given the course of your experience over the preceding hours, this is far from being wholly implausible. You had become accustomed to enjoying audio-visual experience without bodily experience, and bodily experience without audio-visual experience; furthermore, you had become used to your body and Head being located in different places. Consequently, is it not likely that when the two 'channels' are activated simultaneously your usual sense of how your audio-visual experiences are related to your body would be disrupted? Perhaps so. But let us suppose that this is not what happens: when both channels are activated you have the impression that your bodily and audio-visual experiences are spatially related to one another in the usual way, for example you feel that you could point in the direction of the bird you see and hear to your left. You feel this even though you know that your Head and body are not in the same place, and you have no idea as to their relative locations. What could account for this abiding sense of spatial connectedness? The most plausible answer is that your *imaginary* audio-visual and bodily V-fields have remained spatially linked. Despite your recent experiences and your knowledge of your scattered condition, and thanks to a combination of instinct and deeply ingrained expectation, the spatial integrity of the relevant imaginary sense-fields remains intact. However, this possibility does not rescue the S-thesis from refutation by counter-example. Since the relevant spatial integration exists only at the imaginary level, the original scenario is easily modified so as to eliminate it. Perhaps spending much longer periods with disconnected sense-fields would lead to the dis-integration of the imaginary V-field. Alternatively, a little neural damage, sufficient to wipe out the misleading instinctive expectations, could certainly do the job.

3.7 Co-consciousness

Returning to our main theme: just what can be said about the relationship of synchronic co-consciousness? Recall first the conclusions of Chapter 2. Since the awareness–content dualism of the A-theorist proved untenable, we cannot explain co-consciousness in terms of a separate awareness. Rejecting the A-theorist's pure awareness does not mean denying the existence of introspective awareness, but we have already rejected the I-theses as accounts of co-consciousness. Likewise the S-thesis: although our consciousness typically does have a spatial form, we cannot equate co-conscious unity with phenomeno-spatial unity, since there is reason to think spatially unconnected contents could be co-conscious. So we seem to be left with only one alternative: we simply accept that diverse experiences can occur together, as co-conscious. That different and diverse experiences are experienced together as co-conscious is a basic fact about the experiential realm. Co-consciousness is a basic experiential relationship, one about which there is nothing more to be said, at least while we confine ourselves to describing how things seem.

In adopting this view, I am, in effect, defending a version of the view that our experiences at any given moment are simply bundles of phenomenal items, items which are not properties of any substance, or at least not of any substance which could be regarded as being experiential in nature. Bundle theories are faced with a problem: what is it that binds the bundled items together? In the phenomenal case we can now see that this is not really a problem at all. A suitable binding agent is available: co-consciousness, conceived as a simple experiential relation between phenomenal contents. This proposal has two merits. It is more economical ontologically, since there is no need for any unifying substance over and above experiences and inter-experiential relations. It is also phenomenologically justified, for there is no denying that phenomenal contents do occur together as co-conscious – they are experienced as occurring together – so there is no need to postulate an undetectable unifying agent (such as a featureless substrate).

In one respect, however, to describe what I am proposing as a 'bundle view' might be misleading, for it might give the impression that there are two distinct kinds of unity within experience: a unity which exists *between* distinct phenomenal objets, and a unity *within* or *amid* phenomenal objects themselves. If this were the case, then co-consciousness would only hold between contents, it would not be responsible for the unity of the contents themselves. This does not seem to be the case. I pointed out in §1.7 that any phase of a stream of consciousness can be divided into parts in many different ways; there is no one 'right' way to divide a subject's overall experience over a given interval into parts. As is plain, no matter which division is considered, all the relevant parts are related by co-consciousness, and this fact alone suggests that it is a mistake to think one unifying relationship holds between contents while another is responsible for the unity of the contents themselves. But there is a more direct way of bringing this point out. Take any phenomenal object you like, a patch of colour, an expanse of sound, a combination of a bodily feeling and a mental image. No matter what the object, if it has discernible parts these are all co-conscious. Every part of a coloured expanse is co-conscious; every part of a spatially extended sound is co-conscious, and likewise for the constituent elements of a bodily feeling and a mental image. Co-consciousness is not limited to binding distinct phenomenal contents, it binds together the contents themselves; it operates both between and within contents. In short, if we confine our attention to the simultaneous contents of a stream of consciousness, co-consciousness is all-pervasive.

While discussing the problems faced by 'bundle dualists', i.e. the problem of finding what Mill called the 'thread of consciousness' that binds together the experiences which belong to a particular mind, Armstrong writes:

> some 'Bundle' dualists have become desperate. They have tried to solve their problem by suggesting that there is a unique and indefinable relationship which holds between items that form part of the same consciousness, and between no other items. It is not similarity, it is not causation, it is not memory, it is not a relationship to a body, it is something else, something we are all aware of, but which we cannot explain in terms of anything else. ...
>
> The genius of Hume disdained this line of escape. He preferred, surely rightly, to confess his incapacity to solve the problem of the unifying principle. For what a triumph this postulation of a unique relation represents for the Cartesian over the 'Bundle' Dualist! 'You objected to my spiritual substance on the grounds that you could observe no such mysterious object when you looked into your mind. Yet here you are forced by your need to find a unifying principle among your experiences to postulate a mysterious unique and indefinable relation. Why did you boggle at my postulating of a spiritual substance? You yourself are postulating a spiritual principle, so my position is at least as tenable as yours.'
>
> (1968: 20–1)

Armstrong provides here a clear statement of the sort of position I have defended on the unifying agent in consciousness, and attacks it on the grounds that it is no better than that which the Cartesian is offering. But of course, although I am suggesting that we recognize the existence of a primitive experiential relationship, I do so from within the framework of moderate naturalism: I am not assuming that experiences and inter-experiential relations are immaterial or 'spiritual' in nature, and so in this sense at least, what I am proposing is different from what the Cartesian offers. But Armstrong's objection is curious for other reasons. He portrays the appeal to a primitive inter-experiential relationship as an act of desperation, and describes the relationship itself as 'mysterious'. If the co-consciousness relationship I have suggested we recognize were wholly mysterious, then I would agree that relying on such a thing would be a desperate manoeuvre. But in what sense is co-consciousness mysterious? If it were transcendental in nature, being neither a physical relationship nor a relationship which exists within consciousness itself, then it would be mysterious in a damaging sense, as we would have no idea at all of the nature of the relationship; we would be positing a unknown quantity, a *deus ex machina*, to solve a problem we could not solve in any other way. However, co-consciousness is not like this at all. It is a relationship that exists in and between experiences; we know what it is like for experiences to be co-conscious. Armstrong himself seems to recognize as much, when he says that it is 'something we are all aware of, but which we cannot explain in terms of anything else'. We are aware of many things in our experience that we cannot explain in terms of anything else, so why should the fact that the co-consciousness relationship falls into this category be thought problematic? And of course, the fact that we are aware of the existence and character of co-consciousness is a further difference between what I am proposing and what the Cartesian is proposing, for we are not aware of any experiential substance in our consciousness.

One final point: what does Armstrong himself have to offer by way of an alternative?

> What, then, does constitute the unity of the group of happenings that constitute a single mind? We are back at the problem that proved Hume's downfall ... I do not see any way to solve the problem except to say that the group of happenings constitute a single mind because they are all states of, processes in or events in, a single substance ... the mind is the brain.
>
> (1968: 336–7)

Assuming it is true that our experiences are produced by or grounded in our brains, how does recognizing this – or going a step further and saying that the mind is the brain – solve Hume's problem? We cannot tell by introspecting that we even have a brain, yet we can tell by introspecting that there is an experienced unity in consciousness. As Armstrong himself accepts, we can conceive of streams of unified consciousness which are not the products of a brain at all; we can also conceive of circumstances in which two (or more) distinct streams of consciousness are sustained by a single brain. If our problem is understanding and characterizing the sort of unity that exists in and amid experience, Armstrong has no solution to offer at all.[5]

We can draw two preliminary conclusions from the discussion thus far: synchronic co-consciousness is a basic experiential relation, and the Simple Conception of experience is preferable to the alternatives. These conclusions are not independent; the claim that co-consciousness is basic is supported by the rejection of the A-thesis that in turn supports the Simple Conception. Indeed, it seems likely that the two conclusions stand or fall together. However, since the discussion thus far has been limited to the special case of simultaneous experience, both conclusions are only preliminary. In Chapter 5 I start to look at how non-simultaneous experiences are interrelated within a stream of consciousness, and as we shall see, the diachronic case turns out to be rather more complex than the synchronic. However, before embarking on this project, there are some further questions concerning synchronic co-consciousness that are worth posing and pursuing.

4 Transitivity

4.1 Co-consciousness as a relation

Co-consciousness may be a basic relation, but what sort of relation is it? Relations can be categorized in a number of different ways; where does co-consciousness fit into the relational scheme of things? There are several different questions here, and while some can be answered quickly, others connect with deeper problems and require a lengthier treatment.

First a rather imprecise, but nonetheless significant distinction. Some relations can be called *material*, in that they consist of a tangible concrete relationship between particular things; other relations are more *formal*, in that they consist of relationships that can exist between abstract as well as concrete things, or alternatively, between only abstract things. Examples of material relations are 'having the same mass as' or 'being in spatio-temporal contact'; examples of formal relations are 'being larger than', or 'having the same number of vertices'. More would have to be said for this distinction to be fully clear, but it is obvious that co-consciousness is a material rather than a formal relation. The relata of co-consciousness are experiences, which are not abstract (even if some people think they are immaterial). Co-consciousness is an experienced relationship between experiences, and as such is a concrete relation between concrete particulars; it is not a relation that can hold between anything other than experiences, and so it is not a relation that can hold between abstract entities.

What degree or 'adicity' does co-consciousness possess? Since there is no reason to suppose there is an upper limit on the number of experiences that can be co-conscious, co-consciousness is a relation of variable degree. As for the question of a lower limit, we could say that co-consciousness is a relation between numerically different experiences, and so must be at least dyadic, a two-place relation. Or we could say that a single experience is co-conscious with itself. This seems the better option. I am using 'an experience' to refer to phenomenal content that is experienced together, as a whole. Given this, all the component parts of a single experience, such as a visual expanse, are co-conscious with each other. So it seems reasonable to say that a single experience is a co-conscious item, and so co-conscious with itself.

Is co-consciousness an all-or-nothing relation, or can it be a matter of degree? It is hard to see how some experiences could be 'more co-conscious' than others. Consider two simultaneous experiences, a visual experience e_1 and an auditory experience e_2. If one is aware of e_1 and e_2 at all, then in virtue of that very fact e_1 and e_2 are as co-conscious as can be – it is not as if one could be aware of both e_1 and e_2 while trying to gauge whether or not they are co-consciousness. But to leave matters here would be to oversimplify. Some experiences we pay attention to, while some experiences pass away at the periphery of the phenomenal background, noticed barely or not at all. The same applies to relations between experiences, co-consciousness included. However, although we can be aware of relations of co-consciousness in different ways, this does not entail that the co-consciousness relationship itself comes in degrees. The issue really hinges on the degree of determinacy that holds in the realm of experience. If e_2 (but not e_1) is so weak or faint that it is indeterminate whether it exists at all, then the co-consciousness of e_1 with e_2 will likewise be indeterminate. For this to be the case, the indeterminacy that afflicts e_2 must be of a deep sort. If it is not clear quite what kind of sound e_2 is – the noise of a passing car or the boiling of a kettle – then the existence of e_2 itself, *qua* phenomenal item, is not indeterminate; all that is indeterminate is its phenomenal type. If we assume, as I do here, albeit tentatively, that there is no half-way house between the experiential and the non-experiential, then the existence of e_2 cannot be indeterminate. Provided there is definitely some kind of experience there, which we label 'e_2', then if we are aware of it while simultaneously being aware of e_1, then e_1 and e_2 are fully co-conscious. The key question is whether, given that both e_1 and e_2 definitely exist, it could nonetheless be indeterminate whether they are co-conscious with one another. Could it be indeterminate as to whether e_1 is experienced with e_2? An appealing initial intuition is that if the existence or non-existence of an individual experience is all-or-nothing, the same applies to relationships of co-consciousness. If e_2 exists at this moment, it is either co-conscious with that ensemble of co-conscious experience I now identify as mine, or it is not; there is no half-way house. Since I can see no way to defend this intuition, I will leave the issue here.

What else can be said about the logical properties of co-consciousness? One important distinction is between relations that are internal and those that are external. This issue is quite a complex one, and I will be discussing it in some detail in Chapters 8 and 9. Where does co-consciousness stand with respect to reflexivity, symmetry and transitivity? I have already suggested that an experience should be regarded as co-conscious with itself, even if this sounds a little strange, so co-consciousness is reflexive. Co-consciousness seems clearly to be symmetrical: if an experience e_1 is co-conscious with an experience e_2, then e_2 is co-conscious with e_1. I can think of no exceptions to this. Transitivity is a more difficult issue. Could there be three experiences, e_1, e_2 and e_3, such that although e_1 is co-conscious with e_2, and e_2 is co-

conscious with e_3, e_1 is not co-conscious with e_3? This is certainly possible diachronically – as we shall see – but what of simultaneous experiences? In this connection the transitivity question is harder to answer. There seems no reason to doubt that our synchronic co-consciousness is usually transitive. My current visual experience, considered as a single experience, can be divided into regions, and all these regions are all co-conscious with one another. Similarly for my auditory or bodily experience, and across modalities: my visual, auditory and bodily experiences are mutually co-conscious. But for co-consciousness to count as a transitive relation, co-consciousness must *always* be transitive. Might there be certain cases where synchronic transitivity breaks down? It is certainly not easy to think of any. The faint sensations at the periphery of consciousness, such as the nagging back-pain that floats in and out of one's attentive awareness, are a possibility. Perhaps the back-pain continues to exist when we are not paying attention to it, and does so detached (experientially) from the rest of our experience. But as we have seen, sensations and experiential relations do not have to be noticed to exist; the fact that the phenomenal background seems to consist of a unified ensemble of experiences suggests that peripheral sensations usually are co-conscious with the remainder of our experience. However, even if most people's simultaneous experiences are mutually co-conscious, we cannot conclude that simultaneous consubjective experiences are necessarily fully co-conscious. Perhaps there are non-human subjects whose typical experience is only partly co-conscious; perhaps the same holds of untypical human subjects. Since these possibilities cannot simply be dismissed, we need to take a closer look at the whole issue of synchronic transitivity.

But before examining the transitivity issue in more detail I want to digress to consider a different question. Thus far I have taken it for granted that streams of consciousness are composed of parts which are unified by the relationship of co-consciousness. The assumption that streams have component parts, and that these parts are particular experiences, is a natural one to make, and reflects the way we commonly talk ('That toothache is bothering me again', etc.). But given that grammar (in this broad sense) is at best an unreliable guide in matters metaphysical, it is worth probing a little more deeply.

4.2 Streams and their parts

Anyone wishing to deny that experiences divide into parts in the way I have been assuming has several options. They could take entire streams of consciousness to be the fundamental units of experience, or they could ascribe this status to brief temporally extended experiences that are experienced as wholes, or even momentary streamal cross-sections. But as will become clearer later, given the temporal characteristics of consciousness – the way one phase of our overall experience flows into another – there are no obvious or natural temporal boundaries between stream-phases, so the first option looks to be the most plausible of the three: entire streams are the basic experiential units. Let us call this doctrine *primitivism*.

Primitivism does not entail the absurd conclusion that streams are homogeneous wholes, which is just false; rather streams would be seen to have distinguishable regions, distinguishable on the basis of their varied phenomenal characteristics. But these regions would be no more able to enjoy an independent existence than the surface or corners of a thin sheet of paper; they would – in effect – be modes or features of their wholes. If we adopted this view some things would change, some would remain the same. The various aspects or regions within a stream would still be connected by co-consciousness; the question of whether or not synchronic co-consciousness is transitive would still arise; as would the issue of whether experiential items linked by co-consciousness are in some way affected by being so related. The most significant change would be with respect to the status of stream-parts: it would no longer be an option to regard these as independent experiential particulars which just happen to be co-conscious with certain other experiential particulars.

Primitivism may not seem very plausible, but it is not without notable adherents. Carnap chose entire streams of consciousness as the basic elements of the constructive system of his *The Logical Structure of the World*, and took them to be non-composite in the sense of having no parts which are themselves experiences. He recognized that we commonly talk as if streams of consciousness have parts that are individual experiences in their own right, and he himself found it useful to work with momentary streamal cross-sections when engaged in constructing his phenomenalistic system, but nonetheless insisted that:

> in this case we do not take the given as it is, but abstractions from it (i.e. something that is epistemically secondary) ... since we wish to require of our constructional system that it should agree with the epistemic order of the objects ... we have to proceed from that which is epistemically primary, that is to say, from the 'given', i.e. from experiences themselves in their totality and undivided unity.
>
> (1967: §67)

Carnap did not think it improper to refer to parts of our overall experience in ordinary discourse, which of course we do all the time ('That toothache has come back'). His claim that streams of consciousness are non-composite applies to discourse conducted within the terms of his system; it is only from this privileged perspective that the parts of experience are nothing more than distinguishable features of essentially unitary wholes, and these wholes are the ontologically primitive units of experience.

How compelling a case for primitivism does Carnap provide? The ability to categorize sub-regions of streams as experiences of particular sorts (e.g. the seeing of a book, the sound of an approaching horse, a pain in the back) involves some degree of convention, and to this extent it is learned with language. This is why Carnap holds that streams 'in their totality and undivided unity' are 'epistemically primary'. But why think that the earliest perspective we have on experience is the truest and most revealing? Later on in life, when experience has long been world-presenting, it is quite natural to suppose hearing a nearby conversation while staring through the window opposite involves two distinct experiences, one visual and one auditory, and there is no obvious reason to suppose this auditory experience could not have occurred without the visual, or vice-versa. This line of thinking can now be extended: we can regard our visual field as a composite of various lesser phenomenal items, and wonder whether each of these could have occurred without the others. Of course, thinking of experience in this way does not come 'naturally,' since the ability to regard what happens when we open our eyes as involving the occurrence of experience at all requires some intellectual sophistication. From the perspective of the natural attitude, world-presenting experience seems to consist of an unmediated access to the surrounding environment, and as such entirely experience-free, if by 'experience' we mean something akin to a thought or sensation, an inner mental production. But the point remains: once we manage to suspend the natural attitude, is there any reason to think a total experience does not consist of logically detachable parts? This sophisticated 'atomistic' conception of experience might be wrong, but the fact that this conception only becomes available at a relatively advanced stage in our intellectual development does not in itself provide a good reason for thinking it is.

Carnap's claim that streams are undivided primitives resulted from a prior decision about what to take as the basic and non-basic elements in a phenomenalistic reconstruction of the world. His choice of primitives was explicitly governed by epistemological considerations: he designed his system to be a rational reconstruction of the learning process, and chose as his basic elements what (he believed) is 'given' prior to any acts of categorization. Since we are not working within the same constraints, we are under no obligation to allow genetic epistemological considerations of this sort to determine our ontology. Consequently, we need some other reason for taking primitivism seriously.

Might simplicity be such a reason? Carnap's system was intended to provide a clear and systematic framework within which streams of consciousness in all their complexity could be described. This is a laudable goal. If taking entire streams as basic experiential units resulted in a simpler and clearer systematic phenomenology, primitivism would be difficult to ignore. But although I think it is fair to say a fully adequate system of this sort has yet to be devised, there is no reason to think Carnap's approach is any simpler than the alternatives. Nelson Goodman's system in *The Structure of Appearance* (1977: part II) goes further than Carnap's in various respects, but takes atomic qualia as basic – i.e. as the minimal discernible phenomenal features in consciousness.

Phenomenal manifolds

There is at least one further way primitivism might be defended. Although I think it too is unsuccessful, it is worth considering briefly if only for the light it casts into some tenebrous territory, and it relates back to one of the themes of Chapter 2. In §2.6, I argued that the notion of a 'substantival awareness' lacked any phenomenological underpinning; subsequent developments have strengthened this claim.

Consider the ontological status of macroscopic physical things, such as rocks, plants, animals and familiar artefacts. Although these are archetypal physical things, are they ontologically basic physical objects? Not necessarily. Suppose our fundamental science were to develop in a field-theoretic direction, and terminate in a basic theory which says, in effect, that the physical universe consists solely of a four-dimensional space-time continuum and a distribution of physical qualities over this continuum. The only physical object in this scheme is the space-time manifold. Consequently, macroscopic physical objects are merely field-time quality distributions when viewed from the ontological perspective of the fundamental theory. One response to this development would be to hold that macroscopic objects such as planets and oceans simply do not exist, but this would be perverse. A more reasonable course would be to hold that macroscopic objects exist, but have the status of ontologically derivative entities, entities that have no place in the ontology of the theory which reveals the underlying character of the physical realm.

This line of thinking is controversial, and could be refined in various ways, but may well be a viable option in some form or other. Could the same line of argument be extended to streams of experience? Just as reflection on the nature of macroscopic physical things could lead us to the view that such entities are not ontologically basic in the physical scheme of things, might not reflection on the structure and composition of our consciousness lead us to the same view of ordinary experiential 'objects', such as pains, thoughts, auditory and visual experiences? A primitivist attracted to this line could start by pointing to the distinctive unity created by co-consciousness. At any given time, each component element of our overall experience is co-conscious with every other element. By analogy with the physical case, could we not take this entire 'field of co-consciousness' to be a quasi-spatial arena in which experiential items are located? As for the experiential items, could we not take these to be composed of field-time distributions of minute phenomenal qualities? If so, we could then take the underlying field of consciousness to be the basic kind of experiential item. Since each stream of consciousness consists of a single field of consciousness and its occupants, streams emerge as ontologically basic entities, of an experiential kind. We need not say that hearing a bell ring is not an 'experience', any more than we need say that bells are not 'physical objects'. But this irenic proposal is quite compatible with also maintaining that only streams should count as experiences, if by 'experience' we mean a unit of consciousness that is recognized at the level of analysis that is metaphysically most fundamental and revealing.

Again, the proposed analogy would need a more careful treatment than I have given here to be at all persuasive, but the rough outline is sufficient for present purposes, for it seems unlikely that the analogy would ever yield a persuasive case for primitivism. We can agree that there is a real sense in which co-consciousness produces a single experience. It is also true that experiences typically possess a spatial or quasi-spatial organization. My current thoughts, bodily sensations and perceptual fields are spatially related: my thoughts seem to occur within my bodily sense-field, from which my visual and auditory fields seem to emerge. Nonetheless, the idea that there is some kind of underlying field of consciousness, a field akin to the hypothetical physical space-time manifold, seems wrong.

If we take physical space-time to be the basic physical object, we are adopting a substantivalist position: we are regarding space-time as an object or substance in its own right, an item whose existence (and perhaps structure) is independent of its occupants. Clearly, the positing of such an object would have to be justified in scientific terms, and there are various ways this could be done. There might be physical phenomena which prove to be otherwise inexplicable; it might simply be that adopting substantivalism makes certain overall theoretical simplifications possible; or space-time might be discovered to possess its own causal properties. But how could we justify positing an underlying *experiential* manifold, a field of consciousness or co-consciousness? There is no direct phenomenological evidence for the existence of an underlying field of consciousness; the Humean point that all we find in experience are particular experiences has as much validity in this connection as it does with that of the Pure Ego. As we saw in Chapter 3, the phenomenal space our experience occurs within is usually a V-field rather than a P-field. P-fields possess an intrinsic phenomenal character, V-fields do not, they are phenomenal vacuums, so to speak. A subject whose experience was confined to a single P-field might well be justified in taking this phenomenal space to be a basic experiential item, and experiences occurring within this space as mere modifications of the basic item. But our experience is not like this. Since we have no phenomenological reason for positing an underlying experiential field, and given that such a field plays no explanatory role in understanding why our experience is as it is, there is no reason to believe such a thing exists.

One last point on this. The idea that ordinary physical things should not be regarded as ontologically fundamental is supported by compositional considerations. Although physical entities such as live cats and lumps of cheese seem to be very different kinds of thing, it turns out that they are composed of exactly the same sorts of micro-constituents (e.g. quarks and electrons are the same the universe over). You could turn a lump of cheese into a cat – provided of course the lump is big enough – simply by re-arranging and re-combining the ultimate constituents of the cheese. This lends at least some force to the idea that ordinary physical objects are ontologically derivative in the physical scheme of things (especially if we view particles as mobile disturbances in universe-wide fields of various sorts). This is another line of thinking that is inapplicable to the experiential case. First, there is no reason to think phenomenal objects decompose into anything akin to the micro-constituents of ordinary physical objects. A television picture turns out, on close inspection, to consist of arrays of discrete coloured dots – pixels – which are invisible at normal viewing distances. But the visual experiences produced by watching television do not have a similarly granular structure – hence the 'grain problem' confronting P-materialism. The only phenomenal parts possessed by a phenomenal object are those that are manifest in the experience itself. Second, although it may well be possible to turn a refrigerator into an experiencing human being by reconfiguring its constituent physical constituents, it does not follow that you could turn an auditory experience into a visual experience by reconfiguring the former's experiential constituents. (If a form of L-materialism should turn out to be true, then experiences of different phenomenal types could have the same kind of *non-experiential* constituents.) The phenomenal constituents of a visual field seem to be wholly different in intrinsic nature from those of an auditory sense-field (and the same goes for other pairings of experiential tokens of different sensory-modal types). Hence, from a phenomenological perspective, the division of a total experience into auditory, visual, somatic, etc. components is rooted in the intrinsic nature of the phenomena themselves, and to this extent is well-founded, unlike, say, the purely conventional boundaries that demarcate certain desert nations. Nor is there any reason to think further investigations of a phenomenological kind will reveal anything that would lead us to revise this verdict. Scientific inquiry reveals that physical objects as dissimilar as people and refrigerators have everything in common at the micro-level. But since phenomenological inquiry is restricted to the level of appearances, there is no room for this kind of discovery being made about seemingly disparate modes of experience. What seems different is different so far as phenomenology is concerned.

4.3 Unity and transitivity

Let us return to the main issue: the transitivity or otherwise of synchronic co-consciousness. I will use the expression *total experience* to refer to groups of experiences which are mutually co-conscious. To be more precise, a total experience is a group of experiences which are all co-conscious with one another, and which are not parts of a larger group of experiences which are all co-conscious with one another. So for example, suppose e_1, e_2, e_3 and e_4 are each co-conscious with one other. Although $S = \{e_1, e_2, e_3\}$ is a group of experiences that are mutually co-conscious, S does not constitute a total experience, since e_4 is also co-conscious with all the members of S, without itself being a member of S. I have been assuming that the simultaneous parts of a stream of consciousness are total experiences. Since this assumption may turn out to be false, we need a more neutral term to refer to the complete contents of a stream of consciousness at a given time: *maximal experience* will serve.

Since co-consciousness is symmetrical and reflexive, if it is transitive it will be an equivalence relation. (Throughout this chapter, by 'co-consciousness' I mean synchronic co-consciousness, unless otherwise indicated.) Equivalence relations partition their relata into distinct non-overlapping groups, where each member of any group bears the relation in question to every other member of the same group. For example, 'being of the same age' is an equivalence relation. If we were to divide the people in a large crowd into groups on the basis of their age, we would end up with a collection of different non-overlapping groups, and everyone in the crowd would belong to one, and only one, of these groups. If co-consciousness is an equivalence relation, the totality of experiences at any given time will be divided, without exception, into discrete non-overlapping total experiences. Let us make the plausible assumption that a single subject's experience, at a given time, cannot consist of two wholly separate maximal experiences. If co-consciousness is transitive, and hence an equivalence relation, every maximal experience will be a total experience, and vice-versa. In short, every part of every subject's consciousness at a given time will be mutually co-conscious. We can call a consciousness of this type *fully* or *strongly* unified. Since a total experience is a fully unified experience that is not a part of any larger fully unified experience, each (momentary) total experience will belong to a different subject, and will comprise everything that subject is experiencing at the relevant time. This is a conveniently tidy situation, but it depends on the transitivity of co-consciousness. If it were the case that co-consciousness is non-transitive, i.e. not always or necessarily transitive, there are actual or possible subjects whose maximal experiences at a given time consist of distinct but overlapping momentary total experiences. (These consubjective total experiences must overlap, since we are working on the assumption that a single subject cannot, at a given time, have two wholly separate streams of consciousness.) We can call a consciousness of this type *partially* or *weakly* unified.

A weakly unified consciousness consists of experiences that are linked by the ancestral of the co-consciousness relation, the relation of *indirect co-consciousness*. Two experiences are only indirectly co-conscious if they are not directly co-conscious, but are nonetheless parts of a chain of directly co-conscious experiences. So, for example, e_1 is only indirectly co-conscious with e_4 if e_1 is directly co-conscious with e_2, and e_2 is directly co-conscious with e_3, and e_3 is directly co-conscious with e_4, and these are the only relationships of co-consciousness which connect e_1 and e_4. If co-consciousness is non-transitive, then presumably it is possible, at least within certain limits, for a subject's consciousness to be more or less unified, depending on the proportion of their simultaneous experiences that are directly co-conscious.

In fact, if partial unity were possible, it could result in some very strange experiential structures indeed. In Figure 4.1 below, the circles represent momentary total experiences. Since in this figure each circle represents a collection of experiences which are unified in the way we ordinarily take our experience to be unified, it is clear that if weak unification were possible, there could be minds or subjects the structure of whose experience is radically unlike our own. This is assuming that overlapping total experiences actually belong to a single subject. We could take the view that each total experience, each circle, belongs to a different subject. But if anything, this view is even odder: can we really make sense of the idea that two co-conscious experiences could belong to two distinct subjects?

4.4 Transitivity: the case against

Why should we take the possibility of a partially unified consciousness seriously? There are two main reasons.

The first concerns the unimaginability of partial unity. In evaluating competing hypotheses about the nature or structure of experience, we inevitably begin by testing the claims against our own experience. Since our own experience seems for the most part to be fully unified, we cannot hope to make much progress on the transitivity issue by appealing to introspection. This might not seem to matter, since we are concerned with ways experience might possibly be, rather than with how it actually is. However, in evaluating claims about what is merely possible we rely on what we can imagine or conceive, clearly and coherently. If we try to imagine cases where

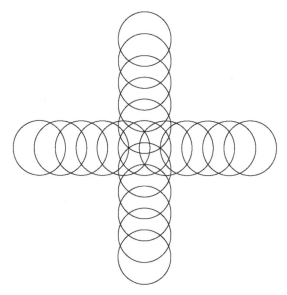

Figure 4.1 Exotic experiential structure

the transitivity of co-consciousness markedly breaks down, we fail. To bring this point home, consider some examples. You have just awoken from a session of brain surgery:

Case 1 Before the surgery your visual field was fully co-conscious. Even while focusing your attention on (say) the extreme periphery of the right-hand side, you had a passive awareness of the central and left-hand portions. Now it is very different: the left-hand side of your visual field is co-conscious with the central portion, and the latter is co-conscious with the right-hand side, but the left and right sides are not co-conscious with each other at all.

Case 2 On awakening you find that your consciousness is, in effect, divided into three portions. Your 'inner' consciousness, consisting of your thoughts, mental images, emotions, etc., is co-conscious with your bodily and tactile experiences, and your smell and taste sensations. You also have visual and auditory experiences, just as before. But there is a difference: your visual and auditory experiences are no longer co-conscious with each other.

Try as I might, I cannot imagine my own experience taking such forms. The impossibility of imagining states of affairs such as these might seem to provide support for the hypothesis that co-consciousness is transitive (i.e. always and necessarily). But it can be argued that it does so to a lesser degree than might be thought.

While it is true that we cannot imagine a consciousness that is very weakly unified, this can be put down to an inbuilt limitation on our imaginative powers. To imagine such a state of affairs we must imagine all three experiences simultaneously; if we do not, we will at most be imagining e_1 being co-conscious with e_2 in the absence of e_3, or e_2 being co-conscious with e_3 in the absence of e_1, etc. However, if we do imagine each of e_1, e_2 and e_3 at the same time, these three experiences will inevitably be present together in our imagination. Although our imaginative abilities are considerable, they are clearly limited in this respect: any simultaneous experiences we imagine are *mutually co-conscious within our imaginations*. Give that our imaginations have this characteristic, we cannot straightforwardly conclude that a partially unified consciousness is impossible just because we cannot imagine it. Of course, we might imagine three experiences and while doing so stipulate to ourselves that although the first is co-conscious with the second, and the second is co-conscious with the third, the first and third are not co-conscious. But since all three experiences would be present together in our imaginations, we would not have succeeded in imagining what it would be like to have a partially unified consciousness, and would have failed to provide the idea of such a consciousness with any phenomenological substance, so to speak.

This suggests we should hesitate before ruling out the possibility of partial unity on the grounds that is hard to imagine. But there is a more positive reason for taking the possibility seriously: it may be the best way of interpreting the empirical evidence concerning split-brains. Michael Lockwood is one philosopher who has argued along these lines.[1]

A normal brain has two cerebral hemispheres, connected by the thick bundle of nerves, the corpus callosum. When thus connected, both to one another and the other parts of the brain, the two hemispheres produce a single, unified stream of consciousness. As is well known, there is evidence to suggest that patients who undergo commissurotomy, an operation which involves the severing of the nerves in the corpus callosum, thereafter have two separate streams of consciousness. This is not wholly surprising, for it is also known that people who have only one hemisphere are nonetheless conscious. One might expect that if a combination of the lower parts of the brain and a single cerebral hemisphere is sufficient for the production of experience, then the severing of all connections between the hemispheres would lead to a split-consciousness, with each hemisphere supporting a distinct stream of consciousness. This said, there is considerable controversy as to exactly how disunified the mind of the typical commissurotomy patient is. The evidence gained from experiments conducted on people who have undergone the operation is puzzling and ambiguous. It is not clear whether the disunity in consciousness is always of the same degree; some commentators have suggested the disunity is exacerbated under special conditions when sensory input to the right- and left-hand sides of their brain are significantly different. Even when care is taken to provide sensory input to only one hemisphere, in some cases it seems information derived from this input is immediately passed on to the other hemisphere. It is sometimes difficult to tell whether this occurs because the stimulus produces an experience that is common to both left and right hemispheres, or whether an experience is produced only in one hemisphere, and information is passed on to the other hemisphere in some other way, sub-consciously. These ambiguities are not wholly surprising, since commissurotomy leaves some neural pathways between the cortices intact (not least the lower brain).

Suppose we make the assumption (not necessarily realistic) that split-brain patients end up with two wholly separate streams of consciousness. Lockwood asks: what would happen if one's corpus callosum were severed quite gradually, while one remained fully conscious? It seems unlikely that the change from a single unified stream to two distinct streams happens all at once. The corpus callosum consists of millions of neurones – could slicing through just one neurone produce a cataclysmic effect of this kind? It seems more likely, argues Lockwood, that as more and more of the corpus callosum is severed, one's consciousness would gradually become increasingly more dissociated. Since at the outset one's consciousness is fully unified, and at the end it is divided into two, if the change between these two extremes occurs gradually, it is hard to avoid the conclusion that during some phase of the process, one's consciousness will be partly unified and partly disunified. How can we make sense of this? It is here that Lockwood appeals to the notion of a breakdown in the transitivity of co-consciousness, which is itself a product of partially overlapping total experiences.

The three pairs of overlapping circles in Figure 4.2 represent the condition of a subject's stream of consciousness at three different times, and register the effect gradual commissurotomy might have. As before, each individual circle represents a total experience. On the left are two circles which represent a stream of consciousness that is close to being fully unified; the degree of overlap of the two total experiences is almost complete: only a small part of the corpus callosum has been severed. In the middle is a depiction of a later phase of the stream, when it is more disunified: the two depicted total experiences overlap to a lesser degree. On the right is a depiction of the stream when it is almost completely disunified: when the severing of the corpus callosum is nearly complete. The overlap of the two total experiences L and R is restricted to the region marked O. Although all the experiences in L are co-conscious with one another, and so with those in O, no experiences in L are co-conscious with the experiences in R except those in O. And similarly for R.

It would no doubt be a mistake to suppose that the only effect of slicing through a conscious subject's corpus callosum would be a progressive disunification of experience. No doubt there would be other effects too. As the brain attempts to accommodate the massive changes being wrought upon it there would probably be all manner of disruptions, in perception, cognition, emotion, memory and so forth, disruptions which could be expected to impact upon the consciousness of the dividing subject in ways that cannot be imagined. It would also be a mistake to suppose the contents of the two sub-streams would be very similar. The two cerebral hemispheres sustain different mental capacities. For example, the left hemisphere in most people has greater capacities for language and abstract thought than the right. This sort of difference will in itself lead to differences between the two part-separated streams of consciousness, even if the sensory input to each hemisphere is the same, which will not always be the case. Nonetheless, it is hard to deny that Lockwood's argument has some force. A gradual commissurotomy, performed on a conscious patient, would do more than create a partially disunified consciousness, but if we adopt a wholly third-person

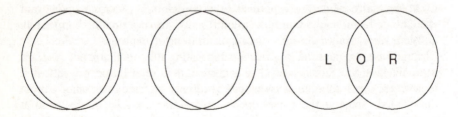

Figure 4.2 Suggested effect of gradual commissurotomy on consciousness

point of view, it is easy to believe that it would at least create a partially disunified consciousness.

If we accept this general picture of what happens in this sort of fictional case, there is room for flexibility as to just how we interpret actual split-brain cases. Real-life commissurotomies leave some inter-cerebral connections intact. This, together with the likelihood that the lower brain is implicated in the production of certain forms of experience, especially emotions, suggests that real-life split-brain patients do not have two wholly separate streams of consciousness, but rather have weakly unified consciousnesses. Perhaps some bodily sensations and emotional feelings are common to both the resulting spheres of consciousness (these would fall within the region O in Figure 4.2). If so, then the operation Lockwood envisages would not result in the creation of two wholly distinct streams of consciousness; we would end up, rather, with two partly overlapping streams. But this scarcely matters, since our concern is precisely with the possibility of a partially unified conscious-ness. Lockwood points out that there is some evidence that this is what happens. In one experiment, pornographic pictures (of a kind tailored to the interests of the split-brain patients concerned) are shown to the part of the visual field which produces experience only in the right-hand hemisphere. The right-hand hemisphere is typically 'mute', having no access to or control over the speech centres. Consequently, when questions are put to these subjects as to what they are seeing, they say they do not know. Yet when the pornographic pictures are shown, these same subjects show signs of embar-rassment and arousal. They admit as much when asked what they are feeling, although they also say they have no ideas as to why they feel as they do. Since it is the left hemisphere that is doing the talking, this suggests that the emotional feelings produced by visual experiences available only to the right hemisphere are also felt in the left hemisphere.

Despite its undoubted initial plausibility, it is important to note that Lockwood's argument is not irresistible. One obvious objection is: how do we know that gradually commissurotomy is compatible with consciousness continuing to be generated in both sides of the brain? Perhaps it is a nomolog-ical impossibility for a subject to remain conscious during such an operation. But this objection does not seem too damaging. On the one hand, there is no reason to believe a commissurotomy patient would not be able to remain conscious. On the other, one of the argument's chief merits is that it provides us with a plausible account of the result of the operation, of what a split-brain patient's experience is like once the operation is complete. So it does not really matter if the operation produces a temporary loss of consciousness.

There is a less obvious, but more interesting objection. In the diagram above, the region O forms a part of two overlapping total experiences, L and R. But what if it were the case that the operation produced two wholly sepa-rate, non-overlapping, total experiences, L* and R*, each of which contain a region indistinguishable from O in all phenomenal respects? In other words, what if the experiences in O are duplicated twice over? Recall the case of the patients whose right hemispheres are shown a pornographic picture; perhaps the resulting sensations of arousal and embarrassment are not shared, but duplicated in two quite separate streams of consciousness. However, although this duplication of experience is certainly a logically possible outcome, it might not be thought to be empirically plausible. Consider the options in the context of the gradual commissurotomy performed while the subject remains conscious. What is the result of severing a tiny section of the corpus collosum? Are we to suppose that this immediately creates two separate streams of consciousness with very similar contents? This seems improbable. But if we suppose that by the time the operation is completed there are two wholly separate streams, with some smaller region (such as O) duplicated in both, at what point does the single stream become two? If the original stream is never in a state of partial unity, then we must accept that at some point, slicing just a few nerves creates a huge change in the brain's production of experience. One moment there is a single stream of experience, the next there are two streams, with very similar contents. Again, while this is not logically impossible, it does seem rather improbable.

It is worth noting that a very weakly unified consciousness is in one sense very hard to imagine, while in another sense it is very easy to imagine. Suppose that the contents of the two overlapping total experiences L and R are broadly similar, i.e. each consists of an ensemble of co-conscious thoughts, perceptions, emotions and bodily sensations. Some emotions and bodily sensations are, let us suppose, common to both L and R (they occur in the region of overlap O). This degree of similarity would not normally obtain, given the fact that the right hemisphere in most people does not have much in the way of linguistic capacities. But a minority of people have equipollent, or co-dominant cerebral hemispheres, that is, each hemisphere can perform similar mental functions. Imagine you are such a person, and your corpus callosum has been cut. In this hypothetical case, the contents of both L and R would be very similar to your actual experience, which we can suppose is fully unified. Because of this, it is easy to imagine what your experience in the hypothetical situation would be like: you can easily imagine the content of L, and you can easily imagine the content of R. Two acts of imaginative projection suffice to capture the complete contents of your weakly unified consciousness. So to this extent there is nothing incomprehensible about the situation at all. But of course, imagining your consciousness in this weakly unified condition required two separate imaginative projections. It seems utterly impossible to imagine, all at once, in a single act of imagining, what this weakly unified consciousness would be like. But it could be argued that this is not surprising; it is only to be expected that the more a consciousness diverges in structure from our own, the harder it is for us to imagine what it would be like to have such a consciousness.

If we were to accept the possibility of partial unity in exceptional cases, could those of us with normal brains be confident that our own consciousnesses are fully unified? I think we would have reason to think the high degree of disunity found in split-brain patients is very unusual, and perhaps only to be found in split-brain cases. Although it is true that the disunity produced by commissurotomy only becomes fully apparent when specially designed tests are conducted, when ordinary people undergo the same sorts of test, they prove negative. But a far weaker degree of disunity would be harder to rule out. Lockwood suggests the situation might be like that shown in Figure 4.3.

The figure on the left represents a set of concurrent total experiences which overlap almost completely. This might be the condition of a normal person. The bulk of their experience is fully unified, but the periphery of their various sense-fields are not. So, for example, although faint bodily and auditory sensations are both co-conscious with the central mass of experience, they are not co-conscious with each other. Such a small degree of dissociation would be hard to detect. Indeed, if there were some small degree of dissociation, it might explain the elusive character of faint sensations at the margins of consciousness: we would rarely, if ever, be experiencing them all at once, as co-conscious. If we assume, as seems likely, that we can only be introspectively aware (whether actively or passively) of co-conscious experiences, it is easy to see why we might sometimes be unsure as to the exact contents of the periphery of our consciousness. In the figure to the right, the total experiences overlap to a lesser extent, so this maximal experience is unified to a correspondingly lesser degree. Lockwood suggests that certain degenerative brain diseases, such as Alzheimer's, might produce a greater dissociation of this kind. Or alternatively, perhaps this degree of dissociation occurs on the borderline of sleep and wakefulness, or during periods of absent-mindedness.

4.5 Transitivity: the case for

There are, then, reasons for taking the possibility of partial unity seriously. However, since these reasons fall short of establishing the possibility beyond all doubt, it is worth investigating whether the possibility of partial unity can be ruled out on other grounds. If partial unity turns out to be unintelligible when subjected to close scrutiny, we would have to think of some other way of interpreting the split-brain cases. In fact, a case can be made for the transitivity of (synchronic) co-consciousness, and not surprisingly it hangs on specific features of the relationship that have already come to light.

 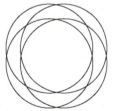

Figure 4.3 Weak dissociations within consciousness

Consider first the accounts of co-consciousness that we have rejected. Suppose a version of the I-thesis were true, i.e. that experiences are co-conscious when they are the actual or potential objects of introspective awareness. We can only pay attention (whether primary or secondary) to simultaneous experiences that are co-conscious; given that the objects of attention are co-conscious, if the I-thesis were true, partial unity would be impossible. But the I-thesis is false. What if the S-thesis were true? The S-thesis says that simultaneous experiences are co-conscious in virtue of being located in a single unitary phenomenal space (P-type or V-type). Since all parts of a single unitary phenomenal space are co-conscious, if the S-thesis were true, synchronic co-consciousness would necessarily be transitive. But the S-thesis is also false. What of the A-thesis? The situation here is more complicated, since the A-thesis comes in quite different forms, but on the face of it, if experiences are only co-conscious when they fall under a single awareness[*], partial unity would be an impossibility. If e_1 is co-conscious with e_2, and e_2 with e_3, then each of these experiences must fall under the same awareness, and all are therefore automatically co-conscious with each other. But this only applies if phenomenal items can only fall under a single awareness, as a matter of necessity. We call the doctrine that this is the case the *confinement thesis*. I imagine that most A-theorists have assumed the confinement thesis to be true (for simultaneous experiences at any rate). But suppose it were not true. This would leave open this sort of possibility: suppose at a given time there are two acts of awareness, A_1 and A_2, and three phenomenal items, e_1, e_2 and e_3. Whereas e_1 and e_2 are co-conscious by virtue of falling under A_1, e_2 and e_3 are co-conscious by virtue of falling under A_2. Although A_1 and A_2 are wholly distinct awarenesses, they have a common object: the item 'e_2' that falls under A_1 is numerically identical with the item 'e_2' that falls under A_2. We now have a situation in which although e_1 is co-conscious with e_2, and e_2 is co-conscious with e_3, the latter is not co-conscious with e_1. In other words, we have a failure of transitivity. Since we have found reason to reject the A-thesis, in all its forms, we do not need to consider further whether there is any reason to reject or accept the confinement thesis. I mention the point only because it is interesting to note that a position which at first glance seems wholly incompatible with the possibility of partial unity may not in fact be so.

In rejecting the I-theses, the S-thesis and A-thesis, I reached the conclusion that co-consciousness is a basic experiential relation. Assuming it to be such, what can we say about the possibility of a partially or weakly unified consciousness? At first sight, it is difficult to see that any definite conclusions can be drawn either way. The I-, S- and A-theses provide accounts of co-consciousness which (sometimes in combination with other assumptions) allow weak unity to be ruled out. But in rejecting these theses, we seem to have removed any grounds we might have had for ruling out the possibility of non-transitive co-consciousness. If co-consciousness is a basic relationship, what is to prevent this basic relationship holding between e_1 and e_2, and also between e_2 and e_3, but failing to hold between e_1 and e_3?

But we should not be too hasty. Co-consciousness may be a basic experiential relationship, it may be a *sui generis* relationship, but we do know *what it is like* for experiences to be so related. Is the possibility of weak unity compatible with what we know co-consciousness is like? An argument to the effect that it is not runs like this:

> When an experience e_1 is co-conscious with a simultaneous experience e_2, these two experiences are in effect *fused* into a single unit of experience, each part of which is co-conscious with every other part. The two experiences are not mixed or blended together, they retain their own distinctive phenomenal characteristics, but all the same their relationship is of a very intimate nature: every part or aspect of e_1 is co-conscious with every other part or aspect of e_1, and with every part or aspect of e_2, and vice-versa. In a manner of speaking, the two are *wholly joined*, there is no 'distance' separating them at all. Since e_1 and e_2 are parts of a single experience in this way, how could it be possible for another experience e_3 to be co-conscious with e_2 without also being co-conscious with e_1? Given that e_1 and e_2 are fused, any experience that is co-conscious with e_2 will automatically and necessarily be co-conscious with e_1 as well. Since the same applies to any combination of simultaneous experiences, partial unity is an impossibility.

As it stands, this reasoning may fail to convince, but the intuition in play has force, or at least it does in the context of what has already been said about the nature of synchronic co-consciousness, as I shall try to show.

Rather than using the term 'co-consciousness' to refer to the relationship between experiences that are experienced together, some writers prefer *co-presence*, or sometimes *compresence*, terms which usefully point to the peculiar immediacy and intimacy of the relationship in question.[2] In assessing the intelligibility of a breakdown in transitivity, it is the precise nature of this intimacy that we need to focus on. Think of a patch of phenomenal colour, such as would result from looking at a large circular expanse of grey on a white wall. This expanse is a single experience; it is sensed as a whole, and each part of it is co-conscious – or co-present – with every other part. Now, it is natural to think of the co-presence of this experience's parts in the way depicted in Figure 4.4.

Because we see the coloured expanse on a wall several feet away, it is easy to assume that because all its parts are co-conscious they are all observed from a single point of view, a point of view which is separate and distant from the wall itself. However, if we take the expanse to be a region of our visual field, this way of thinking is wrong. We do not observe our own visual field from some distance away; the visual field is a part of our overall consciousness. The co-presence of the expanse's parts does not consist in

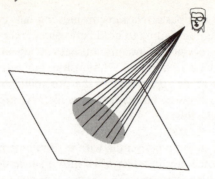

Figure 4.4 A natural way of thinking of the unity within experience

their being presented to a single point of awareness that is distant and distinct from the visual field: this is the awareness–content picture of the A-thesis, which we have rejected. The co-presence of the parts is a consequence of the fact that the parts *themselves* are related to one another by co-consciousness, as I stressed in §3.7. Hence, if we imagine the expanse as being divided into four, we can represent the relationships of co-consciousness between the regions in the way shown in Figure 4.5.

This depiction better approximates the real situation, but still oversimplifies. Call this experience E, and let r_1, r_2, r_3 and r_4 designate the four indicated regions, starting from the upper right. Not only are each of these regions co-conscious with one another, each individual region itself contains parts – the division into four was quite arbitrary. So the upper right quartile, r_1, could be further sub-divided into four (or eight, or 101) parts; each of these

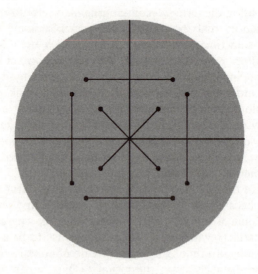

Figure 4.5 A better way

sub-divisions of r_1 is co-conscious not only with every other sub-division within r_1, but with every part of r_2, r_3 and r_4. And of course the same applies to every sub-division of r_2, r_3 and r_4. In short, all the distinguishable parts of the expanse are co-conscious with one another. Indeed, not only are all the parts co-conscious with one another, they are *equally* co-conscious with one another: parts which are spatially distant are no less co-conscious than parts which are closer together. The same applies across the modalities: if I hear a sound to my right simultaneously with a sound to my left, both auditory contents are co-present to just the same extent as the spatially adjacent tactile sensations I have when I tap my hand with two fingers, or my visual experiences of the horizontal and vertical components of the letter T. For the sake of having a convenient label, let us say that an experience is *maximally connected* if all its distinguishable parts are mutually and equally co-conscious.

Now return to E. Could some other experience, call it E*, be co-conscious with just one region of E, say r_1, but not the others? It is difficult to see how. Because it is maximally connected, not only are all the parts of r_1 co-conscious with each other, each part of r_1 is co-conscious with every other part of E, and hence r_2, r_3 and r_4. Since the parts of r_1 are no less co-conscious with r_2, r_3 and r_4 than they are with one another, how could E^* be co-conscious with r_1 without also being co-conscious with each of r_2, r_3 and r_4? By virtue of being maximally connected, the parts of E are enmeshed in a pervasive web of co-consciousness, and hence fused into a single unitary experiential whole, with the result that an experience cannot be co-conscious with just one part of E without also being co-conscious with the rest of it. Since similar considerations apply to any pair of co-conscious experiences, there is reason to think that whenever a combination of simultaneous experiences are co-conscious, they are maximally connected, both within their own boundaries and to one another. In which case, synchronic co-consciousness cannot fail to be transitive.

By way of a contrast, consider some relationships which are non-transitive. One such is 'being attached by a piece of string'. An object A can be attached to B, and B attached to C, without A being attached to C, thus: A–B–C. Physical attachment is symmetrical but non-transitive by virtue of the nature of the relationship in question and the items it holds between: physical objects which occupy different locations in space. The string which links A and B does not link A and C, and this is possible because B and C have different spatial locations. By way of analogy, if we suppose A, B and C are experiences, then because they are co-conscious with one another, B and C would occupy exactly the same place in space, and hence anything attached to B would also be attached to C. It is worth noting that this situation may in fact arise in the case of physical objects. Suppose (as many do) that a statue, *Goliath*, and the lump of clay which constitutes it, *Lumpl*, are numerically distinct objects by virtue of having different identity conditions; since Lumpl and Goliath exactly coincide in space, anything attached to

Lumpl is also attached to Goliath, and vice-versa. But even if physical attachment can be transitive, it is not always so. Co-consciousness is different: whenever two experiences are co-conscious they are maximally connected, and hence so profoundly unified that it is *as if* they were spatially coincident, with the result that any third experience that is co-conscious with one cannot fail to be co-conscious with the other.

Another non-transitive relationship is 'falling under the same beam of light', or *co-illumination*. Three objects, A, B and C, can be such that A and B are co-illuminated, as are B and C, but A and C are not. As in the case of attachment, co-illumination is non-transitive because of the nature of both the relationship and the items related. Physical objects located at different places can fall under more than one source of illumination, and co-illuminated regions can partially overlap. I suggested above that versions of the A-thesis which reject the confinement thesis permit an analogous situation to obtain for phenomenal objects; on this view co-consciousness is non-transitive. But if the Simple Conception of consciousness is true, co-consciousness does not arise as a consequence of diverse contents falling under a common awareness, it is a product of a relationship which holds between the contents themselves, and if these contents are maximally connected there is no possibility of contents falling within regions of co-consciousness which only partially overlap.

There is, then, a case for taking synchronic co-consciousness to be transitive. It rests on, first, the fact that the component parts of a phenomenal object are maximally connected by co-consciousness; and second, the intuition that when several such objects are both co-conscious and simultaneous, they cannot fail to be maximally connected with one another.

A natural objection at this point is: 'Granted we cannot imagine two simultaneous experiences that are co-conscious without being maximally connected, but since we already know that our imaginative abilities are limited in this regard, surely it is illegitimate to go on to say that non-transitive co-consciousness is impossible'. As I pointed out earlier, this objection has to be taken seriously, and there is a sense in which the case for taking co-consciousness to be transitive does indeed rest on the unimaginability of the alternative. But it can also be argued that non-transitive co-consciousness is both unimaginable and inconceivable because we have an intuitive understanding of the nature of co-consciousness itself. Some essential properties of the relationship are known to us simply because the intrinsic character of the relationship is manifest in our experience. And this point too has considerable force. Co-consciousness is such a primitive feature of experience, is it not plausible to think its basic phenomenal characteristics will be discernible through introspection?

A quite different objection takes us back to split-brain cases. If we accept the argument for transitivity, we have to accept that in the gradual severing of a corpus callosum (belonging to a conscious subject) there would come a point when the previously unified phenomenal field suddenly collapses, a short time after which both sides of the brain re-establish their own quite separate phenomenal fields. This is an intelligible state of affairs, but as Lockwood points out, the idea that severing just a few connecting nerves can produce such a dramatic alteration in the brain's functioning seems implausible. Two points can be made in reply. First, to estimate the plausibility of an empirical claim we need a reasonable theoretical understanding of the relevant domain. Since at present we have no idea how the brain generates phenomenal consciousness, such an understanding is absent, and so claims about how the brain is likely to react in highly unusual circumstances amount to little more than guesswork, and need not be taken too seriously. Second, as I pointed out in §1.6, moderate naturalism has implications for the weight given to physical and phenomenal considerations when these are in conflict. If a general claim about experience that is firmly grounded in the phenomenological data conflicts with what we would be led to expect by one or other of the natural sciences, questioning the relevant science is as reasonable as questioning the putative phenomenal truth. If we are serious about taking experience seriously, occasions may arise when it is appropriate to allow purely phenomenological considerations to take the lead when it comes to formulating hypotheses about the relationship between experience and the brain. Since the transitivity of synchronic co-consciousness certainly has the status of a putative phenomenal truth, this may be such an occasion.

4.6 A question of interpretation

There is another way of assessing the intelligibility of non-transitive co-consciousness: could someone convince us that their own consciousness is only partially unified? Whilst we cannot ourselves imagine a partially unified consciousness 'from the inside', we can easily imagine someone else *claiming* that their consciousness is partially unified. Perhaps no one has ever made such a claim, but it is certainly possible that they might.

Actual split-brain cases are not much help. Commissurotomy patients usually claim to be unaware of their unusual condition, which is understandable: since language and analytical reasoning are concentrated in the left hemisphere, at best we will get a one-sided report on the partially divided consciousness. Also, ignoring the various cognitive deficits, if partly overlapping total experiences were to exist in such cases, each would usually contain a full range of perceptual and bodily sensations. So as far as the 'talking' left hemisphere is concerned, there will be nothing dramatically unusual to report. But less dramatic cases of partial unity surely would be noticeable. Consider Case 2, as described above. I can imagine that, after undergoing brain surgery, a subject S tells me that although his 'core' experience is largely as it was before, and is still co-conscious with both his visual and auditory experience, the latter are no longer co-conscious with each other. What should I make of S's claim?

Although I can imagine someone saying this, I cannot myself imagine what it would be like to have the sort of consciousness S describes. Since this can be put down to a limitation on my powers of imagination, if we leave the phenomenological argument out of the picture, this is not itself a sufficient reason to reject S's claim. After all, strange things are possible. Asked to elaborate on his condition, S might say:

> I know you must find it difficult to believe that my consciousness is as I describe it to be; before my brain surgery, I would not have imagined such a thing to be possible either. But now the overall structure of my consciousness is different from how it used to be, in just the ways I claim. At the moment, I am having both auditory and visual experience. I also know that my auditory and visual experiences are not co-conscious: although at any moment I have both visual and auditory experiences, these are just not experienced *together* or *co-present* in the way they used to be. The only way to know what this is like is to experience it yourself. Trying to explain the structure of my experience to you is like trying to explain what seeing colour is like to someone who has always been blind.

This reply, were it made, would have to be treated with some respect. Since it is difficult to rule out the possibility of there being forms of consciousness very different from our own, how can we rule out the possibility of a partially unified consciousness? After all, there are well documented mental disorders which produce alterations in experience that are at least equally hard to imagine. There are visual agnosias which render subjects unable to recognize objects they can clearly see (e.g. the case made famous by Oliver Sacks, of the man who could see his wife and his hat but not tell which was which). It is hard to imagine what it would be like to suffer such a deficit. Even harder to imagine are the conditions known as *anosognosias*, which render one both deficient in some aspect of experience and unaware of the deficiency. In one variant, subjects no longer have colour vision but fail to notice that anything is amiss. Even more incomprehensible is Anton's syndrome: the failure to acknowledge or recognize the onset of total blindness.

But I might still be sceptical about S's claim. S maintains that his auditory and visual experiences are no longer co-conscious with each other. How can S *know* that his experience has this bifurcated structure? One thing seems clear: S's claim cannot be a phenomenal judgment about the character of his experience. Since his visual and auditory experience are no longer co-conscious, he cannot possibly attend to both simultaneously. This means he cannot have an introspective awareness of the fact (assuming it is one) that he is usually *having* both auditory and visual experiences at any given time. Whenever he is introspectively aware of seeing something, he will have no introspective awareness of hearing anything, and whenever he is introspectively aware of hearing something, he will have no introspective awareness of seeing anything; and this applies irrespective of whether the introspection is active or passive.

A second reason for scepticism about S's claim stems from the fact that the argument from neurological disorders can be run the other way. If synchronic co-consciousness is transitive, a partially unified visual field is impossible, but it does not follow from this that a subject's cognitive awareness of their visual field could not be impaired. There are visual agnosias which render a subject unable to make phenomenal judgments about more than a small portion of their visual field. Sufferers from this sort of condition apparently have full visual fields – they are able to point to or grasp all the objects one would expect a normal person to see when presented with a given scene – but they are unable to describe more than a small portion of what they see at a given time. So, for example, on glancing into a box containing a plate and a cup, they would be able to recognize the plate but not the cup, or the cup but not the plate. After looking into the box for a few seconds, they would recognize that it contained both a cup and a plate, but maintain that they still could not see both objects simultaneously. Clearly, this pattern of response is compatible with both objects continuously featuring in the subjects' overall visual experience. Although the subjects are unable to cognize or attend to more than a small part of their visual field at a given time, the remainder of their visual field is there, but as part of the phenomenal background to which they have even less cognitive access than a normal person. Perhaps S is suffering from a similar affliction. His experience is fully unified, but he is not cognitively aware of the fact.[3]

This sort of argument can be taken a step further. If nothing in his experience could lead S to make his claim, what could explain it? We might reasonably interpret S's predicament along these lines: S's experience is in fact always fully unified. At any one time, S is having either visual or auditory experience, but never both (contrary to his claim). He believes he is having both for two reasons. First, he can switch back and forth between the two modes at will. If at a given time he is having visual experience, he can decide to listen, and as soon as he does so he starts to have auditory experiences, and stops having visual experiences. Similarly, if he is in auditory mode, he can decide to switch to visual mode at will, and when he does so he ceases to have auditory experience and starts to have visual experience. Second, S possesses both an acute blindsight and an acute 'deafhearing'. People with so-called blindsight typically have large blind areas in their visual field, areas within which they have no visual experience at all, yet under certain circumstances they can make accurate statements about objects that are shown to them – objects that would appear within the relevant areas of their visual field if they could see normally. Although blindsight subjects claim not to see the objects presented to their blind fields, when prompted to make guesses about the location, shape, size and movement of these objects, they often guess correctly. It seems clear that a certain amount of sub-conscious processing of visual stimuli is going on, and that some of the resulting information (in non-sensory form) is being made available to the subjects' cognitive centres and hence their consciousness – even though the subjects have no idea how it is getting there, and are not consciously aware of its presence. Now, it is easy to imagine a more acute form of blindsight – call it super-blindsight – in which subjects have no visual experience at all, yet are able to form confident judgments about their surroundings at will, and these judgments are just as accurate as any normally sighted persons. Acute 'deafhearing' is the auditory equivalent of super-blindsight. I do not know of any cases of deafhearing, but they seem perfectly conceivable. If our subject S possessed such faculties, it is easy to see why he might believe that he was continuing to have both visual experience and auditory experience, even though in actual fact, at any one time he has one but not the other. As we have already stipulated, he is able to switch back and forth between the two modes of experience at will. In addition, when S is in visual mode (having visual experience) he continues to have conscious beliefs about what he is hearing – although he has no auditory experience; similarly, when he is having auditory experience, he continues to have conscious beliefs about what he is seeing – even though he has no visual experience.

We have been considering one particular way a consciousness could be partially unified, but I think it likely that the claims of subjects who maintain that their consciousness is only partially unified in other ways could be interpreted in similar fashion. Since we cannot make sense of the idea that these subjects can be introspectively aware, actively or passively, of the disunity in their consciousness, the alternative interpretations should be taken seriously. Given the strength of the purely phenomenological case against the possibility of partial unity, I will tentatively conclude that synchronic co-consciousness is a transitive relation.

5 Phenomenal time

Problems and principles

5.1 Time in experience

The investigation so far has suggested that the primitive relationship of co-consciousness is the key to understanding the unity of consciousness. This finding is at best preliminary, since the investigation has so far been concerned only with the unity within experience at a given moment, and this is only half the story: there is unity in experience over time as well as at a time. A typical stream of consciousness is a continuous succession of experiences which lasts for some hours. How are these successive experiences related? What is it about them which makes them parts of the same stream, or *co-streamal* (for want of a convenient expression)? It may well be that answering these questions will amount to more than half the story about the unity of consciousness, for as I have already remarked, to even consider synchronic unity in isolation is to risk a distorted view of the phenomena. Consciousness is not a static but a flowing thing, it is never still but always on the move. To gain a full understanding of the unity within experience we must take the plunge, into the turbulent dynamics of the stream of consciousness proper.

My aim is to establish that the diachronic unity of experience is no different, in essentials, from the synchronic: both are the product of co-consciousness. Just as simultaneous experiences, such as a thought, a bodily sensation and a visual experience, can be experienced together, so can successive experiences, experiences occurring at different (but not distant) times. My current experiences belong to the same stream of consciousness as those I had on first waking several hours ago, but they are not directly co-conscious with them; the same applies to experiences I had a minute ago: I am no longer directly aware of these either. Diachronic co-consciousness is a very short-term affair, spanning at most a second or so – the duration of the so-called 'specious present'. But this brevity does not matter: each link in a chain only passes through the links either side of it, but this does not undermine the chain's integrity. Diachronic co-consciousness is what binds together the adjacent phases of a stream of consciousness, and so is responsible for the very existence of the stream as a temporally extended whole.

I will refer to claim that diachronic co-consciousness is responsible for the experienced unity of streams of consciousness from moment to moment as the *DC-thesis*. Why think the DC-thesis is true? One reason is the fact that change and persistence are directly experienced. Change and persistence both take time. How could we directly experience change and persistence unless experience itself encompasses a temporal interval?

Consider some basic data. If I hold my hand in front of me and rotate it at the wrist, I see this rotation as clearly as I see my fingers: my hand's movement is as much a part of the intrinsic phenomenal content of my experience as its colour, shape or size. Whenever we see movement, our visual experience has a temporal character; the content of such an experience is as much temporal as it is spatial. It is not just in perception that we directly experience change. Thinking, as an activity, involves a continuous succession of occurrent thoughts and mental images, irrespective of whether the content or subject matter of these is continuous or fragmented. Moreover, the succession of thoughts and perceptions is itself something we experience; the succession is not just a succession of experiences, it is a succession within experience. I said that we also directly experience persistence, a fact which may be slightly less obvious, until it is pointed out. Think of what it is like to hear an unvarying auditory tone. Even though the tone does not vary in pitch, timbre or volume, we directly experience the tone *continuing on*. It is as though, from moment to moment, there is a continual renewal of the same auditory content, a renewal which is directly experienced. Or think of an unvarying yet enduring pain sensation; for as long as the pain is felt, it is felt as a continuous presence; this presence is not static but dynamic, it is an enduring presence. This experienced flow or passage is common to all sensations; indeed, a sensation lacking this characteristic seems inconceivable – perhaps this is why a strictly durationless sensory experience, existing all by itself, seems impossible to conceive. I have been concentrating on particular types of experience, but what holds of particular types of experience also holds of the stream of consciousness as a whole: every part of it exhibits the same dynamic characteristics; the stream as a whole, from moment to moment, undergoes passage; it flows as a whole, and it does so for as long as it lasts.

This brief survey has provided some examples of how time manifests itself within consciousness, some examples of what we can call *phenomenal temporality*. The fact that we directly experience both change and continuity suggests that contents spread over a brief interval of time can be co-conscious; the fact that our experience consists of a continuously renewed flow of content, a flow within experience itself, suggests that diachronic co-consciousness plays a key role in the generation of streams of consciousness. But although these aspects of phenomenal temporality certainly provide *prima facie* support for the DC-thesis, they do not establish it as true, for there are a number of alternative accounts which reject the thesis in question. These accounts are attempts to make sense of the sort of data I have just mentioned while rejecting one or both of the following doctrines, (a) that experiences have genuine temporal duration; (b) that successive experiences can be directly co-conscious. The position according to which both (a) and (b) are false amounts to a wholesale rejection of phenomenal temporality; I will call this stance *anti-realism*. Although immediate experience seems to extend a short way through time, the anti-realist maintains that this is merely an appearance which can be explained away. Realists about phenomenal temporality, by contrast, accept both (a) and (b). A third way lies between these two extremes: *partial anti-realism*, the doctrine that although experience is not confined to momentary time-slices, something other than co-consciousness is responsible for the binding of temporally extended total experiences into streams. This position embraces the phenomenal or specious present, but rejects the DC-thesis. My conclusion will be that anti-realism in its various forms cannot provide a coherent and believable account of phenomenal temporality, and that for such an account we need to turn to realism.

The need for a realist account emerges from a series of case-studies. The best way to appreciate the perplexing nature of phenomenal temporality is to look at some attempts to account for it. By examining the various proposals, we will not only discover the general shape of a solution to the problem, we will also be improving our grasp of the problem itself. Although this problem is of fundamental phenomenological significance, it is also very perplexing indeed. As soon as we start to think seriously about the experience of time, as we are forced to do as soon as we make a serious attempt to describe it in detail, then, as Husserl found, 'we get entangled in the most peculiar difficulties, contradictions and confusions' (1991: 3). Because of this I will proceed cautiously. This chapter is taken up with some preliminary groundwork. In Chapter 6 I examine some influential theories – those of Broad and Husserl – in some detail. Although the theories considered are all problematic, in one way or another, bringing their deficiencies to light suggests a way forward, which I explore in Chapter 7.

In the course of the investigation a number of principles and constraints will emerge, but one constraint is so basic I mention it right at the outset. Recalling the phenomenological data outlined above, it is this: our experience of change is just as immediate as our experience of shape or colour. I take this to be an obvious truth, and will refer to it as the *phenomenological constraint*. The constraint is not particularly controversial; most of the accounts of temporal experience we will be considering start from the assumption that change is something that is experienced. But, as we shall see, in attempting to provide a coherent account of how this is possible, this most basic of facts sometimes gets forgotten.

What of the conclusions we have already reached concerning co-consciousness: the primitiveness of the relation and the Simple Conception? These results will, in the end, be retained, albeit transposed into a temporal key. However, I do not presuppose these results when assessing competing accounts of time-consciousness. It would be wrong simply to assume, without further argument, that what holds at a time also holds through time. We should be open to the possibility that an account of the unity of experience across time requires ingredients that are not needed in an account of the unity of simultaneous experiences. Particularly relevant in this context is the A-thesis, the doctrine that all experience involves an awareness–content distinction. Although I have already argued against the A-thesis, I did so while examining synchronic co-consciousness. There is no guarantee that these arguments will still apply in the diachronic case, and indeed, some of the theories of time-consciousness we will be looking at presuppose the A-thesis. Since I will be arguing that these same theories should be rejected, this conclusion completes the case against the A-thesis.

Although my primary concern remains the unity of consciousness, in the course of investigating the diachronic aspect of this unity I will be dealing with some of the various accounts that have been given of the specious present, that brief expanse of immediate awareness which is also known as the living, sensible or phenomenal present, and which Heidegger sometimes referred to as the illuminated clearing within which the world presents itself and we live out our lives. This is an important and contentious topic in its own right, but also a puzzling one, as can be seen from some of the attempts to describe it:

> the practically cognized present is no knife-edge, but a saddle-back, with a certain breadth of its own on which we sit perched, and from which we look in two directions into time. The unit of composition of our perception of time is a duration, with a bow and a stern, as it were – a rearward- and a forward-looking end. It is only as parts of this duration-block that the relation of succession of one end to the other is perceived. We do not first feel one end and then feel the other after it, and from the perception of the succession infer an interval of time between, but we seem to feel the interval of time as a whole, with its two ends embedded in it.
>
> (James 1952: 399)

If it is really necessary to have some image, perhaps the following may save us from worse. Let us fancy ourselves in total darkness hung over a stream and looking down on it. The stream has no banks, and its current is covered and filled with continuously floating things. Right under our faces is a bright illuminated spot on the water, which ceaselessly widens and narrows its area, and shows us what passes away on the current. And this spot that is light is our now, our present. ... We have not only an illuminated place, and the rest of the stream in total darkness. There is a paler light, which both up and down stream, is shed on what comes before and after our now. And this paler light is the offspring of the present. Behind our heads there is something perhaps which reflects the rays from the lit up now, and throws them dimly upon past and future. Outside this reflection is utter darkness ... the now and here, in which the real appears, are not confined within simply discrete and resting moments. They are any portion of that continuous content with which we come into direct relation. Examination shows that not only at their edges they dissolve themselves over into there and then, but that even within their limits as first given, they know no repose. Within the here is both here and there; and in the ceaseless process of change in time you may narrow your scrutiny to the smallest focus, but you will find no rest.

(Bradley 1922: vol. 1, 54–6)

There are questionable elements in each of these descriptions, but both capture something of the phenomenon. We have an immediate experience only of what is present, a present that is surrounded by the comparative darkness of the remembered past and the anticipated future; the experienced present is not momentary, we seem to be directly aware of intervals of time as wholes; within these wholes there is a continual flow of content, and each experienced whole seamlessly gives way to the next. The question is: how and to what extent can we make sense of any of this?

5.2 Continuity in question

Thus far I have taken it as a given that in talking of consciousness the stream metaphor is apt in at least one respect: just as a stream consists of an uninterrupted flow of water from start to finish, the stretches of our conscious lives that span periods of dreamless sleep consist of an uninterrupted flow of experience. A typical stream does not always flow at the same rate; it is sometimes narrower, sometimes wider; some parts are turbulent, others almost motionless. Although it is dangerous to press any metaphor too far, it is not hard to find counterparts of these features in ordinary experience. The experienced passage of time sometimes slows to a crawl and sometimes speeds along; our sensory experience is far more intense and varied at some times than it is at others – periods of heightened emotion or intellectual activity are counterbalanced by periods of relative quiescence. Such variations are compatible with the idea that our consciousness is nonetheless characterized by continuous flow. But is this basic claim concerning the continuous character of consciousness correct? In a recent article, Galen Strawson has suggested otherwise. His discussion is of interest in its own right, and trying to evaluate it serves the useful purpose of clarifying the manner in which our consciousness is indeed continuous. Strawson writes:

I think William James's famous metaphor of the stream of consciousness is inept. Human thought has very little natural phenomenological continuity or experiential flow – if mine is anything to go by. 'Our thought is fluctuating, uncertain, fleeting', as Hume said ... It keeps slipping from mere consciousness into self-consciousness and out again (one can sit through a whole film without emerging into I-thinking self-consciousness). It is always shooting off, fuzzing, shorting out, spurting and stalling. William James described it as 'like a bird's life ... an alternation of flights and perchings' ... but even this recognition that thought is not a matter of even flow retains a strong notion of continuity ... It fails to take adequate account of the fact that trains of thought are constantly broken by detours – by byblows – fissures – white noise. This is especially so when one is just sitting and thinking.

(1997: 421)

Nothing Strawson says in this passage is incompatible with the claim that our streams of consciousness taken as wholes exhibit phenomenal continuity. He is concerned with conscious *thought*, and on this topic I agree with everything he says. The observation that our thinking is usually fragmented, full of detours and dead-ends, is quite compatible with the claim that there is continuity elsewhere, most notably in perception, mood and bodily feeling, which together constitute the bulk of our experience. Having said this, it is also worth pointing out that short bursts of thinking themselves exhibit phenomenal continuity – most thoughts have some temporal extension. But Strawson continues in a more threatening vein:

When I am alone and thinking I find that my fundamental experience of consciousness is one of *repeated returns into consciousness from a state of complete if momentary unconsciousness*. The (invariably brief) periods of true experiential continuity are usually radically disjunct from one another in this way even when they are not radically disjunct in respect of content. (It is in fact often the same thought – or nearly the same thought – that one returns to after a momentary absence.) The situation is best described, it seems to me, by saying that consciousness is continually *restarting*. There isn't a basic substrate (as it were) of continuous consciousness interrupted by various lapses and doglegs. Rather, conscious thought has the character of a (nearly continuous) series of radically disjunct irruptions into consciousness from a basic substrate of non-consciousness. It keeps banging out of nothingness; it is a series of comings to.

(1997: 422)

This passage is more puzzling. The topic is still conscious thinking, but now Strawson seems to be claiming that the brief passages of continuous thought are surrounded by periods of complete unconsciousness. Thought sequences or fragments are surrounded by experiential blanks, by a 'basic substrate of non-consciousness'. This is not what I find at all. My thinking is often scrappy and inchoate, but it takes place in the context of a relatively constant and continuous mass of peripheral experience, bodily, emotional and perceptual, which together constitute the phenomenal background. The phenomenal background is rarely noticed, but it is nonetheless a constant –

and constantly flowing – presence in our consciousness. When my line of thought takes a detour, for example when without noticing I pass from trying to formulate this sentence to indulging in a few moments of daydreaming, I do not find myself in total silence or darkness or bereft of any bodily feeling; the course of my thinking alters, my mental imagery alters, perhaps the focus of my attention alters, but everything else remains much the same.[1]

Reading on, it is surprising to find – in the light of the preceding claims – Strawson making what seems to be a similar point:

> One works in a room for an hour. Examined in detail, the processes of one's thought are bitty, scatty, and saccadic in the way described; consciousness is in 'perpetual flux', and different thoughts and experiences 'succeed one another with an inconceivable rapidity' [Hume]. And yet one is experientially in touch with a great pool of constancies and steady processes of change in one's environment including, notably, one's body (of which one is almost constantly aware, however thoughtlessly, both by external sense and by proprioception). If one does not reflect very hard, these constancies and steadiness of development in the *contents* of one's consciousness may seem like fundamental characteristics of the *operations* of one's consciousness, although they are not.
>
> (1997: 423)

If one's bitty and saccadic thought processes take place against a great pool of constancies in one's perceptual and bodily experience, with which one is experientially in touch – i.e. the phenomenal background – how can it also seem that one is constantly plunging in and out of periods of total unconsciousness? I do not see how it can, if by 'consciousness' we mean experience in all its forms, and take 'unconsciousness' to refer to the absence of experience in all its forms. Consequently, I can only assume that in these passages Strawson is using the terms 'consciousness' in a restricted way, sometimes meaning conscious thought, sometimes reflective self-conscious awareness. Perhaps, in talking of the *contents* of consciousness, he is referring to the non-introspected phenomenal background, and by the *operations* of consciousness he means self-conscious thought or introspection.

In any event, reading Strawson in this way yields a reasonably realistic picture. For the most part we go about our business in a non-self-conscious way, and our stream of conscious thought is fragmented, taking one detour after another; this all takes place against the continuous presence of the phenomenal background. On occasion, we pause, draw back from whatever was previously occupying us, and introspect – we find ourselves paying attention to what we are currently perceiving, feeling or thinking. The effect is often quite dramatic, so much so that it can seem as though we are suddenly becoming aware of what we were previously not experiencing at all. If I lose interest in a television programme and sink into reverie, and then suddenly become aware that I am staring fixedly at the lamp on top of the set, it can seem as though I have just woken up, even though I have not lost consciousness for a moment (of course sometimes I may actually fall into dreamless sleep, but this is not one of those occasions). This impression is especially vivid if, as is often the case, I have no clear recollection of what I have just been thinking about or imagining. But the impression is misleading: while daydreaming I was not only experiencing a sequence of thoughts and mental images, but the phenomenal background was present too. My eyes were not focused, I was not seeing clearly, but some visual experience was there; likewise for peripheral auditory and bodily sensations.

So Strawson is right to this extent: so far as both conscious thought and self-conscious awareness are concerned, our streams of consciousness contain frequent discontinuities and many a sudden eruption. But they are also characterized by an enduring constancy and continuity, albeit at the level of the largely unnoticed phenomenal background.

5.3 Experience, the present, and presence

There is a simple line of reasoning which, if sound, would immediately establish that our experience is strictly momentary, and hence render an anti-realist view of phenomenal temporality unavoidable. Although I think the reasoning is unsound, it has undeniably exerted an influence.

It is a truism that our immediate experience is limited to the present. Only what is going on now is being directly experienced. If our immediate experience is restricted to the present, how long is the present? Augustine reasoned that the present has no duration whatsoever: evidently, what is present is neither past nor future; take any temporal interval, and make it as short as you like; not all of this interval can be present, because the initial part of the interval occurs before the later part; since the same reasoning applies for any finite interval, no matter how short, it seems that the present, strictly speaking, must be a durationless interface between past and future, between what was but is no more, and what will be but is not yet. Now, if experience is confined to the present, and the present is durationless, it seems experience must be literally instantaneous.

I will call this the *Augustinian* argument (even though in so doing I am not being entirely fair to Augustine). The use of the term 'the specious present' stems from this argument. William James says the expression is due to E. R. Clay, whom he quotes:

> The relation of experience to time has not been profoundly studied. Its objects are given as being of the present, but the part of time referred to by the datum is a very different thing from the conterminus of the past and the future which philosophy denotes by the name Present. The present to which the datum refers is really a part of the past – a recent past – delusively given as being a time that intervenes between the past and the future. Let it be named the specious present, and let the past,

that is given as being the past, be known as the obvious past. ... Time, then, considered relative to human apprehension, consists of four parts, viz., the obvious past, the specious present, the real present, and the future. Omitting the specious present, it consists of three ... nonentities – the past, which does not exist, the future which does not exist, and their conterminus, the present; the faculty from which it proceeds lies to us in the fiction of the specious present.

(James 1952: 398)

Dictionary entries for *specious* include 'in reality devoid of the qualities apparently possessed' and 'appearing to be actually known or experienced'. But we also find 'Of reasoning etc.: Plausible, apparently sound or convincing, but in reality sophistical or fallacious'. A little reflection suggests the term is at least as applicable to the Augustinian argument as it is to the phenomenal present.

It has often been noted that in ordinary usage, the word 'present', and terms connected with it such as 'now', are not used to refer to an instantaneous boundary between past and future. They are mostly used quite flexibly to refer to periods of time of different lengths, periods which include the time of utterance. We talk of present-day trends or standards of living; we talk of the present epoch, the developments now taking place elsewhere, the changes now occurring in the Earth's atmosphere. In doing so, we are obviously not talking about durationless instants; we are referring to processes or states that endure. But I shall not press this point. Although the notion of the durationless present is to some extent artificial, it also seems an intelligible one in certain contexts, for example the description of movement in physics. Instead, let us focus on what is meant by saying that experience is always present.

What does this mean? It does not mean that experience does not *occur* at times other than the present moment, for this is obviously not true. There have been conscious beings on this planet for millions of years, and every experience of every one of these beings was present when it occurred. It is more plausible to say that we cannot, at a given time, be immediately aware of events that are happening at other times. Given the time-lag involved in perception (e.g. the time taken for light to reach us, or for the 'messages' to pass from the sensory cells in the skin to the brain), it could be said that we can only perceive the past, never the immediate present. But there is no such time-lag when it comes to our awareness of our own experiences. A pain-sensation is felt when it occurs. One cannot feel a pain before it begins or after it has ended. But this really only amounts to saying that a pain happens when it happens, or more generally, experiences happen when they happen. This tautology does not establish that experience is necessarily instantaneous, for if there were temporally extended experiences, they too would happen when they happen, i.e. they would occupy one stretch of time rather than another. It is true that a temporally extended sensation would have earlier and later phases, as do all extended processes. But why should adjacent phases not be co-conscious? The earlier and later phases of most processes are related, for example by causation. Relationships as such are not restricted to holding between simultaneous items; why should co-consciousness be any different?

The Augustinian argument seems unsound, but why can it seem plausible? I can suggest two factors. The first is a view sometimes imputed to common sense, namely that only the present moment is real, that the past does not exist, and neither does the future. If we take this seriously, then it clearly does follow that any experience has to be instantaneous, assuming we follow Augustine and regard the present as instantaneous. If the present is instantaneous, and nothing exists in either the past or the future – if as Clay put it, the past and future themselves are nonentities – then anything that occurs or exists will be instantaneous. But this is a highly suspect doctrine. Even if we can make metaphysical sense of the idea that future events and/or times do not exist – and I am not sure that we can – past times and events are surely real enough, and this suffices for the reality of temporally extended happenings and processes.

The second factor is rather harder to make precise, but easy enough to state: a conflation of the present with *presence*. I have already used the term 'presence' to denote the property of being an immediate object or content of consciousness. Everything that is immediately present in a subject's experience possesses presence in this sense: it is just there within one's consciousness. Now, I can see nothing wrong in saying that experience has 'presence' if this is meant only to draw attention to the sheer immediacy of what is being currently experienced. But there are two errors to avoid.

First, it should not be thought that only current experience possesses presence in this sense. This mistake is easily made. The agonizing toothache I had yesterday was throbbingly present at the time, but the pain has now gone, all I have is the memory, and a remembered pain does not hurt. What does hurt is the blinding headache I have at the moment. When I now compare yesterday's toothache, which I can only remember, with my current throbbingly present headache, it can seem as though the property of presence has moved: it was possessed by the pain in my tooth, it is now possessed by the pain in my head, and will soon be possessed by some future experiences. When we focus on the vibrant presence that our current experience has, it is hard to believe that experiences located in the past have this same vibrant property. But of course this is confused: it is a mistake to suppose anything has moved through time, or that anything could move through time. A thing can move through space, by occupying different places at different times, but it makes no sense to say that a thing could exist at different times *at different times* – though of course a thing can exist at different times simply by enduring. To say that a toothache possesses presence is just to say that at the time when it is experienced it possesses the immediacy characteristic of all sensations. As we have already noted, it is clearly wrong to say that experiences exist only in the present. Consequently, *all* phenomenal items possess presence as and when they occur.

The second mistake to avoid is to assume, without further argument, that presence is confined to the present moment. Whereas the notion of an instantaneous present is a concept drawn from a mathematical (or quasi-mathematical) way of thinking about time as a dimension, the notion of presence is connected with experience. The fact that we can think of time as consisting of a succession of durationless instants does not entail that phenomenological presence is instantiated instantaneously. If the sensory present has a non-zero duration, presence will also have a non-zero duration.

5.4 Memory and the experience of time

The Augustinian reasoning is not the only motivation behind anti-realism. We will encounter a more subtle and powerful motivation in a subsequent section, but first I want to take a look at some quite simple ways of accounting for our experience of time. These accounts all appeal, in one way or another, to memory. There is no denying that memory and temporal experience are connected in a number of ways, but it is another thing to hold that memory is largely or wholly responsible for our experience of time. Although it quickly becomes apparent that this is not the case, the reasons why this is so are instructive, and some themes will emerge which will prove relevant later on, when we consider the more exotic accounts.

Memory, more particularly experiential memory, is indisputably crucial to some aspects of our what we might loosely call our 'experience of time'. Experiential memory provides us with a distinctive kind of knowledge of our own pasts. When I remember what I was doing yesterday evening, I remember experiences that I had then, for example how I cut my finger while chopping onions, and what this felt like. We usually know (roughly) when remembered episodes took place: five hours ago, five months ago, five or twenty years ago, as the case may be. Memory thus furnishes us with inside knowledge of how our lives have unfolded over time, and so with a sense of how we arrived at the present moment. Then there is what we might loosely call the 'experience of passage'. We have the impression that our lives are moving forward, in that we live our lives in the present, with future events getting ever nearer while past events recede. Memory plays a role here too. When we recall an earlier experience, we can also remember (if we try) that this earlier experience was followed by later experiences; we can thus anticipate that our current experience will be followed by future experiences. I will not go on: there is no denying that without memory we would have a diminished cognitive and emotional relationship with time over the medium-to-long term. However, it does not follow that our short-term experience of time, from second to second, depends on memory in the same way or to the same extent. Indeed, it does not seem likely that it could.

There is a clear phenomenological difference between seeing a shooting star and remembering seeing a shooting star, and the memorial replay of the experience is itself temporally extended, and so involves the immediate awareness of change. Or so it seems natural to think. To take a different tack, suppose you have been given a drug which over the course of a day gradually and sequentially destroys your experiential memory, without impairing your mental functioning in any other way – for example your factual beliefs are unaffected, your reasoning abilities likewise. First to go are your memories of early childhood; then your school years; soon you can only remember a minute or so back, then a few seconds, then nothing at all. But you continue to be conscious. Although you are now stranded in the immediate sensory present, you hear sounds, you have bodily sensations, you see movement, you feel strangely bewildered. The phenomeno-temporal character of immediate sensory experience is much as it ever was. True, it is impossible to imagine with any clarity what it would be like to be in this condition; but it is easy to believe that one could continue to be conscious, and continue to be directly aware of change. How could this be if the experience of temporality depended on memory? Nonetheless, despite these apparent difficulties, there are philosophers who have assumed that memory can explain the short-term awareness of time (cf. Mellor 1998: 122–3). Let us consider how such accounts might go in a little more detail.

It will help to have a simple example. Imagine the experience of hearing someone play a C major scale on the piano: C-D-E-F … Suppose the scale is played quite quickly, so each note lasts a only short time and is immediately followed by another. Now think of the experience of listening to this scale: a corresponding succession of auditory sensations, C-D-E-F … We hear each tone in turn, but we also hear each tone being followed by another. How could it be that memory is responsible for this experience of succession? One answer comes quickly to mind: when I hear the sequence C-D-E, I have an experience of tone C; this ends and I then hear D while simultaneously remembering hearing C; the experience of D gives way to the experience of E, and while I experience E, I simultaneously remember hearing C and D. But this basic proposal is clearly inadequate. Simply remembering having heard C while I hear D is not enough: this state of affairs is compatible with my having heard C hours or years previously. My memory must register the temporal distance between present and past experiences. What we need to account for is my (apparent) experience that D follows immediately on from C. Likewise for temporal order. I hear C then D then E. The experienced temporal order is something we need to account for. If we try to explain this simply by saying that when I hear E I do so whilst simultaneously remembering having heard C and D, this is compatible with D occurring before or even simultaneously with C.

We might try overcome these difficulties by introducing appropriate *beliefs*. There is no denying that we can estimate both intervals of time and the temporal ordering of events in an intuitive manner. I do not need to look at a clock to know that it is about half an hour since I made coffee, and about three hours since I ate breakfast. Even without estimating the amount of time which has passed, I know that this morning I drank tea before drinking coffee. So we might augment the initial memory-based account along the following lines. When I hear D, after hearing C, I have a memory of hearing C, and accompanying this memory is the belief that C has only just occurred. Similarly, when I hear E, I simultaneously remember hearing both C and D, and the memories of these earlier experiences are accompanied by beliefs: that C occurred just prior to D, and D occurred just prior to E.

But this will not do either. Experiential memories combined with beliefs about the times at which the relevant experiences occurred would certainly provide us with accurate beliefs about our recent experience; we would believe that E was immediately preceded by D, and D was immediately preceded by C. But what sort of beliefs? Before reading this sentence you doubtless believed that the solar system has nine major planets, but this belief was not one you were consciously aware of at the time. We can distinguish between beliefs which we hold but are not conscious of, and beliefs which we are consciously entertaining, between beliefs which are latent and those which are occurrent. Now, we are seeking to account for our experience of succession. According to the proposal we are considering, we are not really conscious of one note following another, we only seem to be. This illusion is the product of a combination of memory and belief. But in order for beliefs to perform the required role, i.e. to act as surrogates for what seems to be a direct experience of succession, the beliefs in question would surely need to be occurrent *conscious* beliefs. The apparent experience of C-being-followed-by-D cannot be explained by the *unconscious* acquisition of a belief, or a non-occurrent belief. The main flaw in the proposal should now be clear: the required beliefs just do not exist. I can hear C-being-followed-by-D without entertaining any conscious beliefs about these notes at all. If experiencing a smooth succession of sensations required us to entertain conscious beliefs as complicated as 'This experience X was immediately preceded by a second experience Y, which in turn was immediately preceded by a third experience Z', we would be unable to think about anything other than the course of our experience; our consciousness would be wholly dominated by these intricate but rather boring beliefs about what we have just experienced. Clearly this does not occur. We experience succession (or seem to) without our minds being flooded with this sort of belief. Of course, it may be true that we acquire (probably short-lived) unconscious or latent beliefs about experience as it occurs, but this sort of belief could not explain our consciousness of change and succession.

Belief is not up to the job of accounting for our awareness of succession, but we have not yet exhausted the potential of experiential memory. Perhaps we can appeal to a distinctive sort of memory: immediate short-term memory. Our memory of very recent experience is usually a lot more complete and accurate than our typical long-term experience-memories. We do not need psychological tests concerning the accuracy of recall over time to tell us this; the difference is quite noticeable. If I look at a photograph for a few moments, even one I have not seen before, and then shut my eyes and recall what I have just been looking at, the resulting memory-image bears a considerable resemblance to the actual experience. The memory-image I can call up a few minutes or hours later is far less realistic. The same applies in the auditory case. If I hear a few moments of music, or a snippet of conversation, and straight away remember what I have just heard, the result is an acoustic memory-image which seems to be almost an exact copy of the original experience. Long-term memory usually lacks this degree of detail and vivacity. There is another reason for supposing that if memory plays a central role in temporal experience, then it is quite a distinctive sort of memory that plays this role. Ordinary long-term experiential memory is to a large degree voluntary, it is subject to our will. Although memories of earlier experiences often invade our consciousness unbidden, we can also choose what to remember. We cannot always recall what we want to recall, but we often can, and we can usually stop remembering when we want to (an exception being so-called obsessive memories). Temporal awareness is clearly not subject to the will in this fashion. Imagine what it is like to hear a piece of harpsichord music: blizzards of notes arriving in fast succession. Imagine trying to *stop* hearing this succession by using your will in the same way as you would to put an end to some unwanted memory. The exercise is futile. Your experience remains just the same, your awareness of the torrent of notes is unaltered. The perception of temporal succession is as independent of the will as any other form of perception (just try altering what you see by exercising your will, without closing or moving your eyes). So how could this perception depend in a crucial way upon memory, which is under the control of the will? The answer can only be that a special sort of *involuntary* memory is involved. Perhaps hearing the initial C-tone in the C-D-E sequence produces a short-term memory which is automatically – i.e. wholly involuntarily – re-played (as it were) as soon as the original ceases.

This is all rather speculative, but assuming that short-term experience-memory is distinctive, in the ways just outlined – which seems plausible – how might it be put to use in accounting for our experience of change? The account could run something like this. First I hear C; I then hear D, the experience of which is automatically accompanied by a short-term memory-image corresponding to my hearing C; I then hear E, and as I do so I have a short-term memory of C-being-followed-by-D. The problem here is that we have posited a short-term memory of an *experience* of succession: 'C-being-followed-by-D'. The sort of experience which the memory-account is meant to eliminate and explain is in fact being presupposed: we cannot remember what we have not already experienced. Also, we must not lose sight of the fact that remembered (and imagined) experiences display the exactly same phenomeno-temporal characteristics as the original experiences. If I remember my experience of hearing C-D-E, three notes occur sequentially in my auditory imagination. I can 'replay' the notes at will, faster or slower, but they always occur in sequence, and I always experience them as occurring in sequence, just as I did when I first heard them. If the memory theorist is prepared to admit that we are directly aware of succession when we remember and imagine, why not admit that we are directly aware of succession in ordinary experience?

To avoid this problem, the memory theorist could posit nested short-term memories. When I hear E, I do not have an accompanying memory of C-being-followed-by-D. Rather, as I experience E, I simultaneously have a short-term memory of hearing D, but this memory is not of the note D alone, it is a memory of hearing D whilst simultaneously having a short-term memory of just having heard C. But as with the belief theory, the complexity of this proposal counts against it. Simply hearing the sequence C-D-E does not seem to involve intricate compound memories of the required sort.

This last point relates to a deeper difficulty. We can distinguish two claims, one weak, one strong. The weak claim is that experiential memory plays a central and indispensable role in temporal awareness. The strong claim is that temporal awareness is *wholly* the product of experiential memory. The various proposals we have considered thus far are all versions of the weaker claim. Why? Because of the example we have been working with: the sequence of tones C-D-E. Each of these individual tones has (it was stipulated) a short but noticeable duration, i.e. a duration which is directly experienced. Since the weak claim recognizes that some experiences possess genuine temporal depth, it falls short of full anti-realism; it amounts only to partial anti-realism. The strong memory theory is fully anti-realist. If phenomenal temporality is wholly the product of memory, there can be no direct experience (or memory) of duration or change whatsoever. This means that our experience of even a single brief tone must be explained in terms of involuntary short-term memories. But memories of what? The answer must be: a succession of strictly durationless experiences. My experience of the tone C consists of a large (infinite?) number of momentary durationless experiences, each (except the first) being accompanied by a large number of nested involuntary short-term memories of other momentary experiences. And what holds of the single tone C also holds of the experience of C-being-followed-by-D. This proposal suffers from a very severe plausibility problem. On the one hand, it is hard to believe that we are not immediately aware of some duration in experience. Is a strictly durationless auditory experience even possible? On the other hand, we are being asked to believe that our experience of duration depends on vast numbers of nested momentary memory-images (for it should not be forgotten that the short-term memories must themselves be durationless). This too is very hard to believe. On hearing the succession of tones C-D-E, are we aware of vast numbers of constantly changing momentary memories? I think not.

5.5 Pulses and binding

The weak memory theorist accepts that we are directly aware of the duration of individual tones (such as C, D and E), and memory only comes into the picture to explain our (apparent) experience of one tone being succeeded by another. If we can be directly aware of the duration of single tones (of the right duration), we can presumably be similarly directly aware of other forms of experience: short stretches of thought, visual experience, and so forth. We are thus led to the view that consciousness itself occurs in short pulses, each of which is experienced as a whole, from which it is but a short step to the view that a stream of consciousness consists of a succession of such pulses, each a short-lived total experience.

A number of philosophers have adopted this view of experience. It finds a quite extreme expression in Whitehead's ultimate ontology: ' "Actual entities" – also termed "actual occasions" – are the final real things of which the world is made up. ... The final facts are, all alike, actual entities; and these actual entities are drops of experience' (1929: 25). Whitehead further claimed that these drops of experience come into being all at once, as wholes; they do not come into being part by part. More recently, Timothy Sprigge has adopted a similar theory as part of his idealist metaphysic (1983: ch. 1). Sprigge takes as his basic ontological unit entities he calls 'momentary centres of experience', a form of words no doubt intentionally reminiscent of Bradley's 'finite centres of experience'. These are taken to be pulses of experience: they are not instantaneous, but have duration, containing earlier and later phases. Despite allowing qualitative changes within single momentary centres to be directly experienced, Sprigge denies that the transition from one momentary centre to another can be experienced in the same way: all experience is confined within discrete experiential units.

The pulse theory amounts to partial anti-realism. It is accepted that experience is not instantaneous; change and persistence can be directly experienced; the earlier and later phases of individual experience-atoms are co-conscious. But since successive co-streamal pulses are not co-conscious, something other than co-consciousness is responsible for linking successive pulses into streams of consciousness. What is this link? Some form of memory is one possibility, but we have already seen that this proposal is problematic. Another possibility is qualitative similarity. Suppose when I hear a fragment of a scale, C-D-E-F, my experience is divided into two distinct pulses, $P_1 = [C-D]$ and $P_2 = [E-F]$, each of which is experienced as a temporal whole. Although these pulses are not linked by co-consciousness, the very last part of the stream-phase to which P_1 belongs is qualitatively very similar (in auditory and non-auditory respects) to the very first part of the stream-phase to which P_2 belongs. Given this similarity, would we not have the impression that the two pulses are directly joined in experience, and hence part of an uninterrupted flow of consciousness? I do not believe that we would, although establishing as much is not entirely straightforward.

Let us look at the matter more closely. Once it is admitted that some changes within experience are directly experienced, it seems phenomenologically unrealistic to maintain that others are not. Consider again the two pulses, P_1 = [C-D] and P_2 = [E-F]. What is the relationship between P_1 and P_2? Since by hypothesis they are not linked by co-consciousness, the transition between the two is not directly experienced. If the pulse theory were correct, we should be able to detect two different forms of transition within our streams of consciousness, one that occurs within pulses, and one that occurs between pulses, yet it seems clear that there is no such thing. When we hear a sequence such as C-D-E-F, the experience of C giving way to D is exactly the same as the experience of D giving way to E, and exactly the same as E giving way to F. According to the pulse theory, this cannot be: since the first of these transitions is directly experienced whereas the second is not, there is bound to be a noticeable difference between them. The fact that such differences are not discernible counts against the pulse theory.

More generally, we are constantly aware of phenomenal contents undergoing passage, there is a constant flow and continual renewal of content. This experienced passage is both continuous and homogeneous: when we witness a continuous change, to the extent that we are directly aware of the change occurring, we are aware of every part and portion of it in the same way. If experience were packaged into discrete units, this would not be the case. Move your hand slowly but smoothly across your field of vision. At each moment you see your hand at a different position; you also see your hand continuously moving. Not only is the movement continuous, but your experience of the movement is continuous: you are directly aware of every perceivable change in your hand's location in the same way. Or imagine hearing a succession of fast clicks. You have an immediate awareness of each individual click, in that you do not hear part of a click and remember or anticipate hearing the rest of it. The click as a whole is apprehended. But is it not the case that each click (except the first and last) is experienced with its immediate predecessor and successor? Is not each click co-conscious with its immediate neighbours? These fact suggests an important principle: that each brief phase of a stream of consciousness is *phenomenally bound* to the adjacent (co-streamal) phases.

The following thought experiment both supports the binding principle and illustrates its significance. Suppose that you have an exact duplicate; there is someone somewhere whose course of experience is indistinguishable from your own. As a result, there exist at the moment two streams of consciousness which are, from moment to moment, qualitatively the same in all respects. I think we can clearly make sense of this possibility, no matter how implausible or unlikely we might think the scenario is. Suppose you are currently watching a pendulum swing slowly back and forth. Your replica is doing the same. The pendulum is currently moving from right to left; it takes a couple of seconds to complete the movement. Imagine your visual experience of this movement is divided into a number of phases [m_1-m_2-m_3 ...

-m_{20}]. Each of these phases is a tenth of a second long. Since you experience the pendulum's movement to be smooth and continuous, each phase consists of the perception of a smooth portion of this movement, and each phase is seamlessly joined to its immediate neighbours. Your replica's experience during this period consists of a corresponding and qualitatively indistinguishable succession [$\mathbf{m_1}$-$\mathbf{m_2}$-$\mathbf{m_3}$ ... -$\mathbf{m_{20}}$]. Now suppose the pulse theory is correct, that experiential pulses are one tenth of a second long, and $\mathbf{m_1}$, m_2, etc. are each individual pulses. Consider the following sequences of phases: $S_1 = [m_1$-m_2-m_3 ... -$m_{20}]$, $S_2 = [\mathbf{m_1}$-$\mathbf{m_2}$-$\mathbf{m_3}$ ... -$\mathbf{m_{20}}]$, and $S_3 = [m_1$-$\mathbf{m_2}$-m_3-$\mathbf{m_4}$-m_5-$\mathbf{m_6}$-m_7 ... -$\mathbf{m_{20}}]$. The first two sequences consist (respectively) of a portion of your experience and a portion of your replica's. The third sequence consists of an alternation of phases from both streams of consciousness, yours and your replica's. Clearly, S_3 is not a real stream of consciousness at all; it is a fictional amalgam of components from two real streams, S_1 and S_2. But according to the pulse theory, from a purely phenomenological perspective, your experience m_1 could be as easily followed by your replica's experience $\mathbf{m_2}$ as your own experience m_2. Indeed, so far as phenomenal factors are concerned, there can be no fact of the matter as to which experiential pulse belongs to which stream; the fictional gerrymandered succession S_3 is every much a genuine stream of consciousness as the streams S_1 and S_2. Moreoever, this remains the case even if the streams S_1 and S_2 do not occur at the same time (thus far I have assumed they do). This seems quite absurd. If we know anything about consciousness, we know that there is a fact of the matter as to which experiences belong to which streams, and we know this in virtue of the purely phenomenal interconnections between co-streamal experiences.

The synchronic case provides a useful contrast. Let us suppose m_1 and m_2 refer to the left and right halves of your visual field at a given time, whereas $\mathbf{m_1}$ and $\mathbf{m_2}$ refer to the corresponding halves of your replica's visual field. The idea that m_1-$\mathbf{m_2}$ constitutes a single experience can be rejected: the relationship between m_1 and m_2 is directly experienced, likewise for $\mathbf{m_1}$-$\mathbf{m_2}$, but there is no experienced relationship between m_1 and $\mathbf{m_2}$, nor between m_2 and $\mathbf{m_1}$. Does the same not apply in the diachronic case? William James puts the point with characteristic verve:

> Neither contemporaneity, nor proximity in space, nor similarity of quality and content are able to fuse thoughts together which are sundered by this barrier of belonging to different personal minds. The breaches between such thoughts are the most absolute breaches in nature.
>
> (1952: 147)

James here is speaking of simultaneous experiences, but as he recognized, the same applies to successive experiences. The intuition that this is the case is grounded, I suggest, in the fact of phenomenal binding.

When presented in this fashion the phenomenal binding principle seems plausible, but there are considerations which run in the other direction. Russell once suggested that nothing in our experience could definitively exclude the hypothesis that the world only came into being five minutes ago. Varying the scenario, does anything in our experience rule out the possibility that our region of the universe has just emerged from a thousand-year total freeze, a period during which all mental and physical processes were completely halted? If our part of the world were simply to stop in this manner, then resume, would we be any the wiser? Arguably not. But if this were the case, the binding principle might seem to be in trouble. Assuming that a total freeze does not discernibly impinge on phenomenal continuity, what connects the last phase of your pre-freeze stream of consciousness with the initial post-freeze phase? Presumably, there is only qualitative similarity and short-term memory. If these are enough to give the appearance of phenomenal continuity, in the absence of directly experienced transitions, the binding principle is refuted.

Far from undermining the case for subscribing to the binding principle, this sort of example in fact strengthens it. The example as it stands is under-described, for there are two possibilities which need to be distinguished: total cessations *without* phenomenal binding, and total cessations *with* phenomenal binding. Returning to our example of the musical scale, in the first sort of case, the transition between notes C and D is not directly experienced. Note C ends, a thousand years pass, then note D is heard; although the hearing of C is remembered as D is heard, there is no experience of the transition between C and D. In the second sort of case, the transition between C and D *is* directly experienced, despite the fact that a thousand years of objective time occurs between the occurrence of C and the occurrence of D. As soon as this distinction is drawn, it becomes plausible to think that only the second sort of case would constitute a wholly indiscernible total stoppage. A total freeze without phenomenal binding would leave its mark on our streams of consciousness; there would be a disruption in experienced phenomenal flow. Of course, we would not be able to tell from the disruption that a long period of external time had passed, but we might well notice that something rather strange had just occurred.

I do not want to insist at this point that the phenomenal binding principle can only be accommodated by holding that adjacent co-streamal phases really are co-conscious – where co-consciousness consists in the same primitive experiential relationship which (I have argued) holds between simultaneous experiences. I am remaining open to alternative proposals. But the principle must be accommodated somehow. The pulse theory fails in this respect, and this failure results in an inadequate description of the stream of consciousness.

5.6 A conflict of principles

Before considering any further attempts to account for our experience of time, I want to consider another general reason for rejecting realism about phenomenal extension. No one denies that we experience change, so why would anyone be tempted to deny that consciousness extends some short way through time? The Augustinian argument is one factor, but not the only one. Philosophers who have tried to make sense of our experience of time have often taken consciousness to possess an awareness–content structure. It is hard to know if they took this view because they already assumed consciousness to have this structure, or whether they found it necessary to adopt this view in order to make sense of phenomenal temporality. Either way, the awareness–content schema has seemed to many to be a natural way of accommodating a basic principle about temporal awareness. But it does so at the expense of making it hard to see how another basic principle can be satisfied. Since the accounts I will be considering in the next chapter can be seen as different ways of implementing and reconciling these principles, it will help to have them clearly in view.

In the chapter of James' (1952) *Principles* devoted to the perception of time, there is a section entitled 'The feeling of past time is a present feeling'. James here discusses (and seems to endorse) a principle concerning the experience of time that has been regarded as self-evident by many philosophers and psychologists.

> between the mind's own changes being successive, and knowing their own succession, lies as broad a chasm as between the object and subject of any case of cognition in the world. A succession of feelings, in and of itself, is not a feeling of succession. And since, to our successive feelings, a feeling of their own succession is added, that must be treated as an additional fact requiring its own special elucidation. ... what is past, and known as past, must be known with what is present, and during the 'present' spot of time.

James also quotes a passage from James Ward:

> 'In a succession of events, say of sense-impressions A B C D E ..., the presence of B means the absence of A and C, but the presentation of this succession involves the simultaneous presence in some mode or other of two or more of the presentations A B C D. In reality, past, present and future are differences in time, but in presentation all that corresponds to these is in consciousness simultaneously.'

It is one thing to have a succession of different experiences; it is another to experience this succession as a succession. Imagine seeing a red flash of light and then seeing a green flash. Call these experiences R and G respectively. If when you see G you have no memory whatsoever of having seen R, if the latter experience is completely gone and left no trace of itself behind at all, then you will see G without any awareness (of any kind) of having just seen R. That is, you will have a succession of experiences but no experience of succession. So what is required for the latter? Let us suppose that you do see G occurring after R – you have an experience of succession. For this to be possible, it might seem that as you see G, you must also simultaneously be aware of just having seen R. It cannot be the other way round: you cannot be aware of G when you see R, since when you see R, G has yet to occur. This is the point James is drawing attention to by saying 'the feeling of past time is a present feeling'. If we are directly aware of the immediate past, this awareness is located in the present. Miller (1984: 109) calls this *The Principle of Simultaneous Awareness*, or *PSA*. This label is in one way apt, in another it is misleading. It is misleading in that R is not experienced as occurring simultaneously with G. The two flashes are not perceived to happen at the same time: they are perceived to happen in succession, first R then G. The label is apt in that as G occurs, one is simultaneously aware of R as having just occurred.

It might seem as though this principle is compatible with awareness having some temporal duration. Could we not be aware of both R and G for some duration of time? This may be an option, but most philosophers who have accepted *PSA* have not taken it up. In part, this may be because they subscribe to the awareness–content model and have simply assumed that acts of awareness are pointlike and so momentary. (We shall see that Broad, initially at least, rejected this idea despite subscribing to *PSA*.) But there are other motivations. Suppose one accepts that to experience a temporally extended content, one must have an awareness of the first half of the content that is simultaneous with one's awareness of the second half. Clearly, this awareness cannot begin earlier than the second half of the content, but could it occur concurrently with it? Not if the second half of the content has some temporal duration, for the same considerations apply. Since by hypothesis one is aware of the latter content as a whole, then one must have an awareness of its first half that is simultaneous with one's awareness of its second half. The same applies for any temporally extended contents, no matter how brief. An adherent of *PSA* is thus driven ineluctably to the conclusion that the acts of awareness which apprehend temporally extended contents are either strictly momentary, or are so brief as to have no discernible temporal extension. A further consideration points in the same direction. When listening to an extended sound, such as a long note played on a cello, is it not the case that throughout this experience we are continually aware of the *continuity* of our experience? We are constantly aware (though not necessarily paying attention to) a flow of sound: the tone goes on and on, and we are constantly aware of this continuity. How can this be? As already noted, a continuity of discrete awarenesses does not amount to an awareness of continuity. One answer runs thus: at every moment we are aware of a temporally extended portion of the enduring note. Again, this is not to say that the constituent phases of the extended tone-portion are experienced as occurring simultaneously; no, they are experienced as occurring in succession. It is one thing to hear a group of notes

C-E-G played in sequence, it is another to hear the same three notes being played simultaneously, as a chord. *PSA* does not deny this difference. What *PSA* does require is that for the succession to be apprehended as a succession, it must be apprehended as a whole in a single momentary awareness. The principle applies generally, right across the stream of consciousness. There is a constant flow of thought, visual experience, bodily sensation. If we are continuously aware of the continuity of our stream of consciousness we must, at every moment, be aware of some temporal extent of it. Or so the argument runs.

But a difficulty now surfaces. Returning to the sequence of flashes R-G, assuming *PSA*, what are you aware of as you experience G that provides you with your experience of succession? Still assuming the awareness–content model, there seem to be two possibilities, one realist, one anti-realist.

The realist option is to say that when G is experienced, an act of awareness occurs which extends backwards a short way, and so takes in the entire succession R-G. Although this act of awareness is momentary, its 'scope' is not: the act is an apprehension of a temporally extended segment of phenomenal content. This might seem impossible: by the time the green flash happens, the red flash is over and in the past: how could there be an awareness of what is past? In response, it might be argued that this is just what is required to make sense of the phenomenological facts: we are immediately aware of change and persistence – how can this be unless awareness is able to take in phenomenal contents which are past as well as contents that are present? Nonetheless, the proposal is somewhat counterintuitive. It runs counter to what Miller calls *The Principle of Presentational Concurrence*, or *PPC*, according to which

> the duration of a *content* being presented is *concurrent* with the duration of the *act* of presenting it … the time interval occupied by a content which is before the mind is the very same time interval which is occupied by the act of presenting that very content.
>
> (1984: 107)

PPC does seem plausible. When I see the red flash being followed by the green flash, or when I hear a sequence of notes C-D-E, my experiencing of the succession does seem to run concurrently with the phenomenal contents which jointly constitute the succession; I am aware of the red flash *before* I am aware of the green flash. Or so it seems natural to say. To this extent, it is counterintuitive to suppose my awareness of the succession occurs an instant after the succession has occurred (or at the very last instant of the succession).

Returning to the problem of accommodating *PSA*, the anti-realist option is to deny that the momentary awareness whose content is the succession R-G actually extends into the past. How then can I be aware of the succession R-G? The answer: I instantaneously apprehend both G (assuming in this context that it is instantaneous) and a *representation* of R, not R itself. Thus, to paraphrase Ward, we might say 'the presence of G means the absence of R, but the presentation of this succession involves the simultaneous presence in some mode or other of R'. Writing more recently, Michael Lockwood suggests that:

> If phenomenal perspectives [i.e. total experiences] lack temporal depth, then something other than temporal separatedness must be used to encode perceived temporal relations between items that are comprehended within a single specious present. Think of the way that a teleprompter screen contains, all at once, a sequence of words that, as spoken, take a period of time to enunciate; on the screen, the words are presented in a spatial order that represents a temporal order. Analogously, so the suggestion would run, if one is listening to music, each instantaneous state of awareness contains, all at once – that is to say, all within the same psychological simultaneity plane – a sequence of phenomenal notes whose external counterparts take a period of time to play.
>
> (1989: 269–70)

If consciousness does lack any genuine temporal depth, then an account along these lines seems unavoidable, assuming adherence to *PSA*. At any instant, we are apprehending a content which although instantaneous also represents or encodes a temporal spread of phenomena, such as a sequence of notes or a perceived movement. When these contents are apprehended, in a momentary act of experiencing, the result is an awareness of a temporal spread of phenomena. A stream of consciousness consists of a continuous succession of these momentary acts of awareness, each apprehending a representation of a temporal spread of phenomena. For obvious reasons, I will call accounts of this type *representational anti-realisms*. Are such accounts in conformity with *PPC*? In one sense they are: the awareness I have at any given instant is instantaneous and only apprehends an instantaneous part of my stream of consciousness. In another and more important sense they are not: at any typical instant my experience *seems* to be temporally extended, for example I am perceiving an extended tone, or an object moving some short distance within my field of vision, so the content of my awareness has at least an apparent temporal depth, a depth which is not possessed by my awareness itself.

The discussion of this section has suggested at least this much: *PSA* and the awareness–content model of consciousness are natural partners. For whether we accommodate *PSA* in a realist or anti-realist fashion, we are positing momentary acts of awareness with phenomenal contents that are non-momentary. If either type of account proves viable, proponents of the A-thesis would be back in business.

6   Broad and Husserl

6.1 A curious tale

This chapter is devoted to the attempts of two philosophers to make sense of our immediate experience of time. A cursory glance at the relevant primary sources, or indeed a more careful scrutiny of some secondary sources, might easily give one the impression that Broad and Husserl had arrived at very similar conclusions concerning temporal awareness. In one sense this would not be too far off the mark, in that it is true that both authors can be found endorsing theories of a similar general form, but a closer look shows the situation to be rather more complicated. Husserl struggled with the topic throughout his long career, and in his various writings several different accounts of time-consciousness can be found; he seems never to have been entirely happy with any of them. Broad proposed an account of temporal experience in his *Scientific Thought* (1923), and returned to the topic in his *An Examination of McTaggart's Philosophy* (1938). Although Broad does not indicate as much, his later account is very different from his earlier effort, despite some superficial similarities. The interesting point is that although the views of both philosophers evolved, they evolved in opposite directions. Broad's later account most resembles a theory Husserl elaborated in his early-mid period, whereas Broad's initial account is in some respects similar to one which can be discerned in Husserl's later writings. Broad's early account is realist, his later account anti-realist; Husserl seems to have moved in the opposite direction. So, to simplify somewhat, far from arriving at the same place, each writer's destination was the other's point of departure.

These curious developments are, I believe, to be explained by the fact that Broad and Husserl both subscribed to certain assumptions – specifically, a combination of an awareness–content model and the Principle of Simultaneous Awareness, *PSA* – and both found it hard to develop an unproblematic account of temporal experience within this framework. The obvious lesson to draw is that at least one of the relevant assumptions must go. As becomes plain in the next chapter, where I look at alternative accounts, the guilty party is *PSA*; it also turns out that when *PSA* is rejected the motivation for subscribing to an awareness–content model disappears.

In expounding the accounts which follow, I have tried to provide as much detail as is required for a proper appreciation of what is on offer; however, when dealing with Husserl I found a hefty measure of simplification was unavoidable, for several reasons. Even a brief detour into the relevant parts of his more general work on perception, meaning, memory, and so on, would have taken us too far afield. Although it is not clear to me that such a detour would shed much by way of useful light on his theory of specifically temporal awareness, I accept that a full appreciation of Husserl's work is not to be had in its absence. Also, Husserl himself never got around to formulating a definitive account of his views concerning time-consciousness, and no doubt this is one of the reasons why his various and voluminous writings on the topic are not easily summarized, and are sometimes obscure. I have not tried to expound in any detail those aspects of Husserl's work which I cannot understand.

6.2 Broad: the early account

Broad's earlier account of temporal awareness is attractively simple, but on reflection baffling. The account is based on an awareness–content distinction: in Broad's terms, there are acts of sensing and their sensible (or phenomenal) contents, or sensa.[1] He makes it clear that we are immediately aware of change and persistence in the contents of our experiences:

> There is no doubt that sensible motion and rest are genuine unanalysable properties of visual sensa. I am aware of them as directly as I am aware of the redness of a red patch, and I could no more describe them to anyone who had never sensed them than I could describe the colour of a pillar-box to a man born blind.
>
> (1923: 287)

In conformity with this, he asserts that 'what can be sensed at any moment stretches a little way back behind that moment. This . ... the Specious present' (1923: 348). In fact, in *Scientific Thought* Broad maintains that the idea of a strictly momentary act of awareness is a fiction, so all actual acts have some small but finite duration. But to make his exposition easier, he begins by assuming that there are momentary acts. The important point is that a typical momentary act has, as its object, a temporally extended phenomenal content. At this point a diagram comes in useful. Figure 6.1 closely resembles Broad's own diagram, but I have altered the lettering.

The top line represents a subject O's successive acts of awareness. The horizontal line beneath represents the contents of these acts. O_1 represents O's momentary awareness at time t_1. The content of this act is represented by the portion of the lower line AC. As will be seen, the content of O_1 is a temporally extended stretch of phenomenal content. The duration of AC coincides with the length of O's specious present. Whatever falls within O's

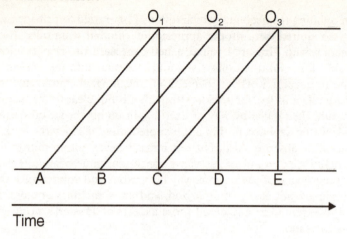

Figure 6.1 Temporal awareness: Broad's early view

specious present is sensed all at once as a whole, but a temporally extended whole. So in a single instant O is aware of a temporally extended phenomenal content, for example an enduring tone, or a patch of light moving some way across his visual field. The fact that O senses the extended content A-C as a whole is represented by the triangle AO_1C. At a slightly later time, t_2, act O_2 occurs, represented by triangle BO_2D. The content of O_2 overlaps that of O_1, the overlap being the content represented by BC. However, the contents of these two acts do not completely overlap: AB is apprehended by O_1 but not O_2, and CD is apprehended by O_2 but not O_1. Then at the still later time t_3 there is the act O_3. The content of this act, CE, does not overlap that of O_1 at all, since these two acts are separated by the length of O's specious present. Or more accurately, the two acts apprehend only the momentary content C. In the diagram, O_2 is situated exactly half-way between O_1 and O_3. If O_2 had occurred closer to O_1, the overlap in the content of the two acts would have been greater; if, on the other hand, it had occurred closer to O_3, the overlap would have been less.

As I said above, Broad believed momentary acts did not exist; any actual act of awareness has some duration; actual acts are continuous processes of sensing. O_1-O_2 is a single extended awareness. As can be seen from the diagram, content BC is apprehended *throughout* the duration of this extended act. B falls in the middle of the specious present of O_1, and C occurs right at the end of the same specious present, so everything between B and C is apprehended by O_1. O_2's specious present begins at B, so nothing prior to B is apprehended by O_2, but everything between B and C is. Although O_2 apprehends content which occurs after C, right on up until D, since O_1 ends at C nothing beyond this point is apprehended by O_1. So the content which is sensed throughout the duration of O_1-O_2 is restricted to their period of overlap, BC. It will be noted that the shorter an extended act is, the greater the overlap in content between what is sensed at the beginning and the end of the act, so the greater the content sensed as a whole throughout the act. The longer an extended act is (up to the limit of the duration of the specious present), the smaller the duration of overlap, so the smaller the duration of content sensed as a whole throughout the act.

Assessment

Broad's theory might seem to provide a neat solution to the problem. But there are obscurities and problems. First the obscurities. Broad says that all actual acts are of some finite duration. If so, how long do they last? There seems in principle to be no limit to how long a continuous process of sensing can go on for; presumably we are continuously aware of *something* for as long as we are awake. The important point, for Broad, is that over the course of intervals of sensing, up to the duration of the specious present, we can be continuously aware of a given stretch of content as a whole. Let us call the content sensed as a whole throughout the duration of an act the *core content* of the act. So in the case of act O_1-O_2, the core content is B-C. In addition to core content, there is what we can call the *total content* of an act, i.e. the sum total of content which is apprehended at some time or other during an act. The total content is always longer than the core content. Remaining with the example of O_1-O_2, A-B is apprehended at the very start of the act, and C-D is apprehended at the very end of the act, so the whole stretch of content between A and D is apprehended at some time or other during the act in question. Broad himself refers to contents such as these as 'penumbra'. Now, as we have seen, the shorter an extended act is, the longer is the act's core content. The limiting case is the duration of the specious present; only a momentary act can apprehend a content with this duration. Since there are no momentary acts, the core content of any actual act will always be shorter than the specious present. If we consider acts which approach the length of the specious present, the core contents of these acts tends to zero. One of the peculiarities of Broad's account is that although core contents have the distinguishing property of specious presents, they are temporally extended and are sensed as a whole, Broad doesn't *call* them specious presents. He reserves this label for the limiting case which can never occur.

But this is only a terminological peculiarity. There are at more significant oddities, and I want to focus now on these. Each of these oddities is the product of Broad's rejection of *PPC*: his premise that acts of awareness have contents which last longer than the acts themselves. To start with, consider what goes on within extended acts. Although Broad refuses to admit momentary acts, he is quite happy with the idea that extended acts contain within them shorter acts of finite duration. Consider again the extended act O_1-O_2. If extended acts contain shorter parts, then O_1-O_2 contains shorter (but still finite) acts. These acts have core contents which last longer than the core content of O_1-O_2. This is illustrated in Figure 6.2. The core content of the longer act O_1-O_4 is Q-R, whereas the core content of the shorter act O_2-O_3 is P-S.

This is a curious result, and so far as I can see, one that does not correspond with the phenomenological facts. When I perceive a continuous process, the extent of the process that I am directly aware of does not seem to change. It does not seem that over very short intervals I am aware of longer stretches of the process than I am over longer periods. If Broad's theory is correct, we surely ought to be able to notice this 'ballooning' of content over short intervals.

A second odd consequence concerns the way temporally extended items enter our awareness. If there are no momentary acts, a short stretch of content such as B-C is apprehended as a whole only by a process of awareness which is temporally extended. B-C is apprehended throughout O_1-O_2. What is strange is that this stretch of awareness *begins* the moment B-C *ends*. Since the extended act O_1-O_2 does not even overlap B-C, we only start to be aware of B-C as a whole from the moment when B-C is wholly in the past. The same applies to all extended contents: they enter our awareness only when they are completed and in the past. This is certainly counter-intuitive. As Mabbot (1951) puts it,

> if my dentist hurts me, he has always stopped hurting me before I begin to feel the hurt. And this has nothing to do with the time taken by nerve transmission; it is a direct corollary of the specious present theory.

And this, he suggests, amounts to an 'unacceptable paradox' in Broad's theory. I am not sure whether this is so or not. Look at the content C-D in

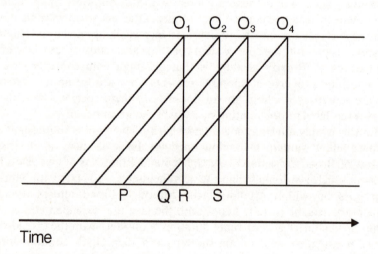

Figure 6.2 Core contents: O_1-O_4 = Q-R, O_2-O_3 = P-S

Figure 6.1. It is true that this content is apprehended as a whole by O_2-O_3, and this period of awareness begins at the same moment C-D comes to an end. But the earlier parts of C-D are apprehended prior to this point, during the period of sensing which ends at O_2. So the difficulty may not be as severe as it first seems. It can also be argued that the objection is simply confused. In Broad's diagram, acts and contents are shown as temporally related: O_1 is strictly simultaneous with C, O_2 is strictly simultaneous with D, and also occurs after O_1 and before O_3. These temporal relations are presumably meant to be wholly objective. But what phenomenological relevance does this objective time-ordering have? When O_1 takes in the spread of content stretching from A to C, would the subject be aware that his awareness was occurring at the end of this content, rather than at the beginning or in the middle? Suppose the extended content A-C is a single tone of brief duration. This tone is apprehended as a temporally extended whole; the content of O_1 is thus of a temporally enduring (if brief) auditory sensation. Since O_1's content is a sensation possessing intrinsic duration, presumably this is all that the subject will experience. The subject will not be aware that his awareness is located at one end or the other of the tone; all the subject will be aware of is the tone itself. To simplify, I have been talking so far in terms of momentary acts of awareness, but the same point applies to extended acts: here too, all the subject will be aware of is the temporally extended content of the extended act, not the act itself, nor its (objective) temporal relationship to the content apprehended.

But Broad's theory is problematic in another, more damaging, way. Let us temporarily suppose that there are momentary acts. Suppose that the content represented by A-E is a constant unvarying auditory tone (e.g. as would result from hearing a sustained note played on a flute), with one exception: the sound of a single sharp click which occurs between B and C. Now consider O_1 and O_2. O_1 is an awareness of the content between A and C; the apprehending by O_1 of this extended content constitutes a single complete experience, call it E_1. The click in the interval BC is a part of E_1. As for O_2, this act takes in content between B and D. Call the resulting experience E_2. The click between B and C forms part of E_2. So the click is heard twice over, once at t_1, when O_1 and E_1 occur, and again at t_2, when O_2 and E_2 occur. This is a disastrous result, since by hypothesis there is only a single click that is experienced by the subject O. Broad's account has the consequence that we cannot hear a single sound just once! In fact, if we take momentary acts seriously, the consequence is much worse: there will be an infinite number of distinct acts between O_1 and O_2, each of which will constitute a distinct experience including the click. So we will hear the click an infinite number of times. This is ridiculous.[2]

Broad does not think there are momentary acts, so let us see whether the problem is avoided by positing extended acts. O_1-O_2 constitutes a single extended act of experiencing, a single extended slice of a stream of consciousness. The extended act O_2-O_3 constitutes a second extended act of experiencing, one which is temporally adjacent to O_1-O_2. Let us once more call these two (temporally extended) experiences E_1 and E_2. The total content apprehended during E_1 includes everything between A and D. As will be clear from our earlier discussion, not all of this content is experienced throughout E_1, but it is all experienced *sometime* during E_1. In fact, the content between B and C constitutes the core content of O_1-O_2, so it is experienced throughout E_1, along with the click. As for E_2, the total content of this act runs from B to E. Again, not all of this content is being apprehended all through this act. Only the core content in C-D has this feature. But the content between B and C, the content including the click, is experienced during the initial part of E_2. So again we have the result that the click is heard twice over, for the first time throughout the duration of E_1, for the second time at the start of E_2. True, the click belongs to the continuously sensed core content of E_1, and only to the earlier 'penumbra' of E_2, but this does not alter the fact that the click is heard twice over. It seems that the problem of repeated contents continues to afflict Broad's theory.

In fact, there is an obvious remedy to this problem. Let us remain with extended acts of awareness. We have seen that an extended act centred on O_1 will apprehend the click, as will an extended act centred on O_2. If these extended acts are wholly discrete, then clearly the click is heard twice over. But what if these acts are not wholly discrete, but overlapping? Suppose the portion of the first act which apprehends the click is numerically identical with the portion of the second act which apprehends the click. The click will only be apprehended once, and the problem of repeated contents is removed at a stroke. However, since Broad never seems to have considered the possibility that acts might share common parts, I will not discuss it further at present. Let us instead move on to see how Broad tackled the problems with his own theory.

6.3 Broad: the later account

Broad prefaces the new account by saying 'I have never seen any account of the Specious Present which seemed even *prima facie* intelligible'. Whether in saying this he intends to refer to his own earlier account is unclear, as he makes a similar remark at the outset of the latter too. In any event, there are significant differences between the two, and it is more than likely that this is due to Broad's having recognized that his earlier account is not without its problems. Comparing these accounts is complicated by certain changes in terminology. Whereas in *Scientific Thought* Broad talks of acts of awareness (or 'sensory acts') and their objects and contents, in *McTaggart* he talks of 'prehending' sensory particulars and other items. As Broad uses the term, 'to prehend' something is to be directly aware of it, in the sense of having it immediately before one's consciousness or awareness. To make matters easier to follow, while expounding Broad's *McTaggart* theory I will continue to speak of 'awareness' and the objects and contents of awareness.

He begins with two assumptions. The first is that the present is a dura-tionless instant, the second that we are directly aware of things changing and remaining unchanged. Each of these assumptions is hard to deny, but if both are true there is a familiar problem: if our awareness is confined to the instantaneous present, what we can be aware of at a given moment in time will be confined to a momentary event, but if this is the case, we would not be able to be directly aware of things changing or remaining unchanged. To solve the difficulty, Broad again suggests that our awareness at any given moment is of finite duration, and extends a short way into the past. So far so familiar. Broad now introduces an additional element into his account: *presentedness*, a psychological characteristic which comes in varying degrees from zero up to a maximum. When we are aware of an extended content C as a whole, the content will seem to be spread through time. The whole of C cannot completely present, in the strict sense, since the strict present is instantaneous. Let us assume that C consists of a compact (dense) succes-sion of instantaneous temporal slices. One of these momentary slices is the presently occurring slice, and this possesses the maximum degree of present-edness. The remaining momentary slices, as we move backwards from the present, possess a gradually diminishing degree of presentedness, tailing off to zero at the point where C no longer falls within the span of immediate awareness. Broad suggests an analogy. We can compare the content of a single specious present with a short strip of paper. At the extreme left edge, the strip is pure black; from left to right this black turns gradually and continuously into ever lighter shades of grey, until at the extreme right edge the strip is pure white. The gradual transition black to white corresponds to increasing degrees of presentedness. Broad does not clarify further what he takes this quality of presentedness to be, but the basic idea seems clear enough. As contents slip into the past, we sense them fading away, they appear less vivid, less intense; or perhaps it is because we are aware of contents losing their intensity that they seem to slip away into the past. I will return to this topic soon. Let us move on to see what Broad does with it.

So far we have been considering what Broad calls the 'extensive' aspect of the specious present: how a single momentary awareness takes in a temporal spread of phenomena. It is time to turn to the 'transitory' aspect, the manner in which specious presents succeed one another, and how they relate to one another when they do so. He makes some simplifying assumptions: that all specious presents of the same subject are of the same duration, that the maximum degree of presentedness is the same for all specious presents, and that the degree of presentedness decreases continuously and uniformly to zero between the later and earlier boundaries of any specious present. He also makes the rather more general claim that 'there is continuity in our experience in respect of degree of presentedness' (1938: vol. 2, 285). He means by this that there are no sudden changes in presentedness, from moment to moment within a single stream of consciousness. There would be sudden changes if immedi-ately successive specious presents were separated by some interval of time.

Consider the most extreme case: successive specious presents are temporally adjacent but non-overlapping. Each specious present is the apprehension of a stretch of content which varies in presentedness from zero to maximum, from earlier to later. Given this, the transition from the later part of the first specious present to the initial phase of its immediate successor would be accompanied by a dramatic drop in presentedness: from maximum to minimum. The same applies to the intermediate cases, where successive specious presents partially overlap but are still separated by some interval: there would still be a sudden drop in presentedness. Clearly, if presentedness is continuous, if we are *continuously* aware of a spread of content, stretching a short way back in time, with uniformly decreasing degrees of presentedness, then co-streamal specious presents must themselves be continuous, there can be no temporal gaps separating them. Thus successive co-streamal specious presents form a compact series: no specious present has an immediate successor, and between any two co-streamal specious presents, no matter how close together, there is an infinity of others.

In considering the implications of all this, a diagram is helpful. Figure 6.3 below resembles the one Broad provides (1938: 285), although I have made a few superficial alterations (e.g. I have depicted variations in presentedness). Between any two overlapping momentary awarenesses there are meant to be an infinity of others. Since these cannot be represented diagramatically, what we have in the diagram is only a small sample of the specious presents that would actually (according to Broad) occur during the period in question.

The lower line represents a continuous stretch of content. O_1, O_2, O_3 are each momentary acts of awareness. Large triangles such as O_1AD or O_3CF represent different specious presents, so the content apprehended as a

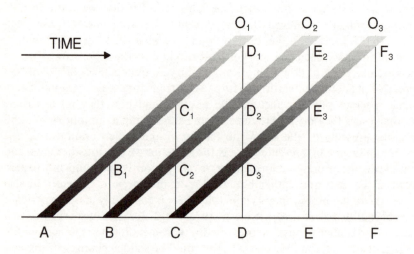

Figure 6.3 Temporal awareness: Broad's later view

temporally extended whole by O_1 stretches from A through to D. Contents earlier and later than A and D are not directly experienced by the subject at O_1, they can only be remembered or anticipated. The thick shaded line A-O_1 represents the gradually diminishing presentedness which this content possesses, with darker shading representing less presentedness. So for O_1, D is experienced as possessing maximum presentedness and A is experienced as possessing minimum presentedness – hence A occurs at the rearward boundary of the specious present, about to slip out of the span of immediate awareness altogether. O_2 and O_3 likewise apprehend extended stretches of content, varying in presentedness: B-E and C-F respectively.

The diagram shows how the same contents are apprehended as possessing different degrees of presentedness in successive specious presents which overlap in content. Look at D_1, D_2 and D_3. D_1 is the momentary content D as apprehended by O_1 possessing maximum presentedness; D_2 is how the same content is apprehended by O_2, possessing a lesser degree of presentedness, and D_3 is how D is apprehended by O_3, as possessing a still lesser degree of presentedness. The same applies to extended contents: C-D is apprehended by O_1 with presentedness ranging from C_1-D_1, by O_2 with presentedness ranging from C_2-D_2, and by O_3 with presentedness ranging from C-D_3 – at this stage the earliest parts of C-D are about to sink out of the specious present. Although a given content is sensed as a whole throughout some finite period of time, throughout this period it will be sensed as sinking continuously into the past.

6.4 Connectedness and presentedness

What are we to make of Broad's revised account? We can begin by noting the implications of the differences between this account and its predecessor. There are two main differences. Broad no longer believes momentary acts are mere fictions; he now takes the view that an extended stream of consciousness consists of a compact series of momentary acts. Then there is the property of presentedness which all contents are alleged to possess to a greater or lesser degree. In the earlier theory, numerically the same content is apprehended *in just the same way* at different positions within successive specious presents. So for example, in the sequence *Do-Re-Mi-Fa-So*, the phenomenal sound-content *Mi* is experienced first as occurring after *Do-Re*, and later experienced as occurring before *Fa-So*. It might be thought that when *Mi* is apprehended from these different temporal perspectives, it will possess different phenomenal characteristics. According to Broad's new account, this is the case: in the specious present [Do-Re-Mi], *Do* possesses close to the minimal degree of presentedness, whereas *Mi*'s presentedness is close to the maximum, while in the specious present [Mi-So-Fa], it is *Mi* that possesses minimal presentedness, and *Fa* that possesses maximal presentedness. As we experience contents from different temporal perspectives, the phenomeno-temporal character of the contents changes.

I will return to the significance of this shortly, but first note how these two modifications provide Broad with solutions to the problems which plagued his earlier theory. Recall the problem of 'ballooning contents'. In the earlier theory, any extended act contains shorter acts as proper parts, and these shorter acts apprehend (as wholes) longer stretches of content than do the longer acts of which they are parts. This may not be incoherent, but it is certainly peculiar, and not phenomenologically realistic. However, if all acts of awareness are momentary, as Broad now holds, this is no longer a difficulty. An extended period of awareness consists of a succession of momentary acts, each of which apprehends the same extent of content; a temporally extended content (shorter than a specious present) will appear in a succession of different acts, but it will appear to be of the same length in each; what changes is the degree of presentedness it possesses. Now recall the problem of repeated contents: successive acts apprehending numerically the same content, with the result that every content is experienced many times over. This problem is also solved, for according to the current theory, although a particular content such as Mi is apprehended by a succession of distinct acts, each act apprehends Mi as possessing a different, and gradually diminishing, degree of presentedness. Although every content is apprehended by uncountably many different acts, no content appears in two different acts under the same temporal mode of presentation. So we do not experience one and the same content repeated over and over; we experience a single content sinking smoothly into the past.

These gains come at a certain cost: a forced shift from realism to anti-realism. If a phenomenal tone Mi has different phenomenal characteristics when apprehended in different specious presents, it makes no sense to think that one and the same phenomenal object occurs in those specious presents. In the earlier theory, Broad held that Mi did not alter its phenomenal characteristics from specious present to specious present, but he now holds that that Mi would have different phenomenal characteristics in different specious presents: it varies in different degrees of presentedness. While this neatly avoids the repeated contents problem, it does make it difficult to see how it is one and the same phenomenal item that is being apprehended throughout this process of sensing. How could a Mi sensed in one specious present with maximum presentedness be numerically the same phenomenal object as a Mi sensed in a later specious present with near-minimal presentedness? Broad continues to talk as though numerically the same phenomenal items are apprehended in different specious presents, but it seems this cannot be.

Faced with this problem, one option is to loosen the individuation conditions for phenomenal contents. We could regard such contents as being akin to enduring physical objects. Just as one and the same house will appear larger or smaller depending upon the spatial distance it is viewed from, so one and the same phenomenal content will appear to possess more or less presentedness depending upon the temporal distance from which it is apprehended. There is a sense in which this revisionary move conforms with appearances. It is natural to describe Mi in successive specious presents as one and the same tone sinking into the past, for it will *seem* to us as though we are apprehending numerically the same tone from a succession of slightly different temporal perspectives – or at least this is what Broad's theory posits to be the case. But even as a revisionary proposal, this is of dubious intelligibility. Suppose that Mi is first apprehended at t_1 by act O_1 with maximal presentedness. Can we make sense of the idea that this phenomenal tone undergoes changes in presentedness over time? Can an item that exists at a certain time t_1 possess *at this time* different and incompatible properties? An item within a sense field, such as a red patch, can change over time; the patch could shrink or expand. We could view the expanding/shrinking patch as a phenomenal continuant, one and the same object possessing different properties at different times. But in supposing that when we apprehend Mi as possessing different degrees of presentedness we are apprehending one and the same tone-content, we are supposing that this content possesses different and incompatible intrinsic properties at the same time. This is impossible. We should conclude, I think, that as 'Mi' is apprehended by later acts O_2, O_3, etc., although it is apprehended as occurring at t_1, given that these acts apprehend 'Mi' as possessing different degrees of presentedness, they are not apprehensions of the same phenomenal item as was apprehended by O_1. But if O_2 is not an apprehension of the originally sensed Mi, what is it an apprehension of? There seems to be only one answer: some kind of *representation* of the originally sensed Mi, a representation which is simultaneous with O_2. (If this representation of Mi occurred simultaneously with the original Mi at t_1, then presumably both contents would be apprehended by O_1, which does not happen.) Instead of successive acts being apprehensions of numerically identical contents, successive acts must be apprehensions of representations of contents, with each representation being apprehended by only one act of awareness. It seems that, knowingly or not, Broad has adopted the second strategy for accommodating *PSA* we discerned earlier: the representational anti-realist strategy. In itself, this does not mean his theory is false, it just means it is not the kind of theory one might initially take it to be.

As an implementation of the representational anti-realist strategy, Broad's theory is not as fully worked-out as Husserl's, which I shall look at next. The theory bears obvious resemblance to the nested short-term memory account we considered in §5.3, and it shares the same drawback: a seemingly unrealistic degree of complexity. When I hear *Do-Re-Mi*, I cannot discern in my experience the complex of representations the theory posits. But since the problem of complexity is even more apparent in the context of Husserl's more fully developed account, I will not dwell further on it now. But I shall mention three points, two of which are also relevant to the Husserlian account.

Recall the remark of Broad's I quoted earlier: 'There is no doubt that sensible motion and rest are genuine unanalysable properties of visual sensa. I am aware of them as directly as I am aware of the redness of a red patch'. This seems true. It is a clear a statement of the phenomenological constraint. But would it be true if Broad's *McTaggart* theory were true? It seems not. For in moving to what is, in effect, a representational theory, Broad has given up the idea that we can be *directly* aware of change, or indeed of anything that has any temporal extent. The line A-F in the diagram represents a continuous stretch of content, and from the diagram it looks as though stretches of this content are apprehended by successive acts. However, when we construe Broad's theory in a representational vein, this is no longer the case. What is actually present to awareness is not the content in A-F, but the representations of past experience in the sloping shaded lines, i.e. A-O_1, B-O_2 and C-O_3. These momentary representations are the real contents of consciousness. True, the contents of these representations are stipulated to be present in experience in a way that contents which have passed out of a specious present are not. But it is nonetheless clear that Broad's later theory does not conform to the phenomenological constraint as fully as the earlier theory. So far as the latter is concerned, it is literally true that we are directly aware of sensible motion and rest, for immediate experience extends over time. According to the later theory, no change or duration can be experienced as *fully* present, since maximum presentedness is possessed only momentarily. This is phenomenologically suspect. Intuitively, there is a clear distinction between, on the one hand, seeing a movement, and on the other hand, remembering or imagining seeing a movement. Visual memories and imagined mental images are very different from visual experience itself. Broad himself recognizes this. Once contents have passed out of the specious present they are available to memory, while in the specious present they are not being remembered – though of course they may occur simultaneously with memory-images. However, since (with the exception of those occurring at the foremost boundary) the contents within a specious presence are not experienced as possessing immediate presence, or maximum presentedness, Broad is introducing a new type of experience that common sense does not recognize: a type that is intermediate between immediate experience, and remembered or imagined experience. Broad could reply (contrary to his earlier position) that we are just mistaken to think that when we see an object move, we are aware of the object's movement over time in the way we are aware of its colour or shape at any given moment. But is this right? The suspicion must be that since there are no solid phenomenological grounds for positing this unfamiliar type of experience, it is being introduced to satisfy some principle or other. Perhaps the principle in question is that only what is strictly instantaneous can be fully present in experience. As we have already seen, this principle is questionable.

Broad's shift to representationalism leads to a further problem. Given that the contents of two successive acts such as O_1 and O_2 are numerically distinct, what is it that connects these two experiences? It seems that there is no direct experiential connection at all. The two acts are qualitatively similar, in that both have in their total content a representation of B-D. This is represented in O_1 by B_1-D_1 and in O_2 by B-D_2. However, since these representations are numerically distinct, the two acts consist of wholly distinct experiences. The same applies to any successive acts which purportedly overlap in content. When interpreted in a representational manner, Broad's theory has the consequence that a stream of consciousness consists of a succession of wholly distinct experiences. The theory thus fails to satisfy the phenomenal binding constraint: the successive phases of a stream of consciousness are not, on this theory, bound together by experience itself. In fact, the problem runs deeper than this. As an act–object theorist, Broad holds that any experience consists of two elements: an act of awareness and a content. In considering the unity of consciousness through time, there are thus two strata to consider, that of acts and that of contents. Even if we were to allow that successive acts can have (in part) numerically the same content, we would only have accounted for the unity of consciousness at one level. What holds the successive acts together? Are they bound together in experience? It seems not: each act of awareness is wholly discrete from its neighbours. These acts overlap in content, but this is all: within a given act, there is no *awareness* of the neighbouring acts. Successive acts of awareness are not aware of each other; all they have in common is their content, to the extent that this overlaps. When we move to the representational construal of Broad's theory (which we must if the theory is to be coherent), then even this limited connection between successive acts evaporates. If Broad's theory were true, a stream of consciousness would consist of a sequence of isolated acts, each having no direct awareness of the adjoining acts. It seems, then, that the theory fails to accommodate the *experienced* unity of consciousness through time.

Let us take a closer look at the notion of presentedness, as it features in Broad's theory. We are told that as contents are apprehended as sliding into the past, they are also apprehended to possess a diminishing degree of presentedness. These two phenomena are not merely correlated: contents appear to be sliding pastwards *because* they are being apprehended as possessing ever-diminishing degrees of presentedness in successive specious presents. The question to consider here is whether variations in the strength of a phenomenal quality could have this effect. Since Broad does not elaborate on what presentedness is, we must consider the various possibilities. One option is simply to equate presentedness with phenomenal intensity. Phenomenal qualities of the same type can vary in intensity, or what Hume called 'force and vivacity'. A sound of a given timbre and pitch can be softer or louder. A patch of colour of a given size, shape and hue can differ in brilliance and/or saturation. Imagine a patch of intense green gradually becoming more translucent until there is no *green* there at all; or a pain becoming less and less intense until it has vanished altogether. But there is an obvious problem with the suggestion that different degrees of presentedness consist of different phenomenal intensities. Presentedness is how *time* is meant to manifest itself in experience. Take two contents, one with more presentedness than the other. The content possessing the lesser degree of presentedness will seem to occur *before* the content possessing the greater degree of presentedness. The difficulty here is that contents of the same type but of different intensity are often experienced together, simultaneously. Imagine looking at a colour chart showing a particular shade of blue varying in intensity, i.e. varying in saturation, or alternatively a combination of saturation and lightness or darkness. Suppose the variation is displayed in a continuous strip, the hue being most intense on the right and least intense on the left. Does the left side of the strip seem to be 'more past' than the right? Obviously not: we see the whole strip at once, and each part seems present in experience at the same time. The same holds of the other sense-modalities. We can hear loud and soft sounds of the same pitch and timbre simultaneously. We can feel several bodily sensations of the same type but varying intensities simultaneously. If differences in presentedness consisted in differences in 'force and vivacity', we would inevitably often be mistaken – or at least seriously confused – as to the temporal order of perceived happenings. But we are not. It is true that over very small intervals (different for different sense-modalities) we are unable to judge with any confidence or reliability which of two sensations occurs before the other, but under normal circumstances this is not the case. We must conclude that it would be a mistake to equate presentedness with Humean force and vivacity.

Since there are no other obvious alternatives, we seem obliged to conclude that presentedness is a *sui generis* phenomenal property. This property would be such that, first, simultaneously presented contents cannot possess different degrees of it; second, any two co-conscious contents which possess different degrees of it seem to be non-simultaneous; and third, the content with the lesser intensity appears to occur before the content with the greater intensity. But this proposal also seems flawed. As I noted earlier in connection with the idea that experiences possess a special quality of 'presence', when we hear a sound while seeing a colour, we are aware of the auditory and visual characteristics of these contents, but we are not aware of any additional phenomenal characteristic that is common to both. The same applies to other cases, e.g. touch and taste sensations. So the problem is that there just does not seem to be any such property. In response, it could be argued that there must be such a property, or else we would not be aware of contents fading into the past. Against this it could be responded that this 'fading into the past' is a postulate of Broad's theory rather than anything we find in experience itself.

6.5 Husserl on the 'consciousness of internal time'

By far the most sustained attempt to describe and understand temporal awareness in the literature is to be found in the various writings which resulted from Husserl's prolonged struggle with the topic.[3] Not surprisingly, given his phenomenological project, Husserl attached the greatest importance to this enterprise. Temporality is the most general characteristic of consciousness; consequently its elucidation is right at the centre of the phenomenological enterprise. However, it is also true that Husserl seems never to have settled on an account of the phenomenon that he could be entirely satisfied with. I will not attempt to summarize all his various positions, some of which I do not understand. What I will do is give a sketch of an account he toyed with at one period, an account which is in significant ways similar to Broad's, though in other ways interestingly different. Since this Husserlian account is also (arguably) an attempt to implement the representational anti-realist strategy, exploring it will put us in a better position to assess this strategy. I will conclude by briefly considering how Husserl later came to change his views.

The basic mechanics of Husserl's account are similar to that of the later Broad. A stream of consciousness consists of a compact succession of momentary experiences. Each of these momentary experiences contains a representation of the preceding stretch of the stream. As one momentary experience gives way to another, these representations change in a systematic manner, such that phenomenal items seem to occur in the immediate present and then sink into the past. However, unlike Broad, Husserl posits a clear distinction between present experience and the representations of recent experiences, which he calls 'retentions' (or sometimes 'primary memories'). Each momentary experience comprises a momentary *primal impression* and a simultaneously apprehended sequence of representations, the retentional modifications of preceding primal impressions. The primal impression is 'the source-point': it is here that all experience of temporally extended objects originates.

> Now within the impression we have to call special attention to the primal impression, over against which there stands the continuum of modifications in primary memorial consciousness. The primal impression is something absolutely unmodified, the primal source of all further consciousness and being. Primal impression has as its content that which the word 'now' signifies, insofar as it is taken in the strictest sense. Each new now is the content of a new primal impression. Ever new primal impressions continuously flash forth with ever new matter.
>
> (Husserl 1991: 70)

Being momentary, i.e. present in the strictest sense, each primal impression is immediately followed by another. But a primal impression does not vanish, it is retained and apprehended with the following primal impression, under the mode 'just past'. As this primal impression in turn gives way to another, the retention of the first primal impression undergoes a further modification: it is apprehended as having occurred slightly further back in time; as new primal impressions continue to occur, it sinks further into the past until it no longer features in retentional consciousness at all. All this is made clear in Husserl's 'diagram of time' (Figure 6.4), which is somewhat different from Broad's.[4]

Here, the central line C-G represents a continuum of primal impressions. F is the current primal impression. The descending verticals represent the continuum of retentions that accompany each primal impression. Primal impression D is retained at E as D_E, and apprehended along with the retention of the earlier primal impression C, which is denoted by C_E. D_F is the retention of D accompanying the current primal impression F. The downward movement of the retentions of D indicate the slippage into the past; the closer a retention is to the horizontal, the more recent it seems to be. At F, the primal impression D is apprehended as further back in the past than E, hence D_F is lower than E_F on the descending vertical; also at F, D is apprehended as being further back in the past than it was at E, hence D_F is further from the horizontal than D_E. Since between D and F there is a continuous series of other primal impressions not indicated on the diagram, the vertical F-D_F should be thought of as consisting of a continuum of retentions. Likewise for the other verticals. Each of these continuums of retentions is a representation of the immediately preceding stream of consciousness. The length of the vertical represents the duration of the specious present: that stretch of the past that is available (in some form) to current awareness.

It is not only momentary primal impressions that sink into the past; temporally extended wholes do so too. Suppose the interval D-E represents the experience of hearing the brief extended tone *Mi*. This experience consists at one level of a continuous sequence of primal tone-impressions, as represented by the horizontal line D-E. But in addition, accompanying each of these primal impressions, is a gradually growing 'comet's tail' of retentions: with each new primal impression, we are aware (in retentional consciousness) of a gradually increasing portion of the tone as past, until

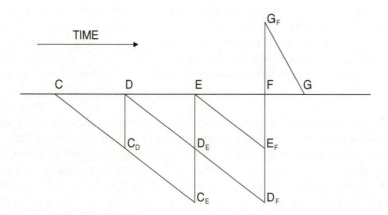

Figure 6.4 Husserl's diagram of time

finally, with the expiration of the final primal impression of the tone immediately after E, we are aware of the entire tone, as a whole, in our retentional consciousness. Now, as the moments pass, this whole tone continues to be apprehended as a whole. The series of verticals which can be imagined to fill the space between E-D_E and E_F-D_F represents the experience of this tone-content sliding into the past. After F, the experience of *Mi* is no longer retained as a whole; increasingly, only the most recent phases of *Mi* are retained, until none are. At this point, no part of *Mi* remains in 'impressional awareness'; the experience is now available only to memory.

With the exception of the emphasis on primal impressions, the similarities between Husserl's account and that of Broad are evident. But there is another difference I have not so far mentioned. Whereas Broad thought it would be paradoxical to suppose we could have any awareness of what still lies in the future, Husserl was more open-minded. In his later writings, he held that primal impressions are typically accompanied by short-term anticipations of *future* primal impressions. He called these 'protentions'. I have included in the diagram a vertical rising up from F, and F-G_F represents the protention of the interval F-G. Again, proximity to the horizontal indicates that contents are being apprehended, or 'protended', as occurring in closer proximity to the present. But now the direction is different: towards the future rather than the past. Retentions are importantly different from protentions. The contents of the former are determined by the primal impressions of which they are the retentions; the content of protentions is often more vague and need not correspond to the actual course of experience: 'The only thing determined is that something or other will come' (Husserl 1991: 111). This qualification is needed, since the course of our experience often takes surprising, and thus unanticipated, twists and turns. On the other hand, Husserl is right to point out that we are not surprised that our experience continues; at any moment we expect that *something* will come next, experientially. But since Husserl does not give great emphasis to the protentional aspect of experience, nor shall I.

Husserl recognized that we are continuously aware of the continuity of our experience. There are two aspects to this. First, the contents of our experience are continuous. This does not mean that we never perceive sudden changes, for of course we do. It means, rather, that while we are conscious, content is always passing through our awareness. The theory caters for this: a given content is retained as successively 'more past' through a continuous succession of acts of awareness. Second, we are aware not only of the flow of content through our awareness, but we are also aware that our awareness is itself continuous. We saw that Broad failed to recognize this: his acts had no awareness of their neighbours. Husserl does recognize the need to unify consciousness at the level of both contents and acts. Accordingly, he holds that retentions and protentions are not simply reproductions and anticipations of successions of past and future primary impressions. They are, rather, reproductions and anticipations of *entire past and future acts*, comprising past and future primary impressions together with their associated protentions and retentions. A particular primal impression becomes first a retention, then a retention of a retention, then a retention of a retention of a retention, and so on, at each successive stage being conjoined with a new primal impression together with new and intervening retentions and protentions (of differing degrees). But individual primal impressions are not retained all by themselves in successive acts; they are retained along with all the retentions and protentions that they were originally apprehended with. This *entire complex* undergoes successive modifications in the succeeding momentary experiences. As a result, we are aware at any given instant of not only our present perspective on a sensory object, but of our past perspectives on it as well – we are aware of how the object was apprehended by previous acts of awareness. Consciousness is thus unified over time at the level of acts as well as contents.

6.6 New words, old problems

So much for the bare bones of Husserl's theory; we can now take a more critical look at it. To start with, recall the objections lodged against Broad. We have just seen how Husserl avoids one of these, but there are two others to consider:

(a) Broad's theory has the consequence that awareness of change cannot be as immediate as the awareness of simultaneity.
(b) How can different intensities of 'presentedness', a phenomenal quality possessed by contents *present* in awareness, give rise to the impression that these contents occurred in the past?

Husserl's criticisms of Brentano's theory of temporal experience shows him to be alert to both these problems. Brentano, at least as Husserl interprets him, held a theory somewhat similar to Broad's. A sensation S occurs, and then ceases; but in occurring, S triggers off the automatic production of a series of representations of itself, a process Brentano called 'original association'. These representations are joined to succeeding current sensations, but in a constantly modified fashion: to each successive representation of S is added a different 'temporal determination', the upshot of which is to make it seem that S occurred at a successively greater remove from the present. Husserl lodges several objections against this account, of which two are particularly pertinent. First, he claims Brentano does not allow for the distinction between directly experiencing change, and merely imagining or remembering it. This is because he locates our immediate experience of change in the realm of imagination-like 'phantasy' representations, rather than in its proper place, our immediate experience. This is similar to objection (a). Second, he asks: how can the representations of S produced by original association give rise to the impression that S is in the past rather than in the present, since the representations are always apprehended as simultaneous with present experience? How could any *qualitative* character-istic belonging to an item presently occurring in consciousness result in our experiencing this item as occurring in the past rather than the present? In response to the reply that the characteristic in question is a 'sign' of the past, Husserl is scathing: 'But this only provides us with a new word', it leaves unexplained how 'a consciousness that is supposed to be now comes to be related to a new-now' (1991: 19). This is similar to objection (b). Given that Husserl was clearly aware of the force of these objections, it is odd to find that his own theory seems vulnerable to them both.

Consider objection (a). Husserl holds that our immediate consciousness of time involves two different kinds of experience: primal impressions and retentions (protentions are similar). Primal impressions are obviously intro-duced in response to the obvious phenomenological difference between immediate and represented experience – remembering or imagining hearing a tone are not the same as directly experiencing the tone. However, whatever direct awareness we have of phenomenal duration and continuity is located in the retentional matrix, rather than at the level of primal impression. Since primal impressions are momentary, there can be no awareness of change or continuity here, for the familiar reason that a succession of impressions is distinct from an impression of succession. As a consequence, Husserl seems to be committed to denying that we are as directly aware of change as we are of colour (which presumably can be apprehended at the level of primal impression), a denial which is phenomenologically suspect.

Now consider objection (b). The retentions of a tone-phase P exist in experiences which occur after P has occurred (after the primal impression of P). Recalling Husserl's criticism of Brentano, how can these retentions present P as being in the past? Husserl's answer: retentions are a quite distinctive type of experiential phenomenon. They are distinct from both 'raw' sensation, in the form of primary impressions, and memory-images and 'phantasms', the products of the imagination. Unlike primary impres-sions, their content is 'intended' or perceived to be past. Unlike memory and imaginings, their content is distinctively real and (in a manner of speaking) present, rather than past or unreal. Retentions *present* the past, memory *re-presents* it. That is, retentions provide us with access to the just-past in our current experience. The past in retentional consciousness is the past directly experienced, the past present in current experience, to the extent that it can be. Memory also furnishes us with contents that occur in current experience, but these contents are presented precisely as having occurred at some other time. Retention generates the original experience of contents occurring and sinking into the past that later memories provide representations of.

This is all well and good, but remembering Husserl's comment on Brentano's theory, we need to ask: to what extent is this explanation merely verbal rather than real? Husserl is *stipulating* that retentions have precisely the properties they need to have for his purposes. Although they occur in the present, they directly intend the immediate past, the past and nothing else.

But how is this possible? 'Memory – and this is equally true of retention – is not image-consciousness; it is something totally different' (Husserl 1991: 36). Husserl tells us what retention is not, and what it does, but provides no explanation as to how it accomplishes this. The Husserlian *concept* of retention is manifestly superior to Broad's concept of presentedness, in that by definition it does not suffer from the latter's deficiencies. But this is not enough. Husserl gives us a 'new word', but nothing more.[5]

This point aside, let us pose a more direct question: is it possible to detect in our own experience the postulated complexes of retentions, primal impression and protentions performing their intricate dance? It is by no means obvious that we can. There are two main problems here: *lingering contents* and the *clogging of consciousness*. Let us start with the lingering contents.

When I see one object eclipse another, as occurs, for example, when I move my hand over the words on this page, the eclipsed object simply disappears from view; the words vanish without trace beneath my hand. Where are the retentions? For a few seconds after the words have disappeared from view I can, if I wish, call up a vivid mental image of them. This image has more detail than the one I can call up after more time has elapsed, but it is nonetheless a perfectly ordinary mental image; qualitatively it is just like any other memory. The same applies in the auditory sphere. If I snap my fingers, I hear the sound of the snap and it is gone. The snap-sound does not linger on in my immediate experience. There may be a faint echo of the snap that lingers on – this depends on the acoustic properties of the environment – but the echo is itself a sound that I am directly experiencing. This is not at all what the theory of retentions leads us to expect.

This problem is most clearly apparent in the case of sudden qualitative transitions, but there is no reason to suppose contents ever move through consciousness in a different way. When I let my eyes sweep round the room, I do have an impression of past contents lingering. But this is explicable without recourse to Husserlian retentions. When I look slowly round the room, I continue to be aware of mostly the same objects; what can be seen at one instant overlaps to a large extent with what can be seen an instant later. This is due solely to the width of my visual field. If I turn my head to the right I will eventually lose sight of the coffee cup to my left. But I do not experience the cup *fading into the past*, rather I experience it moving to the left, towards the periphery of my visual field, until it finally moves out of view. When I lose sight of the cup, I do so completely and all at once. The only 'fading' that occurs is due to the blurring of perception at the peripheries of the visual field. But even the indistinct perception of the cup, as it lingers in my peripheral vision, is completely present. Those with tunnel vision will not have the same impression of contents remaining in consciousness: when they turn their heads what they see will change too quickly. To drive this point fully home, try looking round the room but shutting your eyes while doing so. The moment your eyes close, you will of course stop seeing your surroundings immediately. You may, however, experience something else: an afterimage – a pattern of colour corresponding approximately with what you last saw. But once again, this is in no way the retention, in the Husserlian sense, of a previous primary experience. An afterimage only represents its preceding experience in the vaguest of ways and is itself directly experienced. According to Husserl (and Broad), momentary experiences enjoy their moment of full consciousness, then slip away, becoming less and less present before finally fading altogether – only then, after they have left direct awareness altogether, can they appear in the guise of ordinary memory. This does not seem to happen. Contents depart from immediate experience cleanly, leaving no residue, and become immediately accessible to memory.

The lingering contents objection is of an almost embarrassing naivety, given the sophistication of the theories under discussion, but it is certainly serious. In response, it could be argued that we fail to notice items such as sharp snapping noises lingering on because they are retained for such a short period of time. (Broad could argue that the drop between contents possessing maximum and minimum presentedness occurs very quickly.) But this response is open to an obvious objection: if retentions are so short-lived that they cannot be noticed, why posit them in the first place?

Let us move on to the 'clogging' problem. While discussing Broad, I suggested that while ingenious, his account possessed a phenomenologically unrealistic degree of complexity, similar to that which afflicted the nested short-term memory theory we considered at the outset. This difficulty is far more apparent in the case of Husserl's theory. Whereas Broad supposed only that preceding stretches of phenomenal content were reproduced (always differently) in successive apprehensions, Husserl goes a step further. We retain not only past primal impressions, but our preceding total states of awareness. The latter include not only retentions of the primal impressions which preceded them, but the total states of awareness and their retentional complexes, with these retentions themselves containing retentions of previous total acts and their retentions, and so on. This extra complexity is needed to accommodate the fact that we are *aware* of the continuity of our experience, something Broad's less complex theory failed to accommodate. However, while Husserl successfully plugs this hole, the cost is phenomenological inadequacy of a different kind. A diagram makes the problem clear (Figure 6.5).

On the left of the diagram is a depiction of a short stretch of a stream of consciousness. The line representing primary impressions can be thought of as continuing in either direction (so before D there are A, B and C). As before, the descending vertical F-D_F represents the continuum of retentions that are apprehended simultaneously with the primal impression F. On this line, E_F represents the retention of both the primal impression E and *its* associated continuum of retentions, which will stretch back from E as far as C. This is indicated by the line to the right, E-C. Now, this collection of retentions itself consists of retentions of not only previously occurring primal impressions, but the retentions associated with these. The horizontal

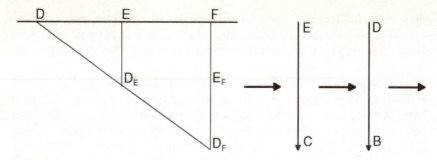

Figure 6.5 A continuum of continua

arrow to the right of this line is pointing to one such retention: that of D. But this retention also comprises a whole continuum of retentions as well as a primal impression D itself. These retentions will stretch from D back to B, as indicated by the next arrow. And so it goes on. To simplify matters, I have not included any protentions in the diagram. So the real situation is rather more complex still.

Commenting on this theory of Husserl's in his translator's introduction, Brough notes 'Obviously, the individual perceptual phase will become quite cluttered'. This is nicely understated: a consciousness which contained this degree of internal complexity would be clogged with different contents to a nightmarish degree. It is manifestly obvious that in the perception of a simple tone, our consciousness is remarkably *clear*: all we are aware of is the tone itself as an enduring auditory item. Husserl was himself aware of the problem:

> Infinities and infinitely many times are encased in one another here. The actually present now encloses memorially a continuum of the past. The new now includes this continuity of memory again, and each subsequent new now includes a new memorial continuum, etc: and this goes on perpetually. We have a continuum of continua, and each attached continuum is different from every other one: The memory of a memory is never identical with a memory pure and simple. Is that not an absurdity? A continuity that includes other continua, even infinitely many continua, is possible.
>
> (1991: 341)

He suggests that retentional modification is of such a nature that 'it is precisely the *essence of this kind of modification not* to allow this infinite regress to arise' (1991: 344), that as the continua arise they 'blend into one another' (*ibid.*), in such a way that they cannot be distinguished from one another. Although Husserl does not elaborate as to how this blending comes about, let us suppose it does. His position is now open, once more, to the objection that his retentional complexes have no phenomenological reality; if they cannot be discerned in experience, why posit them? The account Husserl provides of the most elemental feature of consciousness is a purely theoretical construction going far beyond the phenomenological data. The theory seeks to explain how our experience is possible, but it does so by appealing to forms of experience which do not seem to exist.

6.7 Husserl's change of view

In fairness, it should be pointed out that I have been considering a theory (or rather an interpretation of it) which Husserl himself was unhappy with, in part at least for the reasons we have been considering. In subsequent writings, Husserl came to recognize a different aspect of temporal awareness, which he calls 'absolute time consciousness', or 'the absolute, temporally constitutive flux of consciousness', which he believed to be of fundamental importance. Unfortunately, what he says on this topic is often very obscure.

The idea is something like this. Husserl believed that within the flow of a single stream of consciousness two distinct series of unifications can be discerned, one at the level of phenomenal contents, the other at the level of awareness itself. As we saw in connection with Broad, an act–object theorist has to explain how we have an awareness of the continuity of our own awareness. One option, as we have just seen in connection with Husserl, is to say that later acts retain not only recently elapsed primal impressions, but the complete contents of recently elapsed acts. Husserl came to see another option. Adjacent acts of awareness are retained all by themselves, as pure awarenesses. In addition to an awareness of the sensory contents passing through our awareness, we have an unsullied awareness of the continuity of pure awareness. Husserl calls this new stratum of *absolute* time-consciousness the 'primordial time constituting flux'. Presumably, this is because the existence of this temporally unified awareness is a precondition of anything else being presented in consciousness, for example thoughts and sensory objects. As he saw it, the temporal unity of awareness itself is produced internally, as a necessary adjunct of the awareness of temporal contents. There is no higher-level awareness involved: our consciousness of the temporality of pure awareness is produced by successive acts of awareness being bound together in the protentional-retentional matrix. Husserl finds this remarkable, even 'shocking' (1991: 390), because within the context of his general system, other forms of 'synthesis' are produced by distinct acts of 'constitution'. If this were the case for time-perception, an infinite regression would ensue: given that all forms of consciousness are temporal, if the awareness of the continuity of awareness depended on some further act of awareness, the latter would also be temporal, which would require the positing of a further level of acts, and so on. Husserl's analysis accounts for why the flux of temporal awareness is an exception to his general model of the nature of consciousness.

One of the peculiarities of Husserl's treatment of this topic is that after arguing that we are aware of the succession of our acts of awareness, he goes on to say that we cannot describe this awareness – 'for all this we have no names' (1991: 382). Although we naturally describe the absolute time-consciousness in terms of flow, flux and succession, these are only metaphors; such terms are not literally applicable to absolute time-consciousness. His reasoning seems to be that our ordinary vocabulary for describing temporal phenomena can legitimately be applied to things that appear in time, such as persisting tones or perceived movements. The absolute flux is not a thing that appears in time; rather, it consists of acts of awareness retaining and protending other acts of awareness; since acts of awareness are not things which appear before awareness, they are not things which appear in time, and hence our ordinary temporal vocabulary cannot be applied to them.

How does the introduction of the absolute flow change Husserl's overall account of time-consciousness? It is not at all clear. At the very least, the clogging problem is reduced. Although previous acts are retained, along with just-elapsed primary impressions, the previous acts are retained only as acts of awareness. The retentions (and protentions) that constitute the content of previous acts are not retained in later acts. Even with this modification, all the problems with the notion of retention remain. However, on one interpretation, Brough's, the introduction of the absolute flow is accompanied by a more radical simplification of Husserl's overall account: he abandons his earlier notion of retention. Such a move would not be altogether surprising, since (as we saw earlier) Husserl was himself acutely aware of the problems facing Brentano's theory, to which his own bore a surprisingly close similarity. Since I find the relevant Husserlian writings obscure, I shall quote Brough himself:

> There are no contents on the level of the absolute consciousness. All contents have been expelled from it and deposited on the level of the immanent temporal objects that the flow constitutes. Each of the flow's phases is purely and simply consciousness of the immanent object in immanent time. Retention, therefore, is not constituted by memorial apprehension animating a content somehow present in the actual phase of the absolute flow. Retention is just the direct and immediate consciousness of what is past as it elapses: It 'really contains consciousness of the past of the tone' (324) and nothing else. As pure – or, perhaps better, 'sheer' intentionality, the momentary phase is no longer bloated with apprehension- and content-continua. It therefore escapes the objection that it now really contains what it is supposed to be consciousness of as past or future. On Husserl's mature reading, the absolute flow in each of its phases 'contains' nothing but the impressional consciousness of the past, present, and future phases of the immanent temporal objects it constitutes.
>
> (Husserl 1991: L–LI)

On the upper level, there is the absolute flux (which cannot be described); on the lower level, there are temporally extended contents which are directly apprehended by the awareness at the upper level. If this is right, then Husserl seems to have moved from a representational anti-realism to a full-blown realism. Given the problems and implausibilities with this form of anti-realism, this change of position is readily comprehensible. Unfortunately, since Husserl nowhere elaborates in any detail or with any clarity how at a given moment we can be directly aware of past and future phases of our experience, our positive understanding of time-consciousness could scarcely be said to have advanced.

7   The overlap model

7.1 Foster on the time within experience

If our look at the views of Broad and Husserl has made anything plain, it is that anti-realist accounts of phenomenal temporality face severe problems. This suggests we should take another look at the prospects for a viable account along realist lines.

The only realist theory we have looked at in any detail so far is Broad's early effort. This was, in effect, an attempt to accommodate realism with *PSA*. As noted earlier, *PSA* seems to demand an act–object model of experiencing: how else can the constituent parts of a temporal spread of content be present to awareness at the same time? We saw that Broad's account ran into difficulties; in particular, there was a difficulty with non-existent repetitions: since successive acts apprehend numerically the same contents, the same contents will be experienced many times over. In his *McTaggart* theory Broad tried to avoid this problem by adopting (in effect) a form of representationalism. According to this theory, the sound of a finger-snap is reproduced in the content of successive awarenesses, but never in the same way, always with different degrees of presentedness. But now the repetition problem merely resurfaces in a different form: recall the 'lingering contents' that trouble both Broad's representationalism and that of Husserl. However, when discussing Broad's earlier theory I noted that a solution of a different sort seemed to be available, in principle at least, although Broad did not avail himself of it. The problem of repeated contents arises when we suppose that numerically the same content is apprehended by discrete numerically distinct acts of awareness. If, however, these acts were not discrete, but overlapped each other, the otherwise multiply experienced content would be experienced only once. Although a number of writers have mentioned this idea, the clearest (though regrettably succinct) discussion is to be found in John Foster's various writings on temporal experience.[1]

Foster suggests two reasons for supposing that there are temporal objects and relations in the contents of our experience. The first is empirical: 'duration and change through time seem to be presented to us with the same phenomenal immediacy as homogeneity and variation of colour through space' (1982: 255). The second is conceptual:

> Just as it is inconceivable that there should be a sensation of colour which was not the sensation of a colour-pervaded region, so, equally, it is inconceivable that there should be a sensation of sound which was not the sensation of a sound-filled period.

> (1982: 256)

Foster operates with an act–object model (or at least he seems to initially), and he begins by distinguishing two types of temporal relations, *phenomenal* and *presentational*, one for acts and one for their objects. A 'presentational act' is a particular subject's momentary awareness of a phenomenal object. Particular acts of awareness occur in presentational time, whereas the contents or objects of acts are distributed through phenomenal time. He takes a 'phenomenal object' to be a universal, a pattern of phenomenal qualities that can be apprehended by different subjects at different times. Suppose I hear the rapid sequence of notes *Do-Re-Mi*, and I am directly aware of the entire succession. So far as my consciousness is concerned, *Do-Re-Mi* is a realization of phenomenal qualities that instantiate a particular temporal pattern or organization, in this case auditory succession. Foster suggests that just as phenomenal visual qualities require a phenomenal space in which to occur, the visual field, auditory qualities require a phenomenal time, or *time-field* in which to occur. Of course, it is not only auditory qualities which can be spread through phenomenal time: three quick flashes of different coloured light, sensed as a succession, will also inhabit (or create) a phenomenal time. Once we recognize a temporality that is intrinsic to phenomenal contents, we can – at least in principle – distinguish this time from the time at which these contents are sensed, i.e. presentational time. In brief, phenomenal time is the time *in* experience, presentational time is the time *of* experience. These distinctions drawn, Foster considers how phenomenal and presentational time fit together.

He considers a simple example: the experience corresponding to hearing someone play the C major scale, with no gaps between the notes. Suppose that the scale is played at a speed such that at most three consecutive notes can be directly experienced as a succession; these are complete or total auditory experiences, i.e. single auditory experiences which are not parts of larger auditory experiences. As I hear the scale progress, I am aware of a series of total auditory experiences. Each of these experiences will be an awareness of a content which consists of a temporal pattern of auditory qualities. For instance, the first of these, call it E_1, might be an awareness of the content $P_1 = $ [2 *units of silence before 1 unit of C*], the second, E_2, the content $P_2 = $ [*1 unit of silence before 1 unit of C before 1 unit of D*], the third, E_3 is the awareness of $P_3 = $ [*1 unit of C before 1 unit of D before 1 unit of E*], and so on. (The supposition that there are no other experiences between these is a deliberate oversimplification.) It will be noted that the content of each of these experiences overlaps with that of its immediate neighbours. The content *1 unit of C* is found in all three; the content *1 unit of silence before 1 unit of C* is common to both E_1 and E_2, the content *one unit of C before 1 unit of D* is common to E_2 and E_3, and so forth. This is odd, because it follows that, for example, each content of 1 unit will be heard three times, and each content of 2 units will be heard twice. But surely in hearing the C major scale, we hear each note only once. The situation might well be worse, for if acts of awareness are momentary and awareness is continuous, then between any two acts there may be an infinity of others, so any content will be apprehended an infinity of times. Since phenomenal contents are universals, this repetition is not logically impossible, but it does not correspond with the character of our experience. This, of course, is the now-familiar problem of repeated contents. Foster resolves the problem thus:

> The resolution of this paradox is the key to sensible continuity. The point is that where the temporal patterns presented by successive total presentations overlap in quality, in that some last portion of the first is the same as some first portion of the second, the two total presentations overlap in a corresponding way, in that the component presentations which in their respective totals present this common sub-pattern are themselves numerically identical. In other words, a presentation of a temporal pattern is itself temporally extended, and it overlaps its predecessor and successor in, so to speak, presentational substance to the extent that its pattern overlaps theirs in phenomenal content. It is this double overlap which provides the sensible continuity of sense experience and unifies presentations into a stream of awareness.
>
> (1979: 176)

As a consequence of this double overlap, what Foster calls phenomenal and presentational time are locked together. Take E_1 and E_2. The contents of these experiences overlap by two thirds. So do the experiences themselves: the final two thirds of E_1 are numerically identical with the first two thirds of E_2. To put it another way, the act of awareness whose content is P_1 and the act of awareness whose content is P_2 share a common part, these acts overlap by two thirds. Similarly, since P_1 and P_3 are contents which overlap by one third, the awareness of P_1 overlaps with the awareness of P_3 by precisely one third.

Not only do acts of awareness overlap to an extent proportional to the overlap in their contents, the temporal duration of acts is directly proportional to that of their contents. Note D is not experienced by E_1. So clearly, since the final two thirds of E_1 are identical with the first two thirds of E_2, D could only be experienced in the final third of E_2. Similarly, the initial period of silence is not experienced in E_2. Since the final two thirds of E_1 is identical with the first two thirds of E_2, the first period of silence must be experienced in the first third of E_1, and the second period of silence followed by C must be experienced in the final two thirds of E_1.

Since both acts and their contents endure through time, and endure through exactly proportional periods of their respective times, what reason is there to continue talking of *two* distinct times here? Why not suppose that phenomenal and presentational time are one and the same? This seems to be an entirely natural assumption to make. Once this identification is made, we can take the further step of inserting the unified mental time into ordinary objective time. This is the move Foster makes:

> we have to take each experience to extend over a period of real time in a way which exactly matches the phenomenal period it presents ... the sense in which E_1 precedes E_2, and E_2 precedes E_3, is not that E_1, E_2 and E_3 occur at successive real moments, but that they occupy successive, but largely overlapping, real periods.
>
> (1991: 249)[2]

This is an elegant solution to the problem of repeated contents. It has other advantages too. It posits none of the complexity that made representational accounts so implausible. It is robustly realist: not only do we have a direct experience of temporal relations and temporally extended phenomena, but successive phases of a stream are welded together by nothing other than direct experience. The account thus satisfies both the phenomenological constraint – we experience movement and persistence with the same immediacy as colour – and the binding principle: there is a directly experienced transition between any two adjacent phases of a stream of consciousness. Moreover, in Broad's early theory, the temporal relationship between acts of awareness and their temporally extended contents is problematic. Foster removes the mystery from this relationship. Finally, we have seen how Husserl wrestled with what he called the 'double intentionality' of consciousness, the necessity, as he saw it, of our awareness being unified at two distinct levels, that of content and that of awareness itself. To solve the problem he introduced the obscure notion of the absolute flux. Foster accomplishes the task in a much clearer way: successive acts of awareness overlap both in content and in substance (as he puts it), i.e. successive acts share a common part.

There is a sense in which Foster's account is not what it first seems to be. He starts off from a position which is apparently similar to that of Broad, with individual momentary acts apprehending temporally patterned presentations. This is precisely what is required by *PSA*. The repeated contents problem then leads him to the view that successive acts of awareness overlap to the same extent as their contents. But how can *momentary* acts overlap? A momentary act has no temporal duration, and only temporal durations (or intervals) can overlap. Two momentary acts could no more share a common part than two geometrical points. It seems that if we take strictly momentary acts as our primitive experiential units, the overlap theory seems incoherent. But the problem here is superficial. For of course Foster's conclusion is precisely that awareness is *not* packaged into momentary acts. The idea that acts of awareness are momentary is one that has had to be given up in order to resolve the problem of repeated contents. To make sense of the character of our experience, we have been forced to adopt the view that acts of awareness and their contents exactly coincide in time; they run concurrently.[3] This is the doctrine enshrined in the Principle of Presentational Concurrence, *PPC*. So in the course of reasoning which leads Foster to the overlap theory, he begins by (in effect) assuming *PSA*, and he concludes by endorsing *PPC*.

PSA has seemed to many a compelling principle. But the overlap theory seems, at first view at any rate, to be such an improvement on the available alternatives – theories that are based on the adoption of *PSA* – that it looks as though the principle should be discarded. I shall consider the ramifications of this in due course. But I want first to draw attention to another consequence of the overlap theory.

PSA presupposes or requires the act–object conception of experience. If we give up *PSA*, we may no longer require the act–object conception to make sense of temporal experience. In fact, since the overlap theory turns out to conform to *PPC*, it is clear that the posited acts of awareness are doing no work whatsoever in explaining *temporal* awareness. Specifically, we no longer need to posit acts whose contents last longer than the acts themselves, contents which are apprehended together at a single moment in time. Since, according to the overlap theory, acts are themselves temporally extended and exactly coincide with their contents in temporal extent, nothing would be lost by, as it were, allowing the acts to sink into their contents, integrating awareness with content, in accord with the Simple Conception of experience. Since I have already argued against the act–object (awareness–content) model while discussing the synchronic unity in experience, if it turns out that the model is not required to explain diachronic unity either, these earlier arguments against the model will stand. For this reason, as I move on to explore the overlap theory in more detail, I will adopt the Simple Conception and no longer talk in terms of acts and their contents. Instead of a dual-level act/object overlap theory, I will discuss a one-level, Simple overlap theory. Consequently, although I shall still refer to *PPC*, the latter principle should no longer be taken to imply the validity of the act–object model.

Having taken this step, it is now clear that in the context of the overlap theory, the same basic relationship of co-consciousness is responsible for the unity of consciousness both at and over time. Moreover, it is plain that although only brief and adjoining phases of a stream are co-conscious, co-consciousness is also responsible for the unity of a stream as a whole. Co-streamal experiences separated by more than the duration of the specious present are not directly co-conscious, but they are co-conscious with an intervening succession of overlapping specious presents, which themselves are linked by co-consciousness (e.g. E_1-E_2-E_3-E_4-E_5-E_6). In short, any two experiences within a stream are either directly co-conscious, or related by the ancestral of this relation, *indirect* co-consciousness. Or to put it another way, any collection of experiences linked by direct or indirect co-consciousness constitutes an uninterrupted stream of consciousness.

7.2 Innocent curiosities

The overlap theory may provide an attractively simple and homogeneous account of the unity of consciousness through time, but when looked at more closely it has implications that are intriguing, and which might even seem problematic.

One such concerns the number of different total experiences a single experience may be a part of. Assuming the temporal span of immediate experience is constant, the briefer an experience is, the greater the number of total experiences to which it can belong. Any content which is nearly as long as the specious present will not be included as a whole in very many total experiences; whereas an experience which is much shorter than the span of the specious present will feature in a large number of different total experiences. For example, consider a total experience E_1 divided into three equally sized parts: two units of *Do* and one unit of *Re*. One unit of time later, there is a second experience E_2 which consists of one unit of *Do*, one unit of *Re* and one unit of silence (let us suppose). One unit later, there is E_3 which consists of one unit of *Re* and two units of silence. The comparatively brief *Re* is thus a part of three successive total experiences, whereas the longer *Do* is a part of only one, in that the two units of *Do* are only experienced together in E_1; by the time E_2 occurs, the first half of *Do* has already passed out of the scope of immediate experience.

This may seem counterintuitive, for it does not seem that short contents, such as *Re* in the example, are experienced more than once, or more often than longer contents. But of course, this is just the repeated contents problem once again, to which the overlap theory provides a simple solution. Although the short content *Re* is a part of three experiences, whereas the longer *Do* is a part of only one, *Re* is only experienced once, since the relevant total experiences overlap. Shorter contents can be experienced with a greater variety of other contents, but this is simply because shorter contents occupy less of the limited span of direct experience than longer contents. Look again at the example: *Re* is co-conscious with both a preceding unit of *Do* and a succeeding unit of silence, whereas the two-unit *Do* is co-conscious only with the one unit *Re*. There is nothing surprising here; it is what one would expect to find.

A second point of interest, and of greater significance, concerns transitivity. Returning to our simple example, *Do* is co-conscious with *Re*, and *Re* is co-conscious with *Mi*, but *Do* is not co-conscious with *Mi*. If the overlap theory is true, diachronic co-consciousness is clearly not transitive.[4] Since it is plain that experiences at one end of a long stream of consciousness are not (directly) co-conscious with those at the other, transitivity must break down somewhere along the line; introspection suggests it breaks down over relatively short periods. Is this not a problem, given the apparent incomprehensibility of non-transitive synchronic co-consciousness?

I suggested in §4.5 that when simultaneous experiences are co-conscious they are maximally connected, and so simply too close, in a metaphorical manner of speaking, for transitivity to fail. The problem is, precisely the same considerations might be thought to ensure that diachronic co-consciousness cannot fail to be transitive. *Do-Re* is a temporally extended total experience, the parts of which are all mutually co-conscious; since the same applies to *Re-Mi*, both these extended totals are maximally connected wholes. In the synchronic case it seems inconceivable that two maximally connected phenomenal wholes, W_1 and W_2, could be only partly co-conscious: if any part of W_2 is co-conscious with any part of W_1, then every part of W_2 is co-conscious with every part of W_1, and vice-versa. If the same were to apply in the diachronic case, then every part of *Do-Re* would be co-conscious with every part of *Re-Mi*, since these two phenomenal wholes overlap. However, by hypothesis *Do* is not co-conscious with *Mi*. As a consequence, the principle that any two maximally connected phenomenal wholes that are co-conscious at all are fully co-conscious is not universally valid; at best it applies only to the synchronic case, where the relevant wholes are simultaneous. That co-consciousness is only transitive over short distances of time is a phenomenological fact that simply has to be accepted.

It may seem that in accepting this fact the case for synchronic transitivity is seriously undermined, and in one respect it is. If we want to say that synchronic and diachronic co-consciousness are two manifestations of the same relationship, and there is every reason to suppose this is the case, then clearly co-consciousness is not, by its very nature, transitive. At most it is transitive over short intervals. However, although this means that we cannot appeal to the nature of co-consciousness in arguing for synchronic transitivity, the case for the latter is supported by the fact that breakdowns in transitivity are closely linked, and quite possibly essentially linked, to the way temporality is manifest in experience.

Experiences occurring at different times are separated in a way that experiences occurring at the same time are not. Synchronically co-conscious contents may be spatially separated, but they are nonetheless wholly and completely *present together*. Temporal separation is characterized precisely by the absence of this mode of co-presence: neither past nor future experiences occurring outside the current specious present are co-conscious with present experience. If we try to imagine a being whose experience takes the form of a continuous stream of consciousness, every part of which is fully co-conscious with every other part, we fail; at best, all we succeed in imagining is an array of simultaneous experiences. Even if we stipulate that this array is spread through some duration of time, for example twelve hours or twelve centuries or clock time, a being whose experience took this form would not be aware of phenomenal contents passing through a phenomenal present of short duration. Unlike the static representation of time as a sequence of moments spread along a line, the phenomenal present is characterized by the absence (in immediate experience) of both past and future. Past and future experiences would not be absent in this manner if they were co-conscious. Consequently, if a being of this sort could exist, its experience would not exhibit the range of temporal characteristics with which we are familiar.

So far as co-consciousness is concerned, this suggests (even if it does not prove) that failure of transitivity is essentially bound up with the way we experience time. And if this is right, it is scarcely surprising that we have so much difficulty in comprehending how synchronic co-consciousness could fail to be transitive. If breakdowns in transitivity create the relationships between experiences that are characteristic of temporal separation, how could co-consciousness among simultaneous experiences fail to be transitive?

I will be saying more about these matters shortly, when I consider whether the overlap model can do full justice to another feature of phenomenal temporality: experienced passage. But first there are questions of a different sort to be considered.

7.3 Durations and thresholds

Thus far we have been working with unrealistically simple examples. We have been focusing our attention on just one series of experiences within a single sensory modality – I will return to this point shortly. But our examples have been oversimplifications in another respect. We have only considered the relationship between extended total experiences that are separated by fixed intervals of time. In Foster's example, E_1 and E_2 are separated by one unit of time. This provided a convenient simplification, but does not correspond with the facts: between E_1 and E_2 there would be many other total experiences, for example those occurring at intervals of one half or one quarter units. These will have their own particular contents, for example the experience occurring half a unit after E_1 will have as its content [*one and a half units of Do followed by one unit of Re followed by half a unit of silence*]. Since these intervening experiences overlap, there is no problem with repeated contents, but their existence does raise the question of just how many total experiences occur between any two total experiences which overlap. If total experiences occur in dense successions, then between any pair of them, no matter how close together, there will always be another that is distinct from either. In which case, there will always be an infinity of total experiences between any two, with the consequence that no total experience has an immediate successor.

This strikes me as highly implausible. Take the succession [Do-Re-Mi], where each note is followed immediately by the next (no gaps) and each note is of equal duration. We will assume that the span of immediate experience is two notes long. One total experience, call it E, is centred on the note *Re*. The content of this experience is [one half of *Do*, *Re*, one half of *Mi*]. The very first total experience that occurs is [Do-Re] and the last is [Re-Mi]. Call these E− and E+ respectively. If total experiences were densely ordered, on either side of E there would be an infinite number of distinct total experiences, an infinite number between both E− and E, and between E and E+. If this were the case, the single tone *Do* would comprise an infinite number of distinct phenomenal tone-phases (likewise, of course, for *Re* and *Mi*). This is hard to believe. Can we really distinguish, in introspection, an infinite number of distinct phases of a single short tone, or a perceived movement? Is there any introspective evidence that we can distinguish even a hundred? Physicists currently believe that intervals of time below the Planck duration of 10^{-43} seconds have no physical significance – is it likely that such intervals have any phenomenological significance?

There are also empirical considerations of a more mundane sort, the results of psychological research into time perception. There are three pertinent results. First, when subjects are presented with two stimuli in quick succession (e.g. two clicks, two flashes of light, two taps on the wrist), if the interval Δt between the external stimuli is below a certain level, the *coincidence threshold*, the stimuli are perceived to coincide. The coincidence threshold varies between the modalities. In the case of auditory experience, it is of the order of 2–3msec (milliseconds), in the case of vision 20msec and in the case of touch 10msec. For intervals only slightly greater than Δt, although subjects can detect two distinct stimuli, they are unable to tell which comes before the other. It is only when Δt exceeds this *order threshold* that subjects perceive one stimulus as occurring before the other. Interestingly, the order threshold is the same for all modalities, it is approximately 30msec, i.e. about ten times the length of the coincidence threshold for sound, but only one and a half times greater than the coincidence threshold for vision. Finally, a variety of experiments, on accuracy of short-term recall and time estimation, on speech perception and decision times, suggests periods of about three seconds play a privileged role in our experience of time.[5]

These results suggest, if no more than suggest, the following. First, that in the auditory case, the shortest distinguishable phenomena are of the duration of 2–3msec, and the shortest distinguishable phenomena in other sensory modalities are considerably longer. Second, the shortest distinguishable successions in experience (for all modalities) are of the order of 30msec. Third, that the maximum span of immediate experience will be somewhere between 2–30msec (depending on the type of phenomenal content) and three seconds. If we assume that a total experience is a phenomenal *succession*, then given that the order threshold is around 30msec, we would expect successive total experiences with discernibly different contents to be separated by this sort of interval. In which case, between two co-streamal total experiences E*x* and E*y* separated by a single second (e.g. from the end-point of E*x* to the end-point of E*y*) there is unlikely to be greatly many more than thirty others. Even if these figures are underestimates, they suggest that the number of total experiences between any two others will be quite small, in comparison with ∞. Each of these thirty or so total experiences will have a just-noticeable difference in content.

Of course, if we ignore the requirement that successive total experiences must have discernibly different phenomenal contents, there is a sense in which there is an indefinitely large number of distinct experiences between total experiences separated by a millionth of a second. A stream of consciousness is extended through time, and we can, if we choose, regard time as divided into instants and intervals in exactly the same manner as the real numbers. If we do this, there is no limit on how finely a given stream of consciousness can be divided into different intervals. But the legitimacy of purely formal manoeuvre does not mean that all the intervals thus recognized in thought correspond to anything recognizable in experience.

As for the duration of the specious present itself, this is notoriously difficult to estimate with any precision, and it is not difficult to see why. Psychological experiments which measure the accuracy with which we can recall recently perceived stimuli, or react to new stimuli, do not address the question directly. Since the question concerns the character of our experience, we are obliged to employ introspection, and the continuity of consciousness can easily confuse here. If I listen to a sequence of notes, and try to gauge whether a given pair of notes X and Y are directly experienced together, even if several notes occur between X and Y, I will experience Y at the end of a continuous period of awareness; I will have been *continuously experiencing* from the moment X starts through to the moment Y ends. This fact can, I suspect, easily lead to overestimations of the span of immediate experience. The figure of three seconds mentioned earlier is based on people's ability to discern distinctive, memorable, or pleasing patterns in their experience, *temporal gestalts*: think of how the notes in a musical phrase, or the words in a line of spoken poetry hang together, or seemingly form natural units. However, given that these patterns extend quite some way through time, there is no guarantee that the beginning and end of a given pattern fall within the scope of immediate experience. For my own part, I would tentatively estimate the duration of my typical specious present to be half a second or less.

The remaining oversimplifications in our discussion so far can now be lifted: we can extend the overlap theory to streams of consciousness as a whole. The sequence *Do-Re-Mi* was introduced as an overlapping succession of distinct total experiences, *Do-Re* and *Re-Mi*. Let Σ denote the length of the specious present. Since by definition a total experience is not a part of any larger experience, *Do-Re* and *Re-Mi* must each be of duration Σ. In calling these experiences 'total' we are also implying that these sensations are the complete contents of their subject's auditory experience over the relevant intervals of time, so for example, the notes are not heard against the backdrop of a conversation or traffic noise. This is clearly unrealistic; for the most part our auditory experience is quite complex. To accommodate this, we can expand the definition of a 'total auditory experience' to refer to a complete ensemble of co-conscious auditory experiences through a period Σ. So for example, *Do-Re* and all the concurrent auditory experiences with which it is co-conscious together constitute a total auditory experience. We can define total visual experiences in an analogous manner. Since we can do likewise for all the sensory modalities, we can say that a total *sensory* experience includes the entire ensemble of co-conscious sensory experiences through a Σ-length interval. But our typical consciousness is not exhausted by sensory experience; there are also thoughts, memories, volitions, emotions, mental images, and so forth. A total experience *tout court* includes these in addition to sensory experiences, throughout a period Σ. A typical stream of consciousness consists of overlapping total experiences, in this expanded sense.

I have been working on the (tentative) assumption that co-consciousness at a given moment is transitive. By a 'moment' here, I mean some brief interval that is shorter than the specious present. We have already seen that co-consciousness over time is not transitive. Three total experiences X, Y and Z can be such that X is co-conscious with Y, and Y with Z, but X is not co-conscious with Z. While recognizing this, it is important to note that all the constituent parts of a single temporally extended total experience are mutually co-conscious. So, simplifying again, suppose my current total experience includes *Do-Re* as well as the experience of a bird moving from P_1 to P_2 and from P_2 to P_3 – call these two visual experiences m_1 and m_2. Then not only is it the case that (a) *Do* is co-conscious with *Re*, and m_1 is co-conscious with m_2, it also the case that (b) *Do* is co-conscious with m_1 and *Re* is co-conscious with m_2, and (c) *Do* is co-conscious with m_2 and *Re* is co-conscious with m_1. (Since co-consciousness is symmetrical, all this holds the other way about too, for example m_1 is co-conscious with *Re*, and m_2 is co-conscious with *Do*, etc.) This holds more generally, for the complete contents of a complex extended total experience. Since each part of a total experience is co-conscious with every other part, throughout its duration, a total experience can legitimately be regarded as a single experience in its own right, no matter how complex it is – and our typical total experiences are very complex indeed.

This takes us on to one final point. I have (tacitly) assumed thus far that the interval Σ is the same for all subjects at all times. This may not be true. Perhaps Σ varies between species; perhaps Σ varies between different human beings; perhaps for a single human being Σ varies over time. If such variation exists, it simply means that total experiences will vary in length. A different type of variation provides a more awkward problem. I have also tacitly been assuming that Σ is the same for different types of experience, for example thought, visual experience and auditory experience. Suppose this were not the case. Suppose it were the case, for a particular subject S at a given time, that the span of immediate auditory experience is longer than the span of visual experience, and that Σ for the rest of S's experience falls between these two extremes, call them Σ+ and Σ− How long would S's total experience be, in the expanded sense of 'total'? The answer is clear: Σ−. Only then would every part of a total experience be co-conscious with every other part.

7.4 Symmetry, flow and mode

So far we have seen little to suggest that the overlap theory is confronted by seriously threatening problems. But there is a more serious charge that must be answered: that the overlap theory as it stands is phenomenologically inadequate. Two distinct but related considerations are relevant here.

Co-consciousness within a stream may not be transitive, but it is symmetrical. In the sequence *Do-Re* (without a gap), *Do* is co-conscious with *Re*, but it is equally the case that *Re* is co-conscious with *Do*. Yet when we hear the sequence, we experience the notes as occurring in a definite temporal order: we first hear *Do* and then hear *Re*. But we do not merely first hear *Do*, and then hear *Re* whilst simultaneously remembering hearing *Do* a moment before, we hear *Do* giving way to *Re*, we hear the first note *flow into* the second note. The transition between the notes is directly experienced, and it is experienced as occurring in a particular direction. It is not only the transition from one note to the next that has this feature: an individual auditory sensation itself exhibits flow. For the short time it lasts, the tone seems to be extruding itself forward into the future. All types of experience which possess noticeable duration exhibit a similar characteristic. A pain may be unvarying in its painful character, but it seems to endure in a particular direction, as the same pain-content is continually renewed from moment to moment. The same applies to other bodily sensations. When nothing is changing within our visual field, our visual sensory-contents are also being continuously renewed; even if we do not reflect on the situation, there is a constant (non-attentive) passive awareness of the scene before us continuing on in its unchanged state. When we see an object move, say from P_1 to P_2, then from P_2 to P_3, we see the latter movement as smoothly continuing on from the former. The same applies to remembered and imagined sensations and perceptions. Thought to take place sequentially: we are aware of one thought giving way to the next, then the next. Consciousness as a whole has a phenomenally manifest flowing character; this is why the stream metaphor seems so apt. How can we account for this feature of *phenomenal flow* or *passage* in the context of the overlap theory? Since the temporal asymmetry is phenomenal, we cannot appeal to memory, and since co-consciousness is symmetrical with respect to time, co-consciousness cannot be the answer.

Representational theories of the Broad-Husserl type have no difficulty accommodating phenomenal passage, after a fashion. When *Re* is experienced as present, *Do* will be experienced too, but as possessing a different phenomenal character than it did when it was initially experienced; for example, it will possess less 'presentedness' or more 'pastness'. We can call these perspective-dependent phenomenal properties *temporal modes*. These properties are tailor-made to account for passage. When *Do* is initially experienced under the mode 'fully present', some earlier tone (or a period of silence) is apprehended under the mode 'has just occurred'. When *Re* is experienced as fully present, it is *Do* that is apprehended as just having occurred. But this sort of explanation is not available in the context of the overlap theory, since the theory does not recognize temporal modes. Indeed, the overlap theory cannot incorporate perspective-dependent properties of this kind. When we say that *Re* occurs in two different total experiences, $E_1 = [Do\text{-}Re]$ and $E_2 = [Re\text{-}Mi]$, we are talking about numerically the same experience. If *Re* in E_1 possessed a different phenomenal character from *Re* in E_2, it would make no sense to say that these two total experiences overlapped: the *Re* in E_1 would be a numerically distinct experience from the *Re* in E_2.

So one problem the overlap theory faces is accommodating phenomenal passage. It has also been claimed that the inability of the theory to accommodate temporal modes should be regarded as problematic in its own right. In discussing a basic version of the overlap theory, Lockwood makes just this point. Lockwood believes that any theory of our perception of time must be compatible with Brentano's claim (which influenced Husserl) that when a note is experienced as sinking into the past, 'it appears as one and the same unitary note, which is such that it is apprehended by us as successively with a different temporal mode' (Lockwood 1989: 270, quoting Brentano). Lockwood continues:

> it is not simply that *Do* figures in a succession of distinct phenomenal perspectives. The point is rather that *it is experienced differently in each;* under the mode of presentation *present* in the first, *just past* in the second, and *further past* in the third. In other words, these are different experiences.
>
> (1989: 274)

If *Do* is a different experience in each of the total experiences (Lockwood's 'phenomenal perspectives') it occurs in, it is incoherent to suppose that these total experiences overlap.

This objection to the overlap theory seems insuperable, *if* we suppose that when a particular phenomenal item is apprehended from different temporal perspectives it has different *intrinsic* phenomenal characteristics. But is there any reason to think this is the case? Three considerations suggest otherwise.

1 As we saw in the course of our discussion of Broad and Husserl, the idea that there are phenomenal properties such as 'presentedness' or 'pastness' is problematic. The only obvious candidate is Humean 'force and vivacity', and as we saw, this will not do the job.

2 I have suggested the duration of immediate experience is relatively short, perhaps as little as half a second of clock-time. Suppose there are ten different degrees of 'presentedness' or 'pastness' that each content possesses as it is perceived to sink into the past. It follows that the bearers of these qualities will themselves be of the order of a twentieth of a second long. It is surely implausible to suppose we can discern phenomenal events of this brevity undergoing qualitative alterations. This suggests that the different temporal modes of appearance that concern Lockwood do not belong to the experienced present at all. Rather, they are relate to how things seem in memory. It is true that as a familiar melody unfolds, we know where we are, so to speak, at any given moment; we can remember the portion of the melody that has gone, and anticipate what is still to come. A particular musical phrase can be first anticipated, then heard, then remembered. As it is heard, it will appear under the mode 'present'; just after it has occurred, it will be under the mode 'just past'; and a while later it will be under the mode 'occurred further in the past'. While all this is true, it has nothing to do with the direct experience of time and change. The experience of hearing a single brief tone is very much simpler than that of hearing an entire melody line. From which we can reasonably draw this conclusion: the claim that phases of an individual tone are experienced differently at different times is an illegitimate extrapolation from medium-term temporal experience to short-term temporal experience.

3 Even if we deny that contents which figure in successive total experiences possess different intrinsic properties, they certainly possess different relational properties. Returning to E_1 and E_2 above, when *Re* is experienced in E_1 it is co-conscious with *Do*; whereas when *Re* is experienced in E_2 it is co-conscious not with *Do* but with *Mi*. Might not this be all that difference in temporal mode amounts to over the short-term?

Before we can properly evaluate this suggestion, we need to return to the first problem, that of the intrinsic directional asymmetry in consciousness, phenomenal passage. In hearing *Do-Re-Mi* we experience *Do* flowing into *Re*, and *Re* flowing into *Mi*. How is this directional flow or passage in immediate experience to be explained? The problem seems acute, because although we have explained the unity of experience through time in terms of co-consciousness, the latter is time-symmetrical.

In fact, I do not see that there is anything deeply problematic here at all. According to the overlap theory, most contents of immediate experience are not momentary, they possess some short duration, and consequently these contents possess an intrinsic temporal organization; the contents consist of a temporal pattern. What is the character of these temporal patterns – is it static or dynamic? The answer is clear: it is dynamic, the flow or passage in experience is included in the phenomenal content of experience. The total experience that results from my seeing a ball move between P_1 and P_2 does not consist of stationary image of the ball at two different places. The content is *a ball moving*. Movement or animation is, as it were, built into the content from the start. It is similar for auditory experience. When I hear the note *Do*, the content of my immediate experience is *a note enduring*.

If this is the case, there is no difficulty in understanding why it is that our experience presents itself as ordered and sequential, as possessing uni-directional flow or passage. The experience of the ball moving from P_1 to P_2 is co-conscious with and overlaps the experience of the ball moving from P_2 to P_3. Consequently, we experience the ball moving continuously and unin-terruptedly from P_1 to P_3. It is only because these experiences are co-conscious that we are continuously aware of the ball moving. But we are not aware of the ball moving *just because* the relevant experiences are co-conscious. We are aware of the movement because the phenomenal content of these experiences are temporally patterned: they possess an internal temporal organization, an intrinsic and directed animation. Similarly in the auditory case. A single note that endures through a discernible interval seems to endure in a particular direction; an auditory sensation seems to be an intrinsically flowing phenomenon. Again, over the short term, this flow is simply an aspect of the relevant phenomenal contents, just as spatial move-ment was in the case of the ball's flight. Hence it is scarcely surprising that in hearing *Do-Re-Mi*, we hear *Do* flow into *Re* and *Re* flow into *Mi*. And again, this succession of notes is experienced as fully continuous only because the experience in which we are aware of *Re* is co-conscious with both of the experiences in which we are aware of *Do* and *Mi*.

So we see that the fact that co-consciousness is symmetrical with respect to time is quite compatible with experience itself possessing an inherent direction: all that is required is for co-conscious experiences to have contents which are not symmetrical with respect to time. And clearly, the contents of our experience have this feature.

Let us return to the temporal modes of presentation objection. Is it the case that when *Re* is experienced as following *Do*, it possesses a different phenomenal character than when it is experienced as preceding *Mi*? The suggestion we deferred considering was this: the only difference between these two total experiences is that in the first, *Re* is co-conscious with *Do*, and in the second it is co-conscious with *Mi*. We can now see how this purely relational difference could be of significant phenomenological import, even though *Re* has the same intrinsic character in both total experiences. In the case of $E_1 = $ [Do-Re], we experience *Do* flowing into *Re*, in the case of $E_2 = $ [Re-Mi] we experience *Re* flowing into *Mi*. The fact that *Re* is experi-enced as coming *after Do* (and before *Mi*) is now understandable, without supposing that *Re* possesses any intrinsic properties such as 'seeming to be present' or 'seeming to be just past'. That *Re* has the phenomeno-temporal property of 'seeming to come after *Do*' is simply part of the phenomeno-temporal pattern that constitutes the content of E_1. Similarly for E_2: this experience also has as a content a phenomeno-temporal pattern, but in this case it is '*Re* flowing into *Mi*'. So far as *Re* itself is concerned, viewed as an experience (non-total) in its own right, it simply possesses the directional flow-character that any phenomenal tone possesses. The phenomenal character of *Re*, considered in itself, is exactly the same in both E_1 and E_2.[6]

Accepting this account has implications for the relationship between phenomenal temporality and the transitivity of co-consciousness. If we accept that temporal patterning is an intrinsic feature of phenomenal contents, does the conjecture that phenomenal temporality is essentially linked to non-transitive co-consciousness stand refuted? No, the link remains intact, but we are now in a better position to appreciate its nature. The passage of time, as manifest in our immediate experience, has two distinguishable components. One is the intrinsic dynamic patterning we have been concerned with in this section. The other is structural: only experiences which occur over a brief period of time are fully co-conscious, and these temporally extended wholes overlap. The sense we have that our consciousness is moving through time, or that contents are moving through our consciousness, requires both components. Without the intrinsic patterning there would be no appearance of flow, but without the structural feature, not only would there be no sense that our experience is confined to the present, but we could not be directly aware of one phase of our stream of consciousness giving way to another. Now, although the experience of transition requires appropriately patterned content, which provides direction, it also requires the overlapping of phenomenal presents, which in turn requires a breakdown of transitivity in co-consciousness. Without breakdowns of transitivity, every phase of a stream of consciousness would be fully co-conscious with every other phase. In such an experience there might be directed flow, assuming the contents have this feature, but there would be nothing resembling our phenomenal present: the entire stream, irrespective of its duration, would consist of a single phenomenal whole. Although we cannot imagine what such an experience would be like, we can be reasonably certain that its phenomeno-temporal characteristics would be very different from those exhibited by our own experience.

7.5 Passage within a four-dimensional world

There might be some reluctance to acknowledge that phenomenal passage is real, even at the level of phenomenal content. The reluctance stems from the conviction, shared by many philosophers and scientists, that nothing in reality flows or undergoes passage. If the four-dimensional or 'Block View' of the universe is correct, every moment and event is equally real, the future exists as much as the present or past; there is no such thing as a 'moving present' gliding smoothly forward along the time-line of history; it is not the case that the present is the interface between the expanding realm of being that is the past and the shrinking realm of absolute non-being that is the future. This is not the place to investigate the scientific and metaphysical reasons for adopting the Block View. Let us suppose they are irresistible. Does it follow that phenomenal passage is unreal? It does not. But to see this clearly, two lines of thought need to be distinguished.

The first is that the Block View directly entails the unreality of passage. The argument might run thus. From the vantage point of the Block View, a flowing stream of water consists of a tangle of molecular world-lines strewn through the four-dimensional space-time continuum. There is variation along the length of the stream, but this consists only of the same molecules existing at different places at different times. Viewed as a four-dimensional whole, the stream is as static as a three-dimensional rock. So although the waters in a flowing stream *seem* to flow, this is an illusion. Any flow that we witness occurs only within our stream of consciousness: as we look at the stream, we see the water running by; if we dip our hand into it, we feel the water flowing through our fingers. The resulting experiences possess intrinsic flow in a way the stream of water does not. But what if we think of our streams of consciousness as they are from the perspective of the Block View? Does it not follow that the passage internal to these streams is an illusion too? The answer is no. Since the phenomenal is the realm of appearance, if experience seems to exhibit flow and passage, it does. What does follow, if the Block View is correct, is that experiences are spread through the space-time continuum in the same way as everything else in the universe. The pain I felt on my last visit to the dentist a year ago is every bit as real as the pain I will feel on my next visit, six months from now. Since pain exhibits phenomenal passage, both of these pains, past and future, possess this characteristic as and when they occur. In talking of 'passage' I am referring not to any coming-into-being and departing-from-being that experiences undergo, but to an intrinsic feature that experiences possess as they occur: for example the characteristic flow internal to auditory sensations. The four-dimensional world-view is quite compatible with experience possessing these phenomenal features, provided that experiences always (in the timeless sense) possess them at the times when they occur. A pain that occurs over a short interval i does not come into being at the start of this interval, possess passage for the duration of it, then lose this property as soon as i is finished. That the pain occurs at i is a truth at all times, that the pain appears to flow for the duration of i is also true at all times. I have already drawn attention to the strangeness of the idea that past experiences possess just the same vibrant immediacy, 'presence', as current experiences. But if the Block View is true, past experiences possess presence as they occur; they do not have the property for a short while then cease having it at a later date. Precisely the same applies to phenomenal passage. This too is an intrinsic feature of experience. Although we are naturally inclined to think that in all the universe, from beginning to end, only presently occurring experiences possess this property, if the Block View is true, this is simply a mistake.

The second reason why advocates of the Block View might be reluctant to admit the reality of passage, even as a feature of the phenomenal, is this: it might be thought that such an admission would hinder the attempt to understand how consciousness could be an ingredient of the material universe. If we suppose that nothing that is material undergoes passage, i.e. possesses an intrinsic flowing character, then how could experiences be material, given that they do possess this character? But it would be wrong to think that recognizing the reality of phenomenal passage (as a timelessly possessed feature) creates any additional problems for materialism, any problems that are not already there. Phenomenal passage is no more mysterious than any other phenomenal feature, for example colour. So far as we know, no material particles or fields possess phenomenal colour. Why is it that certain wavelengths of light manifest themselves in our experience as phenomenal red, rather than as phenomenal green? Indeed, why should light produce in us experiences of phenomenal *colour* rather than phenomenal *sound*? If we assume that our bodies and brains are wholly composed of material particles and fields and nothing material possesses phenomenal colour, how can the processes in our bodies and brains create phenomenal colour, or themselves possess this property? Since passage is a phenomenal feature that (we are assuming) nothing material possesses, exactly the same questions arise. In response to these problems, we might opt for a phenomenalized materialism, and hold that the intrinsic nature of at least some parts of the physical world is phenomenal. In which case, some parts of the physical world will exhibit passage. Perhaps the space-time continuum, when energized by the motions of suitably charged particles, takes on phenomenal characteristics, passage included. If some form of liberalized materialism is true, our brains and our experience may turn out to be constituted of the same kind of pre-spatial and *pre-temporal* ingredients. Or perhaps some form of dualism is true; if so, then the material world is wholly devoid of passage – passage belongs only to the non-material realm of the experiential. That the matter–consciousness relationship is deeply mysterious is undeniable, but so far as I can see, phenomenal passage is no more mysterious than any other phenomenal characteristic.

7.6 Time, awareness and simultaneity

It seems, then, that the various objections to the overlap model can be met. The mode of presentation objection dissolves when closely scrutinized, and by taking the temporal patterning of phenomenal contents seriously, the overlap model can accommodate the directional asymmetry of our streams of consciousness. Moreover, the phenomenon of experienced passage is not incompatible with the four-dimensional view of the world. But there is one further issue we have not yet dealt with: what of *PSA*? What would an adherent of *PSA* make of the overlap theory?

PSA can seem compelling for two reasons. The first is the distinction between a succession of experiences and an experience of succession. The
second is the idea that for us to be continuously aware of the continuity of
our consciousness, we must at each instant be aware of some temporally
extended portion of our experience. How can we be continuously aware of the
flowing property of phenomenal sound unless we are at each moment aware
of some extended phase of this sound? We are now in a position to see that
both these points can be accommodated by a theory which rejects *PSA* in
favour of *PPC*.

The difference between an experience of succession and a succession of
experiences poses no difficulty at all, for according to the overlap theory
every temporally extended experience is an experience of succession. The
experience [Do-Re] amounts to an experience of succession for two reasons:
first because *Do* is co-conscious with *Re* (and vice-versa), and second,
because the content of this experience is a phenomeno-temporal pattern, of
Do-flowing-into-Re. There is no need to posit a point-like awareness which
encompasses both tones.

As for the continuous awareness of continuity, in the context of the
overlap theory this clearly cannot consist of a momentary awareness of a
temporal content: the overlap theory embraces *PPC*. So even if we draw an
awareness–content distinction it makes no sense to suppose that an act of
awareness can apprehend a content of a greater temporal duration than
itself. But the idea that we are continuously aware of the continuity of experience can nonetheless be accommodated. The experience of continuity
requires duration; there would be no experience of continuity in a strictly
momentary consciousness. If we assume the Simple Conception, although
there is no longer a duality of awareness and content, in any experience of
some duration there will be experienced continuity. The character of such an
experience will, as we have seen, take the form of a phenomeno-temporal
pattern; this pattern will consist of an experienced flow or succession of
content. Whenever we choose to inspect our streams of consciousness, our
attentive gaze will itself always possess some temporal duration; throughout
this duration we will be aware of content which is continually flowing. Or as
Bradley put it: 'in the ceaseless process of change in time you may narrow
your scrutiny to the smallest focus, but you will find no rest'.

More generally, and somewhat speculatively, the idea that the apprehension of a complex sensory content requires the simultaneous presentation of
all the content's constituent elements, may be the product of an illicit univer-
salization of a single type of experience. Consider your current visual field, a
spatial spread of coloured objects stretching from right to left, seen from a
central point of view. Now conduct an experiment in your imagination:
rotate this spread of content round by ninety degrees, but through time
rather than space – so, for example, the contents on the right-hand side are
perceived to occur later than the contents on the left-hand side. You are now
aware of a temporal stretch of content. In conducting this imaginative exer-

cise, you will doubtless have retained an important element of the spatial case: you are still apprehending the entire spread of content from a single localized point of view. This localized point of view, translated into the temporal case, is a single moment of time, a moment of time in which a temporal spread of phenomena is presented to you simultaneously. It is far from inconceivable that *PSA* derives some of its intuitive force from this sort of manoeuvre. If so, it is a particularly striking example of the oft-remarked dominance of the visual in our thinking about consciousness. From the naive standpoint, vision presents a spatial array of objects to a single spatial point of view. But although such a spatial array can be apprehended at a single time and from a single place, it is clearly problematic to suppose that a temporal array could in an analogous fashion be apprehended at a single time. (There is, of course, nothing wrong in supposing that a temporal sequence of events could be apprehended from the same place.) From a common-sense perspective, at any given time the only events available to immediate perception are those in the surrounding space; events occurring at different times can only be remembered or anticipated, they cannot be directly seen, heard or touched. Experiencing a temporally extended process requires time – just as much time as the process itself takes up. Once the difference between, first, perceiving the occupants of a space at a time; and second, perceiving the changes these occupants undergo over time, is appreciated, the illegitimacy of regarding temporal awareness as analogous to spatial awareness is apparent. Once this is appreciated, the appeal of *PSA* is considerably weakened. The overlap theory does not make the mistake of spatializing temporal awareness. For the overlap theory, change within experience is experienced only as it occurs, over a period of time.

To sum up: as I said at the outset, in investigating our immediate experience of time my main aim was to establish that the unity of consciousness over time is no different, in its essentials, from the unity of consciousness at a time. In both cases, the unity is the product of a primitive relationship of co-consciousness. We have looked at a number of other ways of analysing temporal experience, but for one reason or another, they all proved to be inadequate. The overlap theory, which relies only upon co-consciousness, is markedly superior in all respects. A good deal more could be said about the overlap theory; there are a number of important issues that I have done no more than touch on here. For instance, a fuller treatment would deal in more detail with the various results concerning our experience of time that have emerged from psychological experiments. But since my aim has been the limited one of establishing the general structural characteristics of our streams of consciousness, this is not the place to go into these topics, interesting and important though they are. Two secondary themes from the discussion of synchronic unity have recurred. The non-dualistic Simple Conception of consciousness has emerged strengthened. The awareness–content distinction plays a crucial role in most of the theories we have considered; but once it becomes clear that *PSA* should be rejected in favour of *PPC*, it also becomes clear that the distinction is redundant, from the explanatory point of view. Then there is the transitivity issue. If the non-transitivity of co-consciousness is incomprehensible in the synchronic case, it seems inevitable in the diachronic case. To the extent that our streams of consciousness require non-transitive co-consciousness, it is tempting to suppose that non-transitivity and temporality are essentially linked, and this further strengthens the case for thinking that synchronic co-consciousness cannot fail to be transitive.

8 Phenomenal interdependence

8.1 Bundles and bonds

Is co-consciousness an internal or an external relation? If a collection of items are internally related by a relation R, then the items could not exist just as they are, perhaps could not exist at all, without being so related to one another. This relatively crude formulation conceals further distinctions, which will be drawn in due course, but to address this question, however we formulate it, we need to investigate more deeply the nature of the relationship between experiences that co-consciousness creates, we need to examine in detail the relationship between individual experiences and the co-conscious wholes of which they are parts. Are co-conscious experiences bound together like stones in a heap, or like bricks cemented together into a wall, or are they bonded in some altogether more intimate manner?

As a way of gaining some initial purchase on this issue, it is useful to contrast two extreme positions, at opposite poles from one another: the *Humean* and the *holistic*. Hume recognized that diverse experiences such as thoughts, perceptions and pains are bundled together, but held that each component experience in a particular bundle is a 'distinct existence', i.e. could exist either by itself, as an entirely isolated experience, or as a component of a different bundle:

> what we call a mind, is nothing but a heap or collection of different perceptions, united together by certain relations. ... Now as every perception is distinguishable from another, and may be consider'd as separately existent; it evidently follows, that there is no absurdity in separating any particular perception from the mind; that is, in breaking off all its relations, with the connected mass of perceptions, which constitute a thinking being.
>
> (1978: 207)

If we equate Hume's bundles with our total experiences, the claim is that total experiences are composed of logically detachable parts, in the sense that it is logically possible for the component parts of a total experience to exist as parts of a different total experience, and in the limiting case such parts could exist by themselves, as total experiences in their own right. For the Humean, co-consciousness is clearly an external relation. Items which are in fact related by co-consciousness need not be so related.

The holist, like the Humean, holds that experiences are bundled together, but not like sticks in a bundle of firewood. Although we can distinguish different parts of a total experience, the holist insists that these parts are related in a manner which precludes the possibility of their enjoying a separate existence, either in isolation or in a different total experience. There is thus a sense in which total experiences are simple or non-composite entities: they have an internal complexity, but are not composed of separable parts.

This is what the holist maintains, but on what grounds? There are various possibilities, but one influential route to holism appeals to some degree of phenomenal interdependence or interpenetration. Suppose it were the case that the character of an experience were influenced by the other experiences with which it is co-conscious. Assuming we individuate experiences by reference to their character, if the influence of an experiential whole on the character of its parts were of the right sort, a degree of holism would inevitably ensue. The idea that the character of experiential parts is altered by the wholes of which they are parts is something to which a number of writers have drawn attention, including William James. In a section of the *Principles* dealing with how earlier experiences affect the phenomenal character of later experiences, we find the following passage, albeit in a footnote.

> Honor to whom honor is due! The most explicit acknowledgement I have anywhere found of all this is in a buried and forgotten paper by the Rev. James Wills on 'Accidental Association,' in the *Transactions of the Royal Irish Academy*, vol. XXI, part 1 (1846). Mr. Wills writes: 'At every instant of conscious thought there is a certain sum of perceptions, or reflections, or both together, present and together constituting one whole state of apprehension. Of this some definite portion may be far more distinct than all the rest; and the rest may be in consequence proportionately vague, even to the limit of obliteration. But still, within this limit, the most dim shade of perception enters into, and in some infinitesimal degree modifies, the whole existing state. This state will thus be in some way modified by any sensation or emotion, or act of distinct attention, that may give prominence to any part of it. ... Our mental states have always an *essential unity*, such that each state of apprehension, however variously compounded, is a single whole, of which every component is, therefore, strictly apprehended (so far as it is apprehended) as a part. Such is the elementary basis from which all our intellectual operations commence.'
>
> (James 1952: 156)

If this is correct, and the characters of the various parts of a phenomenal whole are interdependent in the way Wills suggests (and James seemingly endorses), then holism, in some form or other, is a force to be reckoned with. Of course, if the Humean is right, there is simply no question of holism in any shape or form.

The remainder of this chapter and the next will be devoted to trying to find where the truth lies between these two extremes, and a good deal of it is given over to the topic of phenomenal interdependence. The discussion is carried out in phenomenological terms; as usual, where possible I adopt a bracketing policy concerning non-experiential facts and phenomena. The aim is to find out what, if anything, can be said about the relationship between experiential wholes and parts, appealing only to the fact that these items are co-conscious, and what introspection (not necessarily of the attentive sort) reveals about the character of this relationship. The wisdom of this restricted approach depends to an extent on what it can be made to yield by way of results. But even if the yield in this regard should prove meagre, it is not negligible, for no other approach could deliver the same.

8.2 Wholes and parts

The doctrine that parts are necessary for the existence of the wholes of which they are parts is *mereological* essentialism. The doctrine that wholes are necessary for the existence of their parts is sometimes called *hological* essentialism, a particularly strong form of holism. Hological essentialism must be distinguished from the trivial point that, for any given whole, if any of its parts were not a part of it, then none of its other parts would be a part of it either, for the simple reason that the whole would not exist. If hological essentialism applies, the objects which comprise the relevant parts cannot exist when detached from their wholes.

On one construal of the concept of 'a part', the very idea of strong holistic interdependence is incoherent. If by 'part' we mean a component of an object that is (logically) removable from that object, and so able to exist independently of it, there is clearly no question of hological essentialism. To avoid begging the question we need to construe 'part' in a weaker way, a way that carries no implications for the logical detachability of the part from its whole, and this is what I shall do. Some technical uses of 'part' allow a whole to count as one of its own parts, and in these contexts 'proper part' is sometimes used to refer to any part that does not wholly overlap with the whole. I will usually use the term 'sub-part' for this purpose. Since for the most part we will be concerned with holistic relationships, it will help to have some of the various types of holism clearly in view.

First, it could be that holism applies to some parts of some total experiences, but not to all parts of all total experiences. So we can distinguish *complete* holism from *partial* holism. I shall take the latter to include the possibility that holism applies to some (but not all) parts of every total experience.

Second, if some degree of holism does obtain, does it do so necessarily or contingently? If holism applies to certain sub-parts of a given total experience only contingently, then although in the actual world none of these parts can exist without all the others, there are other possible worlds where phenomenally indiscernible parts are not mutually dependent. If the phenomenal character of a subject's contemporaneous experiences were interdependent as a consequence of natural psychophysical law, holism would obtain contingently; under a different nomic regime experiences of the same sort would not be mutually dependent. If holism applies necessarily, however, this is likely to be due to the very nature of co-conscious experience – how else could the relevant experiential elements be mutually dependent in all possible worlds? In which case, a holism which is necessary seems likely to be complete rather than partial.

Third, there is a distinction to be drawn between *type* holism and *token* holism. Both type and token holisms can apply completely or partially, necessarily or contingently. The doctrine of hological essentialism mentioned earlier, the claim that all an object's parts are essentially parts of that object, such that each part is logically undetachable from the remaining parts, amounts to full token holism, of the necessary variety. This is the strongest version of token holism, but not the only version, since there is no obvious reason why token holism could not be partial rather than complete, contingent rather than necessary. Type holism is the weaker doctrine that certain parts can only exist as parts of wholes of a certain type, where two wholes W_1 and W_2 are of the same type if and only if they are globally indiscernible and each part of W_1 has an exactly similar counterpart in W_2, and vice-versa. Type holism too could be contingent or necessary, and hold completely or partially.

Before assessing the implications of any form of experiential holism, we need to settle on the identity criteria for the relevant items, experiences. I have already set out my stall on the individuation issue, in §1.7. So far as their phenomenal type is concerned, only exact phenomenal character matters. As for particulars, token experiences are often individuated in terms of subject, time and phenomenal character, so that simultaneous experiences of the same character can be numerically distinct in virtue of belonging to different subjects. However, in line with my policy of remaining neutral on the precise nature of the relationship between subjects and experience, and focusing as far as possible on purely phenomenological factors, I prefer to take a different approach, and am assuming that token experiences owe their individuality to three factors: their exact phenomenal character, their time of occurrence, and their physical basis.

As I will often be concerned with the relationships between total experiences and their parts, it will help to have available a convenient way of representing these items. Let us represent a total experience E at a given time t thus:

$$E = e_1 \backslash e_2 \backslash e_3 \backslash ... e_N$$

Each of e_1-e_N stands for a component part of E, such as the sensations, perceptual experiences, thoughts, feelings and so on that jointly constitute this total experience, and the backslash indicates that these items are simultaneous. Since strictly momentary experiences probably do not exist, E should be assumed to have some short temporal extent, so each of e_1-e_N also has some short duration, and t is an interval rather than an instant. For the time being I will operate on the simplifying assumption that each of e_1-e_N lasts for the full duration of E. The important point is that all the component parts of E are co-conscious, both at and over time. Since any given total experience can be divided into parts in many different ways, the division of E into e_1-e_N is a conventional matter; there are other possible ways of dividing E into parts, just as there is more than one way of dividing a chair into parts. The possibility that different sorts of whole–part relationships might obtain when total experiences are divided into parts in different ways, is one we shall be looking into in due course.

In virtue of being composed of e_1-e_N, E has a certain overall phenomenal character, and since E is an experience like any other, and given our stipulations concerning individuation, this overall character is essential to it. On the face of it, there are at least four ways the constituents of E at t could be different, and so constitute a different total experience:

1   One or more of e_1-e_N could be absent, leaving a diminished total experience.
2   One or more of e_1-e_N could be replaced by experiences of a different phenomenal character.
3   The group e_1-e_N could be augmented with one or more additional experiences.
4   The membership of e_1-e_N could remain the same, but their mode of organization be different.

The way a total experience's constituent parts are structured is a contributing factor to overall phenomenal character. Organization has two aspects. First, the way contents belonging to a particular sensory modality are arranged, for example a visual field could contain various spatial arrangements of the same coloured shapes, or the elements of perceived succession *Do-Re* could be ordered in reverse, *Re-Do*. Second, the ways in which different phenomenal fields are organized. In Chapter 3 we considered some ways in which visual and bodily sense-fields could be differently organized with respect to phenomenal space while remaining co-conscious. To simplify matters I shall simply assume that $e_1 \backslash e_2 \backslash e_3 \backslash \ldots e_N$ denotes a total experience with a definite but unspecified internal organization.

8.3 Mereological essentialism

There are at least three classes of entity to which mereological essentialism, or something akin to it, is generally thought to apply: sets, quantities (or aggregates) and collectives. The relationship between a set and its members may not be that of whole and part, but since sets are individuated in terms of their members, all the members of a particular set are essential to it. Quantities or aggregates, such as a particular mass of water, are spatially located concrete particulars (unlike sets, which are usually taken to be abstract entities), but they are not countable – we can say how much water is present in a region, but not how many. Quantities have the distinctive feature of being highly, but not always infinitely, divisible into sub-parts, each of which is of exactly the same kind as itself: a quantity of water is composed of lesser quantities of water. Each of these lesser quantities is logically detachable from the whole – the existence of the puddle on my front porch is not bound up with the existence of any other puddles that contribute to the UK's current quantity of puddle-water. Mereological essentialism is evidently true of quantities. Quantities are mereological sums of their parts, i.e. they are strictly identical with the sum total of their actual parts. A particular mass of water would not be the same mass if it contained a different quantity of water, or was constituted from different water. Collectives are particular groups of countable objects. The people currently wholly contained within a two-mile radius of me make up a collective, as do the books owned by these people. Collectives are typically scattered objects, and as mereological sums their identity is dependent upon their parts. Unlike quantities, however, collectives are not indefinitely divisible into entities of the same kind of themselves. A group of people has parts that are not people, for example the bodily parts of the people that make up the group.

Where do experiences and their parts stand in relation to mereological essentialism? More specifically, are the parts of total experiences necessary for the existence of their wholes? It seems so, for what are total experiences (or any experiential wholes) if not sums of parts that are themselves experiences? In saying this, it would of course be a mistake to think just any combination of experiences constitutes a total experience. A total experience is composed of experiences that are mutually co-conscious, and only experiences that are so related can be parts of the same total experience. This noted, it remains the case that a particular total experience is wholly constituted from, and nothing over and above, a particular collection of experiences and their experiential interrelations. These interrelations include the manner in which the component experiences are organized with respect to one another to form a total experience of a particular overall configuration, and include the relationship of mutual co-consciousness. Consequently, there is no reason to suppose mereological essentialism does not apply here. In the case of $E = e_1 \backslash e_2 \backslash e_3$, since E is wholly constituted from e_1-e_3, and the particular way they are organized with respect to each other, it makes no sense to suppose E could have numerically different constituents. Experiences are not continuants that can gain and lose parts, and total experiences are no exception. Since they are experiences, total experiences are not sets of experiences (they are not abstract things); they are more like quantities or collectives, some of whose features they share. Like a collective, a total experience is often composed of countable parts. Like a quantity, a total experience is indefinitely divisible into component parts of the same kind as itself: the components being themselves experiences, albeit not always experiences of a single phenomenal type.

There is another route to the conclusion that mereological essentialism applies to experiential wholes. Suppose for a moment that we have elected to individuate token experiences in terms of subject, time and phenomenal character. The hypothesis that the same experiential whole could exist with different parts quickly reduces to an absurdity. The argument runs thus:

1 Suppose we take as our token total experience E at t. E is wholly constituted from parts $e_1 \backslash e_2 \backslash e_3$. If we suppose E belongs to subject S, each of e_1-e_3 also belongs to S.

2 Suppose e_1^* is a token experience that is numerically distinct from e_1 but of exactly the same phenomenal character; call it a *phenomenal counterpart* of e_1. It is incoherent to suppose e_1^* could replace e_1 in E at t. In any possible world in which e_1^* is part of E at t, it also belongs to S, since we are assuming E belongs to S. In which case, e_1 and e_1^* must be numerically identical, since they are indistinguishable with respect to subject, time and character.

3 Consequently, if E is to possess different parts at t, these parts must differ in phenomenal character from e_1-e_3.

4 But any total experience belonging to S at t which is different in phenomenal character from E would not be E. For as we have already noted, the overall character of a total experience is essential to it.

I will call this the *counterpart argument*. Given the stance I am adopting here on the individuation of experiences, this argument for mereological essentialism is not available, and as we have seen, it is not needed. But the counterpart argument serves a useful role in drawing attention to a consequence of *not* individuating experiences by reference to subjects: a significant possibility opens up that would not otherwise be available.

Consider again E = $e_1 \backslash e_2 \backslash e_3$. From the counterpart argument, it follows that it is incoherent to suppose there could be a component of E that is both indiscernible in phenomenal character and numerically distinct from any of its actual components, e_1-e_3. However, once we grant experiences their ontological autonomy, at least with respect to subjects, there is no longer any obvious reason to reject the idea that e_2 and e_3 could be co-conscious with e_1^* rather than e_1. It might be that a neural structure similar to, but distinct from, the structure responsible for e_1 could generate e_1^* as a component of a total experience comprising $e_1^* \backslash e_2 \backslash e_3$. In such a case, the resulting total experience – call it E^* – would not be E: since a total experience is nothing over and above its constituent parts and their mode of organization, any change in the identity of the parts is incompatible with the whole remaining the same. Yet the overall phenomenal characters of E^* and E are exactly the same; in this respect they are akin to two indistinguishable quantities of water that are numerically distinct in virtue of being composed of different water molecules. The idea that some parts of a total experience could (logically – in other possible worlds) be replaced by phenomenal counterparts now seems to make sense.

Whether this really does make sense depends not on whether mereological essentialism applies to experience, but on whether a sufficient degree of holism obtains. In envisaging a possible world in which e_2 and e_3 are co-conscious with e_1^* rather than e_1, we are envisaging a case in which the parts of one total experience, E, exist as parts of a different total experience, E^*. This is precisely the possibility that the stronger forms of holism rule out.

8.4 Phenomenal interdependence

On the face of it, experiential holism in any strong form might seem a wildly implausible doctrine. The fact that all the parts of a whole are necessary for the existence of that whole does not entail that those same parts could not exist independently of that whole (cf. the constituent parts of a quantity of water). When we focus attention on some insignificant part of our current total experience, such as a dull ache somewhere in the lower back, it seems unlikely that this sensation depends for its very existence on our current visual experience (say) being exactly as it is, and it seems likely that our current visual experience could be just as it is in the absence of the back pain. However, despite the initial implausibility, a number of philosophers and psychologists have defended doctrines which have precisely these consequences.

Suppose, as Wills and James believed, 'the most dim shade of perception enters into, and in some infinitesimal degree modifies, the whole existing state'. If so, what would follow? Suppose a total experience E at t consists of e_1, e_2 and e_3, three different experiences, each of a definite but different (and unspecified) character. We now envisage a counterfactual situation: suppose it were the case that e_1 and e_2 at t had been co-conscious with e_4 rather than e_3, where the intrinsic characters of e_3 and e_4 differ. Two consequences would follow. First of all, since mereological essentialism applies to experiential wholes, E would not exist; in its stead would be a numerically distinct total experience E^*, consisting of e_1, e_2 and e_4. Second, in line with the doctrine of interpenetration, the substitution of e_4 for e_3 would make a difference to the character all of the experiences that are co-conscious with e_4. As a result, e_1 and e_2 would not have the character they had in E. Assuming the identity of an experience depends on its character, it is clear that e_1 and e_2 would not exist in the envisaged counterfactual scenario. The question, then, is whether the characters of the parts of an experiential whole are interdependent in this way.

We can call the doctrine in question the *phenomenal interdependence* thesis, or *PI*. The alleged interdependence concerns the familiar intrinsic properties of experience, for example colour and shape, timbre and volume. This qualification is significant, because in Chapter 9 I will be making a case for phenomenal interdependence of a different sort, an interdependence which does not involve the intrinsic properties of experience, as these are usually conceived. But more on this later.

The doctrine of PI comes in several strengths. First, PI might apply to all parts of a total experience or only some of them, or to all parts of only some total experiences. So we need to distinguish the *complete* phenomenal interdependence thesis, *CPI*, from the weaker *partial* phenomenal interdependence thesis, *PPI*. The latter holds that PI applies only to some parts of some total experiences, or to all parts of only some total experiences. Second, PI might hold as a matter of necessity or only contingently. Third, PI could be necessary but only partial. If co-conscious experiences are necessarily phenomenally interdependent simply in virtue of possessing an experiential nature, then PPI is ruled out – each and every kind of co-conscious experience would be phenomenally interdependent. But it could be that PI applies necessarily to only some kinds of experience, not all.

Finally, given the assumptions we are working with, it seems more likely than not that if experiences are phenomenally interdependent, to whatever degree, this fact will establish at most a holism of the type variety. A combination of PI and the counterpart argument would yield token holism, provided we further assume that experiences are dependent for their identity on their subject, as well as their phenomenal character. But we are not making this assumption; we are assuming that the identity of an experience depends upon its character and its physical basis. So returning to our original example of $E = e_1 \backslash e_2 \backslash e_3$, we can consider an alternative scenario, which features a total experience $E^* = e_1 \backslash e_2 \backslash e_3^*$, where e_3^* is a phenomenal counterpart of e_3, but distinct from the latter in virtue of having a numerically distinct physical basis. No matter what degree of phenomenal interdependence obtains, e_3 and e_3^* are both co-conscious with e_1 and e_2 (and no other experiences). If the characters of e_1 and e_2 are altered in some way by virtue of being co-conscious with e_3, they will be affected in just the same ways by virtue of being co-conscious with e_3^*, for by hypothesis there are no relevant differences between e_3 and e_3^*. Consequently, both e_1 and e_2 can exist in either E or E^*, for their phenomenal characters are the same, irrespective of whether they are co-conscious with e_3 or e_3^*. So, if PI does obtain, co-conscious experiences will be sensitive to each other's types, but they will not be sensitive to each other as tokens. Although I will be considering an alternative way of looking at things, I will assume for now that the holism we are concerned with is of the type variety.

Let us begin by looking at CPI, which itself comes in varying strengths. For an idea of what a very strong version might look like, consider the (very implausible) *holographic conception* of experience: i.e. the idea that the entire and exact character of a total experience is in some manner reflected or encoded in each of its parts. Take any small component of a particular total experience, and you will find it to be imbued with the character of the whole experience of which it is a part. If experience were like this, CPI would clearly obtain: were a total experience in any way different, the difference would be reflected in each of its parts. But no one – so far as I am aware – has tried to defend a holographic conception of experience. (Not even Leibniz, although he may have held that the character of each particular total experience was encoded in every other total experience.) This is hardly surprising. How could the entire complex phenomenal character of my current visual experience be reflected in each and every component of my current tactile experience, or in the character of the smallest components of my visual experience for that matter? Experience does not and cannot possibly interpenetrate in this manner: a simple sensation such as a pain or itch does not possess the intrinsic phenomenal complexity that would be required for the holographic thesis to be true. If the parts of a total experience are phenomenally interdependent, the interdependence is not of this order. But it does not need to be. All the holist need defend is the weaker claim that each part of a total experience would be different in *some* way if any of the other parts were different in character; the difference can be as small as you like. Provided that we grant that an experience's exact phenomenal character is essential to its being the experience it is – and this is the concept of experience we are currently working with – even the slightest degree of global interdependence would yield CPI.

One contemporary philosopher who thinks CPI does obtain is Timothy Sprigge, who also advocates experiential holism on just this basis. Sprigge maintains that the phenomenal character of each constituent of a total experience is affected, albeit in slight and subtle ways, by being a part of a co-conscious whole of a particular kind. He suggests this interdependence of character is manifest in introspection:

> A holistic relation is strong if the kind of whole its terms unite in forming has a character which so suffuses every element that no element with some difference from it in character could be found without a whole of just that sort. ... That some holistic relations are strongly so is readily revealed. Consider the character of a painting and the relation between its parts when the painting is seen as a whole. Consider the painting, that is, as a total presence is someone's perceptual field. ... It is a commonplace of aesthetics and of right-minded psychology, but something we can each discover for ourselves, that every detail in the painting as a complete presentation has some difference, even within its own bounds, from what that detail would have if it were seen apart, or in another whole. ... An eye, as it figures in a certain painted face, will supply a good example. Certainly the same identical shape and pattern of colour can be present in a different whole, but one cannot think of

what lies within the eye's own bounds as having a character unaffected by the whole it helps form. Indeed, the mere place at any moment of any visual phenomenon in the visual field, high or low, to the left or right, gives it a different character. ... All holistic relations between terms actually given in experience appear to be strongly so ... I do not want to rest the point upon conclusions already reached and invite the reader to consider whether he can think of any element within experience as having for its total character something which is untouched by its precise role in the experience as a whole. One surely cannot isolate something which would be only the same, without a shred of difference, rather than something possessing an affinity thereto, if it occurred in another total experience. As a shape passes to the right across the perceptual field it alters in a way which is inherent to what it is. A quality of emotion is different when felt in one state of bodily feeling, or in one perceivable situation, than when felt in another.

(1983: 219–20)

Sprigge suggests this position, or something close to it, was also held by both F. H. Bradley and William James:

Among the more important positions which James and Bradley held in common are the following: 1. Our states of consciousness are wholes such that every element within them is so coloured by the totality that they could not occur again without difference in another state of consciousness.

(1993: 2)

James certainly seems to have had some sympathy with the idea – recall the passage quoted at the start of this chapter. While it is not altogether clear whether Sprigge thinks CPI generates token- or type holism – he says things compatible with both doctrines – he certainly thinks it obtains as a matter of necessity: phenomenal interdependence is a consequence of the essential nature of consciousness in all its forms.

Taking up Sprigge's invitation, can we envisage elements of a total experience having a character that is independent of their broader experiential context? Sprigge's example of a painting has some plausibility. Compare the two eyes in the illustration below (Figure 8.1). The eye that clearly belongs to a cow radiates the familiar mild benevolence; the eye behind the peephole may look distinctly alarmed, even menacing. Yet, if the cow's face is masked off, the two eyes are seen to be indistinguishable.

Modality-specific context-dependent differences of this sort are elusive and hard to describe, but this is not to say they do not exist – I shall be considering some instances in more detail shortly. But this sort of case only supports the *partial* interdependence thesis, PPI. Sprigge claims that phenomenal interdependence extends, as a matter of necessity, to all parts

Figure 8.1 A case of partial phenomenal interdependence

of every total experience. Consequently, CPI requires the characters of co-conscious contents belonging to different modes of consciousness to be mutually dependent, and this stronger claim seems very dubious indeed.

Is there any introspectible evidence for the contention that the phenomenal character of an emotional feeling depends on every last detail of its subject's concurrent auditory and visual experience? I can easily envisage my emotional state being affected by what I see or hear; this happens all the time. But I find it hard to believe that very small variations in my auditory and visual experience would make *any* difference to my mood. Would a sense of melancholy alter in felt quality if the noise of the passing cars was a fraction louder, or the room slightly brighter? The same holds the other way about: would the sound made by the passing cars have a different auditory character if my mood were a fraction brighter? It seems unlikely. Yet this experiential combination (mood + perception) provides more support for CPI than most, since our moods (like our thoughts and memories) are relatively responsive to what we are currently perceiving. Other combinations of experiential types are even less promising in this respect. It is hard to believe that one's current auditory experience is significantly responsive to small variations in one's visual experience, or that the character of one's current tactile experience would be different were one's current olfactory experience other than it is. Quite generally, at any given moment, any pair of co-conscious experiences belonging to different perceptual modalities seem largely – and typically completely – unaffected by each other. Any interdependence that does obtain can often be put down to other factors. If a loud noise had disturbed my concentration at any time during the past five minutes, then no doubt my visual experience (say) would have been different from how it was (in fact no loud noise occurred). But the bulk of this difference would have been due to my attention having been diverted, and my not looking at the same places in the same ways. Suppose I had been expecting the noise, and its occurrence did not disrupt my concentration, nor cause my attention to wander – would the intrinsic quality of my visual experience have been altered by the occurrence of the sound itself? Would there have been any alteration in the colours and shapes that filled my visual field? This seems improbable.[1]

If the character of experiences in different sensory modalities are generally independent, which contrary to Sprigge's claim they seem to be, CPI is false, and complete holism cannot be grounded on phenomenal interdependence. What about interdependence within modalities? There is doubtless some degree of interdependence here. But on the face of it, it seems unlikely that small differences within a single perceptual field would always or even usually impinge on the local characteristics of the remainder of the experience within the same field. If the pile of books to my left were differently located, a centimetre or so further to the right, say, I see no reason to suppose the contents of the remainder of my visual field would in any way be different. And the same applies to small variations in other perceptual fields. This seems so obviously to be the case, the reason anyone could think otherwise is puzzling.

Why would anyone think otherwise? Why would anyone think CPI is true? One explanation runs as follows. As will already be plain, the unity of consciousness is surprisingly elusive for something so familiar; attempts to describe or analyse the character of this unity are sometimes accompanied by suggestive but frustratingly vague metaphors, sometimes by implausible and exaggerated claims which ascribe to consciousness near-magical and certainly chimerical properties. It is tempting to speculate that spending too long in rapt introspection might lead to a condition of intellectual intoxication, call it *consciousness mysticism*, which would have just these consequences. Perhaps advocates of CPI are suffering from this condition.

However, there is another and more charitable explanation, namely that there is an element of truth in CPI; that there are indeed pervasive and far-reaching holistic relations among experiential parts. Some of these are essential, some are contingent; some hold among all parts of all total experiences, some are more local, and restricted to certain types of experience. The advocates of CPI have simply gone wrong in the account they have given of the experiential interrelations which do exist, either by misdescribing them, or exaggerating their extent or depth. In Chapter 9 I will be developing an argument to the effect that co-consciousness itself generates interdependencies between experiences. Does this mean CPI is true? No. Although all parts of every total experience are mutually co-conscious (by definition), the interdependencies due to co-consciousness are not interdependencies of intrinsic phenomenal character of the familiar sort, or so I will be arguing. But before looking at this issue, I want to look at a particular sort of case where it has been alleged that interdependence (of intrinsic character) is both real and significant.

8.5 Interdependence and its limits: sensory wholes

I have suggested that phenomenal interdependence across sense modalities is largely non-existent, and even within modalities is not very significant. But it has been argued that PI is rampant for a particular class of experiential item: psychologists of the Gestalt school believed interactions between context and character to be ubiquitous and far-reaching in the case of so-called *phenomenal wholes*. Their reasons for subscribing to this view are of interest, for if they are right intra-modal interdependence would certainly be a force to be reckoned with. Unlike Sprigge, the Gestalt theorists explicitly propounded a partial interdependence doctrine. They maintained, first, that phenomenal interdependence only obtains with respect to experiences of the same sensory-modal type; and second, that even here (e.g. within a single visual field) it is only the parts of *perceived wholes* that are qualitatively interdependent. They held that there are certain structured or 'segregated' wholes – *gestalten* – sub-parts of total experiences, which themselves possess sub-parts whose characters are interdependent. Both restrictions are plausible, for as we have seen, there is no reason to think slight variations in the periphery of a sense-field affect the more central regions, and there is little or no trace of inter-modal interdependence to be found at all.

As for the notion of 'perceived' or 'segregated' wholes, the term refers to a kind of phenomenal item we have already acknowledged. Gestalt theorists recognized that our experience is world-presenting. The typical visual field is not a flat pattern of coloured points; when we open our eyes, we see familiar objects spread all about us. When we look at a thick brown book on a flat white table, the book does not look like a patch of brown colour smeared over a white plane; what we see is a three-dimensional solid that cleanly stands out from its surrounding space; this phenomenal solid constitutes a perceived or 'organized' whole. Phenomenal organization within the visual field comes in more subtle guises. If a pair of dice are thrown and display a total of eleven spots, we do not need to count the dots one by one, we immediately recognize the familiar patterns of the 5-face and the 6-face. The presence in perceptual experience of two-dimensional patterns and shapes is another instance of phenomenal organization. There are diachronic instances too. Notes of music occur in recognizable temporal patterns (as of course can taps on the skin). We can follow a conversation through a hubbub of ambient noise – the conversation seems to stand out from its auditory surrounds.

What is relevant to our present concerns is the idea that phenomenal context influences phenomenal character, where the relevant contexts are perceived structured phenomenal wholes. That the Gestalt theorists thought there was such an influence is clear from the following passages:

> What is given to me by the melody does not arise as a *secondary* process from the sum of the pieces as such. Instead, what takes place in each single part already depends upon what the whole is. The flesh and blood of a tone depends from the start upon its role in the melody: a 'b' as leading tone to 'c' is something radically different from the 'b' as tonic. It belongs to the flesh and blood of the things given in experience, how, in what role, in what function they are in the whole.

> (Wertheimer 1967)

experience as such exhibits an order *which is itself experienced*. For instance, at this moment I have before me three white dots on a black surface, one in the middle of the field and the others in symmetrical positions on both sides of the former. This ... order ... is concrete and belongs to the very facts of experience. ... One dot is seen between two others; and this relation is just as much a part of the experience as the white of the dots is.

(Köhler 1947: 38–9)

Since [sensory] data exhibit phenomenal features only derived from the configuration into which they are integrated, it follows that *such a configuration cannot be considered as built up out of the 'parts' of which it consists, if these parts are regarded as independent and self-contained elements.* More precisely, *the configuration cannot be accounted for in terms of these properties and attributes which its constituents display when they are extracted from the actual configuration and are taken isolatedly.* The reason is that if a constituent of a configuration is isolated and taken by itself as an independent and self-contained element, it may be affected so radically and by such deep reaching modifications as to destroy its phenomenal or experiential identity, the constancy of the external stimuli notwithstanding.

(Gurwitsch 1964: 114)

Whereas the first two passages draw our attention to (alleged) instances of phenomenal interdependence, the third is concerned with the implications of such interdependence. Wertheimer and Köhler are both concerned with the difference that being part of a structured whole or pattern makes to an experience. Köhler says that in experiencing a structured phenomenal whole we do not just experience a certain arrangement of parts, the structure itself is something we experience: 'experience as such exhibits an order *which is itself experienced* ... [which] is concrete and belongs to the very facts of experience'. If the claim here is that we experience the structure or organization of a whole as a separate or additional ingredient in an experience, it seems plainly wrong. The parts of a phenomenal whole may be structured in certain manner, but we do not perceive the structure as a separate element of the whole, in some manner superimposed on the other elements; all we perceive are the elements organized in a certain manner, for example spatially or temporally. The important claim is that a phenomenal part *gains* something in virtue of being a constituent of an organized whole, hence the notorious slogan: 'the whole is different from the sum of its parts'. This can be interpreted in two ways. If a collection of items that together form a particular whole could be arranged in a different way, there is a fairly trivial sense in which the whole is different from the sum of its parts: it consists in a particular arrangement of parts, one of several possible arrangements those same parts could enter into. It is only on the stronger reading of the slogan that holism enters the picture: a whole can be different from the sum of its parts if its parts are in some way *altered* by being part of that particular whole, or a whole of that particular type. In the third passage, Gurwitsch argues that certain phenomenal wholes cannot be regarded as merely arrangements of phenomenal parts – such wholes are not 'built up' from their parts – because the constituent parts of a phenomenal whole possess features they do not possess in isolation, outwith their actual wholes. A wall is 'built up' from a collection of bricks, but exactly the same bricks could have gone into several different walls, or a wall of a different shape or style. So a wall is 'different from the sum of its parts' in only the weak sense. If the parts that jointly constitute an organized phenomenal whole thereby acquire certain phenomenal characteristics they could not otherwise possess, they could not exist in a differently organized whole, and so the phenomenal whole is not merely 'built up' from its parts; the parts only come into being – i.e. become phenomenal items with a certain specific character – in virtue of constituting a whole of a certain kind.

In assessing these claims, it will be useful to have a few concrete examples on hand. It is trivially true that the overall character of a perceived whole depends on the organization of its parts. Compare (A) with (B) in Figure 8.2: the two gestalts look different in virtue of the different arrangements of their parts.

The non-trivial question is whether, in such cases, the *parts* appear different as a consequence of belonging to different wholes, and in this case at least, it is not clear that they do. But the issue is not straightforward, since if there is a difference, in cases such as this one it is subtle and not easily noticed. In other cases, the difference is much more noticeable. In the Müller-Lyer illusion (see Figure 8.3), the horizontal line is the same length in each case. The presence of inward- and outward pointing arrow-heads produces a difference in the apparent (i.e. phenomenal) length of the horizontals. There are less schematic examples, such as the two exactly similar eyes in different contexts depicted in Figure 8.1 above.

In trying to assess the impact of context on character in cases such as these, a number of points need to be taken into account. Taken together,

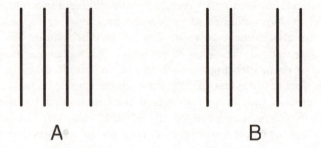

Figure 8.2 Two perceptual gestalts

they suggest that so far as phenomenal wholes are concerned, while there often is a degree of PI, this is less pervasive and dramatic than the Gestalt theorists believed. To start with, let us suppose the Gestalt theorists are right, and that being a component of a perceived whole can make a difference to the part's intrinsic phenomenal features. We can draw a rough distinction between two ways in which the parts of a whole can be influenced by their context, two ways in which the character of a whole can impinge on the character of its parts.

Strong Impingement Phenomenal wholes have certain parts that possess intrinsic phenomenal features that reflect the character of that whole, and parts with the same character could not possibly occur except in a whole of the same or similar type.

Weak Impingement The character of the constituent parts of a phenomenal whole are partly dependent on their being such, but items with just the same intrinsic phenomenal characters as these parts could exist in wholes of a different type, or as perceived wholes in their own right.

It is not very clear which of these the Gestalt psychologists thought applied, but there is certainly no doubt that Weak Impingement exists. Consider the Müller-Lyer again. Although the 'fins' make a difference to how two lines of equal length (on the page) appear, it is not as though we cannot see lines of the same apparent (phenomenal) length in different contexts, e.g. where the 'fins' are absent.

The lower pair of lines are approximately how I see the upper lines, with 'fins' in place. There is no mysterious interpenetration of context and character here. The kind of interdependency illustrated by the Müller-Lyer is obviously contingent, a product of the way our brains generate experience in response to sensory input. That we perceive the same lines as having different lengths is due to the particular way our nervous systems turn physical stimuli into visual experience, and there could surely be subjects whose nervous systems were different in this respect. Indeed, there is some evidence

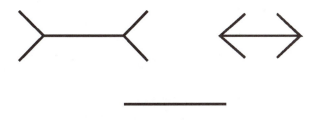

Figure 8.3 Müller-Lyer

that people brought up in an environment lacking straight walls and corners are not so susceptible to illusions of the Müller-Lyer type – which suggests that where qualitative interdependence of this kind does exist, it does not do so in virtue of the nature of experience itself, or the fact that the different elements of a total experience are joined by co-consciousness.

Figure 8.4 below provides another example of Weak (and contingent) Impingement. An equilateral triangle is perceptually ambiguous in that it can be perceived to be pointing in any of three directions, but only in a single direction at any particular time. If you stare at the encircled triangle for a few moments, you will see it point first in one direction, then another (in fact, the 'flips' in orientation can often be produced at will – it may help to mask off the figure to the right). However, when a triangle is perceived amid other triangles, or in a rectangular box, there is a strong perceptual bias: we tend to see the triangle point in the direction of the axis of symmetry of the whole figure, as seen below (if the presence of the figure on the left somewhat dilutes the effect, mask it off).

There is a degree of holism here; the appearance of a single triangle is affected by the character of the surrounding visual context. This is not in question. What is in question is whether the phenomenal whole confers on its constituent parts a phenomenal character they could not possess in isolation or in a different whole. This is what would be needed for Strong Impingement. Focus on any of the three triangles enclosed by the box. Would it be possible to perceive a phenomenally indistinguishable triangle all by itself, in isolation? The answer is clear. Nothing more than Weak Impingement is at work in cases such as these.

The examples we have been looking at are of course exceptional; effects as striking as the Müller-Lyer are notorious precisely because they are unusual. This is not to say that effects of this kind may not be rather more common than is commonly believed – this is a topic for empirical inquiry – but there is no reason to believe they are very common. Casual observation suggests as much, as does the phenomenon of perceptual constancy: there are well known instances in which our perceptual systems strive to preserve phenomenal appearances despite changes in context and stimuli. But the most significant thing about Weak Impingement is the lack of mystery. In cases of Weak Impingement, there is no enigmatic interpenetration of whole with part. Although how the part (regarded as an external stimulus) is

Figure 8.4 Perceptual bias: Weak Impingement

perceived is affected by its context, the effect of context on character is not so far-reaching that a phenomenally indistinguishable part could not be experienced in a different context.

8.6 Strong Impingement

Strong Impingement is a more interesting doctrine. If phenomenal wholes Strongly Impinge on their parts, then phenomenally indistinguishable parts could not exist except as parts of the same or similar wholes. In this kind of case, the putative impact of context on character is profound. If Strong Impingement were a universal feature of phenomenal wholes, qualitative inter-dependence would be both more widespread and far deeper than it initially seems to be. The Strong Impingement doctrine is reminiscent of the holo-graphic conception of experience mentioned earlier, but less stringent. The claim is not that the exact character of the whole is reflected in the character of each of its parts, no matter how insignificant, but that *some* parts of the whole are imbued with a distinctive character they could not possibly possess on their own or in a whole of a markedly different type. Strong Impingement yields a partial type holism of the necessary variety. If it obtains whenever we perceive a structured whole, so does this form of holism.

But is there any reason to believe Strong Impingement *does* obtain? Although examples of Weak Impingement are easy to find, examples of Strong Impingement are not. Certain cases which one might initially take to be instances of Strong Impingement look dubious when considered in more detail. Or so I shall argue.

I have already acknowledged that there is something right about the idea that a tone of a certain pitch, loudness and timbre sounds different when heard in isolation from when heard as a component of a melody. This case is the auditory and diachronic counterpart of the claim that a visual feature looks different when seen in isolation – think of Sprigge's example of seeing an eye featuring in a portrait and seeing it reproduced alone on a blank white canvas, and the two cow-eyes depicted in Figure 8.1 above. The question is whether these differences consist of variations of intrinsic phenom-enal character. And if they do, is the phenomenal impact of the whole on the part of a sort which sustains Strong or Weak Impingement? The differ-ences between perceiving the part in isolation from perceiving it in context may seem so massive in such cases as to suggest Strong Impingement. But there is ample room for doubt on this score.

In the context of a portrait, two eyes clearly have a greater expressive potential than they do in isolation; in the former context the eyes might look manifestly gentle and benevolent whereas in the latter they may lack any definite expression at all, or they may look alarming and menacing. But consider: is the expressive power of the eyes in their normal context a phenomenal feature of the eyes themselves, of their intrinsic visual appear-ance, or a matter of how the image as a whole affects our overall state of mind, for example the emotions it incites, the beliefs we form in response to perceiving it, the conscious judgments we make? The latter hypothesis is surely the more plausible. There may be some slight difference in how the eyes themselves appear when set in the context of a facial portrait – a difference compatible with Weak Impingement – but the difference in their expressive power (or what they express) is largely due to the fact that we are looking at a depiction of a face of a certain type, rather than a pair of eyes. We can see a lot in a face or portrait, but a good deal of what we 'see' in this sense amounts to judgments about character traits and other matters that go beyond the phenomenal character of the visual experience itself. The same applies in the auditory case. The individual tones that make up a melody are heard as parts of a whole that evokes various responses in us. We might recognize that the notes form a melody without recognizing the melody as one we have heard previously. Or the melody might be familiar: as we listen we can anticipate the notes to come. In either case, the melody might produce affective and aesthetic responses, for example we find it beautiful but sad, or pleasurable but hackneyed. But as in the visual case, these responses involve our broader state of mind – they are not confined to the phenomenal characteristics of our perceptual experience – and they are produced by the melody as a whole, as it unfolds, rather than any particular note. Consequently, it remains unclear to what extent, if any, the intrinsic phenomenal characteristics of the constituent notes would be different if they were heard in isolation. Quite generally, while it is obvious that experiential wholes produce effects on our overall state of mind that their constituent parts perceived in isolation would not, it does not follow from this that belonging to an experiential whole Strongly Impinges on the phenomenal character of the constituent parts. We certainly do not need to posit any such Impingement to explain why the whole has a greater cognitive and affective impact than its parts: there is simply more to the whole than there is to any of its parts. The fact that wholes do have greater effects than their parts does not, in itself, establish the doctrine of Strong Impingement.

Although I think this argument is applicable to many of the cases where one might think Strong Impingement is in play, there are other cases where different and additional factors are at work. Let us consider an instance of a type of case that was a favourite of the Gestalt theorists.

If you stare for a few moments at the six equally spaced parallel lines below (Figure 8.5) you will probably see them 'arrange themselves' into different patterns.

You may briefly see three pairs of lines, as in a depiction of three railway tracks running side by side, before two groups of three lines emerge. Or you may begin by seeing six lines side by side, with no grouping at all, and then see a central cluster of four emerge, with an extra line at each end. Or maybe another permutation of these variants. Each aspect-switch involves a subtle difference in the phenomena, an alteration in the character of your visual experience. But do you see anything more than the six parallel lines? As the lines 'organize themselves' into different structures, are these structures also present as an additional ingredient in your experience?

'Yes', you might say, 'I see the lines grouping themselves together in different ways, and this "grouping together" is not reducible to changes in the appearance of each line taken singly. Consequently, there is a sense in which structure is as much a feature of visual experience as colour, just as Köhler says'. But can this be right? How can structure be an additional ingredient in experience? I noted above that this is at best an obscure claim, and I think we can account for the 'grouping' phenomenon without endorsing it.

As already noted *ad nauseam*, our visual experience is structured to the extent that our typical visual fields contain well defined phenomenal objects of familiar sorts (which we automatically take to be occupants of the surrounding physical world). We are used to seeing lines of six stakes planted in the ground, pairs of rails disappearing into the distance, gates consisting of three vertical bars, and suchlike. If this is what is meant by seeing 'structures' or 'organized wholes', then we certainly see such things. When the six vertical lines shown below appear as two groups of three, the lines constitute two familiar patterns which appear next to one another – they look somewhat like two three-membered gates standing side by side. When the lines appear as three groups of two, they constitute three familiar patterns, which again appear in a row – they look rather like three railway tracks, seen from above, running in parallel. So there is a perfectly anodyne sense in which structure and organization can be present in perceptual phenomena, and in this sense the six lines can be seen as possessing different structures. Far from being additional ingredients in experience, these structures consist of nothing more than familiar configurations of colour, shape and size amid the three dimensions of the visual field.

So far as Strong Impingement is concerned, the crucial question is whether the constituent elements of a particular phenomenal pattern could exist separately or in a pattern of a different kind. Suppose that you are seeing the six lines as two groupings of three. Each line has a particular phenomenal character. Focus on the line at the extreme right. Could you see an exactly similar line appearing all by itself? There is no reason to think not. The right-hand line, considered in itself, has a certain phenomenal character,

Figure 8.5 Gestalt-switching

and you could easily see a line possessing just this character which was not paired up with two other lines, or which was part of a pattern composed of four or more lines instead of just three. Consequently, this example (and others of the same ilk) provide no reason to think context impinges on character. Why would anyone think differently? Two possible reasons come to mind.

When you see the right-hand line as one of a group of three, you are seeing a familiar pattern of objects, and you can only see this pattern because you see its constituent parts; to this extent each of these parts is 'implicated' in a whole. Now, if the other parts were not present in your experience, you would not see the pattern, and the character of your visual experience would be markedly different. But this undeniable difference in your visual experience is a difference in what you are seeing in the region surrounding the right-hand line, it is a difference of a relatively global kind. Your experience being different in this way is quite compatible with the character of the right-hand line remaining just as it is. True, this line now occurs within a region of your visual field which has a different overall character. This overall difference is a product of certain phenomenal items being absent (the two missing lines); there is no reason to think the intrinsic character of the experience which remains (the right-hand line) need be any different. If the character of the region is different there will be some difference within it, but this is quite compatible with the character of some of its parts remaining exactly the same. The overall character of a whole depends on the character of each its constituents. But it is an obvious fallacy to think this entails that any change in the character of the whole results in a change in the character of all its constituents; a change in any single constituent would suffice to produce a change in the whole.

But I suspect another factor is relevant here, an artefact of this particular sort of case. The six lines on the page are equally spaced and exactly similar. If you succeed in seeing them as they are, this is how you see them. But you can also see them as forming two groups of three, or three groups of two. If you pay attention, you may notice that with each re-grouping the appearance of the lines changes slightly. There may be small variations in the gaps between the lines, or the lines may vary slightly in thickness or relative saliency, or you may perceive certain lines more or less sharply as the focal point of your eyes shifts with each change of gestalt. If so, in this example at least, 'change in aspect' is accompanied by a change in the phenomena: the lines as perceived, as elements within your visual field, do not remain constant. Now focus again on the right-hand line. As a phenomenal item in your visual field, the right-hand line appears differently when featuring in different groupings (let us suppose). The holist may offer this as an instance in which context Strongly Impinges on local phenomenal character: the alteration in character is due the line's being part of a cluster of two rather than a cluster of three (say). But there is a different explanation.

We know that our visual systems 'interpret' and 'clean up' incoming optical data, so as to provide us with visual images that are clear and unambiguous.

The six lines readily lend themselves to different visual interpretations, as is evident from the different ways they appear to us. As we stare at the lines, our visual systems try out a succession of different (sub-conscious) 'working hypotheses' as to the source of the incoming optical stimulus: three pairs of two, two pairs of three, and so on. With each hypothesis, the incoming data are 'cleaned up' in an appropriate and corresponding way, and the result is an experience that conforms to the currently dominant hypothesis. When the 'three pairs of two' hypothesis is dominant, the resulting experience has a different phenomenal character from when the 'two pairs of three' hypothesis is being entertained. Since the lines on the page provide an approximately uniform stimulus throughout, our visual systems can only succeed in creating experiences that conform to the successive hypotheses by to some extent misrepresenting what is on the page, perhaps by altering the gaps between lines or the appearance of individual lines. Consequently, it is hardly surprising that individual lines appear somewhat different in different wholes, for example the extreme right-hand line looks somewhat thicker and denser when appearing as one of a group of two than it does when appearing in a group of three. But this variation in phenomenal character is only indirectly connected to the individual line's belonging to wholes of different types. The variation is the product of a visual system's struggling to create an experience that accords with a perceptual hypothesis for which the incoming stimuli provide only ambiguous support. Of course, the relevant hypotheses are about the type of organized wholes that are currently being perceived. But the only reason the constituent parts of these perceived wholes vary in character is because the incoming stimuli remain constant, and so have to be misrepresented (in different ways) if our experience is to match the current perceptual hypothesis. There is no mysterious interpenetration of whole and part.

Suppose we were dealing not with printed lines on a page, but with a row of six indistinguishable but easily moved matchsticks on a tabletop. You begin with the matches arranged vertically in a row of six, just as in the figure we have been discussing. Without moving the extreme right-hand match, you then discard two matches and position the remaining three around the right-hand match so as to make a square. If you constantly focus your eyes on the right-hand match, you will probably not notice any variation in its perceived character, even though this match is being perceived as a part of different gestalten. There is no reason why you should. Since the 'hypothesis' that the matches are arranged in a square is both suggested and supported by the position of the other three matches, there is no need for the appearance of the right-hand match to alter in any way whatsoever for perceptual experience and perceptual hypothesis to agree. In this case, and the many others like it, context does not Strongly Impinge on character. The six-lines case does provide some support for the Gestalt theorists' claim that the characters of constituents of structured phenomenal wholes are affected by their being parts of such wholes, but this sort of case is far from typical, and supports at most only Weak Impingement. If one were looking for a convincing example of phenomenal objects altering their character in response to changes in their perceived wholes, it would be hard to find a better example than cases of this kind; it is surely no coincidence that Gestalt theorists were so fond of them.

I have suggested that in most of the cases where one might think Strong Impingement, or something akin to it, might obtain, the only Impingement that is really to be found is of the Weak variety. But there are a few cases where it looks as though Strong Impingement might occur. Here is one candidate, another visual illusion: Kanisza's Triangle (Figure 8.6).

The triangle is an integral part of this phenomenal whole, and is clearly dependent upon the other parts: mask off two of the 'pies' and the triangle vanishes; leaving all three 'pies' in place but altering their orientation produces the same result. The sensitivity of the triangle to changes in context is understandable. For although *qua* phenomenal object the triangle is a clearly distinguishable part of the whole, *qua* perceived object, there is nothing on the page (no external stimulus) to which it corresponds and which could exist (and so be perceived) independently of the whole. Take away the three 'pies' and there is nothing left, by way of triangular stimulus on the page, to be perceived. However, this sort of dependency is compatible with Weak Impingement. What suggests Strong Impingement in this case is the difficulty of envisaging a phenomenally indistinguishable triangle occurring in a markedly different phenomenal whole. The triangle is 'illusory' because its apparent boundaries (between the 'pies') are not perceived in response to anything on the page, which is plain white. Yet the triangle does seem to have boundaries which cross these gaps. These phenomenal boundaries consist, in effect, in a quite distinctive kind of *distortion* of phenomenal space. These distortions are also parts of the boundary of a triangle which seems to be superimposed on three black circles. It is hard to see how this exact combination of effects could be produced in a different way.

Figure 8.6 Kanisza's Triangle

The same may be true of similar cases, where a perceived whole includes distortions which are parasitic on the surrounding context. But while such cases may be instances of Strong Impingement, they are also rare. The question of just how rare is an empirical one, and would no doubt merit further investigation. However, since my aim here is the more limited one of distinguishing different kinds of qualitative interdependence, I will not press further into these areas.

8.7 Interdependence and its limits: meaning

I want to comment, in a fairly cursory manner, on sensory wholes of a quite distinctive sort, those which possess meaning. To what extent, if any, does the presence of meaning in an experience, over and above sensory characteristics such as phenomenal colour and sound, give rise to phenomenal interdependencies? The sort of meaning I have in mind is *experienced* meaning, the sort of meaning that is associated with understanding-experience, of the sort discussed in §1.3. Before considering this question, there is a preliminary issue to consider: exactly what sorts of experience constitute or give rise to understanding-experience?

This issue is in some respects a controversial one. It is sometimes said that perceptual experience in general is meaningful, in that it possesses 'representational' or 'intentional' content. If so, then does not the vast bulk of our experience 'possess meaning'? I am sceptical about this, in that I can see no reason to believe that our typical auditory, visual or bodily experiences *themselves* possess anything like the sort of meaning that our thoughts possess, or that occurs in the perception of speech or writing. Some writers use the expression 'perceptual experience' in a more restricted way than I have been doing: they equate 'perception' with 'perception *that*'. For these writers, a person has a 'perceptual experience' when they perceive that the world is thus and so, i.e. when they form a belief about the world in response to their current experience. This is not how I have been using the term: in talking about perceptual experience, I have been referring to *all* our sensory-perceptual experience, irrespective of whether we are noticing it, or forming beliefs in response to it. Most of our perceptual experience, especially that which constitutes the phenomenal background, goes wholly unnoticed; it occurs without provoking any conscious beliefs or judgments. What happens when we do make a judgment about what we see or hear? Does the relevant experience become imbued with meaning? Again, I am sceptical. We often use propositional idioms when thinking about, or reporting on our experience, for example, 'I can see that Jim is taller than Mary', but it is one thing to describe a perceptual experience using words or sentences which express propositional meaning, it is another for a perceptual experience itself to possess propositional meaning. The visual experience I have when I look at Jim standing next to Mary has a certain overall visuo-phenomenal character. Would this visual character have been different if I had thought 'Oh, there's Mary'? Would this visual character have been any different if I had not formed any belief about it at all? Would it have been any different if I had been quite incapable of reporting on it? It is reasonable to say that an experience has 'representational content' if it disposes its subject to make certain phenomenal judgments, or form certain beliefs, where these beliefs and judgments are about what the subject takes himself to be perceiving, and grounded in the phenomenal character of the perceptual experience itself. But this is compatible with, first, a perceptual experience occurring without actually provoking any beliefs or judgments; and second, perceptual experiences of the same intrinsic phenomenal type disposing different subjects to form different beliefs or make different judgments. I am also inclined to think that a subject could have perceptual experience just like mine but be incapable of making any conceptual judgments about it at all – I am thinking here of infants and animals. But I will not enter into these issues, interesting though they are. I will restrict my attention to those experiences which *obviously* possess meaning (or one aspect of it) as an intrinsic phenomenal characteristic: conscious thoughts (construed widely so as to include conscious beliefs, intentions, wishes, etc.) and those perceptual experiences that are most intimately connected with linguistic meaning, namely speech perception (and production), reading and writing.

Consider a typical case of speech perception: you hear someone utter the sentence 'Earthquakes can cause avalanches'; call this token utterance S_1. As you hear S_1, you hear it as meaningful, you understand what is being said; the meaning you understand is present in the utterance itself; the meaning is not present in a thought you think shortly after hearing the sentence (even if hearing S_1 does result in your thinking a thought with a similar content, you would have heard S_1 as meaningful even if you had not had this thought). If this general picture is along the right lines, it seems clear that the experienced-meaning is a phenomenal quality which S_1 possesses in addition to its purely auditory qualities. Let us refer to the experienced-meaning of S_1 as m_1. What sort of part/whole phenomenal interdependencies might occur in cases such as this?

Suppose you were to hear a different sentence, S_2: 'Avalanches can cause earthquakes'. The experienced-meaning is different here, so call it m_2. Although S_1 and S_2 contain (some of) the same words, due to the rhythms of speech it is likely that there will be some differences in the purely auditory characteristics of the same words, for example 'avalanche' may well sound different when it occurs at the start of a spoken sentence rather than the end; perhaps the same applies to 'cause', perhaps it will sound different when the next word to be uttered is 'earthquake' rather than 'avalanche'. Having recognized this fact, let us ignore it; what I want to focus on is the differences in the intrinsic phenomenal character of the individual words, that is due solely to their occurring in sentences which as wholes express different meanings. When the word 'cause' is heard in S_2, it is experienced as part of a sentence expressing the meaning m_2, whereas when the same word (type) is heard in S_1, it is experienced as part of a sentence expressing the meaning m_1; does *this* difference impinge on the phenomenal character of the word in question?

If my own experience is anything to go by, it does not, certainly not to a significant extent. I cannot detect any differences in the experienced-meaning of the individual words in S_1 and S_2. There is a plausible explanation of why this should be so. Although S_1 and S_2 are experienced as expressing different meanings, and the experienced-meanings are phenomenal features of S_1 and S_2 themselves, the difference in meaning is due to the constituent parts and their organization, the order in which the words occur. The meaning is possessed by the wholes, and the meaning possessed by these wholes is very different; but then the wholes themselves are different. To account for the fact that S_1 expresses or possesses m_1, and S_2 expresses or possesses m_2, we do not need to suppose the words themselves possess a different experienced-meaning in the two sentences. In this respect, the case is similar to that of the six lines we looked at earlier. The character of the whole depends on the character of the parts; remove one or two lines, and the character of the perceived whole alters; but it does not follow from this that changes in the character of the whole result in changes in the characteristics of its constituents: the lines which remain look just the same; the change in the appearance of the whole is due to the disappearance of some lines, not changes in the character of the lines which remain. In both cases, there may occasionally be some alteration in the character of the parts, but when this does occur, the change is relatively slight.

A more theoretical consideration points in the same direction, and suggests that if the experienced-meaning of a word is affected by its sentential context at all, the Impingement will usually of the Weak rather than the Strong variety. What would Strong Impingement amount to in the case of understanding-experience? Presumably this: the experienced-meaning of a word is a function of the sentences in which it is experienced, so different tokens of the same type of word have different meanings in different sentences. This clearly gets things the wrong way about. If we abstract from pragmatic considerations, sentences mean what they do because their words mean what they do; sentence-meaning is a product of word-meaning and word-order. We would not be able to use familiar words to express unfamiliar meanings ('Sunspots are caused by the sneezing of whales') if the meaning of words were a function of the sentences they occur in. This said, there are certain special cases where context has a more significant affect. Imagine hearing S_3 = 'Banks contain money' and S_4 = 'Banks contain rivers'. Here, context (the presence of the words 'money' and 'rivers', together perhaps with the conversational situation) makes it clear what sort of bank is the subject of discussion. But even in this sort of case, the influence of context is limited: the sound or inscription 'bank' means either 'place or institution where money is deposited' or 'the side of a river'; context merely makes it clear which of these meanings is intended.

So far as meaningful phenomenal wholes are concerned, the impact of context and character may be relatively small, but there is nonetheless a difference between the sensory and linguistic cases. The (purely visual) experience of looking at six vertical lines is not very different from the experience of looking at five vertical lines; removing a line does not lead to dramatic phenomenal variation. In the linguistic case, changes of a comparatively small kind at the sensory level can be accompanied by very significant changes in experienced-meaning. The visual character of the sentence 'The man was bitten by the dog' is not dramatically different from 'The man was smitten by the dog', but the two sentences have very different meanings. Similarly for 'The man swallowed' and 'The man swallowed the dog'. This difference is not difficult to explain: it is due to the very nature of symbolic representation. The meaning of a sentence depends upon the meaning of its words and the order in which the words occur, and quite small alterations in the ordering of words, or the presence or absence of a single word, can produce significant changes in the meaning of the resulting sentences, even though the auditory and visual changes are relatively insignificant. Similarly, the meaning of a word is only arbitrarily connected to its sensory characteristics, in that cases of onomatopoeia aside, a word's meaning is quite unrelated to its auditory and visual properties. The difference in meaning between the phrases 'Success is a mile away' and 'Success is a smile away' is not proportionate to their visual (or auditory) differences.

Experience, meaning and reference

There is another sort of case that should be mentioned. We can think and talk about our own experiences. Does demonstrative reference to one's own experience generate a significant degree of interdependence or Impingement? Suppose I have a thought T about an experience E; the thought is 'That hurts!' and the experience is a twinge of toothache. T and E are co-conscious experiences, they are parts of a phenomenal whole. Is the character of T dependent upon the character of E, or vice-versa?

It seems clear that the character of E would not be significantly different if T had not occurred – the vast bulk of our experience occurs without being thought about. Although there are attention-dependent variations in experience, if I paid attention to E, and had a thought with a different content, for example 'I wonder what caused this pain?', it seems unlikely that the character of E would be significantly different. But what of T? Would this be different if E did not exist, or if I were referring to an experience of a different sort? There are several different aspects of 'meaning' that are relevant here.

In thinking 'That hurts!', I understand the meaning of what I am asserting or thinking. I understand that I am referring to a particular sensation, and asserting of this sensation that it hurts. Since I am also aware of E, I realize that what I am thinking is true: E does hurt. Suppose I think 'That hurts!' while referring to a slight tickling sensation, call it F. I realize that this thought, call it T^*, is false, and so my overall state of mind is different in the two scenarios. But is the experienced-meaning of T^* itself different from that of T? In one sense it is, and in another it is not. In thinking T^* and T I am referring in thought to different experiences, and in each case I am aware of the character of the experience to which I am referring, so there is a difference in semantic content, a difference that is registered in understanding-experience. T asserts '[that pain] hurts', whereas T^* asserts '[that tickle] hurts', and the two thoughts have different contents; they are attributing the same property to different phenomenal objects. But there is also a similarity: T^* and T both mean 'the experience to which I am referring hurts', which is why I know that T is true and T^* is false. Similarly, when I think 'That hurts!' and have no particular reference in mind, the thought is neither true nor false, and it could be said that I am not thinking a thought at all – I am not expressing or asserting a proposition with a specific content. Yet the thought-token 'That hurts!' still has an experienced-meaning of a sort, in that I know or understand what I would be asserting of a sensation if I were to say that it hurt.

To make sense of this situation, a distinction needs to be drawn between what a sentence (whether spoken, read or thought) means, and what a sentence is used to say. If we allow the term 'utterance' to refer to token thoughts, as well as sentences that are heard, spoken, read or written, we can formulate the distinction we need in terms of 'utterance-meaning' and 'utterance-content'. T and T^* have the same utterance-meaning, but different utterance-contents; both utterance-meaning and utterance-content register in understanding-experience.

Since T and T^* have the same utterance-meaning, despite the fact that the experiences referred to are very different, utterance-meaning is independent of phenomenal context. Utterance-content is clearly very different. When I think, T = 'That hurts!', intending to refer to a particular token pain-sensation e_1, the utterance T is co-conscious with e_1, and since I understand that I am referring to e_1, T would not have the experienced content it does have if e_1 were absent. Similarly, the experienced utterance-content of T differs from that of T^*, where the intended referent is a token tickle, e_2.

At this point the type/token distinction rears its head once more. Consider a case where the intended reference of a token utterance, $T^\# =$ 'That hurts!', is a phenomenal counterpart of e_1, namely e_1^*. Being phenomenal counterparts, e_1 and e_1^* have an indistinguishable phenomenal character, but a different physical basis. Although e_1 and e_1^* are numerically distinct experiences, since they are phenomenal counterparts, there would be no discernible difference in the phenomenal characteristics of T and $T^\#$. Does this mean that T and $T^\#$ have the same experienced-meaning? It depends how we choose to individuate utterance-contents. To employ the standard terms, we can say that T and $T^\#$ have the same narrow (or type-specific) content, but a different broad (or token-specific) content. Since differences in broad content are not phenomenally discernible, it might be thought that the notion of broad content has no role to play in an account of experienced-meaning. How could a phenomenologically irrelevant aspect of meaning have a role to play in the phenomenology of meaning?

It could be argued that this is something of an oversimplification. Although the difference in content between the thoughts T and $T^\#$ would not be discernible within experience, it seems right to recognize that T and $T^\#$ do have different contents, for in both cases the intention is to pick out a particular token experience, and the token experiences picked out are in fact numerically distinct. Moreover, while it is true that the difference in content here is not phenomenally manifest, and this difference is due to purely relational factors, the relational factors in this case concern *experiences*. T is related (refers) to e_1, whereas $T^\#$ is related (refers) to e_1^*. Does this not suffice to render the *experiential* content of T and $T^\#$ distinct? The distinction between broad and narrow content is usually drawn in cases where the external references of utterances are different. If I think 'Tom is unhappy' and my counterpart on Twin-Earth has a similar thought, our thoughts are phenomenally indistinguishable, but they are thoughts about different people: I am thinking about the Tom I know, the Tom on Earth; my counterpart is thinking about the Tom he knows, the counterpart of Tom who lives on Twin-Earth. This sort of example may suggest that, first, the referential component of meaning transcends experience, and second, that if we are concerned with the purely experiential aspects of meaning, referential considerations are irrelevant, and so third, that utterances whose content is phenomenally indistinguishable must have the same experiential meaning. However, in the Twin-Earth case, the reference is external to consciousness, whereas in the case we have been considering, the reference is *internal* to consciousness. Since T and $T^\#$ refer to numerically different *experiences*, is it not legitimate to hold that T and $T^\#$ have different experiential contents?

We need not reach a decision here, for both options are viable. If we insist on the principle that thoughts which are phenomenologically indistinguishable must have the same experienced-meaning, then T and $T^\#$ do not differ in experiential content; if, on the other hand, we allow that relations between experiences can make a difference to experienced-meaning, T and $T^\#$ have different contents. Construed narrowly, the notion of 'experiential content' (or 'experienced-meaning') is type-specific; construed broadly, it is token-specific. The important point is that demonstrative reference does give rise to a degree of phenomenal interdependence within total experiences. When we refer to some part of our overall experience, the intended reference is itself an experience, and this experience is relevant to the experienced content of the relevant thought. However, while it is important to recognize that intra-experiential demonstrative reference does generate a species of phenomenal interdependence, it is also important to recognize that the interdependence in question is a limited one, in two respects. First, as noted above, it seems unlikely that the meaning-bearing wholes in general (such as thoughts or spoken utterances) have phenomenally interdependent parts, at least insofar as we are concerned with the experienced meaning of these parts, as opposed to their other phenomenal characteristics. Second, we can and do think and talk about our experience, but not very often: most of our experiences are not the objects of thought or attention.

9 The ramifications of co-consciousness

9.1 Co-conscious wholes

Phenomenal interdependence generates only a limited, often localized, form of experiential holism. I will bring matters to a close by exploring a direct route from the simple fact that experiences are co-conscious to a wide-ranging holism: complete, necessary, and applying to both types and tokens.

The wide-ranging holism I have in mind is in one respect similar to CPI, in that it posits a wide-ranging form of phenomenal interdependence, but the kind of interdependence is very different: it requires us to recognize that experiences have phenomenal properties of an unfamiliar sort. So as to make this clear, I will temporarily assume that both CPI and PPI are false; that is, I will assume that when two experiences are co-conscious, that they are co-conscious does not impinge on their intrinsic phenomenal characters. I will call this the *Indifference Principle*. This departs some way from the truth – I have already acknowledged that a degree of phenomenal interdependence exists – but in isolating the effects of co-consciousness *per se*, the Indifference Principle provides a useful simplification.

We can begin with a simple example. Watching television with the sound on produces an audio-visual experience. Consider a brief token audio-visual experience E at t, with visual component v_1 (of type F) and auditory component a_1 (of type G). We will assume that E is a total experience, so all its component parts are mutually co-conscious; we further assume that its component parts are of the same duration (that of the phenomenal present). As before, we express the fact that these components are both simultaneous (or concurrent) and co-conscious thus: $E = v_1 \backslash a_1$. So far as the televisual experience $E = v_1 \backslash e_1$ is concerned, the Indifference Principle has the consequence that had the sound of the television been turned off, the purely visual character of v_1 would have been just as it is, and similarly, had the screen been darkened, the purely auditory character of a_1 would have been just as it is.

Now focus on v_1. If we consider this to be a token experience in its own right, what would a full phenomenological description of it include? If v_1 constituted a total experience it would suffice to describe its visual characteristics – 'F-type' – there would be nothing else to describe. But v_1 is co-conscious with a_1, and this makes a definite difference. The subject who experiences v_1 also and necessarily experiences a_1; if you were the subject of v_1 you would automatically be aware of a_1 too. You might not be attentively or introspectively aware of a_1, but at a minimum this experience will be part of the phenomenal background, which is itself unified by co-consciousness. Since $v_1\backslash a_1$ is a total experience, it comprises a complete conscious episode in the sense that there is nothing else going on at this time in the consciousness of the subject of this experience (an implausibly oversimplified situation admittedly, but this will not affect the point).

The fact that v_1 *is co-conscious with* a_1 is a clearly a phenomenological characteristic, something manifest in consciousness, at least in the minimal sense just noted. Yet the co-consciousness of v_1 with a_1 is not a separate and additional experience, an experience over and above $v_1\backslash a_1$. We have already stipulated that nothing else is going on in the subject's consciousness in addition to $v_1\backslash a_1$. If we were to subscribe to the awareness–content model, there would be an additional component, a separate awareness of v_1 occurring with a_1, but we have already rejected this model of consciousness. If there were an occurrent phenomenal judgment that v_1 is co-conscious with a_1, there would also be a third component in the total experience, but by hypothesis there is not (and if there were, the same issue would arise concerning the co-consciousness of the phenomenal judgment with the audio-visual experience). So we are left with the problem of how to take into account the fact that v_1 is co-conscious with a_1. Since we cannot posit any additional token experience, or any higher-level awareness, the only solution is to accept that v_1's co-consciousness with a_1 is a phenomenological feature that is rooted in v_1 and a_1 *themselves*. If we accept that (i) the co-consciousness of v_1 and a_1 is a phenomenal feature of the total experience $v_1\backslash a_1$; and (ii) this phenomenal feature belongs to v_1 and a_1 themselves (it does not depend on a separate awareness of the two experiences), then it seems that the phenomenal characters of the component parts of $v_1\backslash a_1$ must be different in *some* way as a consequence of their being co-conscious. I am assuming that the phenomenal effect of the co-consciousness of v_1 and a_1 is distributed between both experiences, rather than being localized in one or the other, but this seems obligatory: since the effect in question is wholly the product of co-consciousness, and co-consciousness is symmetrical, the phenomenal consequences of co-consciousness will surely be symmetrical too.

In line with the Indifference Principle, if the purely visual characteristics of v_1 are not affected by its being co-conscious with a_1, how can being co-conscious with a_1 make a difference to v_1's experiential character? Similarly, how can the fact that a_1 is co-conscious with v_1 make a difference to a_1's experiential character? The key lies in the distinctive character of co-consciousness itself. If two experiences are co-conscious, they are related in a distinctive and immediate manner; in virtue of being so related they are parts of a single unified experiential episode. But although there is undoubtedly 'something it is like' for experience to be unified in this way, this mode of togetherness seems to be a primitive and unanalysable phenomenon, and this is what I am taking it to be here. Co-consciousness itself is not an ordinary qualitative feature of experiences and their parts; it is unlike any sensory property, it is distinct from attentive or introspective awareness and is not dependent upon the making of any cognitive judgment. Since we are assuming that co-consciousness does not alter or augment the 'ordinary' qualitative characteristics of an experience, but is nonetheless an experienced relation that holds between token experiences, we could call it a 'non-qualitative' feature of experience (i.e. of experiences that are co-conscious). But since co-conscious unity is also a phenomenal feature of experience in its own right, albeit one with its own *sui generis* character, to call this feature 'non-qualitative' would be somewhat misleading.

To avoid any confusion, we can continue to refer to the 'ordinary' intrinsic phenomenal features of an experience as its *local* character, and refer to the additional phenomenal features it gains in virtue of being co-conscious with other experiences as its *global* character. The local qualitative properties of v_1 are its purely visual characteristics; in virtue of being co-conscious with a_1, it also has a global property which we can roughly characterize as 'being co-conscious with an G-type auditory experience, a_1'. The auditory experience in question, a_1, has a corresponding global property, 'being co-conscious with a F-type visual experience, v_1'. This characterization of global properties is not meant to be exact; quite how these properties should be construed is a question I shall turn to shortly.

However, one possible objection can be addressed straight away. In specifying the global character of v_1 (say), do we need to specify in any detail the experience (or experiences) it is co-conscious with? Could we not simply say: v_1 is an F-type experience that is co-conscious with *some* other experience or experiences? I think not. We are forced to recognize global character in order to accommodate the phenomenal fact that v_1 and a_1 are mutually co-conscious. This particular phenomenal fact is not explained or accommodated by recognizing that both v_1 and a_1 have the phenomenal property of being co-conscious with one or more other unspecified experiences. Since the co-consciousness of v_1 and a_1 is a phenomenal fact which depends solely upon the phenomenal characters of *these* two experiences, a full description of the character of either must in some manner register the presence of the other. Also, we saw in §4.5 that synchronically co-consciousness experiences are maximally connected. It is a mistake to think that when two experiences such as v_1 and a_1 are co-conscious they are only (as it were) in partial contact: every part of v_1 is co-conscious with every part of a_1, and vice-versa. This profound phenomenal *proximity* can only be captured by specifying global character in the way I have suggested. Anything less would fail to capture the complete phenomenal character of the experiences concerned.

As a general (but not yet fully precise) description of total experiences and their constituents, this seems unobjectionable. The difference co-consciousness makes is of a *sui generis* yet phenomenal kind. This may sound rather mysterious, but is not really; the phenomenon of co-consciousness is as familiar as can be. All we are being asked to accept is the claim that when experiences are co-conscious, that they are co-conscious is a property of the experiences themselves. The claim that co-consciousness is a phenomenal feature of experience in its own right seems an inevitable consequence of the Simple Conception. Given that co-consciousness is a phenomenological feature of experience, if it is not a feature superimposed by a separate awareness[*], it follows that it must be a feature belonging to the experiential items it binds. There is simply no other option.

Acknowledging global character takes us a significant step closer to a wide-ranging holism. The global features of an experience are phenomenal features in their own right, and so can be taken to be relevant to the identity of an experience. In so taking them, we are simply applying one of the usual criteria for the identity of experiences – phenomenal character – and extending its range of application to a type of phenomenal characteristic that is relatively unfamiliar. The phenomenal characteristics usually taken to be relevant to experiential identity are purely intrinsic, the characteristics an experience has in itself, irrespective of how it is related to other experiences. Think of looking at a yellow circle on a white wall, and call this experience Y. The intrinsic properties of this experience are what is found within its perimeter: Y is a particular shade of phenomenal yellow, of a certain shape and size. A shape with the same intrinsic phenomenal character could be experienced by itself, or next to a shape of a different colour, or in combination with an endless variety of auditory and bodily experiences, not to mention any number of different thoughts, memories, visual images, and so forth. Since the same yellow shape can be co-conscious with a vast variety of different experiences, why take any further properties to be relevant to the identity of Y? The intrinsic properties of Y are what matter.

I would not disagree with this. Experiences with the same local character can be experienced in total experiences of different overall types. An experience with the same local character as Y can be co-conscious with any number of other experiences, of different local types. However, if we take it that the *intrinsic* properties of an experience are relevant to its identity, it is not clear that Y's intrinsic properties are restricted to the phenomenal features found within its borders. Suppose that Y is co-conscious with an auditory experience Z (a buzzing noise), which is heard to be located some distance away from Y. Z is not something which occurs within Y's borders, but is it wholly extrinsic or external to Y? I suggest not. Co-consciousness is more intimate than this: as I have already argued, if Y and Z are co-conscious, they are so in virtue of phenomenal features of Y and Z themselves. Co-consciousness is a relation, but it is not a relation which has its own independent phenomenal character, and which can be observed (or introspected) in its own right, as an external connection between otherwise independent experiences. Co-consciousness connects or holds between experiences, and so in one sense is external to any one experience, but when experiences are co-conscious, they are not joined by anything external to either of them. Co-consciousness is a phenomenal feature which is neither fully 'intrinsic' nor fully 'extrinsic', as these terms are usually understood. It is therefore at least an option to take an experience's global characteristics to be akin to its local (or purely intrinsic) characteristics, and hence regard them as a factor relevant to experiential identity.

We have been looking at an artificially simple example, a single audio-visual experience divided into only two concurrent parts, but the same line of reasoning extends to each and every division of any total experience into parts. By definition, each component of a given total experience is co-conscious with every other part. Think of the sensations located along the sole of your right foot (I am assuming your foot is on the ground or in a shoe and currently providing you with some sensations). This sensation is co-conscious with each part of your visual field, each part of your auditory field, the remainder of your bodily sensations, your current thoughts, mental images and feelings. Each part of your current total experience contributes to the global character of your current foot-sensation, and so is relevant to the latter's identity; and since co-consciousness is symmetrical, the same holds in reverse, your current foot-sensation contributes to the global character of every other part of your current total experience. Then there is the temporal element. Each phase of a stream of consciousness overlaps (and so is co-conscious with) earlier and later phases (except, of course, for the first and last phases of a stream, which are only co-conscious with later and earlier co-streamal phases respectively). These relationships of co-consciousness are rarely attended to, but exist nonetheless; as we have already seen, the fundamental structures of our total experiences are neither affected nor created by acts of attention.

9.2 Global character: type holism and token holism

To be clear on the species of holism we might be dealing with here, we need a clearer idea of the nature of what I have been calling 'global character'. We can begin by distinguishing relations from relational properties. Relations hold between individuals. Two-place relations hold of pairs of objects, for example in the case of 'Jim loves Mary', the '... loves ...' relation holds between Jim and Mary. A relational property, unlike a relation, is monadic rather than dyadic or *n*-adic: Jim has the property of loving Mary, and it is Jim who possesses this property, though not necessarily exclusively. The same monadic property can be possessed by many people: Harry might love Mary too. Although this property is not itself a relation, it contains (or essentially involves) a relation, since any person who has it bears the relation '... loves ...' to Mary. We can further distinguish *particularized* relational properties, such as being R to Mary, from *generalized* relational properties, such as being R to something that has a property F. Particularized relational properties are token-specific, they involve being in a relation to some specific individual, whereas generalized relational properties do not. Admiring Churchill is a token-specific relational property, whereas admiring a prime minister is only type-specific. Different individuals can possess the same generalized relational property by bearing the same type of relation to different objects: lots of people possess the type-specific property of being in love with someone called Mary.

Co-consciousness is a relation, its terms are experiences, and so far as individual total experiences are concerned, it is reflexive, symmetrical and transitive; each total experience is a partition of the totality of experiences at a given moment created by co-consciousness. The global character of a particular experience, on the other hand, is a relational property rather than a relation. In the case above, v_1 possessed the relational property of being co-conscious with a_1. Let us take a slightly more general case, featuring a particular total experience E_1 at t comprising three concurrent experiences, e_1, e_2 and e_3, of intrinsic (local) types F, G and H respectively. The remainder of my simplifying assumptions remain in place: I will ignore temporal considerations, and work on the assumption that E_1 stands alone. This simplification will be lifted in due course.

The fact that E_1 comprises three simultaneous experiences that are mutually co-conscious can be expressed thus:

$$E_1 = e_1 \backslash e_2 \backslash e_3$$

The backslash '\' again indicates that we are dealing with concurrent co-conscious experiences. Focusing on e_1, we can distinguish two relational properties that it possesses, which we can represent thus:

$$P_1 \, Cp \, [e_1 : e_2 \backslash e_3]$$
$$P_2 \, Cg \, [e_1 : Gx \backslash Hx]$$

The letter 'C' indicates co-consciousness here. Cp is a particularized, token-specific relational property, and P_1 expresses the fact that e_1 is co-conscious with the token experiences e_2 and e_3. Cg is a generalized, type-specific relational property, and P_2 expresses the fact that e_1 is co-conscious with a G-type experience (Gx) and an H-type experience (Hx), where these 'types' refer to the local characteristics of the experiences concerned. Any number of different token experiences can possess the latter property, but only e_1 possesses the former. P_1 entails P_2; that is, since e_2 is essentially of type G, and e_3 is essentially of type H, it follows that e_1 possesses its Cg-property in virtue of possessing its Cp-property. Each of e_2 and e_3 possess corresponding pairs of properties, for example e_3 possesses both Cp $[e_3 : e_1 \backslash e_2]$ and Cg $[e_3 : Fx \backslash Gx]$.

Since e_1 possesses both these properties, we are faced with a choice as to what we take the global character of e_1 to be. So, focusing on e_1, we have to ask which property is relevant to e_1's phenomenal features. It seems clear that the *types* of experience with which e_1 is co-conscious contribute to the latter's global character, on the assumption that it is legitimate to recognize global character at all; all that is in question is whether the particular *token* experiences e_1 is co-conscious with are relevant to its phenomenal character too.

Someone might argue: How could e_1 possibly be co-conscious with experiences that are both phenomenally indistinguishable from e_2 and e_3 and numerically distinct? Any experiences co-conscious with e_1 are also consubjective, both with one another and with e_1, since co-conscious experiences are clearly consubjective. So consider the hypothetical scenario in which e_2^* and e_3^*, phenomenal counterparts of e_2 and e_3, are co-conscious with e_1. Since e_2^* has the same phenomenal character, time and subject as e_2, it must surely be e_2, and likewise, *mutatis mutandis*, for e_3^* and e_3. So the claim that Cp-properties are relevant to global experiential character is simply incoherent. However, this now-familiar reasoning, the counterpart argument, relies on the assumption that experiences are individuated by reference to subjects. This assumption is one we are not making. Consequently, there is no logical problem in supposing that e_1 could be co-conscious with experiences that are qualitatively identical but numerically distinct from e_2 and e_3.

There is a simple argument to the conclusion that global character must be type-specific. In trying to characterize the global character of an experience, we are trying to characterize its complete phenomenal character. As a matter of fact, e_1 is co-conscious with e_2 and e_3. Suppose instead that e_1 is co-conscious with phenomenal counterparts of e_2 and e_3, i.e. numerically distinct G- and H-type experiences e_2^* and e_3^*. In this counterfactual scenario, the relation of co-consciousness holds between e_1, e_2^* and e_3^*. Would the purely phenomenal character of e_1, whether local or global, be any different as a result? As soon as we pose the question in this way the answer seems clear. How could the *phenomenal* character of e_1 be in any way different were it to be co-conscious with phenomenal counterparts of e_2 and e_3? Surely, the only features of e_2 and e_3 that are relevant to e_1's phenomenal character are their phenomenal features. By definition, phenomenal counterparts have the same phenomenal features; any relevance e_2 and e_3 have to the character of e_1 will be replicated by e_2^* and e_3^*. If this is right, it seems that we must conclude that the global character of e_1 consists in the type-specific Cg-property, P_2, rather than the token-specific Cp-property, P_1.

This conclusion would be unavoidable if the only phenomenal properties experiences can have are those which make a difference to their discernible phenomenal features. In the case just considered, the total experiences $E_A = e_1 \backslash e_2 \backslash e_3$ and $E_B = e_1 \backslash e_2^* \backslash e_3^*$ have exactly the same phenomenal features, they are qualitatively indiscernible, phenomenologically speaking. In this sense it is true that they possess the same phenomenal characteristics. The same applies to their parts: e_2 and e_2^* have exactly the same phenomenal features.

However, recalling the verdict we reached on narrow and broad experience-meaning, if we take a wider view of what can count as a legitimate phenomenal *property*, we arrive at a different picture of what can constitute the global phenomenal characteristics of an experience. The token-specific Cp-properties are genuinely *phenomenal* properties, of a relational sort. Experiences linked by co-consciousness are joined by a concrete relation of a phenomenal kind, a species of relation which can only hold between experiences. Now, there is no denying that e_1 has the same phenomenal character irrespective of whether it is co-conscious with $e_2 \backslash e_3$ or $e_2{}^* \backslash e_3{}^*$. But is there not a genuine sense in which e_1 has different phenomenal properties in these two scenarios? In each scenario, e_1 is linked to a numerically different experience by an experiential relationship. In recognizing properties of this sort, we are rejecting the principle that qualitatively indistinguishable experiences cannot differ in phenomenal properties. But once we admit the existence of relational phenomenal properties, as recognizing the existence of co-consciousness forces us to do, this principle seems dubious anyway. It is worth emphasizing again that co-consciousness is a genuine relation between experiences. By way of illustration it suffices to recall the discussion of the phenomenal binding constraint in Chapter 5. There is clearly a fact of the matter as to which experiences belong to which streams of consciousness, and it seems plausible to think co-consciousness plays a crucial role here. Suppose I have a replica, whose experience is exactly like mine in character. If my total experience at the present time is $E_1 = e_1 \backslash e_2 \backslash e_3$, my replica's is $\mathbf{E_2} = \mathbf{e_1 \backslash e_2 \backslash e_3}$, that is, my replica is also enjoying a total experience consisting of parts with characters F, G and H. The total experience $E_3 = e_1 \backslash \mathbf{e_2} \backslash e_3$ is a gerrymandered fiction, comprising as it does two components of my current experience and a component of my replica's. The non-existence of E_3 is entailed by the simple fact that $\mathbf{e_2}$ is co-conscious with $\mathbf{e_1}$ and $\mathbf{e_3}$ rather than e_1 and e_3. Co-consciousness is a real and concrete relation between token experiences.

If we accept this line of reasoning, the global properties of experience can ground a holism of the token variety, a holism which is again necessary and complete. This is as strong as holism gets. It has the consequence that total experiences do not possess any logically separable parts, which in turn means that total experiences are metaphysically simple entities. Saying this does not entail that total experiences cannot be complex; in our case, they usually are. But it does entail that it makes no sense to suppose that the various parts that compose a particular experience could exist in a different total experience, even a total experience of the same overall type.

There is no need to choose between the two options we have been considering. Again recalling the verdict we reached on understanding-experience, we can individuate experiences narrowly, in terms of their type-specific global phenomenal features, or we can individuate them broadly, in terms of their token-specific relational properties, of a phenomenal sort. Individuating by way of Cp-properties is more discriminating than individuating by way of

Cg-properties – two experiences can be identical by the latter criterion but different by the former – but both modes of individuation seem legitimate, both are options. What we must do, however, is draw a clear distinction between phenomenal character and phenomenal properties. Phenomenal character is type-specific; phenomenal properties can be token-specific; an experience's phenomenal characteristics do not exhaust its phenomenal properties.

We can represent an experience's phenomenal properties in various ways. To start with narrow global characteristics, we could say:

$$Fe_1: Cg\,[Gx\backslash Hx] \qquad [1]$$

Meaning: e_1 is a token of an F-type experience that is co-conscious and simultaneous with experiences of types G and H. Given that co-consciousness is a reflexive relation, or at least can reasonably be taken to be such, we could express the same fact in the following manner, using bold type to indicate the local character of the experience being described:

$$e_1 : Cg\,[\mathbf{Fx}\backslash Gx\backslash Hx] \qquad [2]$$

This formulation describes the same state of affairs as [1]. Since e_1 is a component of a maximally connected, mutually co-conscious ensemble of experiences, of local types F, G and H, there is nothing wrong with characterizing e_1 in this way; e_1 is an F-type experience that is co-conscious with itself, a G-type experience and an H-type experience. If we adopt the same policy for e_2 and e_3, we have a clear manifestation of holism:

$$e_2: Cg\,[Fx\backslash \mathbf{Gx}\backslash Hx] \qquad [3]$$

$$e_3: Cg\,[Fx\backslash Gx\backslash \mathbf{Hx}] \qquad [4]$$

Each experience in the total experience E = e1\e2\e3 has exactly the same Cg-property; thus is the character of the whole reflected in each of the parts.

The same applies when we characterize the broad, token-specific, Cp-properties of an experience. Adopting the same conventions yields:

$$e_1: Cp\,[\mathbf{F(e_1)}\backslash G(e_2)\backslash H(e_3)] \qquad [5]$$

$$e_2: Cp\,[F(e_1)\backslash \mathbf{G(e_2)}\backslash H(e_3)] \qquad [6]$$

$$e_3: Cp\,[F(e_1)\backslash G(e_2)\backslash \mathbf{H(e_3)}] \qquad [7]$$

We are now in a position to clarify in a preliminary way the sort of holism we have been moving towards. We can distinguish two levels at which a sub-part of an experience can be characterized: a partial characterization, which only takes into account local qualitative properties, and a complete characterization, which also includes the experience's global phenomenal properties. These global properties can themselves be characterized in two ways, narrowly or broadly, i.e. in terms of Cg- or Cp-properties, the latter being token-specific, the former type-specific. To simplify, we can refer to properties of both sorts as *C-properties*. The C-properties of an experience are determined by the other experiences with which it is co-conscious, and the particular form a C-property takes reflects the character and composition of the total experience as a whole. Consequently, and still ignoring temporal considerations, every part of a given total experience will have exactly the same C-properties, both broad and narrow.

If we individuate solely with respect to local properties, holism does not enter the picture: the experience could conceivably have had these same phenomenal properties in the context of a different total experience. If, on the other hand, we take global phenomenal characteristics of the narrow sort to be relevant to the identity of an experience, type holism ensues. The global character of any experiential sub-part is determined by the global character of the total experience to which it belongs, so any variation in global character alters the global character of each sub-part. In the case of $E_1 = e_1 \backslash e_2 \backslash e_3$, if we imagine a case in which e_1 is part of a different total experience, $E_2 = e_1 \backslash e_2$, its Cg-property would be different: Cg [**Fx\Gx**] rather than Cg [**Fx\Gx\Hx**]. If we take it that an individual experience is individuated by reference to its entire (narrow) global character, then e_1 does not exist in the imagined situation – in its stead is an experience e_1* of the same local type as e_1, but of a different global type. So e_1 can only exist as a component of a total experience of the same global type as E_1. Clearly, the same applies to every part of every possible total experience, and does so necessarily. Any experience that is a sub-part of a total experience can only exist as a component of the same type of total experience, i.e. a total experience with sub-parts of the same local type. This is complete holism, and while only of the type-variety, rooted as it is in co-consciousness, it applies to all total experiences and all of their parts necessarily – since all sub-parts of any total experiences are mutually co-conscious. A stronger, token-specific form of holism is available if we elect to individuate by reference to the broad phenomenal properties an experience has. In doing so, we appeal to a more liberal sense of 'phenomenal property', and allow that phenomenal properties are not restricted to what is discernible by introspection. This token-specific holism is also complete and necessary, and has the consequence that total experiences are metaphysically simple entities. For convenience, I shall refer to these forms of experiential interconnectedness as *C-holism*. Strong C-holism is the token-specific doctrine, Weak C-holism is the type-specific doctrine.

Having drawn the distinction between phenomenal character and phenomenal properties, where the latter can be purely relational and token-specific, we can – if we choose – extend the distinction to cases involving phenomenal interdependence at the level of local character, for example cases of

Strong or Weak Impingement among the parts of sensory wholes. Local interdependencies too can give rise to holism of the token variety.

How strong is the case for C-holism? Both forms presupposes a particularly stringent identity criterion for experiences, since it is only when we recognize global phenomenal properties, and incorporate these into the identity criteria for individual experiences, that the case for C-holism emerges. Strong C-holism is particularly guilty in this regard. For most everyday purposes there is clearly nothing wrong with adopting a far less stringent concept of what counts as a particular experience. Since there is no practical utility in adopting the more exacting concepts, whatever interest they have is theoretical. But to the extent that we are interested in phenomenology rather than practical utility, the case for C-holism, especially in its Weak form, seems strong. Although C-holism rests on a somewhat idiosyncratic concept of experience, the holist can nonetheless maintain that this concept captures or reflects a universal feature of the relationship between experiences and their parts, and that if we overlook or ignore this feature, our understanding of the purely phenomenological nature of the unity of consciousness will be at best superficial.

9.3 Space and character

Co-conscious experiences have non-local features because co-consciousness is a relation rooted in the phenomenal character of the experiences it relates, or so I have argued. However, most total experiences have parts which are related in additional ways; a description of a total experience which only mentioned the C-properties of its parts would leave a lot out. In considering the impact of C-properties on phenomenal character, I assumed that the experiences in question possessed a definite but unspecified mode of organization, and left this out of the picture. Synchronic experience, especially of the sensory kind, usually has a spatial organization. As I stressed in Chapter 3, our typical total experiences are fully spatially integrated. My thoughts seem to occur within my body; my bodily sense-field seems part and parcel of the space through which my senses of sight and hearing range. When my attention is drawn to a distinctive bird-call in the garden, I can turn and see the bird responsible; I hear the bird's call coming from the place where I see the bird to be. Adopting the projectivist perspective, rather than that of naive realism, we interpret this situation thus: my experience is distributed through a single unified phenomenal space; phenomenal objects of diverse modal types exist at various locations within the same phenomenal space. Given that the parts of a total experience will usually have various spatial properties, how should we think of these? In particular, what is the relationship between these spatial properties and the C-properties we have been discussing? A case can be made for the following answer: an experience's spatial properties are not wholly distinct from its C-properties, they are among its C-properties, at least when these are more fully described.

To be experienced in some spatial relation, phenomenal items must be co-conscious; if they were not co-conscious, they would not be experienced together, and so would not experienced as being in some spatial relation to one another. Quite generally, and necessarily, any experiences that are directly phenomeno-spatially related will also be co-conscious. Although co-consciousness is not a spatial relation, it seems reasonable to say that one of the ways experiences can be co-conscious is by being phenomeno-spatially related. We might even say that spatial relatedness is a *mode* of co-consciousness – provided, of course, that we bear in mind the fact that experiences which are not spatially related can also be co-conscious. Phenomenal items are co-conscious when they are experienced together, but there are different ways for phenomenal items to be experienced together; being experienced as occurring in some spatial relationship is one such way.

If this way of thinking is along the right lines, it seems that a complete (or fully specific) description of an experience's C-properties would specify any spatial properties the experience possesses. In describing these spatial properties, we are simply describing the C-properties in more detail. Thus, if a total experience E comprising $e_1 \backslash e_2 \backslash e_3$, of types F, G and H, consists of parts which are spatially related to one another, a full description of E will mention (i) the fact that e_1, e_2 and e_3 are mutually co-conscious; and (ii) the particular spatial properties of these experiences.

If we let 'S' stand for these properties, whatever they may be, then the overall character of E could be expressed in this form:

$$E = S \, [e_1 \backslash e_2 \backslash e_3]$$

The global character of the parts of E could be expressed in a similar form. Taking e_1 as one such part, its global character could be expressed in either of these ways, depending on whether we are concerned with its narrow or broad features:

e_1: Cg {S [**Fx**\Gx\Hx]}   [1]

e_1: Cp {S [**F(e$_1$)**\G(e$_2$)\H(e$_3$)]}   [2]

Again, the S indicates that e_1 possesses certain specific spatial properties, which again are left unspecified. [1] is type-specific, whereas [2] is token-specific.

It is plausible to suppose that a collection of co-conscious experiences of the same local type could possess different spatial properties and relations (I am still assuming the Indifference Principle). To take a simple example, suppose you see a square situated a few inches above a triangle. You close your eyes, open them a few moments later, and see the same triangle and square, but the shapes have swapped positions: the triangle is now above the square. If we wanted to take into account the change in spatial relations, we might describe these two total experiences thus, where 'Above [x,y]' means 'x is above y':

$(E_1) = \{\text{Above [Square\textbackslash Triangle]}\}$

$(E_2) = \{\text{Above [Triangle\textbackslash Square]}\}$

Suppose we wanted to describe the global character of the triangle-experience, in both E_1 and E_2. Restricting ourselves to type-specific properties, we could describe each of these experiential parts in the same way:

(E_1) e_1: Cg [Square**Triangle**]

(E_2) e_1: Cg [Square**Triangle**]

A global characterization of this sort registers all the other experiences with which the target experience happens to be co-conscious, but it ignores (or abstracts from) the way these experiences are organized with respect to one another. Hence e_1 has the same global character when it occurs in E_1 and E_2, even though its spatial relations with respect to e_2 are different. But there is nothing to prevent our providing richer, more detailed, global characterizations of individual experiences. Hence:

(E_1) e_1: Cg {Above [Square**Triangle**]}

(E_2) e_1: Cg {Above [**Triangle**\Square])

Here, the characterizations of the e_1-type experience make the phenomeno-spatial relations explicit.

These *enriched* Cg-properties amount to a finer-grained way of individuating experiences. Once we have recognized that experiences have both local and global characteristics, there is nothing to prevent our adopting a more fine-grained way of describing their global characteristics.

We saw in Chapter 3 that it is possible for co-conscious experiences to be spatially dis-integrated, for example be divided between two spatial structures, S_1 and S_2, which are not themselves spatially related in any way. If e_1 is itself part of such a total experience, we can express this thus:

$$e_1: \text{Cg } \{S_1 \text{ [Fx\textbackslash Gx\textbackslash Hx]}\}/\{S_2 \text{ [Ix\textbackslash Jx\textbackslash Kx]}\} \qquad [3]$$

Here, Fx\Gx\Hx and Ix\Jx\Kx are each a spatially structured collection of experiences, which are co-conscious, but which are not spatially connected to one another. A formulation of e_1's broad (token-specific) global character would take a similar form.

Finding a systematic way of describing in any detail the various spatial properties experiences can have would be a substantial task. P-fields differ from

V-fields, and the kinds of spatial relationships experiences can have will depend on the kind of phenomenal space they are located within. But these are matters of relative detail which need not detain us here. The important point is that phenomeno-spatial relations among experiences can be taken as ways of being co-conscious, and as such, they contribute to the global characteristics of experiences.

9.4 C-holism and succession

We can now move on to consider slightly more realistic cases, those involving temporal succession within experience. Temporality can be taken to be another mode of co-consciousness, in that being temporally related is another way for experiences to be co-conscious. Indeed, time is even more general characteristic of experience than space, in that we can conceive of non-spatial experiences (e.g. non-imagistic thoughts), but any stream of consciousness will necessarily be composed of experiences which endure and are temporally interrelated. To simplify the discussion I will concentrate for the most part on global properties of the narrow, type-specific sort.

Suppose E_1 is a temporally extended total experience consisting of two successive auditory experiences, a_1 and a_2. We represent succession thus: a_1-a_2, i.e. the convention is that a hyphen indicates succession whereas a backslash indicates concurrence. E_2 is a neighbouring and partially overlapping auditory total experience, comprising the succession a_2-a_3. Experiences a_1, a_2 and a_3 are of local phenomenal types C, D and E respectively. Now consider the global characteristics of each of these experiences.

a_1:   Cg [**Cx**-Dx]   Cp [**a₁**-a₂]   [1]

a_2:   Cg [Cx-**Dx**-Ex]   Cp [a₁-**a₂**-a₃]   [2]

a_3:   Cg [Dx-**Ex**]   Cp [a₂-**a₃**]   [3]

Focusing on the narrow characterizations, line [1] expresses the fact that a_1 is a C-type experience that is co-conscious with and precedes a D-type experience; [2] expresses the fact that a_2 is a D-type experience that is co-conscious with a preceding C-type experience and a succeeding E-type experience; [3] expresses the fact that a_3 is an E-type experience that is co-conscious with a preceding D-type experience. Each Cg-property is now an extended phenomeno-temporal pattern. In order to make it clear that a_2 features in two total experiences, we can reformulate [2] thus:

a_2: Cg [Cx-**Dx**, **Dx**-Ex]   [2]*

Doing so clarifies the point that the content of type Cx-Dx-Ex is divided between two distinct (but overlapping) total experiences.

More complex global characters can be represented in a similar fashion.

In [4] below there is a representation of the constituents of a phase of a simple stream of consciousness s consisting of a succession of concurrent auditory, visual and gustatory experiences. Experiences in the same vertical column are concurrent, for example a_1, v_1 and g_1 are concurrent, as are a_4, v_4 and g_4. The local types of these experiences are specified in [5]; a_2 is a D-type auditory experience, g_3 is a R-type gustatory experience, and so forth.

$$
s = \begin{array}{l} a_1\text{-}a_2\text{-}a_3\text{-}a_4 \\ v_1\text{-}v_2\text{-}v_3\text{-}v_4 \\ g_1\text{-}g_2\text{-}g_3\text{-}g_4 \end{array} \quad [4] \qquad \begin{array}{l} Cx\text{-}Dx\text{-}Ex\text{-}Fx \\ Gx\text{-}Hx\text{-}Ix\text{-}Jx \\ Px\text{-}Qx\text{-}Rx\text{-}Sx \end{array} \quad [5]
$$

We can represent the Cg-property of just one of these experiences, v_2, in either of these ways:

$$
v_2\text{: Cg} \begin{array}{l} Cx\text{-}Dx\text{-}Ex \\ Gx\text{-}\mathbf{Hx}\text{-}Ix \\ Px\text{-}Qx\text{-}Rx \end{array} \quad [6] \qquad v_2\text{: Cg} \begin{array}{l} Cx\text{-}Dx,Dx\text{-}Ex \\ Gx\text{-}\mathbf{Hx},\mathbf{Hx}\text{-}Ix \\ Px\text{-}Qx, Qx\text{-}Rx \end{array} \quad [7]
$$

As can be seen in [7], experience v_2 of type H is a constituent of two complex overlapping total experiences, the first is Cx-Dx\Gx-Hx\Px-Qx, and the second is Dx-Ex\Hx-Ix\Qx-Rx (the backslash indicates simultaneity). Each of these maximally connected total experiences is an entire temporal cross-section of stream s. It will be seen that all the experiences in each of these cross-sections is registered in v_2's global character. Each such cross-section is a total experience, and all the constituent parts of a total experience are mutually co-conscious. So for example, the auditory experiences a_1 and a_3 of types C and E occur before and after v_2; since they are co-conscious with v_2, their phenomenal types are included in the latter's global character; hence the presence of Cx and Ex in v_2's Cg-property, along with Dx, which represents the local character of a_2, which is simultaneous with v_2. Similarly with g_1 and g_3, and of course v_1 and v_3. In short, each of the constituents of matrices [6] and [7] is co-conscious with v_2.

The experiences which are concurrent with v_2, namely a_2 and g_2, will have exactly the same Cg-property, since they are co-conscious with just the same experiences as v_2. So (in the succinct mode) we have:

$$
a_2\text{:}\quad \text{Cg} \quad \begin{array}{l} Cx\text{-}\mathbf{Dx}\text{-}Ex \\ Gx\text{-}Hx\text{-}Ix \\ Px\text{-}Qx\text{-}Rx \end{array}
$$

$$
\begin{array}{lll}
 & & \text{Cx-Dx-Ex} \\
v_2: & \text{Cg} & \text{Gx-}\mathbf{Hx}\text{-Ix} \\
 & & \text{Px-Qx-Rx}
\end{array}
$$

$$
\begin{array}{lll}
 & & \text{Cx-Dx-Ex} \\
g_2: & \text{Cg} & \text{Gx-Hx-Ix} \\
 & & \text{Px-}\mathbf{Qx}\text{-Rx} \hspace{3em} [8]
\end{array}
$$

In the simplified synchronic case, we saw that the overall character of a total experience is reflected in each of its sub-parts. We now see, in the diachronic case, that when two total experiences temporally overlap, the character of both totals is reflected in each experiential component in the region of overlap.

We have been concerned so far with the (narrow) global characters of individual experiences which are sub-parts of total experiences. What of total experiences themselves? These too have global characters; they are, after all, experiences in their own right. By way of example, consider the central two columns of the matrix in [4] above, consisting of a_2-$a_3\backslash v_2$-$v_3\backslash g_2$-g_3. This is a single, temporally extended total experience, we can call it E_T. The global character of this experience is thus:

$$
\begin{array}{lll}
 & & \text{Cx-}\mathbf{Dx}\text{-}\mathbf{Ex}\text{-Fx} \\
E_T: & \text{Cg} & \text{Gx-}\mathbf{Hx}\text{-}\mathbf{Ix}\text{-Jx} \\
 & & \text{Px-}\mathbf{Qx}\text{-}\mathbf{Rx}\text{-Sx} \hspace{3em} [9]
\end{array}
$$

Here the middle two columns represent the local character of E_T, and the first and fourth columns represent its global character. If we want to make the division into overlapping sub-totals clear, we can reformulate thus:

$$
\begin{array}{lll}
 & & \text{Cx-}\mathbf{Dx}, \ \mathbf{Dx}\text{-}\mathbf{Ex}, \ \mathbf{Ex}\text{-Fx} \\
E_T: & \text{Cg} & \text{Gx-}\mathbf{Hx}, \ \mathbf{Hx}\text{-}\mathbf{Ix}, \ \mathbf{Ix}\text{-Jx} \\
 & & \text{Px-}\mathbf{Qx}, \ \mathbf{Qx}\text{-}\mathbf{Rx}, \ \mathbf{Rx}\text{-Sx} \hspace{3em} [10]
\end{array}
$$

I have been concentrating on the type-specific Cg-properties, but similar points could be made in terms of token-specific Cp-properties.

9.5 C-holism and temporal modes of presentation

A point of some interest is the manner in which the global character of an experience reflects the character of the earlier and/or later experiences with which it is co-conscious. Returning to our initial example, of a_1-a_2-a_3, the global character of the D-type a_2 includes a C-type and an E-type experience. Since we are assuming (artificially) that the Indifference Principle holds without exception, the fact that a_2 is preceded by a C-type rather than a B-type experience makes no difference to the local character of a_2, similarly for the fact that a_2 is followed by an E-type rather than an F-type experience. The impact of a_1 (and a_3) on a_2 is limited in this respect, but is nonetheless real: the global character of a_2 would have been different had it been preceded and/or succeeded by experiences of a different local type. To this extent, the identity of an experience is sensitive to the characters of the earlier and/or later experiences with which it is co-conscious.

What we have here is a vindication, after a fashion, of the doctrine of temporal modes of presentation. As we saw in §7.4, some analysts of temporal experience have held that the character of an experience will be influenced by the earlier (and possibly the later) experiences with which it is co-conscious – Lockwood saw this as a problem for the overlap theory. In response, I argued that in an experienced succession such as *Do-Re-Mi*, the phenomenal character of *Re* in the two total experiences [Do-Re] and [Re-Mi] would be exactly the same. This still holds true, but only so far as the local character of *Re* is concerned. Now we have recognized global character, we can see that the temporal context of an experience *does* impact on its character, and so its identity (assuming that we take the global character of an experience to be relevant to its identity). Although the local character of an experience is unaffected by the adjacent experiences with which it is co-conscious, its global character is sensitive to the local character of the adjacent experiences. Suppose that *Re* had been followed by *Fa* rather than *Mi*. The global character of *Re* would reflect this fact: it would be of the form 'a *Re*-type experience preceded by a *Do*-type experience and succeeded by a *Fa*-type experience', as opposed to 'a *Re*-type experience preceded by a *Do*-type experience and succeeded by a *Mi*-type experience'. And this holds generally, across (or along) the stream of consciousness as a whole.

The recognition of global character introduces a new element into our account of the temporal dimension of experience. But does this new element pose a problem for the overlap theory? No, for all the overlap theory requires is that successive total experiences can have a common sub-part. In the case of a_1-a_2-a_3, the central experience a_2 must have exactly the same phenomenal character in the two successive overlapping total experiences T_1 = [a_1-a_2] and T_2 = [a_2-a_3]. If a_2 has a different character in the former than it does in the latter, it makes no sense to suppose 'a_2' refers to numerically the same experience in T_1 and T_2. So far as local character is concerned, there is obviously no difficulty here, since a_2 has the same local character in T_1 as it does in T_2. What of global character? The global character of a_2 is Cg [Cx-**Dx**, **Dx**-Ex]. Does it make sense to say that a_2 possesses *this* character in both T_1 and T_2? Since a_2 does have the property of being co-conscious with both a C-type experience and an E-type experience, there is no problem here either: an experience with this global character is a common part of *both* T_1

and T_2, hence a_2 has the local character D and the global character [Cx-**Dx**, **Dx**-Ex] in both T_1 and T_2. The crucial point is that a_2 does not *change* its global character, it has exactly the same character in both T_1 and T_2.

Still, it might be thought odd to suppose that a_2 has the element of global character 'being co-conscious with an E-type experience' when it occurs in T_1. From the perspective of this total experience, a_3 has yet to occur, and so is yet to be experienced. Similarly, from the perspective of T_2, a_1 is in the past and is no longer being experienced, so it might seem peculiar to suppose a_2 in T_2 has the element of global character, 'is co-conscious with a C-type experience'. However, like all mid-stream experiences, a_2 is Janus-faced, being co-conscious with both earlier and later experiences. Once this is recognized, the situation no longer seems peculiar or problematic; it is simply an inevitable consequence of the fact that distinct total experiences overlap.

To reflect this fact more clearly there is nothing to prevent our introducing another level of content-characterization. In addition to complete and partial characterizations of an experience's content, which take in global and local content respectively, we could recognize *perspectival* characterizations. These register only the global character an experience has from the perspective of a given total experience, with the global character it has in virtue of being co-conscious with other total experiences bracketed off. From the perspective of T_1, a_2 has global character [Cx-**Dx**], and from the perspective of T_2, this same experience has global character [**Dx**-Ex]. But since these perspectival characterizations are incomplete, the fact that a_2 has a different perspectival character in T_1 than in T_2 does not mean that a_2 has undergone a change in global character, or that a_2 itself has different characteristics in different totals. For the identity of a_2 is fixed by its entire global character. And this means there is no obstacle to taking a_2 in T_1 to be numerically the same experience as a_2 in T_2, which is what the overlap theory requires.[1]

One further point pertaining to the temporal aspect of C-holism is worth mentioning. We can envisage a counterfactual case in which the stream of consciousness to which a_1-a_2-a_3 belongs takes a somewhat different course. Instead of a_1-a_2-a_3 we have a_1-a_2-a_4, where a_4 is a F-type auditory experience rather than an E-type. In the original case, the stream-phases included two total experiences $T_1 = [a_1$-$a_2]$ and $T_2 = [a_2$-$a_3]$. What difference does the occurrence of a_4 instead of a_3 make here? To start with, instead of T_2 we have a new total experience $T_2^* = [a_2$-$a_4]$, comprising auditory experiences of types D and F. Originally, a_2 had global character Cg [Cx-**Dx**, **Dx**-Ex]; it now has global character Cg [Cx-**Dx**, **Dx**-Fx]. Since the global character of a_2 has changed, so has its identity; we can now refer to it as a_2'. As one would expect, the substitution of a_4 for a_3 has impacted upon the character of the immediately preceding (and co-conscious) stream-phase. But what of a_1? This is not directly co-conscious with either a_3 or a_4, so it would be odd to find that the occurrence of a_4 in place of a_3 would have any impact on the identity of a_1. Yet in the counterfactual scenario, a_1 is co-conscious with a numerically distinct experience a_2' rather than a_2. To assess the effect of this, we need to consider only the global character of a_1, since its local character is the same in both cases. But we also need to consider both the broad (token-specific) and narrow (type-specific) ways of characterizing global character.

We can start by viewing the situation from the perspective of narrow characterizations, which we have been working with thus far. In the original scenario, a_1's global character is Cg [**Cx-Dx**]. In the counterfactual scenario, when a_1 is co-conscious with a_2', a_1's global character is also Cg [**Cx-Dx**]. Although the global characters of a_2 and a_2' are different, temporal separation ensures this difference does not impinge upon the global character of a_1. So, although in the two scenarios a_1 is co-conscious with two numerically distinct subsequent experiences, and these experiences have different global characters, the type-specific global characterizations of a_1 remain the same. Consequently, the initial experience in the first scenario is numerically identical with the initial experience in the second scenario.

From the perspective of broad, token-specific characterizations, the situation is different. The initial experience in the original scenario is co-conscious with a_2, whereas in the counterfactual scenario the initial experience is co-conscious with a_2'. Since a_2 and a_2' are numerically distinct, then so too are the initial experiences. Hence we need to distinguish a_1 and a_1', and hold them to be numerically distinct. These two experiences are numerically distinct solely because of the numerical distinctness of a_2 and a_2'. If the latter were distinct because a_2 is co-conscious with a_1, whereas a_2' is co-conscious with a_1', the situation would be viciously circular. But this is not the case: the distinctness of a_2 and a_2' is not due to their relationships with a_1 and a_1', but to the fact that each has a different narrow (and broad) global character, by virtue of the fact that a_2 is co-conscious with the E-type a_3, whereas a_2' is co-conscious with the F-type a_4. This difference does not impinge upon the narrow global characters of a_1 and a_1', but for a difference in broad global character this is not required.

So, the occurrence of a_4 instead of a_3 only impacts upon the identity of the earlier experience a_1 if we choose to individuate in terms of broad rather than narrow global character. The idea that the identity of an experience can be affected by the absence (or presence) of experiences further upstream (or downstream) with which it is not directly co-conscious may seem odd. But since this result only arises when a particularly stringent mode of individuating experience is adopted, it is not surprising that it seems counterintuitive.

9.6 Transitivity revisited

All this puts us in a position to shed a little further light on the vexed issue of the transitivity of synchronic co-consciousness. In Chapter 4 I tentatively concluded that synchronic co-consciousness was transitive, and have been working on this assumption ever since. But for the sake of completeness, let us suppose this assumption is false, and take a look at a partially unified consciousness at the level of global character.

Consider a simple example, a subject S who has at time t three simultaneous experiences, a pain, an itch and an auditory sensation, e_1, e_2 and e_3, of types F, G and H, such that e_1 is co-conscious with e_2, and e_2 with e_3, but e_1 is not co-conscious with e_3. S's overall or maximal experience at t thus consists of two overlapping total experiences $T_1 = [e_1\backslash e_2]$ and $T_2 = [e_2\backslash e_3]$. The global characters of the constituents of these are as follows:

$$e_1 = Cg\,[\mathbf{Fx}\backslash Gx]$$

$$e_2 = Cg\,[Fx\backslash \mathbf{Gx}, \mathbf{Gx}\backslash Hx]$$

$$e_3 = Cg\,[Gx\backslash \mathbf{Hx}]$$

It is clear that everything we said about the diachronic case (which, of course, also involves a failure of transitivity) applies here too. If we envisage a counterfactual case, where e_2 is co-conscious with e_4, an I-type experience, then this would impact on the global character of e_2, which would then be of the form $[Fx\backslash \mathbf{Gx}, \mathbf{Gx}\backslash Ix]$. The experience with this global character would be numerically distinct from e_2, so call it e_2'. Although e_1 is, in this hypothetical situation, co-conscious with e_2' rather than e_2, this does not register in any way upon e_1's local character. Since the local character of e_2' is still Gx, the narrow global character of e_1 remains unchanged, i.e. $[\mathbf{Fx}\backslash Gx]$. Whether or not the identity of e_1 remains unchanged depends upon whether we individuate broadly or narrowly.

The interesting feature of this case is e_2, and its global character (e_1 and e_3 are perfectly ordinary in this respect). As in the diachronic case, the global character of e_2 has two components, $Fx\backslash Gx$ and $Gx\backslash Hx$. These components are (by hypothesis) not experienced together. In the diachronic case this is readily understandable, since the second component occurs at a later time than the first. But the synchronic case is different, since both components occur simultaneously, and this makes it harder to comprehend what is going on. As in the diachronic case, we can give perspectival characterizations of e_2's global character. From the perspective of T_1, e_2 has the character Cg $[Fx\backslash \mathbf{Gx}]$, and from the perspective of T_2 it has character Cg $[\mathbf{Gx}\backslash Hx]$. But neither of these perspectival characterizations fully captures e_2's character; the full characterization of e_2's character is Cg $[Fx\backslash \mathbf{Gx}, \mathbf{Gx}\backslash Hx]$, and it has this character because it is co-conscious with both e_1 and e_3. Is this state of affairs really intelligible? We seem to be attributing to e_2 a phenomenal characteristic which is not actually *experienced*. How can an experience have a phenomenal character that is not experienced?

But this may be moving a little too fast. Although the two components of e_2's global character are not co-conscious with each other, they are both *experienced* at t. For in describing the case, we have stipulated that e_1 is experienced as co-conscious with e_2, and the latter is experienced as co-conscious with e_3. In which case, the entire global character of e_2 is experienced; it is just not experienced as a whole. That is, the global character of e_2 is not experienced as a feature of a total experience all of whose parts are directly co-conscious. So we are not positing a phenomenal feature which is not experienced at all, rather we are positing a phenomenal feature which is distributed, as it were, across an ensemble of simultaneous experiences that are not mutually co-conscious. Whether this is a genuine possibility is another issue. I suggested in §4.5 that experiences joined by synchronic co-consciousness are fused together in such a way that transitivity cannot fail; in §7.2 and §7.4, I drew attention to the distinctive way that breakdowns in transitivity are bound up with aspects of phenomenal temporality. If these arguments are along the right lines, if non-transitivity is indeed the hallmark of temporality, there could not be an experience such as e_2, an experience which simultaneously inhabits two distinct (but overlapping) phenomenal wholes, for the only way an experience could have a global character which is not fully co-conscious is by being co-conscious with non-simultaneous experiences.

To summarize: over the past two chapters we have been looking at the various sorts of part-whole interdependencies which exist among co-conscious experiences. The CPI thesis asserts a complete experiential holism of the type variety at the level of local intrinsic character. This thesis seems false: there are clearly some parts of some total experiences that are not phenomenally interdependent in this manner, the most obvious instances being experiences belonging to different perceptual modalities. This is not to say that there are no instances of phenomenal interdependence at all. I looked at the two special cases: sensory wholes and meaningful wholes. So far as sensory wholes are concerned, while there is no doubt some degree of interdependence in these cases, it seems likely that the Gestalt theorists exaggerated both its depth and its extent. Once we recognize that sensory wholes influence our overall state of mind in ways that their parts taken in isolation do not – think of the images of eyes in and out of their ordinary context – the influence of context on character already seems less mysterious. In a wide range of other cases, the impingement of the character of phenomenal whole on phenomenal part is of the Weak rather than the Strong variety. If Strong Impingement does exist, it is rather unusual. Meaning poses problems of a different sort, and no doubt warrants a more extended investigation, but my comparatively brief examination led me to the (tentative) conclusion that meaning-bearing phenomenal wholes do not in general exhibit phenomenal interdependence, in virtue of the meaning their parts possess. There is, however, at least one notable exception: thoughts which are about experience itself. In this chapter my concern has been with a different sort of phenomenal interdependence, the sort which exists at the level of global rather than local character. Since global character is the product of co-

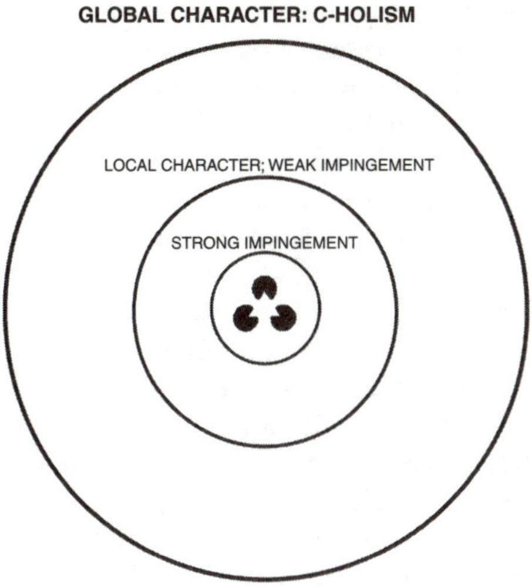

GLOBAL CHARACTER: C-HOLISM

Figure 9.1 Holism: the overall picture

consciousness itself, the relevant interdependence is complete and necessary. We can also, if we choose, distinguish between narrow and broad global features; C-holism can be type-specific or token-specific.

As far as the general issue of experiential holism is concerned, we have the following overall picture (Figure 9.1).

There is complete interdependence at the level of global character. C-holism applies to all parts of all co-conscious experiences, both synchronically and diachronically. There is a partial holism due to phenomenal interdependence at the level of local intrinsic character. For the most part this is intra-modal and contingent, and is perhaps most commonly found to apply to the parts of sensory wholes and in the case of intra-experiential demonstrative reference. Then there is, perhaps, a small degree of Strong Impingement: some parts of some phenomenal wholes may have phenomenal features which are context-linked, features which can only exist in wholes of certain types. Phenomenal items to which either of these kinds of partial local interdependence applies are, of course, also interdependent at the level of global character. C-holism, which can be either type-specific or token-specific, applies without exception to all parts of all co-conscious experiences.

9.7 Conclusion

This brings my inquiry into the unity of consciousness to an end. I have deliberately focused only on the more general, schematic or structural features of our experience. Although this seemed necessary in order to bring these same features into clear relief, it has meant that the astonishing variety, complexity and subtlety of our conscious lives has largely been ignored –

but perhaps a phenomenology which would do justice to all this is best left in the hands of the poets. In any event, what I have been concerned with here is the general framework within which our experience, in all its complexity, occurs and unfolds. Although the inquiry has been largely phenomenological, the results have not been negligible or without interest. The framework in question has turned out to be stranger than might have been thought, involving as it does an intriguing mixture of simplicity and subtlety in its own right.

One aspect of this subtlety lies in the various sorts of holism and interdependence we have been looking at latterly; my discussion has in all likelihood done no more than scratch the surface of these difficult topics. But there are others which should not be overlooked. The unity we find in our streams of consciousness, both at and over time, consists in the simple fact that our experience divides into parts and these parts are co-conscious. Since a given stretch of experience can be divided into parts in any number of different ways, and whatever parts are discerned can themselves be regarded as wholes consisting of further parts, the unifying relationship of co-consciousness is all-pervasive, at least within the confines of the phenomenal present. No matter how a total experience is divided into parts, every part is connected to every other part by co-consciousness. A typical stream of experience thus exhibits a deep and far-reaching unity; and in so far as consciousness has characteristic features, this mode of unity is as distinctive and remarkable as any.

Co-consciousness itself, when viewed as a phenomenal feature of experience, is not susceptible to analysis or explanation, or so I have argued. It does not depend on or require attentive or cognitive awareness, or the Pure Awareness of the act–object theory; it does not require experience to occur within a single phenomenal space or a conscious substance with discernible phenomenal features. Given the irreducibility of co-consciousness, the bond between experiences that is responsible for their unity might seem strange, perhaps so subtle and uncanny a thing that its very existence seems dubious. But nothing could be more wrong, for nothing is so familiar as the fact that experiences are experienced together, Co-consciousness is simply a basic feature of experience, as basic as colour or sound. Then there is the dynamic diachronic aspect of consciousness. Finding a coherent yet believable account of the flux and flow to be found within streams of experience is not an easy matter, as shown by the baroque complexity of some of the theories of time-consciousness on offer. But on examination, the more complex theories seem inadequate to the actual character of temporal experience; a simpler and better account is founded on the basic relationship of co-consciousness.

One lesson to be drawn from all this is that the unity within our experience is an affair that is at once simpler and more involved than it has sometimes been thought to be. A second lesson is that experience is self-unifying, in that to understand the unity we find within experience, we do not need to look to anything above, beyond or external to experience itself.

If my analyses of these matters are along the right lines, the familiar watery metaphors are appropriate. A stream of water is a unified flowing whole, and so is a stream of consciousness. Indeed, in some respects streams of consciousness are more like their liquid counterparts than some enthusiasts for such comparisons have recognized. In a passage quoted earlier, Bradley suggested that if we want an image to assist us in grasping the character of our experience, we could do worse than to imagine ourselves in total darkness, suspended over a stream with no banks, a stream entirely filled and covered with continuously moving things; we are only aware of the stream and its contents because, directly below our faces, is a brightly illuminated pool of light – our now, our present – which reveals to us what the current is carrying away. This image is as appealing as it is mistaken, at least if taken too literally, for it implies a separation of awareness and phenomenal content (a separation Bradley himself did not recognize). If, as I have argued, awareness and content are not separate, consciousness does not consist in an awareness of a passing stream, consciousness is the stream itself.

Aquatic comparisons should not be taken too far. Whereas a stream of water consists of parts unified by proximity and forces of attraction, a stream of consciousness consists of parts compounded by the phenomenal relationship of co-consciousness. Hydraulic flow consists of the same water molecules occupying different places at different times. Phenomenal dynamics are different, and involve a combination of two factors: experiences at different times possessing inherently animated contents, and a breakdown in the transitivity of co-consciousness. If this account of phenomenal temporality is right, another aspect of Bradley's image stands in need of correction. Descriptions of experience commonly invoke light as often as water – Bradley's image incorporates both. As a description of how things seem, or how we naturally take things to be, the image may be as good as any, but it does not correspond with how things are. If we choose to think of phenomenal contents as possessing a distinctive illumination, it is natural to think this illumination is possessed only by contents occurring at the present time, but this is wrong: if we assume that all times are equally real and present, it is possessed by all contents, irrespective of when they occur. Consciousness does not consist of a stream running beneath a spot of light, nor of a spot of light running along a stream; consciousness is the stream itself, and the light extends through its entire length. But if this image of an extended glowing whole better corresponds to how things are, metaphysically speaking, this is not something which can be discerned from within experience; in this respect at least, experience is not how it seems.

As for the broader implications of the various conclusions I have reached, I will mention just two. The first is connected to the point just made. The static view of time, according to which all moments are equally real and present (when they occur), has often been taken to be in tension with time as it is manifest in consciousness. Given that phenomenal temporality is inherently dynamic, all flux and flow, if physical time is static it might seem that consciousness itself could not possibly be physical. However, as we saw in §7.5, this apparent tension can be resolved; the account of phenomenal dynamics I have provided is fully compatible with the four-dimensional Block View of time. Whether or not this view of time is correct is, of course, another story.

If this is a result which makes it easier to see how the phenomenal and the physical might one day be reconciled, another result might seem to have precisely the opposite effect. It has proved hard enough to comprehend how phenomenal properties such as colour and sound could be ingredients of the material universe, but it may prove harder still to understand how co-consciousness fits into the physical scheme of things. Co-consciousness is a pervasive relationship; it holds not only between experiences, but within experience. No matter how a total experience is divided up, all its discernible constituent parts are mutually co-conscious. A counterpart of this unifying relationship in the physical realm would hold only between those portions of matter associated with the production of experience. Needless to say, it is hard to think of any remotely plausible candidates.

To end on a more positive but also more speculative note, there may be one respect in which recognizing the pervasive nature of co-consciousness renders the relationship between the material and the phenomenal easier to comprehend. If we assume that physical items have at least some intrinsic properties, and we further assume that phenomenal properties are themselves physical, we are faced with a problem. What is it that is special or distinctive about phenomenal properties? How do intrinsic properties that are phenomenal differ from those that are non-phenomenal? The problem is made more severe by the following consideration. Conscious beings can no doubt come in many shapes and forms; since conscious beings physically different from us may well have experiences very different in (intrinsic) character from our own, the range of possible (or actual) phenomenal properties might far exceed the range known to us. Once we accept this possibility it becomes harder still to think of a feature which might distinguish the phenomenal from the non-phenomenal.

However, in the light of the main results I have reached concerning phenomenal unity, this problem no longer seems entirely intractable: if there is a real distinction between phenomenal and non-phenomenal properties, surely one of the most significant differences between them will be that the former but not the latter are unified by co-consciousness. From the perspective of the awareness–content model it would certainly be plausible to say that a property should be regarded as phenomenal if instantiations of it are, or could be, apprehended by an awareness, irrespective of the intrinsic character of the property in question. If we reject the awareness–content model in favour of the Simple Conception, experiences consist of contents pervaded by co-consciousness. That this mode of unity is a crucial feature of experience as we know it is easily appreciated: remove this unity from a typical stream of consciousness and what would be left? At most a myriad instances of point-like quality, each so entirely isolated from the rest that, from the point of view of experience at least, they could as well exist in different universes. So might it not be that *any* intrinsic qualities unified by co-consciousness should properly be regarded as phenomenal in nature? The answer to this may depend on the significance we grant to the dynamic temporal patterning our own experience exhibits, a feature of our experience which cannot be explained solely in terms of co-consciousness. In any event, there is no denying that co-conscious unity is *a* if not *the* distinguishing characteristic of the phenomenal. As a consequence, the matter–consciousness problem becomes at once easier and more difficult. Easier because the experiential loses a good deal of what can make it seem mysterious; harder because the physical counterpart of co-consciousness remains as mysterious as anything ever was.

Postscript

In this addendum I will comment on a few issues that were neglected in the hardback edition, and offer some preliminary observations on more recent developments. I defend, expand, clarify (and on occasion modify) various aspects of my position in a *Psyche* symposium devoted to the book – matters dealt with there are not dealt with here.[1]

Co-consciousness: a ghostly connection?

In the course of a valuable discussion in Chapter 5 of *Sensations* (1991) Christopher Hill distinguishes a number of different ways in which experiences can be unified at a given time. Hill's discussion is particularly pertinent because he comes to the conclusion that one putative mode of synchronic unity does *not* in fact exist – and this mode sounds very much like co-consciousness in the form that I have tried to bring to the fore. Although I think Hill is wrong, exploring where he goes astray will prove useful.

Hill begins by arguing that although it can be tempting to think that the unity of consciousness is nothing more than a matter of diverse experiences being owned by a common subject, this cannot be the whole story. There are other relationships which experiences can enter into, and while these relationships obviously constitute modes of unity, they are distinct both from one another and the relationship 'belonging to the same subject'. To start with, experiences can be unified by virtue of falling under a single act of introspective awareness, and experiences which do not fall under a single awareness can nonetheless be unified by virtue of the fact that they could have done: experiences that are not introspected can be introspectible. A further variety of unity is functional. In addition to their purely qualitative or phenomenal features, experiences have causal properties, e.g. in a normal human subject, seeing yellow is apt to cause yellow-related thoughts and beliefs. Being a component of a causally integrated cognitive system is a distinctive mode of unity. Yet another mode of unity is 'being (phenomenally) spatially related'. A patch of yellow and a patch of blue seen to its right in the same visual field are related in this way, as are a toothache and an ache in the ankle that are experienced not only together, but at some distance apart. As we saw in Chapter 3, these spatial relationships are very pervasive indeed in our experience. Finally, Hill suggests (plausibly) that experiences enter into part–whole relationships, and that although experiential parts will often be spatially related to their wholes – as when a patch of yellow is surrounded by a larger patch of blue – this is not always or necessarily the case. When listening to a symphony, the sound of the oboe might be clearly discernible amid the overall sound of orchestra, but it might well not be spatially localized; consequently, although the sound of the oboe is clearly part of the overall orchestral sound, it is not one of the latter's spatial parts. So far so good, but Hill goes on to say this:

> I have sometimes felt that it is possible to discriminate introspectively a form of co-consciousness that is different from all the forms that we have considered up to now. Thus, it has sometimes seemed, when I have been focusing on a pair of auditory sensations, or a pair of sensations associated with different sense modalities, that I was directly aware of the sensations as co-conscious even though I was not aware of them as owned by the same subject, nor as objects of a single state of awareness, nor as standing in any causal or counterfactual relations to one another, nor as parts of some third sensation, nor as linked by any [phenomeno]-spatial relation. I never felt that I was aware of this new form of co-consciousness as having positive differentiae that distinguish it from the other forms. Rather I was aware only that it lacked the positive differentiae that belong respectively to the other forms. Accordingly, it has seemed to me that this form of co-consciousness is pure – that it has no distinguishing characteristics other than its ability to unite sensations.
> [. . .] I now feel this view is wrong. It isn't possible to find this ghostly form of co-consciousness within one's experience. Hence, there is no good reason to believe that it exists.
>
> (1991: 239)

Having rejected co-consciousness in this 'pure' form, Hill argues that we should espouse a pluralistic conception: there is not one way in which consciousness is unified, there are several, each of which is significant, none of which is privileged.

Hill's 'pure co-consciousness' is very much akin to co-consciousness in the form I have espoused in this book. As I construe it, co-consciousness is a primitive relationship of experienced togetherness, a relationship that lacks any intrinsic phenomenal features of its own, but one which forges a phenomenologically real connection between diverse phenomenal contents. Does the fact that co-consciousness thus construed lacks discernible intrinsic qualitative features mean that we have no reason to believe that it exists? I do not see that it does. One reason for thinking that co-consciousness in the pure form exists is that we have reason to believe that experiences can be unified in this way when they are not unified in any other way – or at least, in any other *experiential* way. (And of course I am only interested here in what can be said about the unity of consciousness while remaining in the phenomenal realm.) But before exploring this point there is a further distinction which needs to be drawn.

In assessing Hill's case for pluralism it is important to note that not all the modes of unity he distinguishes are varieties of phenomenal unity, unity that is directly experienced. It may well be that co-conscious experiences belong to the same subject. However, quite what 'subjects' are is much disputed, and unless subjects are things we encounter in our experience – and as Hume noted, it is far from obvious that they are – it is difficult to see how 'belonging to the same subject' could be a unity relation of the phenomenal variety.[2] The same applies to functional unity. Our experiences no doubt are unified in this way, but as Hume also observed, causal relations themselves are phenomenologically invisible (their effects, of course, are not), and consequently such relations cannot themselves be phenomenal unity relations.[3]

The remaining forms of unity distinguished by Hill certainly are phenomenal, so the issue we need to focus on is the relationship between these forms and co-consciousness.

We saw in Chapter 2 that experiences do not need to be introspected or introspectible in order to be experienced together – Hill himself argues persuasively for this – and in Chapter 3 I argued that there are grounds for thinking that experiences can be co-conscious without being phenomeno-spatially related. The thought-experiments used in §3.3 illustrate the latter point in a particularly vivid way, but there are less dramatic ways of arguing for the same conclusion. It is not difficult to envisage circumstances in which contents are fully co-conscious despite being only very weakly related in a spatial way. Imagine that you have been lying in a sensory isolation tank for several hours, while under the influence of disorienting drugs which have robbed you of any sense of distance or direction. All of a sudden you start to hear two droning sounds of an entirely unfamiliar nature. Given your general disorientation, you have no clear impression of the distance or direction of these sounds – the hypothesis that they are coming from very different distances and directions is no more (or less) plausible than the hypothesis that they are co-located. But despite this spatial ambiguity, the sounds are *experienced together* in as clear and unambiguous a manner as any sounds ever are. And this applies irrespective of whether you are introspectively aware of the sounds, or whether they are merely parts of the phenomenal background. In a more mundane vein, there is the relationship of being a non-spatial part of a more encompassing experience to which Hill himself draws our attention. This is unquestionably a unity relationship of a phenomenal kind, and contents that are related in this manner are unquestionably co-conscious – in the example given earlier, the sound of the oboe is experienced together with the sound produced by the rest of the orchestra.

Cases such as this serve the useful purpose of bringing co-consciousness into clearer view: not surprisingly, it is easier to appreciate its distinctive character when other modes of unity are absent or insignificant. Once this character is appreciated, however, it soon becomes obvious that the relationship is pervasive: the same direct and unmediated phenomenal connection binds each and every part of our ordinary states of consciousness at any given time. My thoughts are co-conscious with the sound I hear to my right, with the sensations of pressure on my back, with all parts of the yellow expanse I see in front of me; and when I introspectively scrutinize the sensations of pressure on my back, this experience continues to be fully co-conscious with the remainder of my consciousness.

Co-consciousness unifies contents that are not connected in other ways, but it also unifies contents that *are* connected in other ways. It is because of this that a strong case can be made for regarding co-consciousness as having a privileged role in the phenomenal unity stakes. Consider again the unity relations distinguished by Hill that fall into the phenomenal category. Phenomenal contents that are introspected are obviously co-conscious, and I argued in §2.3 that it is more plausible by far to suppose that acts of introspection detect rather than create relationships of co-consciousness. A content that is experienced as part of a more complex whole is obviously experienced together with the whole, and so the whole and the part are co-conscious. Similarly for contents that are experienced as spatially related: by virtue of being experienced as spatially related, such contents are experienced together, and so are co-conscious. Synchronic phenomenal unity comes in different modes, but these modes all involve experienced togetherness. Being related by co-consciousness is thus a precondition for being related by any other mode of phenomenal unity; indeed, co-consciousness is an ingredient *in* other modes of phenomenal unity.

By way of a further illustration of these points, consider the following passage from Hill:

> As I now see it, when it seems to me that I am aware of a fact involving two auditory sensations, or two sensations associated with different sense modalities, and a ghostly unity relation, I am aware only of a fact that consists of the simultaneous existence of the two sensations. This is the only fact involving the sensations that is given. If it were otherwise, I would be able to distinguish introspectively between the fact consisting of the two sensations and the fact consisting of the two sensations and the putative ghostly unity relation. There would be a detectable difference between these two facts. However, as can be seen from the very ghostliness of the putative unity relation, there is no such difference.
>
> (1991: 240)

Hill is right about one thing: when we are aware of two auditory sensations, so far as the content of our experience is concerned, we are aware only of these two sensations – we are not aware of any ghostly string extending from one to the other. But Hill is wrong to conclude from this that the unity relation in question does not exist. If co-consciousness is nothing more (or less) than the primitive relationship of experienced togetherness, we should not expect to be able to detect it among the contents of our consciousness. This does not mean that we cannot introspectively discern the relationship in question: when diverse contents are experienced together it is perfectly obvious that this is the case. Indeed, the fact that Hill is *aware* of his two auditory sensations *together* is proof of the existence of the co-consciousness relation – or at least it is if the latter is defined purely in terms of experienced togetherness. Accordingly, there would be a very significant difference between the two scenarios Hill describes, between a state of affairs consisting of two sensations joined by co-consciousness, and a state of affairs consisting of two sensations *not* so joined. He is also wrong in supposing that he could have two sensations that are not co-conscious which could also fall under a single act of introspective awareness. If they are apprehended together, they cannot fail to be co-conscious.

So we can see that when co-consciousness is understood in the right way, it is not at all elusive; it makes its presence felt in the most dramatic of ways. Nor is it in any way mysterious. For as I pointed out in §3.7 in connection with Armstrong's objection, we know exactly what it is like for two (or more) sensations to be experienced together – indeed, it is probably true to say that there is no relationship more familiar than co-consciousness. It is also probably true to say that this familiarity is part of the problem. Despite its ubiquity, co-consciousness is easy to miss; the precise manner in which our consciousness is unified can easily go unnoticed.[4]

Duplications and regresses

Hill's rejection of co-consciousness (of the pure variety) was rooted in phenomenology: he looked, but failed to find it in his experience. Others reject the sort of account I have proposed because, for one reason or another, they think it doesn't ultimately make sense to suppose such a thing as co-consciousness exists. I will examine some of the more prominent lines of argument that have led some philosophers to this conclusion.

In a number of writings, Susan Hurley has argued that to make sense of consciousness we must appeal to something 'objective' that is external to consciousness (1998: 62). This is because consciousness is unified, and we cannot – she maintains – successfully or intelligibly mark the distinction between those contents of consciousness that are unified and those that are not without appealing to something external to consciousness: 'The unity of consciousness cannot be determined by the consciousness of unity. If conscious content is understood as subjective or narrow, then it seems that something outside conscious content, and in this sense objective, is needed' (1998: 63).

One of her arguments for this conclusion appeals to the notion of a partially unified consciousness. In a state of this kind, although every part is co-conscious with some other part, there are also parts that are not co-conscious with one another. As we saw in Chapter 4, what makes such states so intriguing is that although they are impossible for us to imagine, there is some evidence (or so some have argued) that split-brain patients have a consciousness with this structure, some or all of the time. While recognizing that the possibility of a partially unified conscious state remains a contested issue, Hurley plausibly insists that an adequate account of phenomenal unity must at least have the means of marking the distinction between full and partial unity. She goes on to argue that if we draw only on phenomenal resources, it is impossible to distinguish cases such as these:

(a) A partially unified conscious state consisting of E_1, E_2 and E_3, in which E_1 is co-conscious with both E_2 and E_3, but the latter are not co-conscious with one another.

(b) A state of affairs comprising two simultaneous but entirely distinct experiences, one of which consists of the co-conscious combination of E_1 and E_2, the other of which consists of the co-conscious combination of E_1^* and E_3, where E_1^* is an experience that is qualitatively identical with E_1, but numerically distinct from it.

More generally, the claim is that if we confine ourselves to a purely experiential standpoint, it is impossible to distinguish the sharing or overlapping of contents (in a partially unified state) from the *duplication* of contents in entirely distinct streams of consciousness.

But as Bayne and Chalmers point out (2003: §6.3), while this may be true if we seek to explain phenomenal unity in terms of phenomenal state *types*, only two of which are needed to describe both (a) and (b), it is ineffective against accounts which favour relationships among state *tokens*. From the latter perspective the two scenarios are clearly distinct: in (a) a single state E_1 is phenomenally unified with tokens E_2 and E_3, in (b) E_1 is unified only with E_2 and a numerically distinct token, E_1^*, is unified with E_3. How could the distinction between the two states of affairs be clearer? Co-consciousness, as I construe it, is a relationship between token experiences.

In reply it could be objected that we need to appeal to something external to consciousness in order to make sense of the claim that E_1 and E_1^* are in fact numerically distinct – given that they are simultaneous and qualitatively identical. Whether this is so or not depends on the position one adopts on the individuation of token phenomenal states. Those who take experiential items to be as real as anything else, physical things included, may well be inclined to regard token phenomenal states as primitive so far as individuation is concerned. Of course, not everyone who takes experience seriously is prepared to go this far. Some would say that to be distinct, states such as E_1 and E_1^* must belong to different subjects, or have different physical bases – as I have been assuming. But while those who adopt stances such as these are appealing to something external to consciousness to *individuate* token states, it is not clear that they are appealing to anything external to consciousness in their account of what *unifies* such states, not if they explicate unity in terms of a distinctive but purely phenomenal relationship, a relationship such as co-consciousness.

Hurley presses another line. She calls it the 'just more content' objection, and summarizes it thus: 'the unity or separateness of consciousness cannot be accounted for in terms of the subjective contents of consciousness because the same question of unity or separateness arises again for any such contents' (1998: 5). It is not difficult to see that this objection menaces some experience-based accounts of the unity of consciousness. The accounts in question are those which hold that experiences are unified if and only if they are connected by *some other experience*. Call the latter 'binding experiences'. Quite what form binding experiences might take is a question we needn't enter into; all we need to know is that they *are* experiences (or phenomenal contents or states) and so have a distinctive and discernible phenomenal character of some kind. In this context the 'just more content' objection is effective. Since the binding experiences *are* experiences, they will presumably be among the phenomenal states that comprise our unified states of consciousness. If so, this question becomes pressing: 'What unifies binding experience with the experiences they connect?' If the reply is 'something other than binding experiences', then since the proposed account applies to some experiences but not all, it is not complete. If the reply is 'additional binding experiences', then the proposed account is exhaustive and consistent, but it is problematic none-theless, for the question now arises as to what unifies the additional binding experiences to the experiences they connect, and since the answer will be 'still more binding experiences', we have evidently embarked on an endless infinite regress. In some contexts such regresses may not be problematic, but in this context they surely are: we have no reason to believe our ordinary states of consciousness include experiential complexes of this kind.

But of course, we have no reason to believe that 'binding experiences' of the envisaged sort exist either. Our ordinary states of consciousness are unified, but they aren't cluttered with experiences which connect other experiences – there are no ghostly threads tying the various parts of our consciousness together, or if there are they do not figure in our experience – we have no introspective awareness of them. As just noted in connection with Hill, co-consciousness as I construe it is *not* an experience or a phenomenal content. It is a relationship which binds experiences, but it has no phenomenal characteristics of its own. When two experiences are co-conscious they are experienced together, and this is all: there is no additional phenomenal content stretching between them. At the phenomenological level, 'experienced togetherness' is a primitive; it is not reducible to, or explicable in terms of, any other form or feature of experience.

If this point suffices to undermine Hurley's 'just more content' objection, it serves a similar purpose with regard to a similar complaint lodged by Michael Tye:

If what it is like to undergo the overall or maximal experience is different from what it is like to undergo the component sense-specific experiences, E_1–E_5, then there must be a unifying relation between the latter experiences that is itself experienced. The experience of the unifying relation is not itself a sense-specific experience. But it is an experience nonetheless; for if there were no experience of the unifying relation, then there would be nothing it is like to have the sense-specific experiences unified. There are, then, it seems, six experiences: the five sense-specific experiences and the experience of unity. However, the maximal experience isn't just a conjunction of experiences. It is a genuinely new unified experience with its own phenomenology. So, what unites the six experiences together? It seems that there must be a further unifying relation that binds the experiences. This relation, however, must itself be experienced. For the unity is phenomenal. And now a regress has begun to which there is no end.

(2003: 22)

Here Tye assumes that the 'unifying relation' must be an experience in its own right if it is to account for the experience of unity. While he is right that a regress looms if the unity relation is an experience, for the reasons just outlined, this is not the only option. Co-consciousness is a relational property of experiences, not an experience, and since it is a *phenomenal* relation, it is by no means absurd to suppose that it can account for phenomenal unity as it is experienced. After all, it is obviously the case that the character of our overall states of consciousness is affected in a significant way by the manner in which the constituent parts of these states are related. A visual experience comprising a patch of blue which bears the 'appearing to the left of' relation to a patch of yellow will be very different in character from an experience where a similarly sized patch of blue bears the 'appearing above' relation to a similarly sized patch of yellow. The experience of a *Do*-tone occurring immediately prior to a *Re*-tone is quite different from the experience of a *Re*-tone occurring immediately prior to a *Do*-tone.

Generally speaking the relational properties of experiences can make a significant difference to the phenomenal character of our consciousness, and co-consciousness is no exception in this regard. Not only is there something distinctive that it is like to experience phenomenal contents occurring together in one's consciousness, being related by co-consciousness is a precondition for contents entering into any other kind of phenomenal relationship that can be directly experienced. In the absence of co-consciousness our experience would be unimaginably different from how it in fact is (cf. pp. 238–9 above). As Tye himself notes, 'Unity is a fundamental part of our experience, something that is crucial to its phenomenology' (2003: xii).

Diachronic unity: two queries

Moving on from these very general matters pertaining to synchronic unity, I want to look at some narrower issues concerning diachronic unity. In his review of the book, Bayne is driven to ask: 'But what *is* the specious present? Dainton makes a number of claims about the specious present, some of which seem to hang together rather uncomfortably' (2001: 87). The tension Bayne goes on to describe is real. I take a specious present to be a temporally extended total experience, i.e. a temporal spread of content whose parts are mutually co-conscious, and which is not part of a more extensive spread of content whose parts are all mutually co-conscious. Although in my discussion of these matters I generally worked on the assumption that total experiences for the different sensory modes are of the same duration, I briefly considered what would become of the specious present if this assumption turned out to be false, and suggested that in this case the specious present would have the duration of the shortest mode-specific total experiences (p. 173), the rationale for this being that only then would every part of a specious present be co-conscious with every other part. Bayne writes:

> this is the appropriate thing to say, but it seems to lead to a strange state of affairs. Take a subject, *S*, who has an auditory experience (a1) and a visual experience (v1). Suppose that *S*'s auditory specious present is longer than her visual specious present. Take two earlier auditory and visual experiences, a2 and v2, that had been simultaneous, where *S*'s specious present includes a2 but fails to include v2. Although a2 is co-conscious with both a1 and v1 – it must be, because it is part of *S*'s auditory specious present – it isn't part of *S*'s current total experience, because it falls outside the scope of *S*'s shortest specious present. But since a2 is co-conscious with the rest of *S*'s current experiences – at least, it is co-conscious with a1 – why shouldn't it be included within (subsumed by) *S*'s current total experience? Surely a2, unlike v2, is part of what it is like to be *S* at this moment. This suggests to me that the length of the specious present cannot be modality specific.
>
> (2001: 87)

So we have a scenario in which two experiences a1 and v1 are fully co-conscious throughout their respective durations, but whereas the preceding a2 is co-conscious with a1, the preceding v2 is not co-conscious with v1. Adopting my policy on the duration of (cross-modal) specious presents would mean that a2 is not a part of the specious present which consists of, or includes, a1 and v1.

Although I agree that there is something strange about this state of affairs, I don't think Bayne has quite put his finger on what it is. He maintains that the specious present which includes a1 and v1 must also include a2 since the latter experience contributes to what it is like to be *S* during the interval of time when a1 and v1 are occurring. In one sense this is true: after all, by hypothesis a1 is directly (diachronically) co-conscious with the immediately preceding a2, and this will impact on the global character of these experiences. But it doesn't follow from this that a2 is part of the specious present which includes a1 and v1. For this to follow something along the lines of the following transitivity principle would have to be true:

> For any three experiences, Ex, Ey, Ez, where (i) Ey and Ez are co-conscious and simultaneous, (ii) Ex occurs just before (or after) Ey/Ez, and (iii) Ex is co-conscious with Ey, then it is necessarily the case that Ex is co-conscious with Ez as well.

Whether this principle is true is an interesting issue. We know that co-consciousness is not transitive over time, at least for durations greater than the specious present. Whether co-consciousness is transitive synchronically is controversial, but in §4.5 I argued (tentatively) that it is. What I did not consider, and what Bayne's query brings into focus, is whether co-consciousness is transitive in situations of the kind we are now contemplating, where a combination of diachronic and synchronic unity is involved.

The truth is not easy to discern. On the one hand, it could be argued that since we know that transitivity fails in the diachronic case, it might also fail in the diachronic + synchronic case. While it is true that diachronic co-consciousness is transitive within specious presents, we are considering the (perhaps only hypothetical) situation in which the specious presents associated with different sensory modalities are of different lengths, and this could easily make a difference. In the scenario outlined by Bayne, for example, although a2 lies within *S*'s auditory specious present at the time when *S* is experiencing a1/v1, it does not lie within *S*'s visual specious present, and it is precisely because of this that it is reasonable to conclude that a2 will not be co-conscious with v1, even though a2 *is* co-conscious with a1. But on the other hand, these matters look very different in the light of the considerations which I suggested might make it reasonable to think that synchronic co-consciousness cannot fail to be transitive. In §4.5 I suggested that if two experiences are co-conscious at a time *t*, then they are *wholly joined* or *fused*: in effect, they are so close together that any third experience at *t* that is co-conscious with one must also be co-conscious with the other. If this is right, then v1 and a1 in Bayne's scenario will be fused in this manner, with the consequence that anything which is in direct phenomenal contact with a1 cannot fail to be in direct phenomenal contact with v1. Similar reasoning suggests the preceding visual experience v2 will necessarily be co-conscious with a1: if a2 and v2 are fused in such a way that any experience that is co-conscious with either must be co-conscious with both, and if the same applies to a1 and v1, then obviously, given that a2 and a1 are co-conscious, all parts of each fusion must also be co-conscious.

But while the latter reasoning may seem compelling, we must not lose sight of the fact that transitivity *does* break down over intervals longer than the specious present, and in the cases we are considering, co-consciousness is 'overstretched' in precisely this manner in *one* of the relevant sensory modalities at least. Although I lean more towards the notion that the specious presents of the different modes are of the same duration, I cannot see how to argue for this in a conclusive manner. Perhaps the issue should remain open, for now.

When Bayne moves on from considering my analysis of individual specious presents to my analysis of phenomenal continuity in entire streams of consciousness, he locates another difficulty, a difficulty afflicting the overlap model. According to the latter, it will be recalled, adjoining co-streamal specious presents overlap by sharing common parts. In the simple case of a succession of auditory sensations, *Do-Re-Mi*, if the sensations are of such a duration that only two can be encompassed by the relevant subject's specious present, then this stretch of experience would include a specious present *<Do-Re>* and a later specious present *<Re-Mi>*, where the 'Re' in the latter is numerically identical with the 'Re' in the former. Bayne objects thus:

> Consider a subject (*S*) who has two token Re experiences at a time, one (*Re1*) is co-conscious with *Do* (and only with *Do*), the other one (*Re2*) is co-conscious with *Mi* (and only with *Mi*). So, the subject's specious presents follow the pattern *<Do, Re1>*, *<Re2, Mi>*. Are these two specious presents continuous? No, because they don't contain any experiences in common. Would they seem to *S* to be continuous? It seems to me that they may well be. If *S* only has introspective access to the phenomenal character of her experiences, then she won't be able to distinguish *Re1* from *Re2* on the basis of introspection.
>
> (2001: 88)

If the overlap model is true these two specious presents will not seem continuous. Given the stipulation that *Re1* and *Re2* are numerically distinct experiences, the specious presents do not possess a common part, and so phenomenal continuity will come to an abrupt halt. But Bayne argues that *S* would in fact experience a *Do*-type experience flowing smoothly into a *Re*-type experience, and a *Re*-type experience flowing smoothly into a *Mi*-type experience. If this is right, then from a purely phenomenological perspective, *S*'s experience in the envisaged case would be exactly similar to the experience she would have had if she had experienced *<Do-Re>* and *<Re-Mi>*. Overlap by way of sharing of numerically identical parts is thus redundant.

In assessing this argument it is useful to start off by taking the subject out of the picture. When we do so, and when we focus on the purely experiential facts and relationships, it is evident that in Bayne's scenario we have two *entirely distinct* streams of consciousness (or stream-phases). It is true that the earlier of these streams *<Do, Re1>* has yet to end when the later stream *<Re2, Mi>* begins; these two stream-phases overlap in time. Nonetheless, given the stipulation that *Re1* is co-conscious only with *Do*, and that *Re2* is co-conscious only with *Mi*, there is no experiential connection between the two phases: neither *Do* nor *Re1* is directly co-conscious with *Re2* or *Mi*. Consequently, so far as inter-experiential relationships are concerned, these streams could as easily belong to different subjects, or occur in different centuries; the temporal overlap is in itself irrelevant to how they are experienced. Your current experiences temporally overlap with billions of other streams of consciousness, but as is obvious, your stream of consciousness, from this point in time on, will not be phenomenally continuous with all these other streams!

Does the situation change when we re-introduce *S* into the picture? So far as I can see, not in the least. Indeed, it is questionable whether *S can* be re-introduced into the picture. Anyone who is committed to the view that subjects necessarily have a synchronically unified consciousness will insist that <*Do, Re1*> and <*Re2, Mi*> must belong to numerically distinct subjects. Not everyone inclines to this conception of subjects. Those who take the view that subjects of experience such as ourselves are human organisms may well look favourably on the possibility that a single subject can have two distinct streams of consciousness at a given time: split-brain patients may well have a divided consciousness of this kind, at least some of the time, and split-brain patients are single human organisms. The fact that there are two *distinct* streams of consciousness in such cases means that they cannot be used to support Bayne's contention that <*Do, Re1*>, <*Re2, Mi*> will (in effect) constitute a single uninterrupted stream of consciousness by virtue of being consubjective. I conclude that we have no reason to suppose that overlap by way of common parts is irrelevant to phenomenal continuity.

Alternative approaches

To bring matters to a close I want to comment on two recently proposed alternative ways of thinking about the unity of consciousness. Each merits a more detailed treatment, but I will confine myself here to some remarks of a fairly general kind.

In §1.7 I recommended the adoption of a flexible approach to the question of what counts as a single experience. Since it is not obvious that there is any uniquely correct way of dividing a typical stream of consciousness into experiential parts, I suggested that the best policy would be to allow any combination of streamal constituents to count as an experience. I also pointed out in §4.2 that alternative policies on the individuation of experiences are possible, and noted that at one stage in his career Carnap espoused the view that only complete streams of consciousness should be regarded as genuine experiences. This position has recently been taken up by Michael Tye in *Consciousness and Persons* (2003). For understandable reasons, Tye calls it the 'one experience' view. The claim of course is not that just one experience exists in the entire history of the universe, but rather that each of us has one single experience from the time we regain consciousness in the morning until the time we lose it again with the onset of dreamless sleep. Carnap's motivation for adopting this policy on individuating experiences was primarily epistemological, while Tye's motivation is more metaphysical: he thinks adopting the one experience view solves (or dissolves) the traditional problem of the unity of consciousness.

If we start from the assumption that our streams of consciousness are composed of a number of individual experiences that are unified in a certain way, then anyone seeking to elucidate this kind of unity will try to discover what it is that holds our streams of consciousness together – the hunt for the phenomenal unity relationship has begun. But the rationale behind this quest will evaporate if the underlying assumption turns out to be false. If the one experience view is correct, and our streams of consciousness are not composed of individual experiences tied together by some elusive string, then it is pointless trying to find this string: it does not exist. Hence it is not surprising that philosophers have found the unity of consciousness a tough nut to crack, nor is it surprising that Hume despaired when he sought to explain how his successive perceptions were unified – he took perceptions to be 'distinct existences'. Or so suggests Tye:

> the proposed view best accounts for the facts of unity at a time and unity through time. Nothing that we ordinarily say about experience needs to be given up. No large bullets need to be swallowed. The view is clear and simple; and it explains in a compelling way why the problems of unity for experience seem so intractable. Begin with the assumption that there are individual experiences somehow bundled together by a phenomenal unity relation to form an overarching experience and you will find yourself either supposing that phenomenal unity is something unique and basic about which you can say nothing else at all except that it bundles experiences together to form a unified consciousness, or you will join Hume in confessing that the problem is too hard to be solved. The latter course of action at least has the virtue of candor, but the best strategy, it seems to me, is simply to give up the assumption.
>
> (2003: 107)

Progress in philosophy does sometimes come from dissolving, rather than solving a problem. Can the problem of the unity of consciousness be dissolved in this way?

Well, Tye is certainly right when he says that the one experience view is clear and simple. It is also true that *if* the view were correct, then it could explain why the problem of unity for experience can seem so intractable; if there is no phenomenal unity relation, it is not surprising that it can seem elusive. It is less clear, however, that he is right when he says that no large bullets need to be swallowed, that nothing we ordinarily say about experience needs to be given up if we accept the view. To take just one example, the senses provide a very natural way of distinguishing between the contents of our ordinary streams of consciousness. As I look at a picture while listening to a piece of music, my overall consciousness contains a purely visual component and a purely auditory component, and as noted in §8.4, in cases such as this there is no obvious interpenetration of auditory and visual phenomenal qualities: if the sound were absent, my visual experience would be unaltered. Not only this: if I continue to look at the picture when the sound comes to an abrupt end, my visual experience *continues on* – or so most of us would find it natural to say.[5] But it is a consequence of Tye's view that 'where there is phenomenological unity across sense modalities, sense-specific experiences do not exist' (2003: 28). If I only ever have *one* experience at a given time, then it is wrong to suppose that my consciousness includes auditory and visual parts that are themselves experiences.[6]

Difficulties such as this are not necessarily fatal – our ordinary ways of talking do not always correspond with how things really are – but Tye's proposal is problematic in further and deeper ways. Suppose we accept that entire streams of consciousness are single experiences that are not composed of lesser experiences. It remains the case that our streams of consciousness have *parts*, and even if these parts are not individual experiences, they are nonetheless *unified* in a distinctive way, and the question of what unifies them remains very much alive. There are various ways in which the unity question can be formulated in the context of the one experience view. We could, for example, opt to talk in terms of 'phenomenal regions' rather than 'experiences'. My current stream of consciousness has an auditory phenomenal region and a visual phenomenal region, and the latter is composed of many smaller visual phenomenal regions. The various phenomenal regions comprising my consciousness are unified in a distinctive way – in a way that the regions of my consciousness and your consciousness are not – so what is responsible for this unity? We want an answer to this question, and since phenomenal regions can be experienced together as easily as experiences, there is nothing to prevent our saying that phenomenal regions are unified by virtue of being co-conscious. So far as I can see, adopting the one experience view does not alter the fundamentals in the slightest.

It is not only possible for a phenomenal unity relation to play a role within the framework of the one experience view, there are reasons for thinking that such a relation is indispensable. I suggested earlier that Hurley might well be right to insist that an adequate account of phenomenal unity must be able to mark the distinction between fully and partially unified conscious states. Tye recognizes the distinction, and argues that partially unified states are in fact perfectly possible (2003: 130–2). Irrespective of whether he is right about this, it is hard to see how the distinction between a partially and fully unified state can be drawn without employing a phenomenal unity relation. A partially unified state is as much a 'single experience' as a fully unified state; the difference between the two is that whereas in a fully unified state *all* the state's regions are phenomenally unified (or co-conscious) in a partially unified state they are not. Unless we can call on the services of a phenomenal unity relation, an important distinction cannot be drawn.[7]

The indispensability of a phenomenal unity relation is equally evident in the diachronic case, which also involves the non-transitivity of the co-consciousness relationship. Tye accepts that we are directly aware of change and persistence over short intervals of time. He illustrates with a musical example: if we hear a succession of notes *Do-Re-Mi*, and each note takes up half the duration of the specious present, then we hear *Do* flowing smoothly into *Re* and *Re* flowing smoothly into *Mi*, but we do not hear *Do* flowing into *Mi* – by the time the latter occurs, *Do* has dropped out of the specious present, and so is no longer being directly experienced. So whereas *Do* and *Re* are diachronically phenomenally unified, as are *Re* and *Mi*, *Do* and *Mi* are not. How can we possibly make sense of this unless we introduce a phenomenal unity relation, in some form or other? In fact, this is precisely what Tye does: he distinguishes between 'direct' and 'indirect' phenomenal unity: the latter 'obtains if and only if the qualities experienced in one specious present are experienced as succeeding or continuing on from the qualities experienced in the immediately prior specious present', whereas indirect phenomenal unity is the ancestral of direct phenomenal unity: two experienced qualities are related in this way if they are not directly phenomenally unified, but are 'linked by chains of direct phenomenal unity' (2003: 100). Clearly, although there is nothing to prevent our calling a stream of consciousness lasting several hours a single experience, if we take this step we must also recognize that not all parts or stages of such streams are unified in the same way. And as is equally clear, we cannot spell out precisely how these parts are related without employing a phenomenal unity relation.

Tye develops the one experience view in the context of a 'representationalist' conception of consciousness. He holds that phenomenal unity is a relationship 'between qualities *represented in* experience, not between qualities *of* experiences' (2003: 36). An important aspect of Tye's representationalism is his commitment to the doctrine of the 'transparency of experience', the claim that we have no awareness of our experiences *per se*, we are aware solely of the objects and properties out there in the world that are presented to us in our experience: 'I am aware that I am having a certain sort of experience by being aware of something other than the experience – the surfaces apparently outside and their apparent qualities' (2003: 24). Since he rejects the notion that we are aware of our experiences, it is not surprising that Tye also rejects the idea that we are aware of our experiences as unified. But again, while these doctrines certainly alter the terms of the debate, I am not at all sure they affect the fundamentals. In the context of Tye's preferred framework, phenomenal unity may be a relationship between 'experientially represented qualities', rather than experiences, but it is not obvious that this makes the relationship any less central to the phenomenology of our experience. In any event, what does seem obvious is that if the one experience view is combined with my preferred framework, the problem of the unity of consciousness remains very much alive.[8]

The approach developed by Bayne and Chalmers in their 'What is the unity of consciousness?' (2003) is in one respect similar to Tye's: it is decidedly 'top-down' rather than 'bottom-up'. Instead of starting off (as I do) by asking what connection exists between the various distinct experiences we have at a given time, they begin by focusing on the relationship between complex states of consciousness and their simpler constituents. My current visual experience, taken as a whole, consists of a large number of simpler parts; the latter are unified by virtue of being constituents of the larger whole. The same applies to the sensations of pressure that I can feel on my back, and the ache I can feel in my knee: they are unified by being parts of my overall field of bodily sensations. Examples such as these suggest that the 'being a constituent of a more encompassing experience' relationship is one of spatial containment, but this is not necessarily the case. Recall Hill's example of being able to discern the sound of an individual instrument, such as an oboe, amid the sound of the whole orchestra; the sound of the oboe is a part of the sound of the whole orchestra, but it is not (or not obviously) a spatial part, and the same would apply to experiencing a particular olfactory 'note' in the overall odour of a perfume, or a hint of garlic in the flavour of a savoury dish. This sort of inclusion extends beyond the particular sensory modalities. My overall visual experience is a constituent of a more complex state consisting of my visual and auditory experience; the totality of my audio-visual experience is included in a more complex state which includes my olfactory and gustatory experience; the latter state is in turn a constituent of a still more encompassing state which includes my bodily experience, my moods, my conscious thoughts and mental images. This hierarchy of progressive inclusion does, presumably, come to an end: it terminates with that maximal state of consciousness which contains *all* my other current experiences as constituents.

Bayne and Chalmers take this relationship of inclusion as the primitive element in their account of the (phenomenal) unity of consciousness. Wary of assuming that this relationship conforms with the principles of standard mereology, they refer to it as *subsumption*, thus:

> it does not seem unreasonable to suppose that there is a single encompassing state of consciousness that subsumes all of my experiences: perceptual, bodily, emotional, cognitive, and any others.
>
> We can think of this last encompassing state of consciousness, for a given subject, as the subject's *total* conscious state. When it exists, a subject's total conscious state might be thought of as the subject's conscious *field*. It can be thought of as involving at least a conjunction of each of many more specific conscious states: states of perceptual experience, bodily experience, emotional experience, and so on. But what is important . . . is that this total state is not *just* a conjunction of conscious

states. It is also a conscious state in its own right. If such a total conscious state exists, it can serve as the 'singularity behind the multiplicity' – the single state of consciousness in which all of a subject's states of consciousness are subsumed.

(2003: §2)

They suggest, very plausibly, that subsumption is a relationship among token phenomenal states that is reflexive, antisymmetrical and transitive. The notion that all of a subject's conscious states at a given time are phenomenally unified can be formulated in this manner: for any set of phenomenal states of a subject at a time, the subject has a phenomenal state that subsumes each of the states in that set.

Bayne and Chalmers are at one with Tye in holding that there is a sense in which we have a single experience at any given time – the maximal state which subsumes all our other conscious states – and that recognizing this fact sheds useful light on the unity of consciousness. But unlike Tye they are not attempting to dissolve or sidestep the problem, they are offering a solution to it: the subsumption relationship is a unity relation, and it is undeniably a *phenomenal* unity relation. We know what it is like for a complex visual state to subsume its simpler constituent states; we know what it is like for a complex visual state to be subsumed in a maximal state. Just as there is nothing in the least mysterious about the co-consciousness relationship, there is nothing in the least mysterious about the subsumption relationship. Bayne and Chalmers argue that it may well be possible to define subsumption in terms of the 'what it's like' in quite a general way: a phenomenal state A subsumes phenomenal state B when what it's like to have A and B simultaneously is the same as what it's like to have A. Since it is widely accepted that phenomenal states are distinguished from non-phenomenal states by virtue of the fact that there is something it is like to have them, we are now in a position to hold that the unity of consciousness depends on precisely the same feature which is responsible for states being conscious in the first place.

The subsumption approach to the unity issue is in some respects a very natural one: it sits well with the phenomenological datum that our ordinary experience takes the form of a unified complex ensemble. Also, as Bayne and Chalmers go on to show, the approach can readily be formalized in various useful ways – see the discussions of 'logical unity' and 'conjunctive unity' (2003: §6). Given all this, the question of the relationship between the top-down subsumption approach, and the bottom-up co-consciousness approach becomes pressing. Is the latter altogether redundant?

It is not obvious that it is. The first point to note is that the two approaches look to be mutually compatible. If two experiences, E_1 and E_2, are co-conscious they automatically constitute a more complex experience W, and in virtue of this E_1 and E_2 are subsumed in W. And what goes for E_1 and E_2 goes for any collection of experiences that are all mutually co-conscious. Looking at it from the other direction, if we know that W is a fully unified experience which subsumes the simpler experiences E_1 and E_2, we also know that E_1 and E_2 are co-conscious. And what goes for E_1 and E_2 also goes for larger collections of experiences.

As for the question of redundancy, we have already encountered one reason for thinking that the services of the co-consciousness relation cannot easily be dispensed with when considering Tye's position. Distinguishing between fully and partially unified phenomenal states is easily accomplished in terms of co-consciousness; it is not so obvious that it can be done if we rely solely on the subsumption relationship. Consider a maximal state W^* belonging to a subject S comprising E_1, E_2 and E_3, where E_1 is co-conscious with E_2, and E_2 is co-conscious with E_3, but where E_1 and E_3 are not co-conscious. Although W^* is unquestionably only partially unified, isn't it also the case that each of E_1, E_2 and E_3 are *subsumed* in W^*? It seems so: W^* is a single complex experience, and E_1, E_2 and E_3 are its constituent parts. In reply it could be argued that the conditions for subsumption are not met in this sort of case. How can E_1 and E_3 be subsumptively related if they are not phenomenally unified? Isn't subsumption supposed to be a phenomenal unity relation? This is certainly what Bayne and Chalmers intend it to be, but there are complications, as this passage reveals:

> We can say that two conscious states are *subsumptively phenomenally unified* (or simply *phenomenally unified*) if there is something it is like for a subject to be in both states simultaneously. That is, two states are phenomenally unified when they have a *conjoint phenomenology*: a phenomenology of having both states at once that subsumes the phenomenology of the individual states. When A and B are phenomenally conscious states, there is something it is like for a subject to have A, and there is something it is like for a subject to have B. When A and B are phenomenally unified, there is not just something it is like to have each state individually: there is something it is like to have A and B together. And the phenomenology of being in A and B together will carry with it the phenomenology of being in A and the phenomenology of being in B.
>
> (2003: §3)

If partially unified states are possible, and W^* is such a state, then there must be something that it is like for S to be in this state, and consequently there must be something it is like to have E_1, E_2 and E_3 simultaneously. So on the face of it these three experiences satisfy the condition Bayne and Chalmers set out for having a conjoint phenomenology in the first part of this passage: the phenomenology of W^* subsumes (or includes) the phenomenology of E_1, E_2 and E_3. We may be unable to recreate this phenomenology in our own imaginations, but since we can put this down to a limitation on our imaginations, rather than a restriction on the possible structures of consciousness, this is (arguably) irrelevant (cf. §4.4); it certainly doesn't follow from the fact that *we* don't know what it is like to be *S* that there is nothing that it is like to be *S*. However, in the second part of the passage we are told that for two experiences to be subsumptively phenomenally unified, in addition to there being something that it is like to have each state individually, there is also something it is like to have both states *together*. If 'together' just means 'at the same time', then it changes nothing. But if it means 'experienced together, or co-conscious', then it changes everything. Since E_1 and E_3 are not co-conscious, they cannot be subsumed in W*. More generally, it is now clear that partially unified states no longer satisfy the criteria for being subsumptively unified. It is equally clear, however, that co-consciousness no longer faces the threat of redundancy: experiences can only be subsumptively related if they are also co-conscious.

Since I am by no means confident that a state of consciousness could be partially unified, I would not want to put too much weight on this line of reasoning. But there is a related and deeper point. Bayne and Chalmers take the subsumption relationship to be intimately related to what it is like to have an experience. Let us follow this through. Suppose a maximal conscious state M subsumes a collection of simpler experiences. What is M itself like? If we try to answer this question in a reasonably comprehensive way we will obviously describe the qualitative character and intentional content of the various simpler experiences which find themselves subsumed in M. We will also mention which parts of M are being introspected, and we will describe any spatial relationships which exist among M's constituents. Is there anything we have omitted? There is indeed. Since the unity of consciousness is itself a phenomenological feature of our ordinary conscious states, and a crucially important one, in order to capture the main phenomenal features of M we also need to describe *the manner* in which the various simpler states subsumed in it are unified. Can we do this entirely in terms of the subsumption relationship? It is not obvious that we can. The relationship of subsumption (or inclusion) finds application in many disparate domains: the set of all animals subsumes the set of dogs; the series 1, 2, 3, 4, 5, 6 . . . subsumes the series 2, 4, 6, 8 . . . the Earth's atmosphere subsumes a vast number of oxygen atoms; the Earth's oceans subsume a vast number of water molecules; a typical beach subsumes a sizeable number of sand particles – and so on and on. In none of these cases are the items subsumed *phenomenally* unified. Since the subsumption relation applies outwith the phenomenal domain, to capture the manner in which M's parts are unified, it won't be enough simply to state that M's lesser parts are subsumed within it, we also need to specify precisely how these parts are *experienced* as unified. And to do this we will need to point out that irrespective of how we divide M into parts, each and every one of the resulting parts is directly co-conscious with every other part: a relationship of immediate experienced togetherness binds all parts of M into a unified ensemble. As soon as we try to spell out what subsumption in the phenomenal domain *is like* as a mode of unity, co-consciousness quickly enters the picture. So it would seem that co-consciousness remains very much alive in the context of the subsumption approach, even if only tacitly. Arguably it is co-consciousness, and co-consciousness alone, that is responsible for the distinctive mode of unity that is to be found within our states and streams of consciousness.

One further issue remains. Even if the unity of consciousness is a product of the co-consciousness relationship, is it possible that top-down approaches better reflect the metaphysics of phenomenal unity? This would be the case if total (or maximal) experiences were in some significant manner more fundamental than their constituent parts. I am by no means hostile to this idea, but I also think the issue is a difficult one, too difficult for anything simply to be assumed without further argument. We saw in §4.2 that although it may be tempting to think of the constituents of our total experiences as local modifications of an underlying phenomenal field, there is no justification for positing such an item, at least if we confine ourselves to phenomenological considerations – and even if such a field did exist, the question would arise as to what unifies its various parts.[9] There is of course at least one other way in which experiential wholes could be more basic than their parts: experiential parts might be unable to exist outside the particular wholes in which they find themselves. But as we saw in the final two chapters of the book, this issue is by no means a straightforward one. Although a potent form of holism is available – C-holism of the strong, token-specific variety – this depth of inter-experiential interdependency comes at a price. As well as requiring the distinction between local and global phenomenal features, we also need to adopt a particularly stringent criterion for the individuation of token experiences. The high price of this mode of holism is not its only significant feature. C-holism comes into view when we give close consideration to the way in which the (proper) parts of our total experience are connected to one another by co-consciousness: if experiential wholes are more basic than their parts, it may well be because of the manner in which their parts are related. Of course, there may be a further route to phenomenal holism. If so, it is not obvious what it is.[10]

Notes

1 Introduction

1   Strawson (1994: 95) says:

> The problem of how experience is possible remains at the heart of the difficulty created by the existence of mind. It is the heart of the difficulty, the rest is easy. All the other things people want to classify as mental pose no more of a philosophical or scientific problem than the classification of experienceless chess computers, or experienceless colour-classification devices.

Fodor (1992: 5) writes: 'Nobody has the slightest idea of how anything material could be conscious. Nobody even knows what it would be like to have the slightest idea about how anything material could be conscious'. See also Chalmers (1995).

2   Recent advocates of P-materialism include Maxwell (1978) and Lockwood (1989: ch. 10); going further back we find Russell (1992 – first published 1927) – Lockwood suggests the same view was espoused still earlier by Schopenhauer, Lundt and Clifford.

3   See Lockwood (1994) for a good discussion of these issues. Also Maxwell (1978) and Foster (1991: 119–30).

4   'A speaker often takes several minutes to disclose one thought. In his mind the whole thought is present at once, but in speech it has to be developed successively. A thought may be compared to a cloud shedding a shower of words' (Vygotsky 1997: 251).

5   In making these remarks I ignore the ways our conception of the material world might be altered by P- or L-materialism.

6   Cf. Russell:

> By examining our percepts it is possible … to infer certain formal mathematical properties of external matter. … But by examining our percepts we obtain knowledge which is not merely formal as to the matter of our brains. This knowledge, it is true, is fragmentary, but so far as it goes it has merits surpassing those of the knowledge given by physics.
>
> (1992: 382)

2 Unity, introspection and awareness

1   The distinction between passive and active introspection I draw here is somewhat similar to Brentano's distinction between inner perception and inner observation:

'It is a universal psychological law that we can never focus our attention on the objects of inner perception' (1973: 30).

2 Although this doctrine has not been at the centre of recent debates, a century ago it was very different. Wollheim (1959: 132) remarks on the 'great lucidity and unbelievable persistence' with which James Ward (a leading A-theorist of the time) attacked F. H. Bradley (a leading opponent of the doctrine) over a period of some forty years (the latter resisted these assaults with 'equal tenacity'). 'Much as Mr Bradley strives to get all his facts into the one plane of presentation, his language continually shows that he has to admit facts outside that plane' (Ward 1887: 569). 'The Ego that pretends to be anything either before or beyond its concrete psychical filling, is a gross fiction and mere monster, and for no purpose admissible' (Bradley 1893: 89). When James wrote 'Does consciousness exist?' in 1904 it was the A-thesis he was arguing against. A survey conducted during a recent conference on consciousness provides evidence that the doctrine remains influential: to the statement 'It is possible for there to be consciousness in which there is awareness but no object of awareness' 73 per cent of respondents replied 'Yes' and only 10 per cent 'No' (Barušs and Moore 1998).

3 Ward is an A-theorist who maintained that *all* our experience is always attended to, albeit not to the same degree: attention fades gradually from wherever it is concentrated and extends to the dim outlying regions of consciousness (Ward 1918: ch. 3).

4 I am indebted here to Nicholas Nathan, who has impressed upon me the merits of this version of the A-thesis.

5 'Emptiness means that state of the imagination of the unreal [= (roughly) consciousness] which is lacking in the form of being graspable or grasper' (Vasubandhu's Commentary on The Verses on Discrimination Between Middle and Extremes, Appendix III [Kochumuttom 1982: 236]).

> How is the definition of emptiness to be understood. ... It is neither [total] assertion. Nor [total] negation. Why not [total] assertion? Because there is the negation of the pair of subject and object. Why not [total] negation? Because there is the assertion of the negation of that pair.
>
> (*ibid*: 239)

For further discussion of non-conceptual awareness and the collapse of the subject–object dualism, see Williams (1989: chs 3 and 4).

6 Griffiths (1986: 13). For more on 'pure' awareness, see Forman (1990).

7 This line of argument will be reinforced by the discussion of phenomenal space in Chapter 3 – for further discussion see the second section of Chapter 4.

3 Phenomenal space

1

> The proposition that all things are side by side in space, is valid under the limitation that these things are viewed as objects of our sensible intuition. If, now, I add the condition to the concept, and say that all things, as outer appearances, are side by side in space, the rule is valid universally and without limitation.
>
> (1980: A27)

2 The idea is also reminiscent of Newton's conception of physical space as God's 'boundless uniform Sensorium'. But this idea should be treated with caution; explaining (or expanding upon) Newton's views to Leibniz, Clarke wrote:

> Sir Isaac Newton doth not say that Space is the Organ which God makes use of to perceive Things by ... he, being Omnipresent, perceives all Things by his immediate Presence to them, in all Space wherever they are, without the Intervention or Assistance of any Organ or Medium whatsoever. In order to make this more intelligible, he illustrates it by a Similitude: That as the Mind of Man, by its immediate Presence to the Pictures of Things form'd in the Brain by the means of the Organs of Sensation, sees those Pictures as if there were the Things themselves; so God sees all Things, by his immediate Presence to them: he being actually present to the Things themselves, to all Things in the Universe; as the Mind of Man is present to all the Pictures of Things formed in his Brain. ... And this Similitude is all that he means, when he supposes Infinite Space to be (as it were) the Sensorium of the Omnipresent Being.
>
> (quoted in Jammer 1993: 114–15)

Throwing caution to the wind, the idea might be that Man's Mind is akin to a spatial field of awareness that acquires phenomenal characteristics in response to changes within the brain brought about by perception.

3

> It seems likely that the young infant is not limited to registering isolated bits of sense data. ... There is probably no time in development in which infants are restricted to modality-specific fragments, sense scraps that are connected through empirical correlation. ... the psychological world of the human newborn is populated by objects and events that can be accessed by more than one modality. When a young baby brings a round rattle before his eyes, he is probably not engaged in discovering what visual sensation is associated with this particular tactual impression; he already knows that. Instead he is fascinated by the additional modality-specific features (the rich colours, visual sheen and shadows that could not have been known by touch alone) of the abstract form that he already apprehended through touch.
>
> (Meltzoff 1993: 228)

See also Piaget (1954: 13). Some of the experimental work Meltzoff's conclusions are based on involved children as young as forty-two minutes.

4   The imaginary aspect of V-spaces can be thought of as a generalization of O'Shaughnessy's notion of a 'long term body image'. See O'Shaughnessy 1995; 1980: vol. 1, ch. 7.

5   At least Armstrong accepts that there is a unity among experiences which needs to be accounted for somehow. After arguing, cogently and correctly, that the unity of consciousness is independent of attention and higher-order thought, O'Brian and Opie (1998) take the step of denying that co-consciousness exists. They claim that a stream of consciousness consists of a number of distinct strands which are quite unconnected and have only representational content in common; on this view there is coherence among experiences, but no connectedness. This bizarre notion, which is immediately refuted by the phenomenological evidence, is perhaps motivated by a reluctance to accept that co-consciousness is a basic feature of experience which cannot be explained in other terms.

4 Transitivity

1 Lockwood 1989: ch. 6; 1994.
2 Describing co-conscious experiences as *compresent* might suggest the following very swift argument for transitivity.

  1 On one view an object consists of properties inhering in a bare particular; those who reject this view, so-called *bundle-theorists*, maintain that an object consists of nothing but a collection of properties bound together by the relationship of compresence.
  2 If we regard properties as tropes, i.e. distinct particulars in their own right, compresence is transitive (it is not if we regard properties as universals).
  3 So if we take experiences to be tropes, co-consciousness (or compresence) must be transitive.

This argument has an appealing simplicity, but it fails. Since co-consciousness relates only experiences but compresence (as the bundle-theorist uses the term) does not, they must be distinct relations. Moreover, all the bundle-theorist means by 'compresence' is 'found together in the same object'. It would not follow from this that compresent experiences are necessarily co-conscious: a partially unified maximal experience could reasonably be taken to be a phenomenal object, despite the fact that it contains experiences that are not co-conscious with each other.
3 For more detail on these agnosias, and reasons for thinking that they leave the visual field (*qua* phenomenal field) intact – unlike blindsight – see Tye (1995: 209–18). Tye himself appeals to a model proposed by Farah (1991).

5 Phenomenal time

1 James himself put the point thus:

> Our own bodily position, attitude, condition, is one of the things of which *some* awareness, however inattentive, invariably accompanies the knowledge of whatever else we know. We think; and as we think we feel our bodily selves as the seat of the thinking. If the thinking be *our* thinking, it must be suffused through all its parts with that peculiar warmth and intimacy that make it come as ours. ... Whatever the content of the ego may be, it is habitually felt *with* everything else by us humans, and must form a *liaison* between all the things of which we become successively aware.
>
> (1952: 157)

6 Broad and Husserl

1 I use the terms 'awareness–content' and 'act–object' in connection with the same model of consciousness, but will increasingly deploy the latter so as to harmonize my terminology with the writers I will be concerned with in this chapter and the next.
2 This problem was noted by Mabbot (1951); see also Foster (1979) and Sprigge (1993: 203–5).
3 See Husserl (1991), which includes the lectures and notes published as *The Phenomenology of Internal Time-Consciousness* (1950), which first appeared in 1928, edited by Heidegger, and a great deal of other material besides.
4 The diagram I provide is not an exact copy of any of Husserl's, but it is similar to most of them.

5   Cf. 1991: 331–6, where Husserl discusses whether contents with the same intrinsic character could be apprehended as having different temporal character-istics – could different *modes* of apprehension be responsible for an identical 'primary' content appearing to be now present, now just past? He concludes that this is not possible, contrary to what he once thought. 'The continuity is a conti-nuity of alterations of consciousness that definitely must not be viewed as products at all times containing a common component – tone c, red, and the like – while the change is attributed to new moments called apprehensions.' But while he rejects this account of retention, he provides no alternative.

7   The overlap model

1   See Foster (1979; 1982: ch. 16; 1991: 246–50). The overlap model is also mentioned briefly by Russell (1984) and critically discussed by Lockwood (1989: ch. 15).
2   It should be noted that Foster only takes this step when he is operating in a non-phenomenalistic mode, and is not seeking to define objective time relations in terms of subjective time, a task he embarks upon in *The Case for Idealism* (1982).
3   The apparent paradox could be avoided in another way. Two geometrical points cannot overlap in part, but they can overlap *in toto*, by coinciding (imagine two points moving through space on intersecting paths). Applying the same principle in the temporal case would have the consequence that an entire stream of consciousness would be apprehended by a single momentary act. This is a bizarre idea, but not one that is unknown in philosophy. We might, for example, adopt a Kantian perspective, and regard the experiencing subject as wholly outside time. Rather than saying that the stream's contents are apprehended in a single temporal moment, we could say they are apprehended by a wholly atem-poral awareness.
4   As far as I know, this feature of temporal experience was first noted by Russell:

> If A, B and C succeed one another rapidly, A and B may be parts of one sensation, and likewise B and C, while A and C are not parts of one sensation, but A remembered when C is present in sensation. In such a case, A and B belong to the same present, and likewise B and C, but not A and C; thus the relation 'belonging to the same present' is not transi-tive. This ... is an independent fact concerned with mental time, and due to the fact that the present is not an instant. It follows that, apart from any question of duration in objects, two presents may overlap without coinciding.
>
> (1984: 78)

Foster also draws attention to this, as does Lockwood (1989: 99).
5   I rely here on Ruhnau (1995) and Pöppel (1985).
6   This is not quite the end of the tale; I have more to say about temporal modes in the fifth section of Chapter 9.

8   Phenomenal interdependence

1   Improbable, but not impossible: Stephen Clark has pointed out to me that some people do sometimes experience slight but noticeable intermodal interferences, for example in colours when experienced with different sounds. But since these alterations occur in special circumstances, when subjects are paying attention to the character of the relevant experiences and are looking out for this sort of modification, the main point stands: generally speaking intermodal interpenetra-

tion is rare, especially among the contents of the unnoticed phenomenal background, which comprises the bulk of our experience.

9 The ramifications of co-consciousness

1 I am assuming here (as elsewhere) that future times and experiences are as real as past and present times and experiences. What if this were not the case? What if times and event-parts (and so experiences) are being continually created, as the present advances and the total content of the world increases? On this view, the global character of an experience would evolve through a short interval. So for example, a_2 would initially have a complete global character [Cx-**Dx**], and then shortly afterwards, have a complete global character [Cx-**Dx**, **Dx**-Ex], as a_3 comes into being. This sort of change is compatible with regarding 'a_2' as referring to numerically the same experience in T_1 and T_2, provided a version of Leibniz's Law is adopted which permits the properties an object has at a given time to be different at different times, a liberalization which this model of time requires.

Postscript

1 To be more specific: in Dainton (2003) I defend and refine my account of diachronic unity and provide some clarifications of my use of the terms 'realism' and 'anti-realism'; I also comment on an interpretation of Husserl. In Dainton (2004a) I defend the claim that it is intelligible to suppose that a subject could have two spatially unconnected sense-fields that are co-conscious, and I offer further elaborations of the thought-experiments used in §3.3; I also comment on unified field theories of consciousness, and respond to the charge that I have left the co-consciousness relationship unexplained and unintelligible. In Dainton (2004b) I discuss the higher-order sense and higher-order thought conceptions of consciousness and their relationship with the A-thesis discussed in Chapter 2, and try to correct some misunderstandings of my arguments against the S-thesis in Chapter 3; I also introduce six forms of self-location. In Dainton (2004c) I attempt to rectify errors and oversimplifications in my rejection of attempts to explicate the synchronic unity of consciousness in terms of introspectibility in §2.3, and respond to an interesting argument, based on split-brain cases, that introspectibility is not sufficient for co-consciousness. The symposium – which includes a précis of the book, can be found at http://psyche.cs.monash.edu.au /symposia/dainton/

2 It would be different if the A-thesis were true. If phenomenal contents were unified in virtue of falling under a centre of pure awareness, and we identified 'subjects' with centres of this kind, then there would be a clear sense in which subjects contribute to the experienced unity of consciousness. But this conception of the structure of consciousness was rejected in Chapter 2.

3 And this applies even if causal relations (in some as yet not understood manner) underpin phenomenal unity.

4 As Michael Tye notes in the preface to his recent book on the topic: 'The epiphany occurred a couple of years ago, as I was sitting in my garden . . . What struck me with great intensity was the unity in my experience, the way in which my experience presented all these things to me *together*. What also struck me was that remarkably this unity hadn't really struck me before, that it was as if I had failed to notice it!' (2003: xii).

5 I am ignoring here the impact of C-holism – but I think it is fair to say that the distinction between local and global phenomenal properties does not figure prominently in our ordinary ways of talking about experience.

6   For more on this see Kobes (2005).
7   Suppose it were possible for a stream of consciousness to divide into two without loss of phenomenal continuity. If a non-branching stream is a single experience, won't a branching stream be so too? It is not obvious why not. This possibility poses a further difficulty for anyone espousing Tye's position. It is plausible to think that it should be possible to distinguish a branching stream of consciousness from a non-branching stream solely in terms of inter-experiential inter-relations. But how are we to do this in the absence of a phenomenal unity relation? The simultaneous experiences in a non-branching stream are all related by co-consciousness (perhaps only indirectly if partially unified states are possible), the simultaneous experiences in a branching stream are not: in such a stream there are some experiences that are neither directly nor indirectly related by synchronic co-consciousness. For more on the problem that branching streams pose for Tye's position, see Kobes (2005) and Bayne (forthcoming).
8   I confess to finding Tye's claim that we can only be aware of our experiences by being aware of things other than our experiences puzzling. I agree that we ordinarily do not think of our perceptual experiences or their contents as being experiential in character; we naturally take ourselves to be directly apprehending the world around us, not states of our own mind or consciousness. But this common-sense stance is not inevitable or inescapable: those who subscribe to the indirect realist (or projectivist) theory of perception reject it. It is perfectly possible to accept that perceptual experience *seems* transparent without believing that it actually *is* transparent.
9   See Dainton (2004a, §8) for more on this theme.
10   My thanks to Tim Bayne, David Chalmers and Bernie Kobes.

Bibliography

Armstrong, D. (1968) *A Materialist Theory of the Mind*, London: Routledge and Kegan Paul.

Ayers, Michael (1991) *Locke*, London: Routledge.

Baruss, I. and Moore, R. J. (1998) 'Beliefs about consciousness and reality of participants at "Tucson II"', *Journal of Consciousness Studies*, 5 (4) 483–96.

Bayne, T. (2001) 'Co-consciousness: review of Barry Dainton's *Stream of Consciousness*', *Journal of Consciousness Studies*, 8 (3) 79–92.

Bayne, T. (forthcoming) 'Divided brains and unified phenomenology: an Essay on Michael Tye's "Consciousness and Persons"', *Philosophical Psychology*.

Bayne, T. and D. Chalmers (2003) 'What is the unity of consciousness?', in A. Cleeremans (ed.) *The Unity of Consciousness: Binding, Integration, Dissociation*, Oxford: Oxford University Press.

Bradley, F. H. (1893) *Appearance and Reality*, London: Swan Sonnenschein.

——(1922) *The Principles of Logic*, Oxford: Oxford University Press.

Brentano, F. (1973) *Psychology from an Empirical Standpoint*, London: Routledge and Kegan Paul.

Broad, C. D. (1923) *Scientific Thought*, London: Kegan Paul, Trench and Trubner.

——(1938) *An Examination of McTaggart's Philosophy*, 3 vols, Cambridge: Cambridge University Press.

Carnap, R. (1967) *The Logical Structure of the World*, Berkeley: University of California Press.

Chalmers, David (1995) 'Facing up to the problem of consciousness', *Journal of Consciousness Studies*, 2 (3) 200–19.

——(1996) *The Conscious Mind*, New York: Oxford University Press.

Dainton, B. (2003) 'Time in experience: reply to Gallagher', *Psyche*, 9 (10).

——(2004a) 'Unity in the void: reply to Revonsuo', *Psyche*, 10 (1).

——(2004b) 'Higher-order consciousness and phenomenal space: reply to Meeham', *Psyche*, 10 (1).

——(2004c) 'Unity and introspectibility: reply to Gilmore', *Psyche*, 10 (1).

Deikman, A. J. (1996) '"I" = awareness', *Journal of Consciousness Studies*, 3 (4) 350–6.

Dennett, Daniel (1981) 'Where Am I?', in D. Hofstadter and D. Dennett (eds) *The Mind's I*, New York: Basic Books.

——(1991) *Consciousness Explained*, Harmondsworth: Penguin.

Farah, M. (1991) *Visual Agnosia*, Cambridge MA: MIT Press.

Flanagan, O. (1992) *Consciousness Reconsidered*, Cambridge MA: MIT Press.

Fodor, Jerry (1992) 'The big idea: Can there be a science of the mind?', *Times Literary Supplement*, July 3.

Forman, Robert (ed.) (1990) *The Problem of Pure Consciousness*, Oxford: Oxford University Press.
Foster, John (1979) 'In *self*-defence' in G. F. Macdonald (ed.) *Perception and Identity*, London: Macmillan.
——(1982) *The Case for Idealism*, London: Routledge and Kegan Paul.
——(1985) *Ayer*, London: Routledge and Kegan Paul.
——(1991) *The Immaterial Self*, London: Routledge.
Griffiths, Paul J. (1986) *On Being Mindless: Buddhist Meditation and the Mind–Body Problem*, Illinois: Open Court.
Goodman, N. (1977) *The Structure of Appearance*, Dordrecht: Reidel.
Gurwitsch, A. (1964) *Field of Consciousness*, Pittsburgh: Duquesne University Press.
Hill, C. (1991) *Sensations*, Cambridge: Cambridge University Press.
Horgan, John (1994) 'Trends in neuroscience', *Scientific American*, vol. 271.
Hume, David (1978) *A Treatise of Human Nature*, eds L. A. Selby-Bigge and P. H. Nidditch, Oxford: Oxford University Press.
Hurley, S. (1998) *Consciousness in Action*, Cambridge MA: Harvard University Press.
Husserl, E. (1950) *The Phenomenology of Internal Time-Consciousness*, trans. J. S. Churchill, Bloomington: Indiana University Press.
——(1991) [1893–1917] *On the Phenomenology of the Consciousness of Internal Time*, ed. and trans. J. B. Brough, Dordrecht: Kluwer.
James, William (1952) *The Principles of Psychology*, Chicago: Encyclopedia Britannica Inc.
——(1995) 'Does consciousness exist?', in *Selected Writings*, London: Everyman.
Jammer, Max (1993) *Concepts of Space*, 3rd edn, New York: Dover.
Kant, I. (1980) *Critique of Pure Reason*, trans. Kemp Smith, London: Macmillan.
Kobes, B. (2005) 'Review of Michael Tye's "Consciousness and Persons"', *Psyche* 11 (5).
Kochumuttom, Thomas (1982) *A Buddhist Doctrine of Experience*, Delhi: Motilal Banarsidass Publishers.
Köhler, Wolfgang (1947) *Gestalt Psychology*, New York: Mentor.
Lockwood, Michael (1989) *Mind, Brain and the Quantum*, Oxford: Oxford University Press.
——(1994) 'Issues of unity and objectivity', in Christopher Peacocke (ed.) *Objectivity, Simulation and the Unity of Consciousness*, London: Proceedings of the British Academy 83.
Lyons, W. (1986) *The Disappearance of Introspection*, Cambridge MA: MIT Press.
Mabbot, J. D. (1951) 'Our direct experience of time', *Mind*, 60; also in R. M. Gale (ed.) (1968) *The Philosophy of Time*, Sussex: Harvester Press.
Maxwell, N. (1978) 'Mind-brain identity and rigid designation', *Minnesota Studies in the Philosophy of Science*, vol. IX, Minneapolis: University of Minnesota Press, 365–403.
McGinn, Colin (1991) *The Problem of Consciousness: Essays towards a Resolution*, Oxford: Blackwell.
McGinn, Colin (1995) 'Consciousness and Space', in T. Metzinger (ed.) *Conscious Experience*, Paderborn: Schönigh Academic Imprint.
McCulloch, Gregory (1995) *The Mind and its World*, London: Routledge.
Mellor, D. H. (1998) *Real Time II*, London: Routledge.
Meltzoff, Andrew (1993) 'Molyneux's babies', in N. Eilan, R. McCarthy and B. Brewer (eds) *Spatial Representation*, Oxford: Blackwell.
Metzinger, T. (ed.) (1995) *Conscious Experience*, Paderborn: Schönigh Academic Imprint.
Miller, Izchak (1984) *Husserl, Perception, and Temporal Awareness*, Cambridge MA: MIT Press.
Moore, G. E. (1922) 'The refutation of idealism', in *Philosophical Studies*, London: Routledge and Kegan Paul.

O'Brian, G. and Opie, Jon (1998) 'The disunity of consciousness', *Australasian Journal of Philosophy*, 76 (3).

O'Shaughnessy, Brian (1980) *The Will*, Cambridge: Cambridge University Press.

——(1995) 'Proprioception and the body image', in J. L. Bermudez, A. Marcel and Naomi Eilan (eds) *The Body and the Self*, Cambridge MA: MIT Press.

Piaget, Jean (1954) *The Construction of Reality in the Child*, New York: Basic Books.

Pöppel, E. (1985) *Mindworks: Time and Conscious Experience*, New York: Harcourt Brace Jovanovich.

Robinson, H. (1994) *Perception*, London: Routledge.

Ruhnau, E. (1995) 'Time gestalt and the observer', in T. Metzinger (ed.) *Conscious Experience*, Paderborn: Schönigh Academic Imprint.

Russell, B. (1984): 'On the experience of time', in *The Collected Papers of Bertrand Russell, Volume 7*, London: George Allen and Unwin.

——(1992) *The Analysis of Matter*, London: Routledge.

Sacks, Oliver (1987) 'Nothingness', in *The Oxford Companion to the Mind*, Oxford: Oxford University Press.

Searle, J. (1992) *The Rediscovery of the Mind*, Cambridge MA: MIT Press.

Sprigge, T. (1983) *The Vindication of Absolute Idealism*, Edinburgh: Edinburgh University Press.

——(1993) *American Truth and British Reality*, Illinois: Open Court.

Strawson, Galen (1994) *Mental Reality*, Cambridge MA: MIT Press.

——(1997) 'The self', *Journal of Consciousness Studies*, 4 (5–6), 405–28.

Tye, M. (1995) *Ten Problems of Consciousness*, Cambridge MA: MIT Press.

——(2003) *Consciousness and Persons*, Cambridge MA: MIT Press.

Unger, Peter (1990) *Identity, Consciousness and Value*, Oxford: Oxford University Press.

Vygotsky, Lev (1997) *Thought and Language*, Cambridge MA: MIT Press.

Ward, James (1887) 'Mr F. H. Bradley's analysis of mind', *Mind*, vol. XII.

——(1918) *Psychological Principles*, Cambridge: Cambridge University Press.

Wertheimer, M. (1967) 'Gestalt psychology', in W. D. Ellis (ed.) *A Sourcebook of Gestalt Psychology*, New York: Humanities Press.

Whitehead, A. N. (1929) *Process and Reality*, Cambridge: Cambridge University Press.

Williams, Paul (1989) *Mahayana Buddhism, The Doctrinal Foundations*, London: Routledge.

Wollheim, R. (1959) *F. H. Bradley*, Harmondsworth: Penguin.

Index

absolute flux 160, 165; time-consciousness, absolute 160
acts of awareness: momentary 137, 145, 165; overlapping 142, 162, 164–5; taking in a temporal spread of content 134
agnostic materialism 8
Alzheimer's disease 103
anti-realism 73, 115, 123, 127–8, 146; representational 135, 161
Anton's syndrome 110
aquatic comparisons 237
archetypal physical things: their ontological status, 93
Armstrong, D. 85–6, 262
aspect-switching 202
A-thesis 42–9, 51–2, 54–8, 86, 104, 106, 108, 116, 135, 261; and naive realism 47; and the will 42; engagement doctrine 52; volitional version 51
attention 30; a more realistic picture 46; dispersed 31; essentially contrastive 51; primary 33, 37, 39, 51; secondary 33, 37
attention-dependency 38, 210
Augustinian argument 120–2, 132
awareness: as 'inner' content as 'outer' 47; as inner eye 45, 50; bare 53; inattentive/passive 32, 173; introspective 34; of continuity 133, 180; searchlight analogy 49; Substantival 55, 80, 93; tangible 51; varieties of 28
awareness* 41–3, 45–51, 53, 55, 57, 104, 217; as featureless locus of pure apprehension 43; bare 48
awareness-content (act-object) model 41, 132, 136, 166, 215, 238, 263; four

variants 48; implications for temporal experience 149, 180
Ayers, Michael 62

bare particular 57, 263
Barušs, I. and Moore, R.J. 261
Bayne, Tim 245, 248–51, 255–8
binding experiences 246
binding problem 4
blending of content-continua 158
blindsight 111, 263; super-blindsight, deafhearing 111
Block View 177–9, 238; compatibility with phenomenal passage 178
bodily experience 2–3, 10, 31, 47, 61, 68, 71, 76, 83, 90, 119, 217; spatially disjointed 79
bodily sense-field: loss of 64; shrunken 65; spatial anchor 67; voids within 76, 79
bracketing policy 185
Bradley, F.H. 117, 128, 180, 193, 237, 261
brain-in-a-vat 4, 63, 66
Brentano, F. xv, 154–5, 160, 174, 260
broad v. narrow content 211, 221
Broad, C.D. xi, 27, 115, 133, 136–57, 59, 162, 165, 174–5; *An Examination of McTaggart's Philosophy* 136, 142, 162; *Scientific Thought* 136–7
Brough, J.B. 158, 160
bundle theory 84, 263

Carnap, R. 91, 92, 251; *The Logical Structure of the World* 91
cessation: condition of 54
Chalmers, David 2, 19, 245, 255–8, 260
change: immediate awareness of 114, 124, 162

characterizations of an experience: partial (local) v. complete (global) 223; perspectival 231

C-holism 223, 224, 259; impact on the identity of experiences in the temporal case 231; Strong v. Weak 223

Clark, Stephen xvi, 264

Clarke, Samuel 261

Clay, E.R. 120, 122

Clifford 260

clogging of consciousness 156, 157, 158, 160

cocktail party effect 38

co-consciousness: a basic relationship 84, 104, 216, 236, 241; a phenomenological feature 215; all-or-nothing? 89; all-pervasive 85, 238, 243; and consubjectivity 25, 96; diachronic 26; examples of 3; in no way mysterious 86, 217, 236, 243; independence from introspection 35; indirect 96; logical properties 89, 96, 219; physical counterpart 239; reflexive 89, 222; symmetrical 89, 215; synchronic and diachronic contrasted 168; unique unifying relationship 27; a ghostly connection 240; pure 241; pluralistic conception 241–2

co-consciousness as a relation 219, 221; 246; internal or external? 89, 183; neither fully intrinsic nor fully extrinsic 218; rooted in experiences themselves 215; why and how it is discernible 244; types versus tokens 245

cognitive access 111

cognitive limitations xiv

co-illumination 108

coincidence threshold 170

commissurotomy 99–103

compresence 105, 263

computation 5

confinement thesis 104, 108

conscious thinking 118

consciousness: ambient inner background 32; analysis of xiv; bi-polarity doctrine 26, 48; contentless 54; generated by pre-spatial particulars 9, 179; Husserl's dual-level unification 154; non-dualistic 54; non-spatial 63; outwardly projecting 16; partially disunified 100; phenomenal 2; reduced to pure diaphaneity 44; unity of 2

consciousness mysticism 195

content: 'ballooning' 140, 146; core v. total 139; representational/intentional 207

co-presence 105

counterpart argument 189, 191, 220

Cp and Cg properties: introduced 218

CPI (complete phenomenal interdependence) thesis 191–5, 214, 234

C-properties 223–5; enriched 226

DC-thesis 114–15

Deikman, A.J. 41

demonstrative reference: to parts of one's experience 210

Dennett, Daniel 20, 66–8

diachronic co-consciousness 113; not transitive 168

drops of experience 128

dualism 10, 179; awareness-content 47; Cartesian 6, 10, 56, 62, 85; property 5–6; substance 5

Eastern traditions 54

eliminativism 5

epiphenomenalism 10

experience: as always present 121; continuous awareness of continuity 153, 157; hallucinatory 16; holographic conception 191, 201; inherent directionality 176; 'inner' and 'outer' 10, 16, 58; marginal/peripheral 30; not merely an appearance of the real 21; perceptual 14; self-unifying 236; taking it seriously xiv, 1; transparency and invisibility of 18; tri-partite identity criterion 24, 189; world-presenting 18–19, 31, 47, 58, 60, 92, 196

experience of succession v. succession of experience 132, 180

experienced temporal order: belief-based accounts 124

experienced temporal succession: involuntary 126

experiences: classifying by type 23; fusions 105, 107; identity and global character 217, 223, 232; identity conditions 4, 23, 186, 191, 245, 251; isolated 58; narrower ways of individuating 24; strictly durationless

127; viewed as disruptions in physical space 7, 19
experiential memory 123

Farah, M. 263
Final Theory *see* theory of everything
Finnish 11, 12
Flanagan, O. 2
Fodor, Jerry 260
Forman, Robert 261
Foster, John xvi, 2, 27, 162–6, 169, 260, 263–4; *The Case for Idealism* 264
functionalism 1

general relativity 6
Gestalt psychology 195
gestalts 198; grouping phenomenon 203; temporal 171
global character 216–19, 220, 223, 225–6, 228–35, 265; and phenomenal proximity 216; as a relational property 218; as relevant to experiential identity 219; narrow and broad 223; spatial aspects 226; temporal aspects 227
Goodman, N. 92; *The Structure of Appearance* 92
grain problem 7, 95
Griffiths, Paul J. 54, 261
Gurwitsch, A. 197–8

hallucinogens: consequences of ingesting xv
Head: adventures of 67; the case reconsidered 82
Heidegger, M. 263; occasional echoes of xv, 116
Hill, Christopher 240–4, 255
Hobbes, T. 64
holism 27; complete v. partial 185; necessary and complete 223; necessary v. contingent 185; type and token 223; type v. token 186, 191, 223
holist v. Humean 183
hological essentialism 185
Horgan, T. 4
Hume, David xiii, 6, 85–6, 94, 117, 119, 149, 183, 242, 252
Humean v. holist 183
Hurley, Susan 244–6, 253
Husserl, E. xi, xv, 27, 115, 136–7, 147, 150–62, 165, 174–5, 263; criticisms of Brentano 154

hyperspheres 77

immaterial soul 4
Indifference Principle 214–15, 225, 230
inherence doctrine 56
inner perception v. inner observation 260
introspectibility: limits of 37
introspection: active 33, 46; non-judgmental 34; passive 33, 38, 46, 51
I-thesis 40, 104; strong and weak forms defined 35

James, William xv, 30, 44, 116–17, 118, 120, 130, 132–3, 184–5, 190, 193, 261, 263; *The Principles of Psychology* 132, 184
Jammer, Max 262
Janus-faced 231
just more content objection 246–7

Kanisza's Triangle 206
Kant, I. 61–2, 264
Kobes, B. 266
Köhler, Wolfgang 197, 203

Leibniz, G. W. 192, 261
Leibniz's Law 265
Liberalized Materialism *see* L-materialism
lingering contents 156–7, 162
L-materialism 8, 10, 23, 56, 95, 179, 260
local character 216–17, 222–3, 228–34
Locke, J. 14
Lockwood, Michael 49, 99–101, 103, 109, 135, 174–5, 230, 260, 262, 264
long-term body image 262
Lumpl and Goliath 107
Lundt 260
Lyons, W. 46

Mabbot, J.D. 140, 263
matter–consciousness relationship xiv, 4–6, 8, 10, 179, 239; non-dualistic approaches 6
maximal experience 233; defined 96
maximally connected 107–8, 216, 222, 228; temporal restriction 168
Maxwell, N. 260
McCulloch, G. 12
McGinn, Colin 2, 8–9
meaning: as present in consciousness 11; draining away 12; experienced 207–10, 212, 221; pure 13

meditation 52, 54
Mellor, D.H. 124
Meltzoff, Andrew 262
memory: drug-induced amnesia 124; experiential 123; short-term 125; weak v. strong theories 127
mental unity 2
mereological essentialism 185, 187, 189–90
mereological sums 188
Mill, J.S. 85
Miller, Izchak 133–4
moderate naturalism 10, 14, 21–2, 25, 56, 85, 109
momentary centres of experience 128
Moore, G.E. 43, 49, 58
Müller-Lyer 198–200

naive realism 15, 18, 31, 45, 47, 224
Nathan, Nicholas xvi, 261
natural attitude 15, 18, 31, 61, 92
nested short-term memories 127, 157
Newton, I. 261–2
non-phenomenal properties 238
nothingness 55, 64, 73, 75, 82, 118

O'Brian, G. and Opie, Jon 262
O'Shaughnessy, Brian 262
oenology 20
one experience view 251–5
order threshold 170
organization: phenomenal 187, 196
other minds 20
overlap theory 264; accommodating global character 230; simple v. dual-level 166
ownership principle 42, 49, 58

panpsychism 7
part: weak construal 185
partial anti-realism 115, 127
partial unity: an impossibility 105; versus duplication 244–6; a problem for the one experience view 253
perceived wholes 196, 199, 205–6
perceptual constancy 200
perceptual experience: presence/absence of meaningful content 207
perceptual gestalts 27
persistence: immediate awareness of 114
P-field 74, 79–80, 82, 94, 226; super-substantival 74
phenomenal background 31–3, 37–40, 42, 45–6, 51–3, 57–8, 89–90, 111, 118–20, 207, 215, 264; as unified presence 36; exploration of 32; unity of 35
phenomenal binding principle 129, 149, 165, 221
phenomenal character 2, 23; complete 220; interdependence 190; local v. global 216
phenomenal characteristics: origin of 5
phenomenal consciousness: not dependent upon attentive awareness 30
phenomenal content 24; awareness*-free 50; awareness-dependent 49; awareness-independent 49; disclosure view 49; exceeds what is noticed 30; intrinsic dynamic patterning 176, 180; self-revealing 57; temporal 114
phenomenal contents: revisionary proposal (Broad) 146
phenomenal counterpart 189, 191, 211, 220
phenomenal dynamics 237
phenomenal features: problem of variety 7, 56
phenomenal fields: sudden collapse 108
phenomenal flow 173, 175–6; an intrinsic feature of content 176; demystified 179; two distinct components 177
phenomenal interdependence 27, 184; demonstrative reference 210
phenomenal judgment 19, 22, 31–3, 39, 110–11, 208, 215
phenomenal objects *see* phenomenal content
phenomenal passage *see* phenomenal flow
Phenomenal plenums *see* P-field
phenomenal present 121, 177; characterized 169
phenomenal properties *see* phenomenal content
phenomenal properties: distinguished from phenomenal characteristics 221, 223
phenomenal space 26, 224; distorted 206; disunified 71, 226
phenomenal temporality 26–7, 114–15, 120, 127, 132, 162, 169, 177, 234, 237
phenomenal time-field 163
phenomenal truths 22
phenomenal voids *see* V-field

phenomenal wholes 196; meaning-
bearing 207
phenomenalized materialism *see* P-
materialism
phenomenological approach:
unavoidability of 4, 185
phenomenological constraint 115, 148,
165
phenomenological tradition xv
phenomenology xiii, xv, 4; conflicts with
science 23, 109; critical 18, 36, 61;
informed 18; naive 18, 36; pre-critical
18
physics xiv, 9–10, 15, 23, 121; intrinsic
nature of the material world 6, 238,
260
PI: phenomenal interdependence thesis
191, 195, 199
Piaget, Jean 66, 262
Planck duration 170
P-materialism 7–8, 10, 22, 56, 95, 179,
260
Pöppel, P. 264
PPC (Principle of Presentational
Concurrence) 134–5, 139, 166, 180,
182
PPI (partial phenomenal
interdependence) thesis 191
presence 122, 178
presentedness, 143–6, 148, 150, 154,
156–7, 162, 174–5; as variations in
'force and vivacity' 149
primal impression 151–8
primitivism 91–4
Principles of Psychology xv
projectivism 14, 16–19, 47, 58, 60–1,
75, 224; counterintuitive consequence
of 17
propositional attitudes 14
proprioception 119
protentions 153–6, 158, 160
PSA (Principle of Simultaneous
Awareness) 133–6, 147, 162, 165–6,
179–81
P-space 74–8, 80
psychology xiv, 23, 192
puddle-water 188
pulse theory 128–31
pure consciousness state 54
Pure Ego 94, 261

qualia 19; atomic 92

realism 115, 161–2, 165

recipe for vanilla ice-cream 12
reductionism 5
refrigerators: what they have in common
with people 95
regress objection 246–7
relational phenomenal properties:
distinguished from phenomenal
characters 221
relational properties: generalized v.
particularized 219
relationism 73
relations: and relational properties 219;
formal v. material 88
repeated contents 61, 129, 141–2
representationalism 254
retentions 151–8, 160, 264
Robinson, H. xvi, 2
Ruhnau, E. 264
Russell, B. 27, 131, 260, 264

Sacks, Oliver 64, 110
Sartre, J.P. xv
Schopenhauer, A. 260
Searle, J. 2
secondary properties 15
self, the xv; as locus of pure awareness*
46
sense-data 19, 55
sense-field: spatial integration 62
sensory anchor 68–9
sensory universes: uncoordinated 66, 69
sets, quantities and collectives 188
Simple Conception 57–9, 86, 108, 115,
166, 180–1, 217, 238
space 60; as boundless uniform
Sensorium 261; phenomenal 62
space and time xiv
space-time 6, 93–4, 178–9; substantival
conception 94
spatial relatedness: as a (quasi-) mode of
co-consciousness 225
specious present 3, 113, 121, 137, 142,
146, 152, 248–51; estimates of its
duration 171; 'intensive' and
'extensive' 143
speech perception 208
split-brains 27, 99, 251
Sprigge, T. 128, 192–3, 195–6, 201, 263
S-thesis 61–3, 65, 72, 78–80, 83–4, 104
Strawson, Galen 2, 8, 11, 13, 117–20,
260
stream of consciousness xiii, 2, 4; and
subjects 96; divisions within 23;

temporal characteristics 114; watery metaphor: apt or inept? 117

stream of water 237

streams of consciousness: as primitive manifolds 93, 251, 259; consist of overlapping total experiences 172; general structural traits 20, 235; single unifying relationship 166

string theory 9

Strong Impingement 199–203, 206–7, 209, 234–5

Strong I-thesis 35, 40, 62

structure: as an ingredient in experience 197, 203

substantivalism 72–4, 94; super- 73

subsumption 255–8

teleprompter: model of temporal awareness 135

temporal modes of presentation 146, 174, 176, 264; global character, 230

temporally extended total experiences: global character 227, 229; number and duration 169

theory of everything 9

Theravada 54

thought: transparent 13

time: phenomenal v. presentational (Foster's distinction) 163

time perception: shortest distinguishable phenomena 170

time-consciousness 27, 115, 236; absolute 159

token holism: grounded in global character 221

total experience: defined 95; simplifying assumptions lifted 172

total experiences: as composed of logically detachable parts 183; as simple non-composite entities 184, 221; character of the whole reflected in each of its parts 222; mereological essentialism applies 188; partitions created by co-consciousness 219; typically spatially integrated 224; in different sensory modalities 173, 248

total freezes (cessations): with and without phenomenal binding 131

transitivity: and global character 232; breakdowns 98, 100, 177; hallmark of temporality 168, 177, 234; of synchronic co-consciousness 27, 89, 104–8

transparency 254

tropes 263

tunnel vision 82, 156

Twin-Earth 14, 24, 212

Tye, M. 263

Tye, Michael 246–7, 251–5, 257, 265–6

understanding-experience 11–14, 17, 53, 207, 209, 211, 221; not a sensory phenomenon 13

Unger, Peter 21–2

unity of consciousness 236; and introspectibility 34; full/strong v. weak/partial 96; not explained by coinstantiation 6; surprisingly elusive 195; synchronic 25; the two strands 26; undescribability of 40; objectivity requirement 244; the problem dissolved 252; top-down v. bottom-up approaches 255

ur-qualities 9

utterance: meaning v. content 211

Vasubandhu 261

V-field: relational 76

virtual reality 18

visual agnosia 110–11

V-space 75–80; absolute v. relative 80; constraints on 77; real and imaginary 81

V-spaces: disjointed 82

Vygotsky, Lev 13, 260

Ward, James 132, 135, 261

Weak Impingement 199–202, 206, 224

Weak I-thesis 35, 37–9

Wertheimer, M. 196–7

Whitehead, A.N. 128

will: naked 53

Williams, Paul 261

Wills, James 184, 190

Wollheim, R. 261

WP-awareness: wholly passive awareness 39–41, 57